THROUGH A SCREEN DARKLY

THROUGH A
SCREEN DARKLY

Popular Culture, Public Diplomacy, and
America's Image Abroad

Martha Bayles

Yale
UNIVERSITY
PRESS
New Haven & London

Yale University Press books may be purchased in quantity for educational, business,
or promotional use. For information, please e-mail sales.press@yale.edu (U.S. office)
or sales@yaleup.co.uk (U.K. office).

Set in Postscript Electra type by Integrated Publishing Solutions.
Printed in the United States of America.

Library of Congress Cataloging-in-Publication Data
Bayles, Martha.
Through a screen darkly : popular culture, public diplomacy, and
America's image abroad / Martha Bayles.
pages   cm
Includes bibliographical references and index.
ISBN 978-0-300-12338-8 (hardback)
1. Popular culture—American influences.   2. United States—Foreign relations—21st
century.   3. Diplomacy.   4. United States—Foreign public opinion.   5. United
States—Social life and customs—1971—Foreign public opinion.   6. Popular culture—
United States—Foreign public opinion.   7. International relations—History—21st
century.   8. Mass media and culture.   I. Title.
E169.12.B332 2013
303.48'273—dc23   2013029404

A catalogue record for this book is available from the British Library.

This paper meets the requirements of ANSI/NISO Z39.48–1992
(Permanence of Paper).

10 9 8 7 6 5 4 3 2 1

To Peter

CONTENTS

THROUGH A SCREEN DARKLY

INTRODUCTION

The back streets of Jakarta were narrow and crowded, nearly impassable. My interpreter and I had taken the precaution of wearing head scarves, and we trusted our driver. But we still felt nervous, because the man we were going to meet, Muhammad Rizieq Syihab, was the leader of Indonesia's most disruptive Islamist group, the FPI.[1] Founded in 1998 after the fall of the dictator Suharto, the FPI claims only a few thousand members in a nation of 237 million. But it seeks headlines by attacking nightclubs, cinemas, casinos, brothels, and restaurants that stay open during Ramadan. It also harasses minority religious and ethnic groups, and lobbies for a sweeping antipornography law that prohibits not just hardcore material but many traditional customs and styles of dress. Reputed to have ties with the police and military, the FPI does not engage in suicide bombing. But it does seek to discredit the many indigenous forms of Islam that have flourished in Indonesia since the thirteenth century, and replace them with the strict, one-size-fits-all version of Islam practiced in Saudi Arabia.

Rizieq invited us to join a circle of watchful aides seated on the carpeted floor of his modest house. Knowing that he opposed Western democracy and capitalism and had studied in Saudi Arabia, I was prepared for some negative responses to my questions about American cultural influence, and I got them. Like many people I have met overseas, Rizieq showed little awareness of America's larger cultural heritage, or even of its "classic" popular culture. To him, American culture consists mainly of the latest commercial entertainment, from rap and rock that "reduces you to the level of animals, making you dance like a monkey," to films and TV shows that "use slogans like 'freedom' to cover immoral behavior like gambling, alcohol, prostitution, and homosexual marriage." He also believed that the US government was deliberately exporting these harmful influences as part of a Western conspiracy to destroy Islam.[2]

It is tempting to say, *Get over it! Sex and violence in the media are the price we pay for freedom, and, compared with living under a dictatorship, it's worth it.* This is the implicit message of many news reports about foreign protests against US entertainment. Typically these reports present only two sides: the freedom side and the extremist side.[3] But this is not the whole story, because in Indonesia and many other countries, there are millions of sensible, down-to-earth people who reject extremism and favor democracy, while also worrying about the impact of American entertainment on their society.

For example, the day after my meeting with Rizieq, I spoke with Rosiana Silalahi, then chief editor at SCTV, one of Indonesia's leading networks. A savvy journalist, Silalahi spoke staunchly in favor of free speech as the cornerstone of Indonesian democracy. But she also expressed dismay at the "cut-throat competition" between TV channels that was leading some to copy the worst aspects of American television. "As a woman, I hear complaints from mothers about the kind of shows that are on when the family is having dinner. One channel showed a *sinetron* [serial drama] right after the 5:30 PM news, where a woman hanged herself, and they showed her in close-up, gagging to death."[4]

The program in question was not American. But Indonesian producers take their cues from the world's most successful entertainment industry—and so do their counterparts in almost every other country.[5] And very often, that means more sex and more violence. Remarking at the speed with which American popular culture was "getting into society," Silalahi told me that just a few years earlier, no young Indonesian girl would have dreamed of dressing in revealing outfits similar to those worn by the American pop singer Britney Spears. As for violence, in 2013 Silalahi told me that a number of Indonesian boys had been injured, even killed, while imitating the American T.V. show *Smackdown!* (an in-your-face fight show from World Wrestling Entertainment).[6]

If these are the sentiments of extremists who reject freedom, then there are a lot of extremists in America, Europe, and Japan, not to mention other democratic countries. According to a 2005 Pew Research Center survey, roughly 60 percent of Americans are "very concerned" about the values that popular culture is teaching their children.[7] Similar worries are found elsewhere in the world. In 2007, Pew's forty-seven-nation survey of global attitudes found roughly 30 percent of Europeans expressing negative views of "US movies, music and TV." Fewer Japanese, Israelis, and South Africans expressed such views, but over 40 percent of South Koreans and Indonesians did. And in Turkey and India, the figure was 68 percent.[8]

Although survey data is unreliable in nondemocratic countries, it is probably worth noting nevertheless that a 2007 report from the World Public Opinion organization showed 78 percent of Iranians holding an unfavorable view of "American culture."[9] And according to Pew, negative views of "US movies, music and TV" are held by majorities in such strategically important countries as Russia, Jordan, Egypt, and Pakistan.[10] Not surprisingly, poll data from most Muslim-majority countries show high percentages believing—with Rizieq—that the US government is using American culture as a weapon against Islam. For example, a 2009 poll by World Public Opinion showed 80 percent of Egyptians agreeing that one of President Obama's policy goals was "to impose American culture on Muslim society."[11]

Because these attitudes are not typically held by English-speaking elites, they tend to be overlooked. In the words of Yuli Ismartono, a senior editor at the popular Indonesian newsweekly *Tempo*, "Americans always miss the point. For most non-Westerners America means fast food, Starbucks, cowboys, and sexual freedom. The real American persona is not well understood. I try to tell people that our traditional values are the same, but TV and movies send a different message."[12]

It is also tempting to dismiss these attitudes as hypocritical, given the tremendous global success of the US entertainment industry. Between 1989 and 2010, foreign sales of U.S. films and TV shows increased fourfold, from $3.6 billion to $14.2 billion.[13] Today, Hollywood's foreign box office earns twice as much as its domestic, and the gap is widening.[14] In terms of impact, we should also count the illegal distribution of US entertainment. This cannot be measured with any precision, but one influential estimate comes from a 2006 report commissioned by the Motion Picture Association of America (MPAA), which estimates that MPAA members lost $6.1 billion to piracy in 2005, much of it due to major pirating industries in other countries, notably China and Russia.[15]

Donny Gahraladian, a professor of philosophy at Indonesia University, recalled for me that, under Suharto, America was officially denounced as "materialistic, individualistic, promiscuous, and dominated by gangsters." So he found it ironic to see those same stereotypes subsequently reinforced by US entertainment. At the same time, Gahraladian noted that his students, who come from diverse backgrounds in Indonesia and Southeast Asia, embrace American popular culture as "the common coin of social interaction, something everyone can talk about in the café or mall."[16] Hearing this, I remembered a meeting in Berlin with the eminent German journalist Günter Hofmann, who commented with a wry smile that part of the glue holding the European Union together was the younger generation's shared passion for American culture.[17]

What should we make of these contradictory reactions? Is American popular culture a destructive force, a liberating one, or both? How do its products shape global perceptions of the nation's ideals, policies, and way of life? There is no simple answer to these questions. But a useful first step might be to imagine popular culture as a fun-house mirror, giving an exaggerated view of America's faults, from sexual immorality to gun violence, political corruption to financial malfeasance. Americans may relish the exaggeration or recoil from it, but either way we automatically adjust the picture in the light of our own experience. A similar adjustment is possible for others who have access to accurate information about the United States, whether from travel, study, or exposure to its larger cultural heritage. The problem is, most human beings have no such access. So they cannot adjust the picture, and while they often find it entertaining, they seldom admire it.

This conclusion is supported not just by global opinion polls but also by the more fine-grained data gathered by media and advertising companies. These data are not available to researchers, but their overall findings were summed up for me by advertising guru Keith Reinhard. What foreigners object to, Reinhard explained, is not just the "pervasiveness" of American popular culture but also its "coarsening." As he noted, "Much of our entertainment is promoting values not in concert with other people's values and morals."[18] Reinforcing this observation is a key finding of the Pew survey cited above. In forty-two of the forty-six nations surveyed, a majority of respondents agreed with the statement "It's bad that American ideas and customs are spreading here."[19] Since only a tiny percentage of the world's people ever visit the United States, the question arises: where did these respondents get their impressions of American ideas and customs? The Pew researchers do not explore the connection, but the answer is popular culture.

The point is borne out by abundant anecdotal evidence. For example, on a 2011 visit to Iraq, columnist Peggy Noonan asked an Iraqi military officer "what was the big thing he'd come to believe about Americans in the years they'd been there." The man replied, "You are a better people than your movies say."[20] In Cairo I met a poet who asked me whether it was true that over 50 percent of American fathers sexually molest their children. Startled, I asked where she had gotten that idea. "It is standard fare on American TV talk shows," she told me. "If it isn't that common, then why are they always speaking about it?"[21] From the comments of Americans working in US international visitor programs, I gather that foreign visitors frequently express surprise at the difference between the Americans they are meeting on the ground and the ones they see depicted on the screen. A report commissioned by the State Department's International Visitors Program offers this summary:

People who watch U.S. television shows, attend Hollywood movies, and listen to pop music can't help but believe that we are a nation in which we have sex with strangers regularly, where we wander the streets well-armed and prepared to shoot our neighbors at any provocation, and where the life style to which we aspire is one of rich, cocaine-snorting decadent sybarites. This is not an accurate description of the U.S., nor is it attractive to many people around the world. . . . The visitors were very clear that their images of America, shaped by commercial media, were inaccurate and distorted, and gave them a negative perception of the United States.[22]

THE SLOW DEATH OF PUBLIC DIPLOMACY

The word *culture* is notoriously hard to define, but the definition offered by historian John Keegan is as good as any. As he writes, culture is "that great cargo of shared beliefs, values, associations, myths, taboos, imperatives, customs, traditions, manners and ways of thought, speech and artistic expression which ballast every society."[23] In these pages, *culture* is used in three main senses: a people's way of life (customs, values, ideals); elite artistic expression (literature, fine arts, performing arts); and popular culture (the products of a commercial entertainment industry). During the Cold War, the US government worked hard to promote culture in all three senses, by supporting activities aimed at "telling America's story" (its ideals and way of life), sharing its high culture with foreign audiences, and even at times promoting certain aspects of its popular culture.

These activities are part of *public diplomacy,* a term that also covers government-sponsored efforts to explain and defend US policies and, more important, project American ideals. Public diplomacy was an early casualty of the post–Cold War era. In the early 1990s, America's victory over the once-mighty Soviet Union seemed to validate not only its economic system but also its political institutions and, indeed, its whole way of life. The nation's mood was "triumphalist," meaning not "triumphant" but something more like "full of it." Pumping our fists, we declared ourselves Number One, and described America as both "the end of history" and "the indispensable nation," able to "stand tall and . . . see further than other countries into the future."[24] While in that triumphalist mood, the US government got out of the business of public diplomacy. As part of a "peace dividend" it slashed funding by one third.[25] And in 1999 it dismantled the agency that had coordinated public diplomacy since 1953, the United States Information Agency (USIA).

Three years later, seemingly out of the blue, a bolt of pure terror struck New

York and Washington. American triumphalism survived that first blow, finding expression in a fierce, impatient call for revenge. But then the mood changed. The memory of 9/11 became a media cliché. Two wars that were supposed to be clean and swift turned out dirty and grinding. In 2008 the nation was hit by a financial crisis that stirred doubts about its continued economic and political viability. Many such doubts were expressed by America's allies and friends, driving home the fact that, even after electing a new and more eloquent president, America had lost its persuasive powers. And despite over forty reports published since 9/11, US public diplomacy remains moribund.

This book was conceived during the nadir of America's reputation, when many people in Washington were saying that the government had made a big mistake by cutting back on public diplomacy. As a long-term observer of popular culture, I wondered whether a bigger mistake had been letting the entertainment industry take over the job of communicating America's policies, ideals, and culture to a distrustful world. Knowing popular culture as I do, its vices as well as its virtues, I questioned the wisdom of deciding, in effect, to make it America's de facto ambassador.

That decision was not dramatic. On the contrary, it unfolded gradually, on a bipartisan basis, over a period of ten years, without attracting any real public scrutiny or media attention.[26] It was also driven by the self-interest of the entertainment industry, personified by one of Washington's most powerful and glamorous lobbyists, Jack Valenti of the Motion Picture Association of America (MPAA); and opposed by a weak and demoralized group of practitioners, whose clout in Washington has never been great, because public diplomacy is largely invisible to the voting public. Finally, the decision reflected a consensus, forged throughout the twentieth century, about the unique ability of popular culture to put flesh on the bones of American ideals.

Ever since World War I, when President Woodrow Wilson called film "a universal language [that] lends itself importantly to the presentation of America's plans and purposes," Washington has regarded Hollywood as a supremely persuasive ally.[27] Repeated many times since, Wilson's sentiment got a boost in the 1990s, when many former Soviet subjects testified to the importance of American movies, jazz, and rock music in sustaining their dreams of freedom. Some of those exports, such as the famous jazz broadcasts on the Voice of America international radio service, were supported by the government. Others, such as the craze for rock music that swept Eastern Europe and the USSR in the 1960s and 1970s, happened of their own accord. But in all cases, the lesson was clear: American popular culture helped free the world from Communism.

Does this lesson still apply? American movies, pop music, and TV shows are still attracting people all over the globe; does that mean they are still winning hearts and minds for freedom and democracy? My answer is a qualified no, because of three important changes that have occurred since the height of the Cold War: transformations in the tone and content of popular culture, in the technology that conveys it to the world, and in the audiences that receive and interact with it.

The first change, in the tone and content of popular culture, dates back to the 1960s, when the entertainment industry began catering to the rebellious, angry mood of the generation that came of age during the civil rights movement and the Vietnam War. That generation ruled the market for a simple reason: it was large and affluent. Before long, the industry was wooing the icons of the 1960s counterculture: first the record labels signed Bob Dylan, the Rolling Stones, and every band that played at Woodstock; then the film studios opened their doors to "outlaw" directors such as Martin Scorsese and Francis Ford Coppola; and, finally, the broadcast networks found ways to address the 1960s generation without "raising the eyebrow" of the Federal Communications Commission (FCC).

The result was a commercialized counterculture that soon lost its radical political edge but retained its compulsion to "shock the bourgeois" by flouting the limits of public propriety. Vulgarity, violence, and vitriol are easy ways to separate adolescents from their dollars, but commercial pressure is not the only reason for the compulsion to shock. After all, it was commercial pressure that kept the entertainment industry *within* the bounds of propriety for most of its history. Nor are vulgarity, violence, and vitriol the inevitable result of democratic taste. Many ordinary people, including adolescents, enjoy these things, but many others do not. The real change is in the sensibility of America's cultural elites. Historically, our elites sought to educate and uplift popular taste. Today, out of a misguided populism that expects people with low levels of income and education to have low morals, elites either ignore the degradation of popular culture or (worse) encourage it.

The second—technological change—is too well known to belabor here. Suffice it to say that for most of the twentieth century, the only US government body with the power to censor the electronic media, the FCC, rarely used that power, because the broadcast networks were privately owned entities that, like the film studios, practiced fairly rigorous self-censorship. But with the massive deregulation of the 1970s and 1980s, to say nothing of the subsequent rise of satellite television and the Internet, the American system of self-censorship has eroded. The networks still enforce certain rules, such as the prohibitions on nudity and profanity. The MPAA still rates movies for theatrical release. And record companies still affix "parental advisory" stickers to certain CDs and MP3 downloads. But as any American ten-year-old can attest, these controls are like a wire fence strung across a river. The American media regime is, in effect, the most libertarian in the world.

Meanwhile, in the former Soviet bloc and many other places where the media had been state-controlled, a revolutionary technology appeared in the 1990s — not the Internet (that came later) but commercial satellite television. Intensely competitive, voracious for programming, satellite television opened new vistas for the American entertainment industry. The result, as we've seen, is a tsunami of movies, pop music, TV shows, and video games coursing through legitimate and illegitimate distribution channels, including pirated videodiscs and unlicensed downloading from the Internet. This situation is unprecedented and bears scant resemblance to the slow, often tortuous diffusion of American popular culture during the Cold War.

This brings us to the third change, which is the audience. No longer is the United States sending jazz and classic Hollywood films into information-starved Eastern Europe and the Soviet Union, as in the early decades of the Cold War. Nor is it sending rebellious youth culture to dissidents who welcome it in the spirit of the European avant-garde, as in the later decades. Instead, America is sending raunchy sex comedies, blood-drenched horror films, and crude talk and reality shows into non-Western societies where the vast majority of the population is socially and religiously conservative. For audiences also exposed to the rougher edges of US foreign policy, this flow adds insult to injury.

Yet the news is not all bad. While researching this book I interviewed more than a hundred American practitioners — public diplomats, trade officials, foreign service officers, soldiers, missionaries, businesspeople, media executives, academics, and artists — as well as over two hundred informed producers, consumers, and observers of popular culture in Britain, Germany, Poland, the Czech Republic, Turkey, Egypt, United Arab Emirates, Oman, India, Indonesia, and China. I did not ask these people what they admired about America, but while describing the distortions of popular culture many of them took the trouble to remind me that America is still greatly esteemed around the world. When asked to elucidate, several of them sketched a picture that is remarkably consistent. What others admire most about America, they told me, is the ordinary citizen, not a big shot or celebrity, who is *hopeful* in the sense of believing that a given problem can be solved, but who is also *prudent* in the sense of being mindful of limits, both material and human.

I call this blend of hope and prudence the American ethos, because while not unique to America, it is uniquely woven into our history. It is also the heart and soul of our culture, and as such provides a useful backdrop to the wide-ranging discussion that follows. I therefore beg the reader's indulgence in offering an overview, as brief as I can make it, of the nature and origins of that ethos.

THE AMERICAN ETHOS

The United States has long been the world's largest exporter of optimism. But this export comes in different grades, from reckless to prudent. At the reckless end, Americans like to believe that the sky's the limit, anything is possible, and every child can become president. In this somewhat inebriated state Americans have done amazing things, and the country's folklore is full of stories about penniless but determined souls triumphing against impossible odds. But the world knows, and Americans know, that not everyone can be a winner. Life is hard, people cheat, and the majority of dreams do not come true. We can despair at this knowledge; we can grow cynical at it (the most common reaction, because it mixes so well with selfishness); or we can follow the American ethos and temper our hope with prudence.

The roots of American optimism are religious, political, and economic. The religious root is captured in the "a city upon a hill" speech made by John Winthrop, the first governor of Massachusetts, to his fellow Puritans while crossing the Atlantic in 1630. For Winthrop, that biblical image evoked a real city that, because it stands on a hill, attracts scrutiny. "The eyes of all people are upon us," he continued. "If we shall deal falsely with our God, then . . . we shall surely perish out of the good land whither we pass over this vast sea."[28]

At the same time, the Puritans shared with their fellow dissenting Protestants (including the Pilgrims, who arrived on the *Mayflower* ten years earlier) a vision of the New World as "a *shining* city upon a hill," a redeemed and blessed Jerusalem that would serve as a light to the world.[29] Endlessly recycled by presidents (John Adams, Abraham Lincoln, John F. Kennedy, Ronald Reagan, Bill Clinton, George W. Bush, and Barack Obama, to name a few), this vision ceased to be purely religious quite early in American history—and also became political.

This political optimism is rooted in John Locke's Enlightenment view of the human condition, the so-called state of nature, as "perfect liberty." In this condition, Locke argued, people are naturally inclined to obey the "Law of Nature" (essentially the Golden Rule) given by God. For Locke, evil is not ingrained in human nature but rather results from human striving, which leads to inequality, which leads to envy, theft, violence, and war. Like his countryman Thomas Hobbes, Locke believed that human reason can devise a social contract to protect property. But unlike Hobbes, Locke did not believe that the price of the social contract must be the surrender of liberty to an absolute ruler. Instead, Locke called for a social contract that would protect liberty—and added that if it fails to do so, then the people have a God-given right to dissolve it. Expressed most eloquently by Thomas Jefferson in the Declaration of Independence, this idea is the key to the American Revolution.

As for the economic root of American optimism, it can be found in Adam Smith's defense of free enterprise. Against the mercantilist view of wealth as finite, Smith argued that wealth can be *grown* if the people have economic liberty. Smith was well aware that greed is a vice condemned by both classical philosophy and Christianity. But he made a moral distinction between greed, which connives to seize the wealth of others and hoard it, and acquisitiveness, which works, earns, and accumulates wealth in a manner that benefits others. For Smith, acquisitiveness was the virtue that opposed the vice of greed.[30] This was also the view of America's iconic entrepreneur, Benjamin Franklin, except that he identified thirteen virtues: temperance, silence, order, resolution, frugality, industry, sincerity, justice, moderation, cleanliness, tranquility, chastity, and humility.[31] No one ever accused Franklin of being too temperate, silent, chaste, or humble. But for millions of his countrymen, he was the exemplar of beneficial striving.

To thinkers who remain attached to an aristocratic tradition, these "bourgeois" virtues are lowly compared with the lofty virtues of courage, honor, and loyalty. But Americans trace a connection between these lowly virtues and the capacity for self-government. Alexis de Tocqueville called this connection "self-interest properly understood," and while he gently mocked the American habit of using it to explain "almost *every* act of their lives," he also praised its cumulative impact, which was less to "inspire great sacrifices" than to produce "a lot of orderly, temperate, moderate, careful, and self-controlled citizens."[32]

Clearly, the optimism grown from such roots is entwined with prudence. And the roots of American prudence are also religious, political, and economic. First is Puritanism, which followed John Calvin in believing that the soul can play no part in its own salvation because before time began God decided which souls will be saved and which damned. By this harsh logic, the whole business of salvation is radically removed from any sort of human agency. Of course, Calvin also held that ceaseless toil, upright character, and material success are the visible signs of God's grace. Hence the Puritan work ethic, which consists of putting in long hours, staying on task, and dealing honestly with others—and then feeling conscience-stricken about the riches that result.[33] The problem was aptly summarized by the Puritan divine Cotton Mather, who quipped in 1702, "Religion brought forth Prosperity, and the daughter devoured the mother."[34]

The political root of prudence is the philosophy of the generation who fought the Revolution and drafted the Constitution. It can be shocking to read the expressed doubts of these men about democracy, and some historians portray them as closet aristocrats. But that is not the point.[35] The framers were students of classical republicanism, which defines politics as an exalted realm that the common people (*demos*) cannot enter, because they lack the breeding, wealth, and education to develop virtue. Rather than endorse that view, the framers sought to create a *democratic* republic, in which the *demos* would rule under a system of checks and balances.[36] To the Puritan objection, voiced most forcefully by John Adams, that it is not possible for ordinary people to develop the virtue required for self-government, the reply was that it *was* possible—as long as they are given a proper education, held to a strict public morality, and assured of a just distribution of property.[37]

This brings us to prudence's economic root. Adam Smith was part of the Scottish Enlightenment, a tradition that did not detach economic analysis from reflection about politics and civic virtue. That's why economist Herb Stein once quipped that "Adam Smith did not wear an Adam Smith necktie."[38] Stein was referring to the cult of Smith as a libertarian for whom free markets and free trade are the only things needful for America to thrive. This was not Smith's perspective, for he had a realistic view of human nature. Indeed, his work is studded with references to dishonest merchants, exploitative manufacturers, corrupt officials, and other cynics out to game the system. Smith also called for robust government interventions, including bank regulation, temporary monopolies to innovative companies, and limits on interest rates.[39] "No society," he wrote, "can surely be flourishing and happy, of which the far greater part of the members are poor and miserable."[40]

If the word *prudence* sounds too sober, let me add another crucial dimension: the debunking spirit of comedy, which, as noted by political thinkers from Aristotle to Tocqueville, is akin to the spirit of democracy. The dry wit of the Yankee, the tall tales of the frontiersman, the sly folktales of the slave, the satire of Mark Twain, the ethnic jokes and pratfalls of the minstrel and immigrant vaudevillian, the riffs of the stand-up comedian, the hilarious antics of cartoon characters from Mickey Mouse to Bart Simpson—all these and more have conditioned ordinary Americans to laugh not only at the high and mighty but also at ourselves. If you doubt that comedy is a form of prudence, consider the humorlessness, indeed the positive antipathy toward humor, found in tyrants and dictators.

Thus rooted, American prudence has proved remarkably tenacious, producing a new round of soul-searching every time the country's optimism goes over the top. But this raises another question: with all this prudence, why does American optimism go over the top?

THE RELIGION OF PROGRESS

In early 2012 the Burmese pro-democracy leader Aung San Suu Kyi warned the international community not to take an attitude of "reckless optimism" toward her country's immediate future. This remark was criticized on the ground that it might dampen the enthusiasm of potential investors. Suu Kyi's response was sharp and commonsensical: "I did not say I was against optimism, I said I was against *reckless* optimism" (emphasis added).[41] This commonsense distinction is rarely made by America's leaders these days. On the contrary, they avoid facing the real problems and skewer those who do face them for being "pessimistic" about America's ever-brighter future. Indeed, envisioning an ever-brighter future is something that leaders in every walk of American life feel obliged to do. And this obligation, too, has deep roots in our history.

Here, too, the story starts with religion. American Protestantism lost its Puritan edge during the First Great Awakening of the 1730s and 1740s, when a new and passionate style of preaching sowed the idea that anyone, no matter how humble (even, in some cases, a woman or an African American), could, if sufficiently fired by the Holy Spirit, out-preach the educated ministers with their advanced divinity degrees. One such educated minister, Jonathan Edwards, charged that this new "religion of the heart" was taking the power of salvation away from God and giving it to man. But that was precisely its appeal. Homegrown, egalitarian, individualistic, affirmative of human agency—the First Great Awakening triumphed because it rode the same political tide as the Revolution.[42]

Then came the Second Great Awakening, which began in the 1790s and consisted of huge "camp meetings" attracting thousands of people, lasting several days, and climaxing in a fever pitch of emotion.[43] Among the churches hosting these events, the Methodists excelled at disciplining the crowds and, more important, giving the proceedings a tangible purpose: a vision of America's destiny as the millennium, or perfected Christian community, that would precede the Second Coming of Christ and final Day of Judgment.[44]

This vision is called *postmillennial*, because it expects the Day of Judgment to occur *after* the millennium.[45] Shared by rich and poor, this postmillennial vision played a crucial role in the reform movements that sprang up in the 1820s and 1830s. Temperance, public education, female suffrage, abolition—all were seen as steps toward the perfecting of God's chosen nation. Postmillennialism also shaped the doctrine of Manifest Destiny, which conferred divine blessing on the nation's westward expansion in the early nineteenth century. Tested by the Civil War, postmillennialism surged back as the faith of the triumphant Union and, at century's end, as the justification for America's imperialistic adventures in the Caribbean and Pacific. A popular novel of 1897, *In His Steps*, begins with a congregation pledging not to act without first asking themselves, "What would Jesus do?," and ends with a mystical dream of the whole human race taking the same pledge at the dawn of the millennium.[46]

But such dreams were soon challenged by massive immigration, labor conflict, World War I, and intellectual currents such as Darwinism, Marxism, and "higher" biblical criticism. In the 1920s the postmillennial vision was replaced by a more secular one, which resembled its predecessor in expecting great things for America, but differed from it in expecting them to come from science, not Christ. This "religion of progress," as historian Christopher Lasch calls it, saw scientific expertise as the key to the perfected future, not just in technology and medicine but also in human affairs, including politics.[47] Yet this vision is an odd amalgam. Mainly, it is not scientific. Claiming the objectivity of science, it expects only positive outcomes. Real science offers no such guarantee: its methods can deliver a distressing verdict as readily as a reassuring one.

To sum up: the American ethos of sustaining hope while coping prudently with harsh reality is admired by others not because it is American but because it achieves better results than despair or cynicism. What is not admired is America's faith, not in the biblical God, who hands down both blessings and judgments, but in the deity of Progress, who hands down only blessings. Not surprisingly, the "ugly American," past and present, is the person who believes that the United States can save the world quickly, easily, and on the cheap. The example on my interlocutors' minds was the catastrophic lack of foresight accompanying the US invasion of Iraq. But that is but one episode in a history of reckless adventures.

The American belief in progress is not always ill-founded. The rapid rise of the United States came at a steep price: millions of human beings conquered, uprooted, enslaved, exploited, and killed. But it was nevertheless one of the wonders of the world. The theologian Reinhold Niebuhr was no fan of reckless optimism; on the contrary, he was one of its sharpest critics. But even he admitted the extraordinary scope of what America had achieved by the middle of the twentieth century: "It had emancipated the individual from irrelevant social restraints and inequalities; it had unloosed the initiative of the common man, particularly in economic pursuits, and had harnessed the forces of nature so that hitherto unknown standards of well-being could be achieved; it had established a democratic political order and vanquished ancient tyrannies."[48]

Faith in progress is still the driving force behind the one aspect of America still highly esteemed in every country of the world: its extraordinary technical achievements. To cite one humble example, Americans began in the early nineteenth century to build houses in a new way, not by joining heavy timbers, as had been done for centuries in Europe, but by simply nailing slender two-by-fours together in a "balloon frame." Disparaged by traditionalists as having "no framing at all" and sure to collapse in the first strong wind, these light, boxy structures proved capable of withstanding the most extreme elements.[49] Today they fill the American landscape, and all it takes to build one are basic carpentry skills, mass-produced nails, and a lot of straight lumber.

But human affairs are different, because, as Kant famously wrote, "out of the crooked timber of humanity nothing straight was ever built."[50] It takes infinite skill, not to mention wisdom, to build something enduring out of the crooked timber of humanity. That is why the writings of the American founders are so fascinating. For all their love of liberty, they fully expected the house they were building—the US Constitution—to be pulled apart by the sheer perversity of human nature. Here we find the main drawback of the religion of progress: it rejects the framers' political wisdom as outmoded, in the same way that their standards of hygiene and methods of transportation were outmoded. This is mistaken. A car may be faster than a horse and buggy, but unless there has been a miraculous transformation since I read the newspaper this morning, the timber of humanity is still as crooked as ever.

FREEDOM AND CENSORSHIP

America's ideals include freedom, democracy, equality, individualism, and the rule of law under a constitution. Yet most of the people I interviewed did not dwell on these lofty abstractions. One reason may be that these ideals are not easily ordered, prioritized, or reconciled. The political scientist Samuel Huntington linked them together in an "American Creed" but also noted that their meanings frequently shift, giving rise to "creedal passions" that divide as often as they unite.[51] This is certainly true of today's blue-state and red-state Americans.[52] Sharing the same creed, they enact the truth of James Madison's warning that human beings are so naturally "disposed to vex and oppress each other," even "the most frivolous and fanciful distinctions" are "sufficient to kindle their unfriendly passions."[53]

This spectacle of political dysfunction gives aid and comfort to the new authoritarians of the twenty-first century. Which raises another reason why the foreigners I interviewed rarely dwelt on lofty words like *freedom* and *democracy*. The new authoritarians stake their claims of legitimacy on these same words, while also giving them an Orwellian twist. For example, the Chinese Communist Party (CCP) affixes the label *democracy* to a form of government that is in fact the opposite. To justify its continuing grip on power, the CCP defines "democratic governance" as "the Chinese Communist Party governing on behalf of the people."[54] When pressed, the CCP defends this in cultural terms as *minben*, the Confucian doctrine holding the ruler accountable for the welfare of the people.[55] The trouble is, this isn't democracy, any more than the divine right of kings in early modern Europe was democracy.

To untwist such meanings, Americans need to engage with the restive populations living under twenty-first-century authoritarianism. But to do so productively, we also need to stop ignoring the elephant in the living room: our ubiquitous popular culture, which reaches into every media market of the world, even those that are ostensibly closed to it. Thus, Part One of this book explores how the most widely known entertainment products represent the lived reality of American ideals. With some noteworthy exceptions, the answer is, not well.

This state of affairs might be tolerable if US public diplomacy were taking up the slack and presenting a more accurate and complete picture of America. But as argued in Part Two, public diplomacy lost its way after the end of the Cold War and has yet to regain it. Part of the problem is public diplomacy's failure to reckon constructively with the elephant in the living room, which is why the conclusion offers a number of suggestions for how this might be done. At the moment, though, it remains the case, as one veteran public diplomat expressed it, that "popular culture is part of the landscape that the Foreign Service and State Department have to deal with, but nobody's thinking about it."

Would thinking about it lead to censorship? When faced with popular culture's more egregious excesses, I admit to feeling a furtive sympathy for the old regime of industry self-regulation. But this book does not advocate censorship, for both practical and principled reasons. The practical reason is that there is no political will for changing America's libertarian media regime. As noted above, a 2005 Pew survey found 60 percent of Americans concerned about what popular culture was teaching their children. Unfortunately, that survey did not ask Americans about what popular culture was teaching the world about America. Instead, it asked what sort of solution the respondents favored, and the results are striking. Eighty-six percent opposed censorship in any form, including self-regulation by the industry. Indeed, the only solution they found acceptable was parental control.[56]

Most of humanity rejects this libertarian view. For example, a young Bollywood actor I met in Mumbai expressed approval of India's state censorship board, because "filtering is needed." Indians strongly support a free press and free political speech, but they distinguish between that kind of freedom and the kind that allows the depiction of graphic sex and violence, because they consider the latter a threat to public morality. There was a time when Americans and Europeans made the same distinction, but no longer.[57] Today many people in the West dismiss as retrograde the idea that political speech is more deserving of protection than shocking or obscene speech. But it is still an important distinction in many societies, including some that are struggling to break free of authoritarian rule.

A further practical reason is this: even if America were to summon the political will to censor popular culture, the cost of doing so would prove prohibitive. This is the age of global piracy and the Internet, and the draconian restrictions required to keep the citizens of authoritarian countries away from forbidden material should be enough to deter any such effort on the part of the US government. American parents, schools, and other institutions are free to impose local restrictions, but any more systematic attempt to impose controls on the online behavior of Americans would violate our essential freedoms.

It is also true that most controls on Internet communication do not work well; there are too many people willing and able to circumnavigate them. This could change, however, as the more sophisticated authoritarians become more adept at using the Internet—and social media—for their own purposes.[58] Hence my *principled* reason for not advocating censorship. If you believe, as I do, that human beings are neither angels nor devils but imperfect creatures who require liberty to flourish, then the only recourse is not to censor but to *censure*, meaning criticize. America's cultural exports are never more persuasive than when showcasing its tradition of free political speech.

A striking example comes from former South African president Nelson Mandela, who while serving an eighteen-year term as a political prisoner on Robben Island was allowed to see a film every six months. One of those films was *In the Heat of the Night* (1967), starring Sidney Poitier as a Philadelphia police detective who gets involved in a murder investigation in racially tense Mississippi. Before showing the film, the prison authorities cut a key scene where the black detective is slapped by a white man and responds by slapping him back. A few weeks later, Mandela heard about the deleted scene and thought: "If America is producing that type of movie, without censorship, then change is possible."[59]

Yet even this fairly recent example does not capture the special flavor of twenty-first-century authoritarian regimes, which differ from their twentieth-century predecessors in not trying to remake human nature for the sake of a future utopia—racial, in the case of Nazi Germany and South Africa; Communist, in the case of the USSR and China; theocratic, in the case of Saudi Arabia and Iran. Today these utopian visions have faded, and the regimes that remain authoritarian seek mainly to perpetuate their own power. Thus they are willing, in the manner of the ancient Roman emperors, to placate the masses with bread and circuses. The bread is a rising standard of living, achieved most spectacularly by China. The circuses are the diversions of popular culture, whether imported, pirated, or locally produced. Not surprisingly, most authoritarian regimes are not very creative artistically, so their homegrown popular culture, like that of most other countries, is copied from American originals.

Popular culture in authoritarian regimes is also censored, needless to say. But here we must differentiate between two kinds of censorship. The first is based on morality and seeks to enforce widely held norms of decency and propriety. This type of censorship is frequently found in countries that, while authoritarian, have not seen their core values gutted by the trauma of war, or corroded by totalitarian ideology. (Some examples might include the United Arab Emirates, Oman, and Singapore.) When such regimes censor on moral or religious grounds, they tend to gain significant public support, even though westernized elites may not approve.

Censorship of popular culture is also driven by the need to stifle political speech by critics and opponents of the regime and is therefore more likely to arouse dissent. It is most prevalent in Russia and the former Soviet republics, where core values have largely given way to pervasive cynicism.

This distinction between moral and political censorship is not cut-and-dried, however. For example, the religious traditions of both Russia and China were long ago gutted by totalitarian rule, and more recently the ideology of Communism has been discredited, too. But both regimes still enjoy a certain amount of public support for censorship imposed in the name of moral values associated with "socialism"—and, of course, nationalism. The point is that popular culture, whether imported from America or copied from American originals, is sometimes censored in authoritarian regimes *with the support of the public.* This point is too subtle for some American pundits, who declare freedom to be a monolithic good, made up of equal parts Thomas Jefferson and Lady Gaga. But it is too important to overlook.

This book does not provide an exhaustive analysis of America's cultural footprint upon the entire globe, much less offer social scientific "proof" of its impact on any given population. My travel was limited to a few countries in Europe and the Middle East, as well as India, Indonesia, and China. I did not make it to Latin America, Russia, Central Asia, or sub-Saharan Africa. And while I pay attention to the cultural dimension of America's relations with Afghanistan, Iraq, Iran, and Pakistan, I could not visit those countries either.

There are also many relevant topics not addressed in these pages, among them sports, consumer goods other than entertainment, and the international flow of elite art and culture. Regarding the latter, I do discuss *cultural diplomacy* in Part Two and the conclusion. Traditionally, cultural diplomacy has meant the elite of one nation sharing its highest literary and artistic achievements with the elite of another. This kind of activity is now deemed ineffective and politically incorrect, not only in the United States but also in Europe. And there is little impetus to see it revived.

This is regrettable, because the world has come close to forgetting that America ever possessed a high culture, or even a classic popular culture. Patrick Spaven, former head of research for the British Council (the organization that conducts public diplomacy for the United Kingdom), told me that America is often ranked lowest of any country in the world in terms of "cultural heritage," because "the loud voice of popular culture drowns out the quieter voice of heritage."[60] Returning to Indonesia for a moment, the novelist Ayu Utami compared the American cultural presence unfavorably with the German and British. Granting the need for heightened security at the US embassy, she wondered why the good people there (whom she had never met) did not try, at least, to offer cultural programs in other locations. "People would really love it if they did," she told me. But then she shrugged: "The attitude, I guess, is *Hollywood does it better.*"[61]

In environmental science, the word *footprint* refers to the amount of natural resources consumed by a particular population. In telecommunications, it denotes the geographical area where a signal is most clearly received. In culture, what does it mean? A bare footprint in sand that will quickly wash away? A heavy boot-sole impression on soil belonging to others? A stiletto heel puncturing sacred ground? All these and more. America's cultural footprint is complex, of varying depth, sometimes welcome and sometimes not. My concern is to do justice to what is truly good about my country. But my method is to follow the tracks wherever they lead.

Part One

———————◆———————

THE FUN-HOUSE MIRROR OF POPULAR CULTURE

PROLOGUE TO PART ONE:
CULTURAL EXPORT—AND PUSHBACK

Hoping to see a part of Shanghai not frequented by foreigners, I let the person I was meeting, a local video artist, choose the location. To my disappointment, she suggested the McDonald's near Zhongshan Park. Arriving early, I bought a Coke and sat by a window covered with posters of American basketball stars, feeling annoyed by the thought that she was mistaking me for the type of American who travels the world eating Big Macs. Watching the chubby teenage boys at the next table scarf down a super-sized order of fries, I wondered whether American fast food was helping to create an American-style epidemic of obesity in China.

When the video artist arrived, she must have read my mind, because she immediately described this McDonald's as "a place of happy memories." One of the first in China, it had opened in the mid-1990s, when she was still in high school, and every afternoon she and her friends had come here to study—because, she explained, McDonald's was a much better place to study than at home: "Our families' houses were cold and dark, so we loved the warmth and brightness, the light music, everything so clean and friendly. We were under a lot of pressure to work hard, so being here helped us stay calm and focus."

This young woman's experience is not unique. Throughout East Asia, customers have turned the Golden Arches into youth hangouts, community centers, even high-prestige venues for romantic dates. And McDonald's has adapted, as it does elsewhere. In France and Italy, for example, McDonald's serves wine. In Russia, customers inured to public rudeness were requested, in the early days, not to feel mocked by smiling McDonald's employees.[1] In Turkey, the menu includes the yogurt drink *ayran*, and the meat is *halal* (permissible under Islamic law)—as it is in Indonesia and the Arab world. In Israel and Argentina there are dairy-free kosher outlets; in India, beef-free ones. In the Philippines,

McDonald's serves a popular Filipino dish reflecting that nation's long-standing ties with America: McSpaghetti, consisting of pasta, sweetened tomato sauce, pasteurized cheese, and a hot dog.

The neutral term for such adaptation is "localization," but the process is not always neutral. It may be just a matter of taste that Filipinos like hot dogs with spaghetti, but it doesn't take long for matters of taste to become matters of custom, even morality. The French and Italians do not just prefer wine, they also look down on people who prefer Coke. The Russians do not just dislike being smiled at, they also find smiling suspicious. And the dietary preferences of Muslims, Jews, and Hindus are part of their religion. I call this kind of localization "cultural pushback." It occurs whenever a foreign market says, "We like most of what you are selling, but don't try to sell us *this*." To succeed in such a market, a company must heed the message. It must ask *what* isn't wanted, and *why*.

The American entertainment industry still dominates the world, earning vastly more revenue than any other. But it is not the only game in town. Indeed, it has some hefty regional and local competitors, most prominently the Indian film industry, or "Bollywood."[2] In terms of the sheer number of tickets sold, the global market for Indian films is estimated to be the biggest, with 3.6 billion tickets sold per year, as opposed to a mere 2.6 billion for Hollywood.[3] As for television, America is still the international leader, but on most overseas channels the trend is toward fewer US programs and more domestic ones.

At the same time, most foreign TV programs are adapted from US originals. A lot of this localizing is done without the permission of US producers. But in the more lucrative markets, co-production with US companies is common.[4] In all events the process resembles the localizing of the McDonald's menu: some items are changed for neutral reasons, others for reasons of custom and morality — as when a host country cuts or alters material deemed offensive to local sensibilities. American companies go along with this cultural pushback when it would hurt their profits to do otherwise. But when their profits are not affected, US companies dismiss cultural pushback as either veiled protectionism or an attack on freedom of expression.[5]

Are they right? Protectionism definitely plays a role, as when the governments of France, Canada, and other nations use the language of "cultural exception" and "cultural diversity" to justify blocking the flow of American cultural products into their domestic markets.[6] Clearly, the desire of such governments is to protect their own publishing and media industries from US competition. But at the same time, that desire is not easily separable from genuine objections to the tone and content of the American imports.[7]

What about freedom of expression? After a century of totalitarian denunciations of American music, films, and other expressive culture as a form of imperialism, dismissing pushback on these grounds is second nature, not only to Hollywood but to most Americans. With remarkable consistency, the dictators of the twentieth century, whether Communist or fascist, likened the inflow of American culture to an enemy invasion, and used every means, including brutal repression, to stem it. But as suggested in the introduction, this is not always the strategy of today's authoritarians. Indeed, they are prone to regale the masses with the circus of popular culture while feeding them the bread of newfound prosperity. Ill-understood by Americans, this strategy is ignored by many US media companies hoping to do business in these markets. The result is a gray area within which twenty-first-century authoritarians encourage the import and localization of US entertainment, as long as it poses no threat to their power — or perhaps even reinforces it.

This strategy plays out differently in different countries. In North Korea, the regime still uses the media to browbeat the masses with old-fashioned propaganda. But in most authoritarian countries the media operate along Western lines, maximizing profit and audience share. The difference is that media companies in authoritarian countries tend to be hybrid corporations, technically private but in fact under state control. In China, for example, "marketized" media are given free rein (in entertainment, not news) until they cross this or that red line — at which point the reins are tightened by the Central Propaganda Department. The Arab media are similar but different. They are similar because most of the major companies are owned by wealthy investors from the Persian Gulf who either are members of their respective ruling families or have close ties with them. So here, too, there is a price for crossing the red lines. But because the Arab market includes twenty-four different countries, no one ruler can exert control. The result is a much more open and competitive media environment than in China.[8]

The point here is that virtually all foreign media, including those in authoritarian states, must pay attention to the tastes, values, and preferences of their audiences. In more lucrative markets, this means Nielsen ratings and other US-style audience research. Such measures are slower to arrive in less lucrative markets, but in virtually every country, media policy is made with substantial consideration for audience opinion, including the reactions of audiences to cultural imports from the United States. For example, both democratic India and undemocratic Oman forbid the release of Hollywood films containing raunchy sex or horrific violence. And while both decisions reflect the priorities of the regime, they also reflect genuine public sentiment — not least because in India and Oman, as in many other countries, movie-going is still a family affair involving everyone from toddlers to grandparents.

Despite the many local variations in its menu, the name *McDonald's* is synonymous with standardization, because every one of its thirty-three thousand outlets around the world offers the same basic package of food, service, and physical setting. There is no denying that certain aspects of this package have universal appeal. For example, in all 119 countries where McDonald's does business, the most popular menu item is the french fries.[9] Equally appealing is the friendly service—and the cleanliness of the facilities. The video artist did not mention the restrooms in the Zhongshan Park outlet, but in countries where public toilets leave much to be desired, the company's insistence on modern, well-maintained restrooms is a key selling point.[10]

The same is true of the kitchens, as I learned from Bambang Rachmadi, the first CEO of McDonald's in Indonesia. In Jakarta Rachmadi told me that when McDonald's was first introduced there, critics charged that it would drive street food vendors out of business. In response, Rachmadi pulled off a public relations coup: he invited the city's street food vendors to participate in a two-day course on hygienic food-handling, followed by a tour of McDonald's immaculate facilities. This made quite an impression, he said, in a city where food-borne illness is common and the majority of restaurants do not clean their kitchens very often.[11]

Stepping back, we can see a pattern. Certain aspects of McDonald's, such as the french fries, are universally appealing but bad for people—*all* people, regardless of where they live and what beliefs they hold.[12] Other aspects, such as the friendly service and clean facilities, are universally appealing and good for all people. Is there a similar pattern discernible in America's exported entertainment? Do certain aspects of our music, movies, and TV shows appeal to all human beings while also affecting them in ways that are either universally harmful or universally beneficial?

I hesitate to say yes, because to make such a claim about McDonald's is already to go pretty far out on a limb; to make a similar claim about popular culture is to cut the limb off. The responses of human beings to expressive culture are a lot more complex and variable than their responses to trans-fats, friendly smiles, and spotless commodes. Not only that, but a great many Americans believe that popular culture has no significant impact on the emotions, attitudes, or behaviors of audiences. Indeed, this is the prevailing assumption of our libertarian media regime.

Has this assumption been proven scientifically? The debate over media impacts is an old one, but over time social scientists have reached a rough consensus: the media do not brainwash us, but neither do they roll off our backs like the proverbial water off a duck. What they do is *condition* us, gradually and slowly, to accept—or at least consider normal—ways of thinking and acting that we otherwise would not. At the same time, social scientists admit it is impossible to quantify the impact of media on the beliefs, customs, and mores within a given society, much less across borders.

Yet the fact that social science cannot measure precisely the conditioning power of popular culture does not mean that rational analysis cannot conclude that this power exists, and that it may be used for good or ill. Nor does a lack of conclusive data prevent billions of human beings from treating their TV, movie, and computer screens as windows onto life in America—and from judging, on the basis of what they see there, whether its ideals and way of life are worthy of emulation or attack.

"RUBBER DUCK" GOES TO CHINA

After the return of Deng Xiaoping to power in 1978, the Chinese government began to allow selected US films to be shown in the country's small number of theaters. According to Dai Xinghue, a professor of literature and film at Peking University, the films were chosen with careful attention to their use as propaganda.[13] Thus, one of the selections was a justifiably forgotten 1978 release called *Convoy*, directed by Sam Peckinpah in his cups and starring Kris Kristofferson as "Rubber Duck," a maverick truck driver who uses the hot new social medium of the time, Citizens' Band (CB) radio, to lead a spontaneous revolt against a crooked, racist sheriff in the southwestern United States.

Asked why *Convoy* was chosen, Dai speculated that it was probably released for the purpose of disillusioning the Chinese people about the supposed high quality of Hollywood films (and because of its low cost).[14] The film also serves the added purpose of making the United States look anarchic. In keeping with the countercultural mood of the 1970s, it shows Rubber Duck leading a mile-long convoy of semitrailers across New Mexico to protest injustice, while also showing that the only way to obtain justice in America is to take the law into your own hands. At one point a headline-seeking governor offers help, but, sensing he's about to be used for a photo op, Rubber Duck spurns the offer and, after surviving a military assault by the National Guard and staging his own death, rides off into the sunset with a sexy new girlfriend in a bus full of stoned Jesus freaks. In true Peckinpah fashion, the final shot is of the crooked sheriff, grinning in recognition of Rubber Duck as a kindred spirit.

Viewed this way, *Convoy* delivers just what the Chinese authorities wanted: a cynical message about America as a place where local officials are corrupt and tyrannical, higher officials clueless and self-serving, and the common man free only when defying the system. But the authorities failed to anticipate the film's impact on a younger professor, Teng Jimeng of Beijing Foreign Studies University. Eyes sparkling, this member of the Tiananmen Square generation recalled how *Convoy* changed his life. I felt like saying, "You're kidding," but I bit my tongue when Teng waxed eloquent on *Convoy*'s depiction of an ordinary working stiff who goes wherever he wants, does whatever he wants, and punches out any thug in uniform who tries to stop him.[15]

Viewed Teng's way, *Convoy* appears a potent messenger, if not of democracy and the rule of law, then certainly of freedom, equality, and individualism, all rolled together. The raw, gut-level urge to bust loose, kick over the traces, and light out for the territory has been a staple of American culture since the earliest days. Immortalized in Mark Twain's *Huckleberry Finn*, Walt Whitman's *Song of the Open Road*, and Jack Kerouac's *On the Road*, it is also a perennial theme of popular music and, needless to say, of Hollywood movies, where it typically involves a fast car, a vast expanse of gorgeous scenery, and a heart-pounding soundtrack.

Of course, the same combination of car, scenery, and soundtrack is also used to sell cars. Indeed, it is rare to see an automobile ad on television or the Internet that does not use this formula. Like it or not, the American love of freedom, equality, and individualism is also identified with our unabashed consumerism. I say "unabashed" because while Americans have always craved material possessions (we are human, after all), we did not always consider that craving a form of citizen virtue. That idea arose at the turn of the twentieth century, when the economist Simon Patten argued that America was creating a new "economy of abundance" to replace the old "economy of scarcity." The son of Presbyterian farmers in Illinois, Patten had been raised to see money as the root of all evil. But as a student of the new social sciences, he came to believe that "science could develop and justify the restraints which would protect abundance from the evils of men's greed and the urges of the flesh."[16]

With this striking claim, Patten made consumerism the centerpiece of America's religion of progress. During the Great Depression this vision gained force in the social philosophy of New Deal intellectual Horace Kallen, who wrote these amazing words in 1936: "So long as men survive, the consumer in them, repressed but indestructible, will push forward to the open day of plenty and freedom which have been the privilege of a few. To be consumers is our birthright." Even more amazingly, Kallen declared that the true goal of human existence was "the living and growing of the personality," with *personality* defined as "the fierce free play of drives and impulses and insights and appetites."[17]

One of the greatest misconceptions foreigners have about Americans is that we have no distance on the advertising that surrounds us every day. This is simply not true. Not unlike the citizens of a totalitarian regime continually hammered by state propaganda, Americans are so barraged by advertising—consumerist propaganda—that we instinctively judge it to be false, unless by some fluke or miracle it should happen to prove true. Nor do most Americans accept the proposition, so dear to the hearts of twenty-first-century authoritarians, that consumer freedom is an adequate substitute for political liberty. Given a moment to reflect, Americans will define freedom and liberty as something far more capacious than is heard in the slogans of advertisers.

Regarding *freedom* and *liberty*, the historian David Hackett Fischer makes the intriguing point that English is the only Western language to include both words. Noting that *freedom* derives from the tribal languages of Northern Europe, and *liberty* from Latin, Fischer traces their different roots: for *freedom*, they are words meaning "beloved" or "belonging," suggesting a birthright enjoyed equally by every member of a tribe; for *liberty*, the root is *libertas*, meaning a specific release from a specific restraint, granted by a ruler and not the same for everyone. Fischer's point, highly relevant here, is that both words connote responsibility to a larger community: *freedom* entails a sacred obligation to the tribe, *liberty* depends on the virtue of the citizen. Indeed, the opposite of *liberty* is *libertinism*, from the Latin *libertinus*, meaning a person who has been granted more liberty than he can handle.[18]

A distinction to ponder, the next time an American president uses the word *freedom* forty-nine times on a single occasion, as George W. Bush did in his second inaugural speech.[19] When listeners around the globe hear such a speech, what images and associations come to their minds: The political wisdom of the American Framers? The giddy personal freedom expressed in a movie like *Convoy*? Or the crass libertinism on display in box-office sensations such as *Hangover, Hangover Part II,* and *Hangover Part III*? In the chapters that follow, I ask the same question about all of America's ideals, and also about its ethos of hope tempered with prudence. And I try to show that the answers matter, not because these attractive aspects of America are useful selling points for the maintenance of its global hegemony, but because they are good for people—*all* people, everywhere.

There I go, cutting off that limb.

———————◆———————

THE AMERICAN WAY OF SEX

Speaking at a conference in London in spring 2011, I suggested that it is one thing to defend the rights of women and quite another to advocate American-style sexual freedom, and that, in some parts of the world, it might be prudent to separate the two goals and concentrate on the first. This provoked vehement disagreement from a young woman in the audience, a US-educated Lebanese who insisted that the two goals were inseparable. When I asked her what she meant by sexual freedom, her reply was blunt: "To have sex with whomever I want, whenever I want." To my follow-up question—"Even after you're married?"—her reply was, "Yes, I plan to create my own marriage, make it unique, an open marriage or whatever." *How naive*, I thought, *how 1970s.* But all I said was, "We tried that in America, and it didn't work."

PLEASURE, COMMITMENT, AND GENERATIVITY

However naive, this outlook thrives in the sweet spot of American culture: the interlude between childhood and adulthood when university-bred youth live apart from their families, presumably starting a career but also enjoying a degree of affluence and personal freedom, including sexual freedom, unknown to most of their age peers around the world. Americans now see this interlude as temporary, a period of transition between the first stage of sexual maturity, which is *pleasure*, or individual gratification, and the second, which is *commitment*, or love and fidelity between partners. The third stage, *generativity*, brings the burdens and joys of caring for children, aging parents, and other relatives. Because generativity is so crucial, most societies give it priority over the other two, especially pleasure. When this meets resistance from the young, as it inevitably does, it is the task of adults to demonstrate, by persuasion and example, the rewards that come with growing up. This task is always hard, but it gets harder when popular culture sends the opposite message.

Recent evidence shows that the families of highly educated Americans are more stable than those of their less-educated countrymen. In a significant change from the 1970s, the well-being of lower-middle-class families has declined, making them almost as fragile as the families of the poor.[1] While this development is presumably related to the growing income disparity between the wealthiest Americans and the rest, it also reflects the cultural changes of the past forty years. The recent economic downturn has been hard on families, to be sure. But in the past even the poorest Americans struggled to hold their families together, because that was what was expected of them. Today the expectation is quite different. Indeed, the loudest message we hear, especially from popular culture, is that sexual autonomy and pleasure constitute the ultimate human good, overshadowing all others. If highly educated families are better at holding together, it may well be because they have the resources to push back against the legacy of the sexual revolution.

The American sexual revolution can be traced to the 1920s, when a generation of artists and writers began self-consciously to reject the strict sexual morality of the nineteenth century. By the 1950s Americans had heard of Freud, and although Freud himself took the tragic view that sexual repression was necessary for civilization, his name was invoked by Paul Goodman, Allan Ginsberg, Herbert Marcuse, William Reich, and other social critics for whom erotic liberation was the key to a radical transformation of the social and political order. This being America, erotic liberation soon acquired a post-millennial flavor. Indeed, in the hands of sexologist Alfred Kinsey, *Playboy* publisher Hugh Hefner, and journalist Helen Gurley Brown, the idea became a quasi-religious summons to smite repression, free the libido, and build an erotic utopia.[2]

Today that summons is all too familiar, and for many of its critics the only solution is to bring back the old puritanical morality of the nineteenth century. This is not my position. That morality was frequently blinkered, biased against women and minorities, and unnaturally strict. Instead of turning flesh-and-blood human beings into saints, it too often turned them into silent sufferers or moral hypocrites. It did, however, have one point in its favor: it expressed a certain prudence toward sex that is more in keeping with the American ethos than the reckless optimism that replaced it.

THE URBAN SINGLES COMEDY

After the attacks of 9/11, dozens of studies were done of America's image in the Arab world. One of these, headed by former ambassador Edward Djerejian, quoted an English teacher in Syria: "Does *Friends* show a typical American family?"[3] The question is puzzling, given that *Friends*, a popular sitcom that ran on NBC from 1994 to 2004, is notable for *not* showing a family. On the contrary, it belongs to a genre of TV show, the urban singles comedy, that focuses on the sweet spot—that is, on the lives of young, unattached men and women living in pleasant urban settings with a comfortable income, a huge amount of personal freedom, and little or no contact with their families or communities of origin.[4] The genre is summed up by the creators of *Friends* in their original pitch to NBC: "It's about sex, love, relationships, careers, a time in your life when every-thing's possible. And it's about friendship because *when you're single and in the city, your friends are your family*" (emphasis added).[5]

When I started my research, *Friends* was not uppermost in my mind. But the more I traveled, the more I saw the extent of its global appeal. The producer of *Friends*, Warner Brothers, estimates that the program has been telecast in 135 countries and "key territories," reaching an average of fourteen million viewers per telecast. And these figures are only for the lucrative markets of Europe, Australia, and East Asia. They do not include a host of other countries where *Friends* is carried by satellite and terrestrial channels.[6] Nor do they reflect the incalculable distribution of *Friends* via illegal downloads and pirated VCDs.[7] When pressed, they estimated that the total number of "hits" (individual view-ings of a single episode) was in the neighborhood of *seventeen billion!*[8]

The people I interviewed cited two obvious reasons for the popularity of this genre. One is the sheer display of affluence. These shows are replete with what the veteran producer Aaron Spelling called "eye candy." In more recent pro-grams produced in the era of high-definition television, such as *Sex and the City* and *Desperate Housewives*, the eye candy is even more enticing. In *Sex and the City*, for example, the four protagonists, single women in their thirties, inhabit a Manhattan whose cutting-edge fashions, trendy apartments, stylish boutiques, hip restaurants, and immaculate streets are made to look as luscious (and lily-white) as possible.

The other obvious appeal is titillation. *Friends* is full of sexual innuendo and (to quote the film rating system) "implied sexual situations." But as a network program, it must respect the parameters set by the FCC. Less restrained is *Sex and the City*, which, as a production of the cable channel HBO, is able to include lascivious language and explicit bedroom scenes. (It does stop short of nudity, however, giving the bizarre impression that promiscuous New York women never remove their brassieres.) In one episode, the lead character, a newspaper columnist named Carrie, asks, "Is sex ever safe?" In this sanitized Manhattan, the answer is yes. Carrie and her friends have frequent encounters with men they scarcely know, but the worst that ever happens is that the sex is less hot than the women had hoped.

But eye candy and titillation are not the main reasons put forward by most of the young people I met overseas. For them, the whole point is a chance to live vicariously in the sweet spot. Here it is worth reporting an observation made by an Indian senior executive working for Sony whom I interviewed in Mumbai. When asked about the general pattern of Indian channels localizing US programs, the executive commented that shows like *Friends* were the exception, because the lifestyle they depict had no equivalent in India. In most countries, young people have neither the resources nor the adult approval to experience the sweet spot. To quote a British editor I met in Cairo: "That bit between family and marriage doesn't exist here."[9]

At the same time, prosperity has brought change. Since the 1990s, writes Kay Hymowitz, a "New Girl Order" has arisen in Europe (including the post-communist countries) and East Asia: "In Shanghai, Berlin, Singapore, Seoul, and Dublin . . . crowds of single young females (SYFs) in their twenties and thirties . . . spend their hours working their abs and their careers, sipping cocktails, dancing at clubs, and (yawn) talking about relationships. *Sex and the City* has gone global." What's driving this New Girl Order, says Hymowitz, is not "American cultural imperialism" but "a series of stunning demographic and economic shifts," including greater educational and work opportunities for women, urbanization, and a worldwide trend toward later marriage and lower fertility.[10]

Hymowitz is right: American culture is not the only factor causing these global changes. But it is arguably an important one. As suggested by her allusions to *Sex and the City*, American popular culture is often the lens through which individuals make sense of social change. For example, a professor at one of China's top universities told me that unmarried Chinese graduate students, male and female, are beginning to share apartments. Adding that most were not telling their parents, the professor unhesitatingly attributed the wish "to cohabit, to not have children, to make their own choices" to "the influence of American culture." Despite widespread belief in America's decline, the United States is still the world's model, both positive and negative, of the future. On the positive side, we could point to the American struggle to fashion a more equitable path to marriage and adulthood. But on the negative side we must ask: how can people learn about that struggle, when their view of America is through the entertaining but distorted lens of television?

To begin, the urban singles comedy makes commitment look next to impossible. In *Friends*, all six characters fail at relationships outside their own circle, and when that happens, they retreat back into the circle. When romance blossoms inside the circle, which it does with dizzying frequency, the lovers immediately lose the ability to communicate, regaining it only when the romance sputters. In *Sex and the City*, the character most scornful of commitment, Samantha, is also the most glamorous, a gorgeous blonde pursuing casual sex as gleefully as Hugh Hefner in a hot tub. Samantha's shamelessness is held up as a foil to her three friends, who yearn to marry before the sweet spot turns sour. But she is also lauded for "putting her sexuality out there." Indeed, in the opening episode she leads her friends in a vow to quit caring and "do it like a man."

Another global favorite, *Desperate Housewives*, focuses on married couples but treats commitment as laughable. Lacking the wit and pizzazz of *Sex and the City*, the show relies on the 1950s-era cliché of sexual secrets simmering beneath the bright surface of a picture-perfect suburb. This seems to strike a nerve among affluent Chinese.[11] A recent college graduate whom I interviewed in Shanghai told me that her friends felt "deprived" when they couldn't watch each new episode of *Desperate Housewives* the day after it aired in the United States.

These shows are played for laughs, of course, and the purpose of comedy is not to depict exemplary behavior but to exaggerate and perhaps correct human folly. Most Americans, knowing our own society, take these programs in that spirit. We understand that they are distorting reality in order to make a point. Lacking this understanding, many foreigners take these programs at face value. For example, a Chinese media executive told me that many Chinese viewers do not see these programs as comedy but rather as therapy: "A lot of Chinese people have emotional problems with sex, and there is very little psychiatry available. So shows like *Sex and the City* offer a way for people to deal with their problems."

If this comment can be taken seriously, then what is the therapeutic message being delivered by *Sex and the City*? It could hardly be more clear: put off commitment as long as possible, and avoid generativity like the plague. To be sure, the four characters in *Sex and the City* do marry and bear children, but rarely in that order, and never without a freight of anxiety more suited to a suicide pact than to a wedding or birth. Of the four, only Charlotte wants children; the others shudder at the mere thought of attending a baby shower. When Miranda gets pregnant by her ex-boyfriend Steve, she decides to have the child only if he promises not to play a fatherly role. Eventually Miranda and Steve marry, but to judge by the two feature films that followed the series, their happiness is far from assured.

Generativity also extends to the old, and here the young people I interviewed pointed to a stunning disconnect. In Cairo, a former exchange student from a Bedouin village who had spent a year in an American suburb told me that she was astonished to see how much time Americans spend with their families. "In the media," she said, "there are no families, just individuals." Through firsthand contact with American society, this young woman understood how dramatic some media distortions really are.

I heard similar comments in Turkey, the Arab Emirates, India, Indonesia, and China—often accompanied by a description of how the speaker's own life was enmeshed in a tissue of extended, multigenerational family relationships. These comments opened my eyes to this aspect of American popular culture. In *Friends*, for example, the families are kept strictly offstage, the only exceptions being the brother-sister tie between Ross and Monica, and an awkward encounter between Phoebe and her estranged birth mother. In *Sex and the City* the few parents depicted are made to look ridiculous, manipulative, pathological. And all other relatives—siblings, grandparents, aunts, uncles, cousins—are airbrushed out.

It is true, of course, that single city-dwellers tend to hail from other places and have little daily contact with the folks back home. But these shows turn distance into willed oblivion. "My family lives in Philadelphia and I don't like them," says Miranda in *Sex and the City*. Charlotte is devoted to the idea of having a family, but at her joyful wedding to the equally devoted Harry, we get nary a glimpse of the families that presumably instilled that devotion. Most astonishing is Carrie, who seems to have sprung from the pavement of East Seventy-Third Street, as Aphrodite from the sea foam. Midway through the fifth season, Carrie mentions in passing that her father abandoned the family when she was small. But in ninety-four episodes, two feature films, and two weddings in which she is the bride, there is no mention of Carrie's mother or any other family member.

How to explain this disconnect? One answer is the abiding prejudice against old people found in America, and American media. So pervasive is this prejudice I was startled, when watching television in India, to see gray-haired grandmothers in commercials for fruit juice and house paint. On American television there are no gray-haired women. And if you see a gray-haired man, he's either the villain of the piece or selling Viagra.

Another explanation, noted by *Time* magazine, is that "gay writers . . . are behind the TV shows that are most provocatively defining straight relationships."[12] To some degree, the estrangement from family life historically suffered by gay Americans has been projected onto these non-gay characters. For example, when Miranda's mother dies, her grief seems mainly directed at her family for rejecting her as "a single woman in my thirties." The pastor mischaracterizes her as a sister-in-law, and the only person willing to escort her from the church is her friend Carrie.

This note of exclusion, even shame, at being single may strike a chord in societies where women are still expected to marry by a certain age. But it rings false in 1990s America, and the only way to make it ring true is to imagine Miranda as a lesbian. The awkwardness of her family, and the distance from family and community felt by characters like Miranda, are best understood in terms of the old Hollywood saying, "Write gay, cast straight." Today that saying is less heard, because Hollywood is more inclusive of gay characters. But the habit of treating familial estrangement as the norm persists—and the price of doing so, at home but especially abroad, remains high.

There is also a rich irony here. Reflecting the contemporary push for gay marriage, the second feature film in the *Sex and the City* franchise (*Sex and the City 2*, 2010) devotes an hour to the campy, extravagant wedding of Carrie's gay friend Stanford to his true love, Anthony, and at one point the camera zeroes in on Anthony's elderly parents, affectionately toasting the happy couple. The irony is not that this fond parental tribute occurs at a gay wedding, but that no comparable tribute occurs at any of the show's four heterosexual weddings.

Burdened by the demands of their own extended families, my young overseas interlocutors were fascinated by urban singles comedies. Some likened them to a drug, alluring but enervating. In Egypt, where educated youth have trouble finding jobs, a recent graduate of Cairo University told me that most of her classmates were "just living at home, doing nothing but watching *Friends*." The preoccupations of young Egyptians have changed drastically since the upheavals that began in 2011, but, at the time, this young woman worried that for some of her peers, *Friends* was "becoming an obsession."

Others drew a sharp contrast with their own values. In Sharjah (one of the Arab Emirates) I asked an engineering student about his personal goals, and he replied forcefully that his "chief aim was to help his family and to live in this world with a positive footprint, because there's more to being here on earth than seeking the pleasure of the moment."[13] In India, I heard praise for all things American, veiled with polite rejection of the hyper-individualism portrayed in its entertainment. A journalist in Delhi told me that educated young Indians,

even those who study in the United States, are eager to return home and become part of "the joint family, three generations, living in the same house."

This may sound like wishful thinking, given how many non-resident Indians
(NRIs) do not return home. But a top executive with a Mumbai-based media
company told me that for many working women, the Indian family was superior
to the American, "because granny is there." Khozem Merchant, an executive
with Pearson India, predicted that while American culture was making inroads,
the joint family would not soon disappear: "It would be a mistake to underestimate the force of this traditional and customary way of life."[14]

I heard less about tradition and custom in China, where sixty years of Communist rule have left a "values vacuum." Chinese media officials are dismayed
by the spectacle of American entertainment rushing in to fill that vacuum, so
they scrutinize the American product, hoping to adapt it for their own use. In
Beijing I interviewed Sun Jin, a professor of "media axiology," a field he described as "the study of how the media construct social values." In this professor's view, urban singles comedies were "typically American" but "not a model
of how Chinese youth should behave."[15]

Seeking to construct a better model, China has become one of the few countries to try localizing *Sex and the City*. According to a memo sent to me by a
graduate student in communications, one such effort, a program called *The
Desire to Fall in Love*, keeps the idea of "modern girls searching for true love
in the big city," but "filters out almost all the sex elements," because "it would
offend Chinese audiences to express the sex problem in the same way as in *Sex
and the City*."

It's hard to imagine *Sex and the City* with "all the sex elements" filtered out.
What would be left? To Americans, the urban singles comedy draws a more
or less amusing caricature of life in the sweet spot. To others—not media officials in China, but millions of ordinary men and women—this caricatured
aspect is harder to discern. Without a doubt, foreigners enjoy watching the
erotic shenanigans of Americans on television. But their enjoyment is tinged
with a voyeurism that should give us pause. Are they laughing at Americans
as fellow human beings, struggling in all our comic frailty to achieve a more
equitable path to commitment and generativity? Or are they laughing at alien,
even grotesque creatures who refuse to acknowledge any sexual good beyond
pleasure?

THE WORLD PUSHES BACK

When it comes to portraying sex, love, marriage, and family in a way that appeals to global audiences, the urban singles comedy has three major rivals: the

Latin American telenovela, the Middle Eastern Ramadan series, and the Indian Bollywood romance. All have much in common with older forms of American popular culture, but they have been adapted for local audiences in ways that make them very different from contemporary American fare—and the differences are illuminating.

The Latin American Telenovela

The North American ancestor of the telenovela is the soap opera, a genre that first appeared in Chicago during the Depression, when that city's elites were worried about the impact of hard times on the large blue-collar population, which included many recent migrants from Europe and the Deep South. Thus, when radio station WGN persuaded two local companies (one a soap maker) to sponsor a fifteen-minute drama aimed at working-class housewives, all parties understood that the goal was not just to sell soap but also to convey morally uplifting messages. The result, *Painted Dreams*, about an Irish widow helping her unmarried daughter stay out of trouble, was a hit. And the second-generation American who created it, Irna Phillips, went on to create many other classic soaps, including the longest-running series in broadcast history: *The Guiding Light*, which ran on NBC radio and television from 1937 to 2009.

During that seventy-two years, the soap changed beyond all recognition. Phillips's original "guiding light" was the lamp in the window of Rev. John Ruthledge, a character modeled on a Chicago minister who had helped her recover from an out-of-wedlock pregnancy. For the next thirty years *The Guiding Light* had a moral center: first a succession of pastors, then Papa Bauer, the patriarch of a German immigrant family. But by the 1970s the show was no longer an uplifting saga watched by tradition-minded women struggling to hold families together. Instead, it was a lurid parade of adultery, divorce, addiction, suicide, and crime watched by an audience that included many teenagers and college students.

Then, in 1973, the sexual revolution arrived in the form of a soap aptly titled *The Young and the Restless*, followed in 1987 by an even more successful spin-off, *The Bold and the Beautiful*. The best way to describe these shows is to note that *The Bold and the Beautiful* started out with a romance between a poor girl named Brooke Logan and a rich boy named Ridge Forrester and that, twenty-three years and six thousand episodes later, Brooke had been married five times to Ridge, three times to his father, and once to his younger brother—a trajectory that brings to mind the old minstrel routine in which a man explains how, through various tangled kinship relations, he ended up being his own grandfather.

Next came the "prime time soap," an upscale version of the daytime soap that focused on rich, quarreling families at the head of business empires. Beginning in the late 1980s, the most popular prime time soaps—*Dallas, Dynasty, Falcon Crest*—were snapped up by foreign media scrambling to compete in newly deregulated markets, and by 1990 *Dallas* was airing in fifty-seven countries to an audience of three hundred million.[16] Several daytime soaps also made their way into the global market—and some remain there. For example, *The Bold and the Beautiful* is currently airing in 110 countries.[17]

Yet these successes have not made the US soap "the number-one form of human entertainment on the planet."[18] That accolade, delivered by the BBC, was for the Latin American telenovela, which began by conquering prime time on its continent of origin, then went on to build an estimated global audience of two billion, stretching from Russia and Eastern Europe to the Middle East and Malaysia.[19] One reason for this global popularity is price: telenovelas cost less than most US soaps. But there's a more compelling reason: unlike soaps, which run as long as ratings and revenues permit, telenovelas run between six and twelve months, then reach a conclusion in which all the loose ends are tied up.

This limited run preserves what literary critic Frank Kermode called "the sense of an ending." Inherent in any form of storytelling is the expectation of a morally satisfying resolution, in which good is rewarded and evil rebuked.[20] The most beloved telenovela of all time, a 1969 Peruvian production called *Simplemente María* (Simply Maria), is all about a morally satisfying resolution: a village girl goes to work as a maid in the city, only to be seduced and abandoned by a rich medical student. Fired from her job, she supports herself and her son while learning to read and sew. Eventually she marries her kindly teacher and becomes a successful fashion designer.

When first broadcast in Peru, *Simplemente María* was so popular, ten thousand people showed up for the taping of the wedding episode. More significant, there was an uptick in the number of housemaids enrolling in adult literacy and sewing classes. When *Simplemente María* had a similar impact in other Latin American countries, a Mexican producer named Miguel Sabido had the idea of getting private media companies and governments to cooperate in making telenovelas that would not just make money but also convey uplifting messages to struggling women trying to hold their families together amid disruptive change. In other words, Sabido took the genre back to its roots.

After producing five successful telenovelas in Latin America, Sabido exported the idea, cooperating with the Indian government to produce *Hum Log* (We People), which aired in 1984 on the state network, Doordarshan.

Some of the messages *Hum Log* hoped to convey, such as family planning and greater assertiveness for women, were not well received. Indeed, one of the characters intended to be a negative role model—a submissive, self-sacrificing grandmother—was cited as *positive* by 80 percent of the viewers. But other messages, about the need for husbands to respect their wives, and for parents to consider the wishes of their daughters when arranging marriages, were better received. And *Hum Log* was a ratings success, attracting an average audience of fifty million (out of eighty million Indians with access to television at the time).[21]

"Entertainment-education," as Sabido calls it, is not unknown in America. For example, the ABC network's *Afterschool Specials,* airing between 1972 and 1996, offered positive life lessons to teenagers in a deliberate attempt to push back against the negative drift of youth culture. In the 1990s, a TV host named Sonny Fox joined forces with Secretary of Health and Human Services Donna Shalala to persuade soap producers to include socially beneficial messages. One result was the inclusion of an AIDS subplot in the 2001 season of *The Bold and the Beautiful,* which prompted thousands of viewers to call a posted 800 number.

The short-term impact of such messages is acknowledged every time a trade group or nonprofit presents an award to a show for supporting a worthy cause. What is not acknowledged is the *long-term* impact of American soaps that spend decades spiraling down the proverbial toilet. The open-ended format wasn't a problem in the old days, when the "guiding light" character kept tabs on the others. But when that moral center dropped out, the lack of an ending became an excuse to "push the envelope" beyond all credulity.

The Middle Eastern Ramadan Series

Entertainment-education doesn't sink to this level, but it has other problems, especially when taken up by the hybrid media in authoritarian regimes. Typically the telenovelas created by the Chinese, Iranian, Russian, and Arab media are designed to attract "eyeballs" and ad revenue, while also shaping public opinion. These goals can be tricky to reconcile, as evidenced by the recent history of the Ramadan series (*musalsal* in Arabic).

The Ramadan series is a major feature of Arab satellite television, airing at sunset during the holy month of Ramadan, when families gather for *iftar,* the meal that breaks their daily fast. Before the mid-1990s, iftar was devoted to feasting and storytelling; today it is devoted to feasting and television. During the later hours, when the children are asleep, the adults choose among many competing musalsal. In the early days, these were produced by Lebanese and Egyptians, the old masters of Arab entertainment. Today the Saudis contribute historical epics such as *Omar*, a lavish series about a companion of the Prophet Muhammad who became the second caliph of the Arab empire.[22]

But before 2011, the leader in cutting-edge musalsal was Syria. Indeed, Syrian TV producers gained a reputation for being able to dodge the flack coming from government officials, financiers, religious leaders, and audiences, not only in Syria but also in the other twenty-four countries that make up the Arab media market. In 2010, Syria produced thirty successful musalsal, some touching on controversial topics such as women's rights, corruption, and terrorism.[23] Not surprisingly, this dominance ended with the Syrian civil war that began in 2011.

The Arab market has also welcomed Ramadan series from Iran. Before the "green" protests of 2009, Tehran's state-controlled television had become quite adept at producing historical serials with political subtexts that resonated with Arab viewers. But those productions were shut down during the violent repression of the green protests, and in 2011 it seemed highly unlikely that Iran would produce any serials touching on political upheaval, even the kind that places contemporary themes in remote historical settings.

Another non-Arab player is Turkey. Deregulated in the 1980s, Turkish television aired a lot of soaps and telenovelas before gearing up to produce its own localized serials, a genre that often dramatized the tension between secular Kamalist values and resurgent Islam. One of these, a 2005 serial called *Gümüş* (Silver), enjoyed a modest success in Turkey, then got sold to the Saudi-owned company that dominates the Arab market, the Middle East Broadcasting Center (MBC). All ten MBC channels are free-to-air, meaning nonsubscription, so they reach everyone in the region who has access to a satellite signal. Thus it was a major event when *Gümüş*, translated as *Noor* (Light), became the most-watched serial in the history of Arab television—with the final episode attracting eighty-five million viewers, including more than fifty-one million adult women, roughly half the total female population of the region.

The plot of *Gümüş/Noor* is pure telenovela. A village girl agrees to an arranged marriage to the son of a wealthy Istanbul family, only to discover that her handsome new husband still pines for another. Like María in Peru, the heroine of *Gümüş/Noor* is devastated, but then pulls herself together, learns to sew, and embarks on a career in fashion. In the end, she succeeds not only in winning her husband's heart but also in turning him into the very model of a modern egalitarian husband.

One measure of the serial's impact was an abrupt rise in tourism between Arab countries and Istanbul, where thousands of Arab wives dragged their husbands on "*Noor* Tours," in the hope of making them more appreciative and supportive. (It is also worth noting that thousands of Arab husbands went along with this.) Is *The Bold and the Beautiful* having the same sort of positive impact? Most Arabs and Turks would say no, and they'd be right.

The Bollywood Romance

In the Middle East it is hard to separate criticism of American popular culture from hostility toward US foreign policy. But what about India, a country where public opinion is generally favorable toward the United States, but unfavorable toward our popular culture? In the same Pew survey cited earlier, 59 percent of Indian respondents expressed a favorable opinion of America, as opposed to 29 percent expressing an unfavorable opinion. (This was in 2007, a low point in America's global reputation.) At the same time, only 23 percent of Indians said they "like American music, movies, and TV," with 68 percent saying they disliked them.[24]

One reason for this split is simply that Indians prefer their own popular culture. India is still a poor country, with 750 million of its more than 1.2 billion people living in villages without functioning roads, elementary education, or basic health care, and 40 percent of its urban population crowded into slums.[25] Yet this huge population lives on movies. Hindi-speaking Mumbai (Bollywood) is not the only center of film production in India, but it sets the tone for all the others. "Hindi cinema's culture is quite different from Indian culture," says screenwriter Javed Akhtar, "but it's not alien to us, we understand it."[26]

So do over a billion non-Indians. Sixty percent of Bollywood's total audience is outside India, and that includes not only diaspora Indians but also Africans, Central Asians, Russians, East Asians, Indonesians, and many others.[27] After the Taliban were driven from Kabul in 2002, the first film to be shown was a Bollywood production.[28]

What does this huge swath of humanity see in Bollywood? Dev Benegal, an independent filmmaker who grew up in the industry, answered this way: "Bollywood knows its audience. Those 1.2 billion people, no matter where they are, do not want American-style stories with sex and violence. What they want are the ingredients that once defined classic Hollywood: beautiful stars, lavish costumes and settings, singing and dancing, strong emotions, melodrama and—most important—a very clear and simple moral lesson."[29]

According to one scholar, that lesson is typically that "family relationships" are "inclusive of, but much broader than, the true romance that provides [the] storyline."[30] A prime example might be the huge 1995 hit *Dilwale Dulhaniya Le*

Jayenge (The Brave Heart Wins the Bride). *DDLJ*, as it is affectionately known, is the story of Raj, who is the playboy son of an Indian millionaire living in London and who falls in love with Simran, the daughter of an Indian shopkeeper. Simran's father longs for India and has betrothed his daughter to the son of an old friend back in the Punjab. So when Simran begs her father to let her marry Raj, he refuses.

The rest of the story unfolds in the Punjab, where the family goes for the wedding. Following them and concealing his identity from everyone but Simran (her parents have not met him), Raj proceeds to turn the situation around by ingratiating himself with every member of her extended family. This includes Simran's mother, who guesses his identity and urges the couple to elope.

This is the high point for Indian audiences, but it is not a scene likely to appear in an American film. Raj refuses to elope without the blessing of Simran's father. In tears, he tells Simran's mother that beneath his Westernized exterior he is a true child of India who would never dream of defying the wishes of his elders, who know what is best for their children and must always be respected and obeyed. A little later Raj makes the same speech to Simran's father and the would-be groom's family. The film climaxes at the railroad station, where, in a typical Bollywood flourish, Simran's father waits until Raj's train is under way to release his grip on his daughter's arm. The music swells as she runs after the departing train and is hoisted aboard by her "brave heart" Raj.

AMERICAN RAUNCH INVADES BOLLYWOOD

When I show these scenes to my students, they smile at the "cheesy" emotion. But they also marvel at the difference between *DDLJ* and a Hollywood film they know well: *Wedding Crashers* (2005). Both are about a lovable rogue who woos a sheltered young woman, is rejected by her family, and wins her in the end. But there the resemblance ends, because while family relationships are the whole point in *DDLJ*, they are beside the point in *Wedding Crashers*.[31] John, the rejected lover, finally wins the lovely Claire during the wedding of her sister. But unlike Raj, who spends days courting Simran's many relatives, John simply barges into the church and interrupts the ceremony with a declaration of love. No one protests except Claire's unpleasant fiancé, and as for the relatives in the pews, they might as well be props. They sit gaping until the lovers kiss, and then in a typical *Hollywood* flourish, they applaud.

One of my students made the apt observation that if some guy pulled a stunt like that at a wedding in her family, he'd be thrown out on his ear. What better example of popular culture as a fun-house mirror?

Of course, the point of *Wedding Crashers* is not weddings or families but the antics of John and his pals, whose favorite pastime is seducing women at the weddings (and funerals) of strangers. In this vein, the film offers plenty of the raunchy humor that has come to dominate American youth culture.

There was a time, not too long ago, when romantic comedy and raunchy humor were two separate genres, the former aimed at female and adult audiences, the latter at adolescent males. What's happened, in essence, is a merging of the two, with raunchy humor taking up residence in romantic comedy. The process dates back to the 1998 film *There's Something About Mary*, in which the love affair between an awkward young man named Ted and his dream girl, Mary, is thwarted first by a freak accident in which Ted's penis becomes stuck in his zipper, and then by a scene in which, after masturbating, Ted greets Mary with a gob of his own semen hanging from his ear. ("What is that," she asks, "hair gel?")

Semen jokes have been around forever, along with excrement and vomit jokes, and they never lose their appeal for adolescent boys (and others) who must struggle to reconcile bodily impropriety with social propriety. But only recently has this "gross-out" humor become the staple of film comedy. Consider the *American Pie* series, which began in 1999 with a randy teenager named Jim masturbating with a warm apple pie, and continued through 2003, with Jim and his girlfriend meeting Jim's father in a restaurant while the girlfriend performs oral sex on Jim under the table. It is characteristic of this new genre—the raunchy romantic comedy—that the father's reason for joining the couple in the restaurant is to deliver an engagement ring, so Jim can propose marriage while hitching up his pants over an erection.

Jim's father smiles benignly on these escapades, thus prefiguring this genre's next phase, which was to make the parents raunchier than the kids. The 2000 film *Meet the Parents* takes the usual path, focusing on a bumbling young Jew who makes a terrible impression on his WASP girlfriend's crypto-fascist parents.[32] But then the producers had the bright idea of making the bumbler's own parents, the Fockers, half-crazed sex therapists. Both sequels, *Meet the Fockers* (2004) and *Little Fockers* (2010), were box-office hits.

Steering the raunchy romantic comedy in a more promising direction was Judd Apatow, the writer-director of *The 40-Year-Old Virgin* (2005), *Knocked Up* (2007), and *Bridesmaids* (2011), three celebrated films whose laughs arise less from bizarre concocted situations than from the natural awkwardness of being human. The humor is no less raunchy for that, but it is also funnier, and better integrated with the romance. Apatow's success was heartening, but it hardly spelled the end of the gross-out humor, which, after all, takes very little talent to produce and reliably provokes guffaws and sniggers from the all-important teenage market.

Of the films in this genre, only *Meet the Fockers* appears on the list of top 100 international hits (at number 97).[33] But the genre's global reach should not be underestimated. Every film that is commercially successful in the United States is also aggressively marketed, legally and illegally, to every possible Western and non-Western audience. And that includes millions of people who share India's high regard for the family.

In Mumbai, I heard many positive comments about Hollywood, but for the most part these focused on business and technical matters. For most of its history, Bollywood has been dominated by small, family-owned studios whose main source of capital was organized crime. This changed in 2001, when the government granted official industry status to the studios, making it much easier for them to raise capital and do business with foreign investors. Soon forward-looking studios such as UTV were embarking on joint ventures with US-based entertainment firms such as Warner Brothers, Sony (Columbia Tristar), Paramount, Fox Star, and Walt Disney.[34] This has led to improvements not only in business methods but also in technical skills such as cinematography, lighting, sound, and production design.

Along with these technical improvements has come a loosening of traditional controls over content. For years it was standard practice to remake Hollywood films in the image of Bollywood—which meant not only adding song-and-dance sequences but also expanding the plot to include many more family members and neighbors, and deleting explicit sex scenes.[35] Today this practice is changing because the audience is changing. Instead of making films to please everyone, from the poorest villager to the most affluent city-dweller, today's Bollywood is making films for an increasingly segmented market.

Of the millions of Indians attending a film on a given day, the majority are poor villagers paying about five US cents a ticket at an old-fashioned single-screen theater. But a growing number (three hundred million and counting) are young, middle-class urbanites paying four or five times that amount at an upscale urban multiplex.[36] Thus, a relatively small number of multiplexes are generating an increasing amount of the film industry's revenue.[37] Equally important is the huge market for Indian films outside India. Made up of non-resident Indians (NRIs) and many others, this audience is also more affluent—and less conservative—than the masses back home.

This shift is affecting the content of Bollywood romances, according to two seasoned observers I met in Mumbai. One, writer and documentary filmmaker Nasreen Munni Kabir, put it this way:

> In films today there is great emphasis on young people as decision makers, and less presence of older family members as key characters. This is because over five hundred million people in India today are under the age of thirty-five. And they are the main cinema-going audience. The older films relied a lot on subplots and a number of characters carrying the narrative. As these have been more or less eliminated, the story lines are linear and often dance numbers fill in the gaps to the detriment of the story.[38]

In other words, the focus has shifted away from the relatives, neighbors, child-hood companions, and loyal retainers whose intertwined stories were once viv-idly brought to life by seasoned character actors and (at times) nonprofessionals.

The other observer was Mumbai editor Rauf Ahmed, who reminded me that Bollywood films are not getting any shorter. "They are still three hours long on the average," he noted. "They've got to fill the time with something." In a clas-sic Bollywood romance, that something would have been the many secondary characters—indeed, it takes a village to build up all the rich comic and tragic layers of a film like *DDLJ*. But now that these layers have been removed, the tendency is to fill the time with "items," meaning song-and-dance sequences that have only the remotest connection to the plot. And because these "items" serve double duty as music videos on MTV's Indian channel, Ahmed noted that "there is pressure to add ever more stand-alone video clips to any given film." The result, he added, is an "epidemic of mindless distraction," which, rather than help audiences "reason through basic questions," gives them "a circus of titillation, some emotional, some comic, but with no linear development."[39] The general understanding among billions of Bollywood fans around the world is that this circus was made in America.

THE AMERICAN WAY OF SEX

"The American condition is a state of unease."[40] The words were written in the 1970s by the eminent man of letters Ralph Ellison. But they could have been written at any time in American history, because Americans have always been a restless, mobile people longing to reconcile our prized personal freedom with our craving for lasting connection. This unease arises naturally from the nation's distinctive social fabric, which is at once loose-weave and cohesive. It is loose-weave in the sense that Americans are willing to leave home in search of new opportunities and experiences; it is cohesive in the sense that we are welcoming to strangers and capable of reaching beyond family, faith, and ethnic group to cooperate with fellow citizens in pursuit of common goals.

Some attribute America's loose-weave cohesion to self-selection, arguing that the country was populated by go-getters, not stay-putters. Others ascribe it to a history of religious liberty and geographical expansion. Still others judge it a dehumanizing adaptation to the relentless churning of capitalism. Whatever the explanation, most Americans understand that the bright threads of our affability—our *friendliness*—are interwoven with dark strands of loneliness, detachment, anomie.

The same is true, with special poignancy, of the American way of sex. Closely related to our willingness to form cooperative bonds with strangers is our willingness to have sexual relations with them. Americans have more sexual partners than do the populations of other Western democracies, and we also marry and divorce more often.[41] We allow our young people wider latitude to follow their desires, explore their emotions, and (eventually) choose their mate. Of course, we also expect that at some point the pursuit of pleasure will modulate into the well-being of commitment and generativity. Most young Americans are eager to achieve this outcome, and there is significant evidence to suggest that married couples have happier sex lives than their unmarried counterparts.[42] But as the period of sexual freedom becomes more prolonged, the transition from pleasure to commitment becomes more difficult.

Further complicating the situation is a definition of marriage based more on the needs of the expanded self than on any sense of reciprocal duty and responsibility. In a 2001 survey conducted by Gallup and Rutgers University, 94 percent of single Americans said they wanted their future spouse to be a "soul mate" and "best friend," rather than a good provider and parent. And only 16 percent thought the main purpose of marriage was to raise children.[43] As interpreted by Barbara Dafoe Whitehead, these findings reflect both a "heightened desire for emotional intimacy" and "a diminished role for . . . many of the larger social, economic, religious, and public purposes associated with marriage."[44]

The cultural critic Morris Dickstein once described the American sexual revolution as a "gospel" in which sex became "a wedge for reorienting all human relations."[45] This is not an exaggeration. First taken up by the beats of the 1950s, the gospel of erotic liberation was then embraced by the hippies of the 1960s and followed by millions of ordinary Americans in the 1970s. The 1980s brought a backlash, as social conservatives sought to restore the morality, not of the puritanical nineteenth century, but of mid-twentieth-century America. But it was too late. As noted by a young woman I spoke with in Cairo, "What Americans mean by conservative is not what Egyptians mean by conservative." On a State Department–sponsored trip to Washington, this young Cairene had been "surprised by the way so-called conservatives acted, drinking heavily and wearing clothes that were very revealing."

To millions of thoughtful Americans, including those who are old enough to remember the gospel of erotic liberation in its heyday, the real legacy of the sexual revolution is not utopia (far from it), but a continuing struggle to fashion a more equitable path from pleasure to commitment and generativity. This struggle would be of great interest to others around the world who are experiencing similar upheavals. But it is not being conveyed by some of America's most popular cultural exports.

EMPIRE OF SPECIAL EFFECTS

"He doth bestride the narrow world like a Colossus." Shakespeare's line about Julius Caesar applies equally well to the American film industry. In some countries, notably China, the import of American films is restricted by law. In others, notably India, it is limited by audience preference for the domestic product. But in the most lucrative markets (Europe, Japan, Australia), Hollywood earns the lion's share of the total box office. Foreign elites tend to blame this dominance on Washington's aggressive trade policies. This is a valid point, but the main driver of American dominance is a unique, self-perpetuating cycle of gigantic capitalization and profitability. No other film industry can spend hundreds of millions of dollars to produce a single film, advertise and distribute it through channels it controls, and, when the profits start to flow, make sure they flow back to the source.

For many years, Hollywood's technical wizardry has been the envy of the world. Today many countries' traditional film craft is as good as or better than Hollywood's. But when it comes to special effects—magical transformations of real landscapes and figures, dazzling animation, entire worlds spun from computer-generated imagery (CGI)—Hollywood is still the chief wizard. And the blockbuster—the massive "movie event" or series such as *Avatar, Pirates of the Caribbean,* and *Harry Potter*[1]—still takes by far the largest portion of global box office receipts. Other countries, notably China, dream of competing in this sphere, but so far those dreams have not been realized.

State-of-the-art special effects are used in other forms of American entertainment in addition to the blockbuster. For example, they play a key role in the countless violence-saturated films, TV shows, and video games that, like blockbusters, reach global audiences in many different ways—from theatrical distribution to DVD sales, satellite television to pirated VCDs and illegal down-loads. In these areas, too, Hollywood's technical wizardry stands out. The only difference is that these ever more gruesome depictions of murder and mayhem are resented as much as they are envied.

REALMS OF FANTASY

With the exception of *Titanic*, the most popular blockbusters are set in fantasy worlds full of CGI wonders and terrors.[2] Yet, in the present context, what is most striking about these films is their lack of explicit sex and violence. Some blockbusters are more family-friendly than others, but all exercise a remarkable degree of self-censorship compared with American popular culture as a whole. They never contain nudity, and while some contain graphic bloodletting, it is typically edited down to brief glimpses in fast-moving battle sequences. The reasons for this restraint are practical: theatrical release in many countries is controlled by government censors, and moviegoing, for many of the world's people, is still something families do together. But the happy result is an unusual regard for foreign sensibilities.

The main complaint I have heard overseas about American blockbusters is that their moral imagination is not as rich as their visual imagination. This is similar to the complaint lodged against *The Lord of the Rings* in 2001, when the BBC voted it "the greatest book of the 20th century." For British critic Andrew O'Hehir, J. R. R. Tolkien's trilogy was "boyish," in the sense that "boys can have access to a nobility and moral clarity, an uncloudedness of motive, that disappears with the arrival of devious and lustful manhood."[3] Thus, Middle Earth is saved by a pair of boyish hobbits, Frodo and Sam, who take the Ring of Power back to the volcano where it was forged, so it can be destroyed before falling into the hands of the Dark Lord Sauron. Both hobbits are swayed by the Ring, but (contra Lord Acton) they are not corrupted by it. Moral clarity triumphs in the end.

But as O'Hehir suggests, such a moral universe is too simplistic for grown-ups. O'Hehir concludes that Tolkien's main achievement was to set this tale in an extraordinarily detailed fantasy world—and the same can be said of the Hollywood blockbuster. *The Lord of the Rings, Star Wars, Harry Potter,* and many other such films offer settings that are visually rich and inventive, but moral universes that are simplistic: good guys noble, bad guys demonic. And while the good guys are sometimes swayed by the Ring, the Dark Side, or the evil Voldemort, they always return to the Light before Armageddon—that is, before the eye-popping apocalyptic battle sequence that is the dream of every special-effects wizard.

But here we run into a problem, because with the exception of the movie *Troy*, which borrows from Homer's *Iliad* the insight that war is something that occurs between human armies, most blockbusters follow Tolkien's formula of having one army composed of blue-eyed, English-speaking heroes and their allies, and the other of vile subhuman monsters along the lines of Tolkien's Orcs. Needless to say, this simplistic formula makes it easy for the heroes to kill thousands while maintaining their boyish nobility.

Of course, no one on earth identifies with Tolkien's Orcs. More troublesome is the blockbuster in which the vile enemy is identified with a real nation. Case in point: 300 (2007), a retelling of the battle of Thermopylae, in which three hundred Spartans held off a much bigger invading Persian army for three days. Based on a comic book, 300 serves as an object lesson in how not to make a global blockbuster.[4] As noted by one irate historian, the Persians are depicted as "a bunch of veiled towel-heads who remind us of Iraqi insurgents, a group of black cloaked Ninja-esque warriors who look like Taliban trainees," while the "300 handsomely sculpted men of Sparta . . . look like the Marine Corps advertisements on TV" as they "fight for freedom and their way of life."[5]

The reaction was equally vehement in Iran, where, in a case of bad timing, the film was released on the eve of *Nowruz* (Persian New Year), when Iranians focus on their proud heritage as a three-thousand-year-old civilization. Not surprisingly, 300 was denounced by the Iranian Academy of the Arts, the Iranian mission to the United Nations, and Iran's embassies around the world. More troubling was the popular reaction. The Iranian people are generally more sympathetic to America than their government, and young Iranians are attracted to our popular culture. But as noted by one journalist, "the hullabaloo over 300" did the regime a favor by creating a "common cause between people and their estranged government. . . . For the first time in a long while, taxi drivers are shaking their fists in agreement when the state news comes on."[6] When the film was banned as "hurtful American propaganda," the public was more supportive than not.[7]

LET A HUNDRED BLOCKBUSTERS BLOOM

In terms of overseas revenue, 300 is far from the top of the list.[8] But before taking comfort in this fact, we should consider that the number one blockbuster of all time is *Avatar*, directed by the Canadian director James Cameron, who also directed *Titanic*. Released in 2009, *Avatar* tells of a lush distant moon called Pandora, inhabited by blue, ten-foot-tall humanoids called Nav'i, and invaded in the year 2154 by mercenaries working for a greedy corporation. The identity of the invaders is made clear by their American swagger and stated intention to "fight Terror with Terror" by using "shock and awe" tactics against the "tree-hugging" natives. A few sympathetic Americans help the Nav'i, but in political terms the film reads as payback for Iraq, with audiences invited to cheer whenever another ugly American invader is destroyed.

This anti-American message may explain some of *Avatar's* success, but being set in a fantasy realm, it is open to multiple interpretations. For example, when *Avatar* took off in China, the regime found itself in a bind. *Avatar* was hugely profitable for both its American and Chinese distributors. And the anti-American message was fine with Beijing—indeed, for many years it has been official policy to admit Hollywood films thought to contain such messages. But Beijing did mind when reports began to circulate that, instead of interpreting *Avatar* in the correct manner, Chinese audiences were interpreting it as an allegory about the forced evictions of people from their property by corrupt officials in their own country. As one blogger wrote, "I am wondering whether Cameron had secretly lived in China before coming up with such an idea."[9]

Soon *Avatar* was pulled from 1,600 of China's 2,500 theaters, ostensibly to make room for *Confucius*, a $22 million tribute to the revered sage scheduled to open on Chinese New Year. But when *Confucius* flopped, even with the schoolchildren who were bused to theaters by local officials seeking to fill empty seats, the State Administration of Radio, Film, and Television (SARFT) admitted defeat and let *Avatar* back into the theaters, where it became the top-grossing foreign film in China's history.

Avatar is about as tragic as a blockbuster gets, which is to say not very, because tragedy requires a grown-up moral universe. In some blockbusters, however, this lack is more than compensated for by a welcome comic sense. Confined to minor characters in the Tolkien-inspired blockbusters, comedy takes center stage in the *Pirates of the Caribbean* franchise, whose hero is not a blue-eyed boy but a mischievous pirate named Jack Sparrow, played by Johnny Depp. These films have no plot to speak of—as one critic wrote, they are "precisely what you'd expect of a movie based on an amusement park ride."[10] But when enlivened by Depp's antic spirit, the ride is a crowd-pleaser.

The true home of comedy is the animated blockbuster, and sure enough *Ice Age*, *Shrek*, *The Simpsons Movie*, *The Incredibles*, *Finding Nemo*, *Toy Story*, and others all rank near the top of the global box office. The appeal of these films seems obvious. Hasn't the world loved cartoons ever since Walt Disney first put pen to paper in the 1920s? A less obvious but highly significant part of the story is the power of one animated feature in particular to perturb Chinese officialdom even more than *Avatar* did.

The story begins in 2000, when Taiwanese director Ang Lee released *Crouching Tiger, Hidden Dragon*, a $15 million US-Hong Kong co-production that grossed $214 million worldwide. Galled by the success of a film set in the Qing Dynasty but produced outside the People's Republic, the Chinese government decided to let a hundred blockbusters bloom. Some of China's leading directors, including some who had made their names as independent spirits, were commissioned to copy those aspects of *Crouching Tiger* judged most commercially appealing: *wuxia*, or heroic martial arts, enhanced by CGI and practiced by women as well as men; and a gorgeous, eye-candy version of the fabled Chinese past.

Thus, two Chinese directors, Chen Kaige and Jang Yimou, and a Hong Kong director highly regarded in Hollywood, John Woo, were recruited to make Chinese blockbusters of the same high quality as America's. The results made money but did not exactly bust the block. Woo's two-part war saga *Red Cliff* (2008–9) grossed $248 million worldwide, Zhang's *Hero* (2004) $177 million. These figures compare with *Crouching Tiger* but are hardly in the same ballpark as *Avatar* ($2.8 billion), *Titanic* ($1.8 billion), and the final *Harry Potter* ($1.3 billion).

Then came a painful shock. In 2008 a DreamWorks Animation film called *Kung Fu Panda* grossed $631 million worldwide, $26 million of it in China. For a cartoon about a pudgy panda who leaves the noodle shop of his father (a kindly goose) and against all odds becomes the wuxia master who saves the Valley of Peace from an evil snow leopard, *Kung Fu Panda* prompted a surprising amount of soul-searching in China. Indeed, a top-level committee of the Chinese Communist Party held a special session to ponder the question posed by Wu Jiang, president of the National Peking Opera Company: "The film's protagonist is China's national treasure and all the elements are Chinese, but why didn't we make such a film?"[11]

In truth, several individuals of Chinese background did work on *Kung Fu Panda*: Jackie Chan, the legendary Hong Kong actor who first combined martial arts with comedy; American actors James Hong and Lucy Liu; art director Tang Heng; and several others. But Chinese background was not at issue. The point was that, once again, China had been beaten by Hollywood. Concluding that "there is no secret ingredient" to explain Hollywood's success, the authorities recommended more funding and less oversight. The funding was forthcoming: $690 million for a new animation facility in Tianjin.

Yet there *is* a secret ingredient to the success of such American films: a commitment to creative freedom that gives free rein to the unruliness of talent, especially comic talent. As noted by some of the uncensored online commentary on *Kung Fu Panda*, no state-approved Chinese director would have made Po, the panda hero, fat and lazy—much less given him a goose for a father.[12] Likewise, no state-approved actor would have been allowed to unleash the antic energy of a Jack Black, the actor who voices the part of Po.

This lack of creative freedom is clearly on display in the first production of the new Tianjin studio. Released in June 2011, *Legend of a Rabbit* pulls off the neat trick of slavishly imitating *Kung Fu Panda* while also attacking it. The hero is a pudgy rabbit who leaves the home of his father (a kindly rabbit who works as a cook) and against all odds becomes the wuxia master who saves China from an evil . . . panda. In a mocking review, one Shanghai critic wrote: "Why didn't anyone think of this earlier? It sounds like it'd be a hit!"[13] This review may not reflect the views of the moviegoing masses, but their opinion was amply reflected at the box office, where *Legend of a Rabbit* was trounced by (you guessed it) *Kung Fu Panda 2*, which grossed $663 million worldwide, $92 million of it in China.

It would be nice to let the matter rest here, with an affirmation of Hollywood's winning combination of creative freedom and profitability. But *Kung Fu Panda 2* was not really an example of that. In 2008 DreamWorks CEO Jeffrey Katzenberg visited the city of Chengdu, home to the world's largest breeding center for giant pandas, and promised his hosts to make the sequel to *Kung Fu Panda* more authentically Chinese than the original.

No doubt Katzenberg was eager to enter the Chinese market, with its rapidly rising number of new screens, its 30 to 60 percent annual increase in box-office revenue, and its passion for American entertainment that government officials cannot deflect toward domestic alternatives, especially in the all-important upscale market.[14] It's no surprise that, faced with such a dazzling prospect, a shrewd CEO would cut a deal with the Chinese government.

The question is, what sort of deal did Katzenberg cut? There are some striking differences between the original *Kung Fu Panda* and *Kung Fu Panda 2*. For example, the sequel contains much less American-style irreverent comedy, and a lot more spectacular action, than the original. Not only that, but the sequel also contains a dutiful, even reverent tribute to Chinese culture—and an explanation of why Po's father, the delightful noodle-cooking goose, is not really his father.

In February 2012, DreamWorks Animation announced plans to build a $330 million studio, Oriental DreamWorks, on the outskirts of Shanghai. Like all such enterprises, this one will be majority-owned by its Chinese partners, and the distribution rights will also be controlled by Chinese firms—which is to say, by the Chinese government.[15] What does this portend for its first production, scheduled to be (you guessed it) *Kung Fu Panda 3*? Will DreamWorks cede even more creative control to the Chinese authorities? When *Kung Fu Panda 2* premiered, one Chinese website quoted Katzenberg calling it "a 'spokesman' for Chengdu."[16] Will the third film be even more of a spokesman—for China?[17]

Without the freedom to unleash the comic spirit, the mighty edifice of the Hollywood blockbuster would collapse under its own weight. Here is what one award-winning Chinese film maker, Lu Chuan, had to say about the experience of trying to create a short animated film for the Beijing Olympics:

> During that year, I kept receiving directions and orders from related parties on how the movie should be like. An important part of the instructions was that the animation should promote Chinese culture. We were given very specific rules on how to promote it. And some were not flexible about "promoting the Olympic spirit," "promoting Chinese culture" or "rich in Chinese elements." Under such pressure, my co-workers and I really felt stifled. The fun and joy from doing something interesting left us, together with our imagination and creativity. The planned animation was never produced.[18]

The comic spirit is akin to that of democracy, so comedy is not the preferred material of authoritarians building cultural castles in the air. The Chinese authorities want to delight audiences the same way Hollywood does, but delighting audiences is an art practiced in freedom, not a technology commanded by the state. In the words of Liu Xiaobo, the imprisoned winner of the 2010 Nobel Peace Prize: "The grins of the people are the nightmares of the dictators."[19]

MEAN STREETS AND ROTTEN INSTITUTIONS

A journalist whom I interviewed in Delhi told me that when he was a boy in the 1970s, "everyone saw America as a lawless, dangerous place, based on Hollywood movies." Today, he added, many middle-class Indians have direct contact with Americans, so "we realize you are not criminals but people like us. You work hard, have families, and worry about daily problems." It's always reassuring to hear that contact with real Americans serves as a corrective to the distortions of popular culture. But the majority of people in India, and the world, never meet an American. And as the distortions of popular culture become more extreme, they become harder to correct.

The image of America as lawless and dangerous is conveyed by five time-tested action genres: the gunslinger western, the gangster saga, the detective story, the medical or legal "procedural," and the "whistleblower" drama in which a lone citizen stands up for what is right. None of these genres seeks to discredit America. On the contrary, they seek to thrill audiences by exposing the dark underside of human nature and various threats to the social order. All involve violence, because all explore fundamental questions such as: What are the sources of public order? What justifies the use of force? What does the individual owe to society?

In classic American popular culture, these questions were foregrounded and violence was backgrounded. This was because, contrary to what many people assume today, the chief concern of Hollywood's self-imposed Production Code was the depiction of "Crimes Against the Law," including murder, drug trafficking, and kidnaping. In 1956 a new section, "Brutality," stipulated that "excessive and inhuman acts of cruelty and brutality shall not be presented."[20] In 1968 the Production Code was replaced by the ratings system we have today. That system is supposed to limit the exposure of young people to graphic violence and explicit sex, but it also allowed the production of more such material (under the "R" and "X" ratings). With the advent of home VCRs and cable television in the 1970s, the ratings system became unenforceable except at movie theaters. And today there are few, if any, restrictions on the representation of criminal acts, sadistic violence, or corpses in a state of mutilation or decay.

GUNSLINGERS, GANGSTERS, DETECTIVES, PROCEDURALS, AND WHISTLEBLOWERS

The increase in artistic freedom that followed the collapse of the Code has been justly celebrated, because without it many of the best films of the past fifty years could not have been made. But like all freedoms, the freedom to depict violence has been subject to abuse. What follows is a brief examination of how this occurred in all five action genres.

To begin with the gunslinger western, the hero of these films is typically a loner too hardened by soldiering or gunfighting to settle down. But he is also too noble to let innocent settlers or townspeople be terrorized by rustlers, outlaws, or hostile Indians. So when settlers or townspeople who would normally shun the gunslinger beg for his help, he gives it, reluctantly but fiercely. And after doing his bloody work he spurns their gratitude and rides off into the proverbial sunset. Some gunslingers, notably the nameless protagonist of *The Virginian* (1946), stay and become pillars of society.[21] But in such classic films as *Shane* (1953), *The Searchers* (1956), and *The Man Who Shot Liberty Valence*

(1962), the gunslinger dispensing the necessary justice is ill suited to community life but is also its brave and selfless defender.

This changed in the mid-1960s, when the Italian director Sergio Leone cast Clint Eastwood as the nameless gunslinger in A *Fistful of Dollars* (1964), *For a Few Dollars More* (1965), and *The Good, the Bad, and the Ugly* (1966). Even before the collapse of the Code, Eastwood's gunslinger, described by one critic as "icy and cynical" and "in no way devoted to justice or aiding the good against the bad," caught the imagination of Hollywood.[22] And the gratuitous violence of Leone's "spaghetti westerns" inspired what film historian Edward Buscombe refers to as a "general increase in the level of violence and the obsessive detail with which it was filmed."[23] Both trends, the cynical antihero and the stepped-up violence, spelled the end of the western and the revival of a genre that had flourished in the pre–Production Code era: the gangster saga.

Gangster films first took off in the early 1930s, with films such as *Little Caesar* (1931), *The Public Enemy* (1931), and *Scarface* (1932). The heroes of these films were cocky, defiant, ruthless in their pursuit of money and power, and destined for a bad end. They were also the sons of immigrants and, as such, quasi-heroes to a popular audience hard-pressed by the Depression and irate at the hypocrisy of the rich. With the arrival of the Code in 1934, these themes became muted, but after 1968 they returned with a vengeance. To appreciate the change, we need only compare the original *Scarface*, directed by Howard Hawks, with the 1983 remake, directed by Brian De Palma. Both were criticized for excessive violence, but the difference between them is striking. In the 1932 version, bodies are knocked over by gunfire as bloodlessly as tenpins by a bowling ball. In the 1983 version, state-of-the-art techniques such as blood squibs, latex body parts, and prosthetic devices are used to show a man being dismembered with a chainsaw, numerous point-blank shootings, and a grand finale of bodies being blasted apart by a grenade launcher.

I realize that none of this will shock most twenty-first-century readers. I also realize that the same techniques were used in such superb gangster films as *The Godfather* (1972) and *The Godfather Part II* (1974). But consider: the main focus of those films was not the gore, it was the moral clash between the Mafia's code of honor and the American legal system. Over time, this theme has become attenuated, and gangster films have come to portray the gangsters and the law as equally corrupt, ruthless, greedy, and hypocritical. Indeed, it is normal to show American police officers, lawyers, judges, and politicians as no better, and usually worse, than the criminals they deal with.

My point is not that the American legal system is a citadel of virtue; clearly, it has problems. But even its most vociferous critics would not trade it for the legal system in Iran, Russia, or China. This is the relevant point of comparison here, and on this point it is troubling to consider how this popular entertainment genre distorts American institutions to the point where, to foreign eyes, they look as rotten as those of the worst dictatorship.

More redemptive is the detective story, which typically focuses on a maverick law enforcement officer, sometimes a cop and sometimes a private eye, who resembles the classic gunslinger in being a loner with a strong sense of honor. Notably, this was the type of role given to James Cagney and Edward G. Robinson, two actors famous for their portrayals of gangsters, after the Production Code was established in 1934.[24]

The post-Code template was laid down by Clint Eastwood (again), playing a San Francisco police detective known as "Dirty Harry" in several popular films, including *Dirty Harry* (1971), *Magnum Force* (1973), *The Enforcer* (1976), *Sudden Impact* (1983), and *The Dead Pool* (1988). True to his own code and hardened by experience, Eastwood's detective is committed to catching the bad guys but also doomed to constant battle with incompetent, arrogant, and hypocritical higher-ups. Recycled in the character of John McClane, the police detective played by Bruce Willis in the *Die Hard* series, and in countless other films and TV series, this figure is more appealing than the bloodthirsty gangster, needless to say. But it has a similarly distorting effect. Dirty Harry, John McClane, and their innumerable successors have courage and integrity, but in order for these sterling qualities to stand out, the environment surrounding them must be made to look as un-sterling as possible. So here, too, we have the portrayal of every institution responsible for public safety—police, courts, and legislature—as inept, corrupt, and worse.

A different angle of vision is taken in the "procedural" genre, typically a TV series about a team of professionals working together to diagnose disease (as in the medical show *House*), prosecute crime (as in the long-lived *Law and Order* franchise), or engage in state-of-the-art forensics (as in *CSI* and its offshoots). At their best, these series exemplify the American ethos: the characters are pragmatic, full of quirks and foibles, skeptical toward human nature, and mindful of the gap between reality and their professional ideals; yet they also work tirelessly to find the cure, see that justice is done, and establish the true facts.

Yet this genre, too, has succumbed to violence and cynicism. Turning the procedural on its head is *Dexter*, a popular, award-winning show whose main character is a "bloodstain pattern analyst" for the Miami police who spends his off-duty hours tormenting and "executing" criminals who have eluded justice within the system. Having witnessed the murder of his mother as a child, Dexter is obsessed with blood, and on this contrived basis the producers indulge their own fascination with the red stuff, drenching whole scenes with it and artfully splashing it on the show's logo. In 2007, when CBS bought the rights to rerun episodes of *Dexter* (which originated on the cable channel Showtime), the Parents Television Council pressured the network to cut some of the gorier bits. The council asked why CBS would want "to air material that effectively celebrates murder."[25] The question fell on deaf ears, however, because violence and cynicism have now become the norm, even on network television.

This brings us to the final action genre: the "whistleblower" drama, in which an ordinary citizen speaks out against the malfeasance of big business or big government. Long a favorite of the Hollywood left, this genre fares poorly in the current climate, for the simple reason that it is not rooted in cynicism. The classic example is *Mr. Smith Goes to Washington* (1939), in which a plucky principled junior senator successfully challenges corruption and cronyism in the US Senate. Some later whistleblower dramas are darker. For example, *Silkwood* (1983), a fact-based film about Karen Silkwood, a nuclear power plant safety activist, ends with her being killed in a suspicious car crash on her way to meet a reporter from the *New York Times*. Yet the majority of whistleblower dramas end with the malefactors being exposed by a free press, then suitably investigated by the appropriate authorities and tried in a legitimate court. For example, *Erin Brockovich* (2000) ends with the heroine, a lowly legal assistant, winning a class-action suit against a polluting public utility.

The fun-house-mirror aspect of this genre is its failure to highlight the social and institutional backdrop required for a whistleblower to make a difference. In the case of *Silkwood*, the film ends with Karen Silkwood's death, not with the subsequent *New York Times* exposé and million-dollar settlement won by her family. But even when these films end happily, they tend to take for granted the institutional contexts that make possible the saving presence of investigative journalists, sympathetic editors, independent investigators, honest prosecutors, brave witnesses, and disinterested judges and juries.[26]

This institutional context does not exist in authoritarian countries, a point illustrated for me when I learned how Chinese students responded to some American films shown by the Public Affairs Section of the US Consulate General in Shanghai. Among the films screened was *Erin Brockovich*, and to the surprise of the Americans present, the students understood the part about a large public utility engaging in pollution, but missed the part about the underdog being able to make a difference. This is hardly surprising, given that China is a country with no free press, no political accountability, and a rigged court system. In such a regime, whistleblowers are heard only when those in power are disposed to hear them.

The whistleblower drama has not faded entirely, but in recent years it has struggled against the rising tide of gratuitous, graphic violence that has affected not just the action genres but all of American entertainment. This tide may have reached its high watermark, for reasons discussed below. But it could hardly have been more ill timed. Occurring at the same time that America was waging its unpopular "War on Terror," this sanguinary tide managed to do some real damage to the country's reputation.

THERE WILL BE BLOOD

The quintessential action hero is John Rambo, the character created in 1982 by actor Sylvester Stallone, whose original appeal is akin to that of the gunslinger and maverick detective: a rugged individual who loves peace, Rambo is fully capable, when called upon, to blast his way through entire phalanxes of enemies. This well-known character provides a useful yardstick by which to measure the tide of violence engulfing American films. The first three Rambo films were released in the 1980s,[27] and the character did not return to the big screen until 2008, when Stallone made a comeback of sorts in a film simply called *Rambo*.

During that twenty-year hiatus, the action genre became far more violent. Indeed, when the 2008 film was released, an enterprising journalist devised a "Rambo Kill Chart," comparing it to the 1988 film, and the differences in the numbers are dramatic. The total number of people killed rose from one in 1988 to 236 in 2008; the number killed per minute rose from 0.01 to 2.59; and the interval between the beginning of the movie and the first killing dropped from thirty minutes to three minutes.[28]

What happened during those two decades? From an East Asian perspective, the answer would likely be a name: John Woo. In 1993, when that renowned Hong Kong director finished editing his first Hollywood film, *Hard Target*, the studio refused to accept the edit on the ground that it was too bloody to receive the desired "R" rating. This annoyed Woo, who had made his career choreographing fast-paced gun battles in popular Hong Kong films. For Woo, this kind of action was the next step in an East Asian cinema devoted to capturing the spectacle of *kung fu*, a generic term for several different martial arts. Traditionally, kung fu films required the skills of martial arts masters like Bruce Lee, Jackie Chan, and Jet Li. But with Woo the emphasis shifted from performer to director. What Woo did was hire ordinary actors, give them powerful weapons, and rely on deft camera work and editing to create dazzling "gun fu" battles. Not surprisingly, this idea caught on in Hollywood, where skilled martial artists were scarce and directors craved a rationale for cranking up the mayhem. When gunplay acquires the aura of East Asian martial arts, only an ethnocentric philistine would dare to criticize it.

Yet according Meaghan Morris, an Australian film scholar whom I met in Hong Kong, this new "gun fu" genre led to a troubling transformation. Citing such classic kung fu films as *The 36th Chamber of Shaolin* (1978), Morris noted that the young hero must labor to acquire thirty-five separate fighting skills, each more difficult than the last, before being permitted to fight. Not only that, but the actual fight scene is quite short—because, as she explained, "The classic stories were about the education of the warrior, his 'soul formation' under the tutelage of his master. All this changed when Woo went to Hollywood. Now the hero is like an American—charging in with weapons and showing everybody else how it's done."[29]

Happy Blood Splatter

This is certainly what Rambo does. But here the story takes a more dispiriting turn, because during the 2000s even the goriest action films paled beside the new, cutting-edge genre dubbed "torture porn."[30] Torture porn is the latest iteration of the "splatter" film (so called to distinguish it from horror films, which rely on suspense as well as on gore). The bad guys in splatter films often enjoy mutilating their victims before killing them, but not until the commercial success of *Saw* (a series spanning 2004 to the present), *Hostel* (2005), *Turistas* (2006), and three films released in 2007—*Hostel Part II, Borderland,* and *Captivity*—did the vivid simulation of torture go mainstream. Thanks to advances in the chemistry of fake blood and body parts, close shots of bodies being cut, burned, flayed, disemboweled, and dismembered are now found in many different films, including the action genres just discussed.

This new level of screen violence is hard to criticize, because ever since 1992, when Quentin Tarantino's *Reservoir Dogs* made casual cruelty look cool, the accepted attitude is that when violence goes over the top, it ceases to be shocking. Why this should be so is never explained. Indeed, the question is infra dig to both the filmmakers and their fans, who take a flippant, inverted pride in the most horrific scenes. For example, the director of *Saw IV* bragged to the media that the film contained "a scene . . . where I physically regurgitated in my mouth."[31] The director of *Hostel* and *Hostel Part II* told an interviewer that "on the days we're shooting the gore . . . I'm just extra happy. I try to have that same excitement and enthusiasm for every scene, but when we're doing some really disgusting scene I'll catch myself gleefully jumping up and down."[32]

This flippancy is uglier than the horror itself. After all, the same techniques have been used to make serious war films more realistic, beginning with *Hamburger Hill* and other 1980s films about Vietnam and continuing with more recent films about World War II, such as *Saving Private Ryan* (1998) and two HBO series, *Band of Brothers* (2001) and *The Pacific* (2010). The difference between these films and torture porn is made evident by Tarantino's *Inglorious Basterds* (2009) and *Django Unchained* (2012). Claiming to be dealing with weighty themes—the Nazi Holocaust and American slavery, respectively—these films do little more than repeat Tarantino's usual formula, which is to borrow the plot of an old B movie and jazz it up with talented actors, clever if pointless dialogue, and a soundtrack designed to produce maximum moral dissonance between what the audience is hearing (sprightly music) and what they are seeing (gross bloodletting).

Did the weighty themes of the Holocaust and slavery force a moral framework into Tarantino's formula? Yes, but the effect was to change a nihilistic cartoon into a melodramatic one. That is, instead of inviting the audience to cheer when one low-life character blasts a hole in another, *Inglorious Basterds* and *Django Unchained* invite the audience to cheer self-righteously when a cartoon hero blasts a hole in a cartoon villain.

What is most objectionable about Tarantino's films is not the violence per se, but the flippant attitude with which we are invited to watch it.[33] This attitude tends to blunt criticism of the increasingly dark portrayal of evil in American films. In 2008, the same year that Rambo made his comeback, the talented actor Heath Ledger played a terrifying villain, the Joker, in *The Dark Knight*, the second film in director Christopher Nolan's *Batman* trilogy. Writing about that film, British movie critic Jenny McCartney commented that "the greatest surprise of all—even for me, after eight years working as a film critic—has been the sustained level of intensely sadistic brutality throughout the film."[34] It may not be possible to draw a direct causal relationship between the disturbing cruelty of this character and the mass shooting that occurred four years later on the opening night of the third Nolan film, *The Dark Knight Rises*, in a movie theater in Aurora, Colorado. But when the shooter announced himself to the police as "the Joker," it is hard to deny any connection.

Video Game Violence

Similar concerns have been raised about violent video games. The world's young people, especially the males of the species, now spend countless hours blasting virtual enemies to smithereens through the deft manipulation of such handheld devices as Game Boy, Nintendo DS, and Playstation Portable. Unlike films, even torture porn films, violent video games invite the "gamer" to join in the fun of killing. That is why a court in California upheld a 2010 statute making it a crime to sell violent video games to minors. The defenders of the statute argued that, just as there is a law against sexual obscenity, there should be a law against violent obscenity. This argument was not without merit. It is an offense to human dignity to make an impersonal spectacle of human flesh, as hard-core pornography does. But as suggested by the term *torture porn*, such spectacles need not be sexual in nature.[35]

When the California case went before the US Supreme Court in 2011, Justices Samuel Alito and John Roberts noted that video games go beyond mere spectacle: "There is a world of difference," they wrote, "between someone who reads about the murder of a character in a book and another person who can *participate virtually in that murder and receive sensory feedback*" (emphasis added).[36] In the event, the Supreme Court struck down the statute, on the ground that "violence is not part of the obscenity that the Constitution permits to be regulated."[37] But many Americans continue to worry about the participatory aspect of popular video games such as Grand Theft Auto, in which the whole point of the game is to kill as many human enemies as possible.

When this "first-person shooter" type of game first appeared in the 1990s, its participatory aspect proved sufficiently controversial that the industry formed a self-regulatory body, the Entertainment Software Ratings Board, to label games by age group. The most common label, "Mature," is supposed to limit the sale of the game to players over seventeen years of age. But by all accounts, its real function is to advertise that a given game contains plenty of "intense violence, blood and gore, sexual content and/or strong language."[38]

The production of video games is multinational, with games often created in one country, programmed in another, and produced in yet another. The main producers are the United States, Japan, and Great Britain. It goes without saying that most video games operate in a moral universe that makes blockbuster films look like Shakespeare. The technology needed for smooth and flexible "gameplay" is incredibly subtle and complex. But the purpose itself is simple: destroy or be destroyed.[39]

Yet even within this limited moral universe, the American producers of video games seem to have been working hard to make their own country look bad. Several video games have nonhuman targets, usually robots, aliens, or monsters. Significantly, these are found more often in the colorful, cartoonlike style associated with Japan than in the grittier style associated with the United States. The latter is also more likely to feature realistic settings and lifelike human bodies to shoot at. Further, American games encourage "free play," in which the gamer assumes the role of a lone shooter, as opposed to that of a member of a team.

It is therefore an unspoken assumption among gamers around the world that America is the natural backdrop for games featuring free play with powerful weapons that turn human bodies into fountains of blood.[40] This assumption is hardly surprising, given the nature of American entertainment. But it is also troubling. Violent video games may not cause young people to commit violent acts, but, along with the rest of popular culture, they do create the impression overseas that American society is a lot more violent than it actually is. Ironically, this impression is muted in countries that censor the most violent fare. In a conversation about the Chinese government's severe restrictions on the import of US action and horror films, the film scholar Teng Jimeng told me: "I don't like censorship, but it does help to sanitize the image of the US in China."[41]

In 2006 a video game was released based on *Reservoir Dogs*, in which the player is invited to take a hostage, then decide whether to shoot him right away or to burn his eyeballs with a lit cigar, chop off his fingers with a cigar cutter, or hack off his ears with a scalpel—all the while enjoying a soundtrack in which the hostage begs for mercy and screams in pain.[42] This game was not a commercial success. And to date, no video game involving active participation in graphically vivid acts of torture has succeeded commercially. According to my gaming informants, this is because torture doesn't require the same high level of eye-hand dexterity that makes video games challenging and fun.[43] That's good to know, but I would also like to know if there is an ethical barrier to the commercial success of such a game. I fear that if such a barrier does exist, we can have little confidence in its durability.

IMAGES OF A SUPERPOWER

Like the majority of people I have met overseas, the Australian film scholar Meaghan Morris was very critical of the Bush administration's "War on Terror." It was all the more striking, then, to hear her remark that "the United States doesn't have a national cinema anymore, so it doesn't represent itself as a distinctive global superpower in any effective way."[44] This remark is correct on both counts. Despite a long history of government involvement in the entertainment industry, America has never had a national cinema of the kind found in countries where the government subsidizes the production of films and to varying degrees controls the content. For evidence of this, we need only look at the way most Hollywood films depict America's role in the world. What government would pay for such a dark, conspiratorial portrait?

Yet quite a few American movies and TV shows *are* made under government auspices. Indeed, some producers, usually so outspoken in defense of their artistic independence, gladly submit scripts for prior approval, and promise to deliver flattering portrayals of their government partners—all for the chance to use government property, equipment, and personnel in a way that tells the audience, "This is real, this is important, this is big stuff."[45] If this sounds outlandish, even un-American, just substitute the word *military* for the word *government* in the preceding passage. In Hollywood there are few outside forces as powerful as the Department of Defense's Film Liaison Office, and in recent years its cooperation has frequently made the difference between box-office success (devoutly to be wished) and critical acclaim (nice at Oscar time but otherwise not a priority).

Consider the blockbuster series *Transformers*, in which US armed forces join with friendly fifty-foot-tall robot aliens to defend Earth from an invasion of hostile fifty-foot-tall robot aliens. These productions are made with the cooperation of the Defense Department, and utilize real soldiers, tanks, aircraft, and locations from airfields and bases to the Pentagon itself. As for why the Defense Department would support what is basically a supersized comic book, the director of the Film Liaison Office, Philip Strub, had this to say: "I know that it's a bit ridiculous to be talking about realism when we're talking about superheroes and giant robots from outer space. . . . But we focus on how the military people, how the individual men and women react to each other, relate to each other, interact with each other."[46]

Meanwhile, Hollywood films about actual contemporary wars tend to be made without the blessing of the Film Liaison Office. For example, *The Hurt Locker*, the 2009 film about an explosive ordnance disposal (EOD) team in Iraq, lost its Pentagon support quite early, before the production was under way, because the director, Kathryn Bigelow, insisted on portraying the main character as a reckless thrill seeker. On this question Strub's reply cuts to the heart of the matter: "One of the things that we encounter is the tendency of filmmakers to stick to proven stereotypes. Whether they're in uniform or not, *they seem particularly fond of the loner who must disobey the rules, thwart his or her own organization and kind of go rogue in the name of achieving justice or redemption or whatever the goal might be*" (emphasis added).[47]

Echoing this observation is Sean Morrow, an army major who served in Iraq in 2003 and 2007. In a conversation about Iraq war films, Morrow shared with me his opinion of *The Hurt Locker:* "It was a good movie, and the setting in Jordan was realistic. But it was typical Hollywood in the way it just stuck those guys out there all alone. Nobody does EOD without a ton of unit support."[48] If *The Hurt Locker* had been made under Pentagon auspices, then that "ton of unit support" would have been in evidence, and the main character would not have been what one EOD officer in Iraq describes as "a run and gun cowboy type."[49] But without such a main character—a violent, cynical maverick—*The Hurt Locker* would have been less likely to win the Academy Award for Best Picture.

The tension between accuracy and "proven stereotypes" is hard enough to re-solve in military-themed entertainment. It is even harder in films and TV shows about US power more generally. In 2004, amid the global backlash against the invasion of Iraq, filmmaker Michael Moore released *Fahrenheit 9/11*, the most commercially successful "documentary" in history. Released in forty-three countries, the film was widely accepted as the definitive statement of what had occurred on September 11, 2001, and what the US government was doing about it.[50] Hundreds of German schoolteachers took their students to see it, and it was aired on public television in Great Britain, Hungary, Denmark, Norway, New Zealand, the Netherlands, Belgium, and Brazil.

Stated plainly, the message of *Fahrenheit 9/11* is that the Bush family, the bin Laden family, Halliburton, the Carlyle Group, the Unocal company, and other corporate entities conspired to kill three thousand people on September 11, 2001, in order to launch a perpetual—and profitable—war. Moore knows better than to say such a thing plainly, so the film cloaks this conspiracy theory in a clever, inventive, skillfully edited polemic. This is one reason for its success. But another reason is that *Fahrenheit 9/11* filled a vacuum. The world was starved for solid information about what was happening, and the US news media were not providing it. Indeed, only the most sophisticated readers of English-language print publications were aware that America was even debating the issue. As for Washington, the first five years of the twenty-first century were a low point in its capacity for global communication.

In Part Two I will discuss how the US military were invited to fill the commu-nication vacuum of the immediate post-9/11 years. Unfortunately, this has come to mean even closer cooperation with Hollywood. For example, in 2012 the Pentagon produced its first feature film, *Act of Valor*, about the heroic exploits of a top team of Navy SEALs. That same year saw the debut of an NBC-TV program called *Stars Earn Stripes*, in which minor celebrities are teamed with soldiers to compete in real military exercises.

Like the deals being cut by US companies desperate to enter the Chinese market, this entertainment-propaganda represents a serious, and underscrutinized, departure from the American tradition of privately owned, independent media. The only comfort is that its appeal seems to stop at the water's edge. Like the entertainment-propaganda churned out by authoritarian regimes such as Iran, Russia, and China, these Pentagon productions satisfy a certain segment of the domestic audience, but they have zero traction at the all-important global box office. For example, *Act of Valor* earned 87 percent of its revenue domestically and only 13 percent internationally. Not that it's particularly comforting to consider that *The Dark Knight Rises*, the movie associated with the mass shooting in Colorado, did very well overseas, earning 49 percent of its revenue domestically, 51 percent internationally.[51]

Jack Bauer to the Rescue

For all its popularity, Michael Moore's *Fahrenheit 9/11* was not the main source of information provided to the world by America during the first decade of the "war on terror." That honor goes to a character in a TV series: the archetypical American counterterrorist, Jack Bauer. Played by Kiefer Sutherland, Jack Bauer is the hero of *24*, the Fox TV series that thrived for ten seasons (2001–10) and still attracts viewers with its heart-stopping suspense and maverick hero who does whatever it takes to stop the next terrorist attack.

It was incredibly poor timing to have torture porn appear at the same time that the Bush administration was facilitating covert torture overseas, but at least that benighted genre does not defend torture in a political context. The same cannot be said for *24*. Bauer gets no kicks from torturing prisoners, but he does so anyway—sixty-seven times during the first five seasons. Why? Because it works. Indeed, Jack Bauer can maul a captive and get actionable intelligence faster than the rest of us can put a dollar in a vending machine and get a Diet Coke.

The standard defense of these scenes is that Bauer is a scrupulous professional who resorts to torture only in "ticking time bomb" situations, when catastrophe is seconds away. The trouble is, such situations are exceedingly rare. As one thirty-year veteran of military intelligence commented in 2007, they are "a mythology."[52] The same can be said for the idea that scrupulous professionals can control the use of torture. The opposite is true: torture has a corrosive effect on every military and law enforcement organization that has ever used it.[53] After twelve years in Soviet prisons, labor camps, and coercive "psychiatric hospitals," former dissident Vladimir Bukovsky had this to say: "Investigation is a subtle process, requiring patience and fine analytical ability, as well as a skill in cultivating one's sources. When torture is condoned, these rare talented people leave the service, having been outstripped by less gifted colleagues with their quick-fix methods, and the service itself degenerates into a playground for sadists . . . incapable of solving the simplest of crimes."[54]

In 2007 General Patrick Finnegan, dean of West Point, and Joe Navarro, an expert FBI interrogator, traveled to Los Angeles to urge a change in the way 24 was depicting torture. These seasoned practitioners had a practical complaint: that cadets and trainees steeped in 24 were turning a deaf ear to instructions about the illegality of torture and its limited effectiveness. The show's creator, Joel Surnow, declined to meet with the visitors. But others, including Sutherland, did meet with them. And in the changing political climate of 2008 and 2009, the series took a more chastened approach to the subject of torture.[55]

For all of its timeliness, 24 was evasive about the identity of the terrorists hunted by Bauer. For the first three seasons they were Serbian war criminals, conniving Americans, Latin American drug dealers, and a grudge-holding British spy. In the fourth, the show dared to feature an Arab villain aided by a Turkish-American family, only to raise howls of outrage. After that, 24 retreated to the safer ground of Russian nationalists, Chinese spies, and, of course, such stock American villains as military contractors and power-mad vice presidents.

Why the evasiveness? When it comes to representing the reality of twenty-first-century terrorism, the US entertainment industry faces a dilemma. In neither the domestic nor the international market is there a consensus about who the bad guys are. Some TV series, notably *Sleeper Cell* (2005–6) and *Homeland* (2011–13), manage to acknowledge that the main threat today is from violent Islamists, without simply equating terrorism with Islam. These programs have also tried to reveal the flawed humanity of both sides without resorting to stock American villains. The success of these programs is heartening, but their global impact is negligible compared with that of the violent and cynical mainstream, which continues to reinforce the image, purveyed in recent years by friend as well as foe, of the United States as a borderline rogue state whose citizens take unseemly pleasure in real and imagined bloodshed.

WHEN PUSHBACK BECOMES PROPAGANDA

The couple are glowing, the wedding party is joyful, and, in keeping with Iraqi custom, the men celebrate by firing rifles at the sky. But all is not well in this idyllic village. Nearby, an American officer sneers, "Now they are shooting, so now they are terrorists." The Americans attack, killing whole families and herding the survivors into a sealed truck, driven by a gum-chewing sergeant.

When a fresh-faced soldier worries that the captives will "suffocate in there," the sergeant rakes the side of the truck with automatic weapon fire, quipping, "Now they won't suffocate." When the soldier protests, he too gets blown away. Then it's off to Abu Ghraib, where a semicrazed Jewish-American doctor scolds the sergeant: "If you don't stop killing my patients so I cannot remove their organs properly, I'll kill you!" With that, the doctor goes back to harvesting kidneys and hearts and placing them in cold transport containers marked: New York, Los Angeles, London, Jerusalem, Tel Aviv.[56]

Oliver Stone's latest? Perhaps a co-production with Michael Moore? No, these scenes are from a Turkish film, *Valley of the Wolves, Iraq* (*Kurtlar Vadisi Irak*). Released in 2006, *Valley of the Wolves, Iraq* was the costliest film ever produced in Turkey ($10 million) and one of the most profitable. In the first two weeks it sold over two million tickets, a record for the Turkish market. It was also praised in high places: Deputy Prime Minister Bülent Arınç, a member of the Islamist Justice and Development Party who was then chair of the Turkish parliament, called it "an extraordinary film that will go into history."[57] The film also did respectable business in fourteen other countries, including Germany (where it drew criticism from across the political spectrum and was eventually pulled from some theaters).[58]

A political consultant whom I met in Istanbul explained to me that *Valley of the Wolves, Iraq* was based on a popular TV series about a heroic Turkish special-ops team, and that its portrayal of Americans was considered payback for negative stereotypes of Turks in US entertainment—not just in 24, but going back to *Midnight Express* (1978) and *Lawrence of Arabia* (1962).

The political consultant also noted the disrespect shown to the proud Turkish military by US diplomats who, during the run-up to the invasion of Iraq, "did not *request* Turkish support, they *demanded* it."[59] He further recalled that when the Turkish parliament voted against supporting the invasion, "the Americans seemed nonplussed, as though they weren't aware that we are a democracy!" And finally, he noted that the public resentment of American arrogance peaked in July 2003, when US troops arrested eleven Turkish soldiers at the Iraqi border, put hoods over their heads and handcuffs on their wrists, and displayed them to the media as "suspected terrorists."

Valley of the Wolves, Iraq begins with a reenactment of that incident, followed by a foray into Iraq by the heroic special-ops team from the TV series, who end up fighting to protect the Iraqis (depicted as pure and devout) from the Americans (depicted as vile and savage). The film has not been distributed in America, but in Istanbul I watched an English-subtitled DVD with a colleague who teaches at Koç University. It was an unnerving experience, to say the least.

I am as accustomed as any American to seeing my countrymen portrayed as stock villains and evil deviants. But not until that moment did I realize what a difference it makes when these portrayals are not homegrown.

A few days later, I had the privilege of meeting Halit Refiğ, the eminent film-maker who pioneered Turkey's National Cinema movement and revolution-ized Turkish television. A man of considerable learning in both Turkish and American culture, Refiğ smiled when I asked him about *Valley of the Wolves, Iraq*. Then he made a wonderful comment that could serve as a punch line to this whole chapter. He called *Valley of the Wolves, Iraq* "the most anti-American movie ever made outside the United States."[60]

3

TELEVISION BY THE PEOPLE,
FOR THE PEOPLE?

On a pleasant spring day, the kind when the sea breeze tempers the desert heat in the United Arab Emirates, I was given a tour of the American University of Sharjah by Hisham El Shaarani, an engineering student about to graduate. Hisham was born in the tiny emirate of Sharjah and considered it home, but as the son of Egyptian immigrants he could never be a citizen. He and his family belong permanently to the majority (80 percent) population of noncitizen expats.

As we strolled the immaculate campus, with its shimmering mosque and pristine if understocked library, I asked Hisham whether his status as a noncitizen had any bearing on his future plans. Not really, he said. His future lay in the private sector, where (in his words) "politics added no value to your business and can simply be ignored." Then, with no prompting from me, he added that the UAE had "a version of democracy"—a radio talk show called *Live Line*, in which everyone, Emirati and expat alike, could call in and express grievances to a well-connected host who could bring serious complaints to the attention of the royal family, even of Sheikh Sultan himself.[1]

As an American, I felt tempted to lecture Hisham on the difference between genuine democracy and a radio talk show, even one sponsored by a ruler as benevolent as Sheikh Sultan. But as a researcher, I opted for a question: What would happen if Sharjah's next ruler was not benevolent? Would there be any *Live Line* then? Probably not, Hisham admitted. Well, I said, that's the whole point of democracy: the freedom of the people depends on durable political institutions, not on the largess of one ruler. At that point I was lecturing, but if Hisham objected, he was too polite to say so.

Live Line was one of several similar programs on Arab radio at the time whose lineage could be traced to the Arab custom of petitioning the sheikh as much as to Western media. Still, the radio talk show is an American invention, part of a decades-long shift from "scripted" programs utilizing the talents of professional writers, directors, and performers to "unscripted" programs inviting the participation of ordinary people. One striking aspect of unscripted programs is how easy they are to localize. Instead of foreign media companies buying the rights to show an entire scripted series (for example, *Sex and the City*), they simply buy the rights to an unscripted "format" and adapt it to local conditions.[2]

To some observers, these changes in TV entertainment seem like ancient history compared with social media, which have been nurturing grassroots politics since 2008. That was when a Colombian civil engineer named Oscar Morales used Facebook to organize demonstrations against the terrorist group FARC. Subsequently the world grew accustomed to the idea of social media nurturing grassroots politics. Many nations—Iran, Tunisia, Egypt, Libya, Syria, Israel, Burma, China, Russia—have seen popular protests facilitated by Facebook, Twitter, YouTube, and the ubiquitous cell phone.

Yet social media did not come out of a vacuum. On the contrary, for most of the non-Western world, social media appeared on a stage that had already been set by the decisive new medium of the past quarter century: satellite television. And satellite television has transformed millions of lives by bringing not just news through channels like Al Jazeera, but also entertainment, including unscripted talk and reality programs. Hisham is hardly alone in associating these shows with democratic values such as freedom, equality, and individualism.

To their detractors, talk and reality shows are inherently degrading, because to put nonprofessionals in front of a camera is to encourage exhibitionism and blur the line between public and private. There's plenty of evidence to support this view. But a glance at older talk shows—and reality show precedents such as *Queen for a Day, What's My Line,* and *Candid Camera*—reveals that, while these programs sometimes embarrassed participants, they never degraded them. The same can be said of the better talk and reality shows today. The degradation of unscripted entertainment has a deeper cause.

Since 1934, America's privately owned radio and TV networks censored themselves, albeit under the watchful eye of the Federal Communications Commission (FCC). That system of indirect government control was criticized by some for departing from the country's tradition of press freedom. But because the electronic media were thought to have greater persuasive powers than print, most Americans accepted it. That system was challenged in the 1960s and '70s, when generational upheaval, carried out in the name of protest and liberation, occurred at both the elite and the popular levels of culture.

That upheaval tested the limits of public propriety. So predictably it provoked a backlash. Yet surprising as it may sound to a non-American, that backlash did not lead to a regulatory crackdown. During the Reagan administration there were calls for stricter censorship, but in keeping with the business-oriented libertarian spirit of the American right, what occurred was a massive deregulation of the electronic media, which over the course of the 1980s and '90s rendered the system of indirect government control all but obsolete. As Reagan's first FCC chair, Mark Fowler, opined in 1981, "Television is just another appliance. It's a toaster with pictures. . . . Why is there this national obsession to tamper with this box of transistors and tubes when we don't do the same for *Time* magazine?"[3]

The resulting competition was good for business, but it also led to what the old Hollywood moguls called "a race to the bottom." This lowering of moral and artistic standards was defended as the necessary price of freedom. In Fowler's summation: "We let the marketplace and the viewers decide what goes out there."[4] Yet the irony of the tale is that this shift from scripted to unscripted material was driven less by viewer preferences than by new technology and narrowing industry priorities.

In the 1970s the "big three" networks (NBC, CBS, and ABC) began to lose audience share to cable channels and the videocassette recorder. In the early 1980s the full scope of this loss was revealed by new audience measurement techniques. Advertisers began to pull back, and the production studios found themselves running deficits of up to $100,000 for a half-hour sitcom, $300,000 for an hour-long drama. To survive, the studios began to hire nonunion crews and use cheaper locations, many in Canada. But it was too late.[5] As the competition heated up, the key to short-term success became unscripted fare less costly to produce and sufficiently sensationalist to catch the eyes of distracted viewers. Daytime television followed suit, with soap operas yielding ground to unscripted talk shows.

In the 1990s a similar dynamic occurred on a global scale. The advent of satellite technology and the opening of huge new markets brought heightened competition, and cheaply produced, easily localized talk and reality shows became the programming of choice. This chapter will trace the rise and global spread of, first, the American talk show, and then the American reality show. The fact that these shows are relatively inexpensive to produce does not mean that they are necessarily sensationalist. Some are, some aren't. Indeed, there is an important distinction to make between talk and reality shows that bring out the best in people, and those that bring out the worst. It matters greatly which type of show we are talking about, because throughout the world, this kind of unscripted programming is associated with American values such as democracy, freedom, equality, and individualism.

AMERICAN TALK SHOWS

The American talk show harks back to the 1930s, when radio networks featured on-air interviews with prominent writers, scholars, and public officials. When television arrived in the 1950s, the genre continued in the same highbrow vein on state-owned channels overseas, while on America's commercial channels it became middlebrow, with late-night hosts such as Jack Paar and Johnny Carson combining serious interviews with live performances and celebrity chat. Not till the 1970s did the talk show become part of US daytime television, when Phil Donahue challenged the soaps with a show focusing on issues of concern to his largely female audience. Donahue's oft-noted innovation, stepping off the stage and circulating among the audience to solicit individuals' opinions, was in fact a staple of revivalist preaching. But it worked no less well in this secular context.

In 1986 the talk show was taken to a new level by Oprah Winfrey, who quickly surpassed Donahue in the ratings. At that early stage, Winfrey specialized in the TV equivalent of the nineteenth-century "sob sister" reporter, hosting noncelebrity guests with sad, traumatic, sometimes sensationalist tales to tell.[6] But as her success spawned imitators, a different tone emerged, and soon "trash TV" hosts such as Ricki Lake, Jenny Jones, Geraldo Rivera, Maury Povich, and Jerry Springer were filling the screen with guests whose lives were twisted by poverty, ignorance, and every conceivable human failing from incest to obesity, pedophilia to bestiality—and then goading those unhappy souls to lose what little self-respect they still possessed. A former producer describes the job of booking for these shows:

> I remember being on the phone with the mother, saying, you know, "The best thing for you to do is to come on this show and tell your story," that whole bullshit. It was going to be therapeutic, everybody's going to learn from it. I'm a good liar. I mean, I was convincing this woman to talk about the fact that while she was getting married to this guy, he was upstairs fucking her five-year-old daughter and giving her HIV.[7]

This was never Winfrey's approach. On the contrary, she believed she was helping people, especially women, to deal with problems they would otherwise suffer in silence. In the mid-1990s she announced she was "tired of the crud" and vowed to transform her show into "Change Your Life TV."[8] Thus began a

transformation that culminated on September 23, 2001, when thousands of trau-
matized New Yorkers gathered in Yankee Stadium to pray for the victims of the
World Trade Center attacks. Present were leaders from Protestant, Catholic,
Jewish, Muslim, Hindu, and Buddhist communities; but the mistress of ceremonies was Winfrey—in the words of one scholar, the only person in America
with the right combination of "spiritual leadership, celebrity recognition, and
consumer popularity" to preside over such a momentous occasion.[9]

Among Winfrey's many critics, the most cogent are the religious scholars
and American historians who place her in a line of "mind cure" healers and
"positive thinkers" stretching back to Mary Baker Eddy and Norman Vincent
Peale. Like those predecessors, Winfrey abandoned the Calvinist faith of her
fathers (she was raised a Southern Baptist) to wander in the wilderness of a free-
form spirituality called New Thought in the nineteenth century, New Age in
the twentieth and twenty-first. The trappings of this spirituality have changed,
but its quasi-gnostic message remains the same: it is more important to connect
with one's inner spark of divinity than to beg mercy from a remote, judgmental
God.[10]

To Catholic writer Amy Wellborn, this message amounts to a shift from God
to Self and, as such, betrays Christianity's concern for "sin, redemption, sacrifice, conversion, humility, worship, holiness, and Jesus Christ."[11] Others refer
back to historian Christopher Lasch's critique of "the culture of narcissism,"
or sociologist Philip Rieff's account of "the triumph of the therapeutic."[12] The
essential point in these criticisms is that Winfrey's "change your life" ministry
is part of a general loss of that mindfulness of human wickedness, and of the
profound otherness of God, that gives the American ethos its starch.

Yet there is another side to the story. Historian Stephanie Muravchik finds
this antitherapeutic charge too extreme, because it fails to recognize "the degree to which psychotherapeutic ideas and techniques changed as they were
popularized." In America, she argues, God and Self travel a two-way street: "As
psychology moved into the mainstream, the mainstream—with its considerable
religiosity—moved into psychology. Believers harnessed therapy to their own
purposes."[13] If Winfrey and her trash-talk rivals are seen in this light, the difference between them becomes clear: Winfrey is the one with the starch.

In every TV market on earth, locally produced talk shows are now busy exposing human frailty by two different paths: the Oprah Winfrey path, which seeks
to redeem it in the context of quasi-religion; and the trash-talk path, which
milks human frailty for crude thrills and laughs. The choice of which path to
pursue depends on three factors: the priorities of media players, the degree of
state censorship, and, most important, the solidity of the society's core values. In

the early twenty-first century there is no society on earth whose core values have not been eroded in some way.[14] But in some, that core remains solid enough that a full-scale race to the bottom is resisted not just by official censors but by the general public.

MUSLIM TALK SHOWS AND *FITNA*

Such resistance is found in those Muslim-majority countries where the general population is more religious than the elites. Emre Erdogen, an opinion researcher in Istanbul, told me that in Turkey, "What doesn't work are talk shows that are too frank and reveal too many intimate details."[15] Similar objections are heard in the West, needless to say. But they have special force in Muslim-majority societies, where the public exposure of wrongdoing—through exhibitionist behavior, slander, or gossip—is considered worse than the wrongdoing itself, because it can lead others to commit the same acts.[16]

Echoing this sentiment was Ayu Utami, a popular Indonesian novelist whom I met in Jakarta. When discussing the use of talk shows to attract advertisers, she noted that certain mainstream Islamic organizations, such as the Nahdlatul Ulama, "suggested that Muslims not watch gossip programs, because gossip causes fitna."[17] The root meaning of *fitna* is "trial," but over time the word has come to mean any test of Muslims' faith and probity, including sexual temptation and civil discord. The public discussion of sexual matters is therefore to be avoided, because, as fitna, it is perceived as a threat to the unity of the Muslim community.[18]

This concern for fitna plays out dramatically in the twenty-four-nation Arab TV market, where despite the Western obsession with news channels like Al-Jazeera, the most popular fare is entertainment. Historically, the main producers of Arab entertainment have been Egypt and Lebanon; since the 1990s the main financial and political players have been Saudi Arabia, the United Arab Emirates (especially Dubai), and Qatar. Because of its transnational nature, this huge media market, which now includes over six hundred channels, operated with surprisingly few controls until 2008, when the Arab League drew up a charter attempting to impose standards.[19] That document is nonbinding, and some of its provisions, such as the requirement "not to offend the leaders," are clearly intended to stifle rising political opposition.[20]

But other provisions are rooted in public sentiment. Despite the political conflicts raging across the Arab Muslim world in the early twenty-first century, there is no doubt that the charter spoke for a majority of the population when it called for TV channels "to conform with the religious and ethical values of Arab society and take account of its family structure." And the same can be said of the requirement to "protect Arab identity from the harmful effects of globalization," though that provision also addressed the economic self-interest of regional TV industries.[21]

Despite these provisions, the key to talk-show success in the Arab market is to flirt with taboo subjects, on a live broadcast if possible, while inviting the audience to call, text, e-mail, and tweet. But to succeed in this way, the host must know exactly where the limits are, because to cross them is to pay a price.[22] For example, one of the most popular hosts in the region, Egypt's Hala Serhan, rose to fame discussing topics like rape, homosexuality, domestic violence, and female masturbation. But in 2007 she went too far, persuading some female members of the studio audience to pose as prostitutes and pretend to be interviewed by her. A scandal followed, and Serhan was forced to leave Egypt for a four-year sojourn in Dubai.[23] Her career appeared over, but in summer 2013 she was back in Cairo, starting a new show using social media.[24]

Serhan has been called the "Oprah Winfrey of the Arab world," but there are likelier candidates for that title. One is Heba Kotb, an Egyptian who dispenses frank but religiously correct sexual advice on the basis of a firm conviction that "sexual ignorance" causes more fitna than does sexual awareness.[25] Another is Nashwa al Ruwaini, whose career began on MBC1, the premier channel of the Saudi-owned Middle East Broadcasting Center (MBC), and now continues on her own company, Pyramedia. Defending her candid discussion of sex education, homosexuality, incest, divorce, masturbation, terrorism, and the veil, al Ruwaini says: "There are many taboo topics, but someone has to discuss them. . . . It is all about how you approach a topic. We don't try to sensationalize, otherwise we wouldn't have anyone who would be willing to speak about these issues."[26]

Still, the best candidate for the title "Oprah Winfrey of the Arab World" is Winfrey herself. Until its final broadcast in May 2011, *The Oprah Winfrey Show* was the most popular talk show in the world, with a sizable following in 149 countries—including the 24 countries in the transnational Arab market. For example, just a few months after being introduced in 2004, Winfrey's was the highest rated show among Saudi women under twenty-five.[27] This inspired MBC to make it the centerpiece of MBC4, a new channel described by one executive as embodying the "intellectual and cultural sophistication" to which modern Arab women aspire.[28]

In the spring of 2013, two and a half years after the Egyptian uprising of 2011–

12, I asked Nimet Naguib, an Egyptian former employee of the US embassy in Cairo, what had happened to the talk shows on Egyptian television. Here is her reply:

> The number of talk shows has greatly multiplied and their focus is now on do-mestic political issues, events, opinions, making them a significant platform for the huge pull and push between Muslim Brotherhood (or other Islamist-based ideology) and everyone else. The public is quite fed up with all this talk, talk, talk. But these shows remain, along with Twitter, Facebook, YouTube and other Internet sites, a major source of insights into the state and psyche of the nation, which, I might add, is rather terrible and frightening.[29]

The transformation described by Naguib may or may not lead in the direction of a stable democratic government in Egypt. But surely it is better to have a passionate public debate, one that includes terrible and frightening opinions, than to have no debate at all. Naguib's linking of TV talk shows with social media suggests that the latter are not the first to stoke democratic aspirations in the region.

TALKING TRASH IN RUSSIA

In Russia we see not the Oprah Winfrey path but the Jerry Springer path: talk shows that degrade their participants. This may sound surprising, given that the Russian media, especially television, are closely monitored by the state. But Russian society is different from the Muslim-majority societies of the Middle East, in the sense that its core values were hollowed out by eighty years of Soviet rule, followed by the near anarchy of the 1990s. Since consolidating power in the early 2000s, Vladimir Putin has sought to fill the vacuum with suspicion toward the West, disparagement of dissidents, and racially tinged hostility to-ward ethnic minorities—sentiments that reinforce the need for strongman rule. What Putin has not encouraged is social trust and the growth of civil society, the necessary prerequisites for democratic reform.

These are the priorities driving Putin's media policy, which began with his crackdown on the wide-open freedoms of the immediate post-Soviet era, when reporters and pundits engaged in aggressive political reporting, fierce public de-bate, and barbed criticism of the powers-that-be. Today the Russian media have two goals. The first is to craft Putin's image as a strongman, but not the kind of strongman who ruled Russia in the dull old Soviet days. Instead, Putin is held up as what Russia scholar S. Frederick Starr calls a "hip tyrant, a cross between

Arnold Schwarzenegger and James Bond." As Starr explained to me, "The last thing Putin wants is to come off as an old geezer like Brezhnev."[30]

The second goal of the Russian media is to facilitate the country's "managed democracy," in which the trappings of campaigns, elections, and the like are paraded before the citizenry while their basic rights and liberties are denied. The mastermind of that parade, Vladislav Surkov, fell from power in 2012, as the second Putin presidency reverted to more straightforward police-state tactics.[31] But the management of the media continues apace, with television being the most important medium by far. This is why opposition leader Aleksei Navalny, speaking to the tens of thousands gathered in Moscow on Christmas Eve 2011, referred to television as "the zombie-box."[32] To one participant, the most important thing about that demonstration was that "people have torn themselves from off their couches."[33] Many young Russians involved in the demonstrations chose to ignore the zombie-box in favor of the Internet TV channel *Dozhd* (rain).[34]

But Russia is vast, and its would-be liberal reformers are outnumbered by a far-flung populace with little inclination toward politics. Indeed, the writer Peter Pomerantzev describes Dozhd TV and its print counterpart, *Snob* magazine, as part of "a very Moscow mix of hip, rich and political," adding that "the Kremlin is generally very happy to have the opposition seen as westernised Muscovites. That way the 'real Russia' can hate them all the more."[35] As for the "real Russians," Putin's media policy is to make sure they don't develop any capacity for, or interest in, politics. To that end, Russian TV producers have been encouraged to fill the airwaves with crude, vulgar programs, including trash-talk shows, in the hope of attracting audiences and ad revenue — and in the process contributing to the demoralization of Russian society.

Like American trash-talk shows, the Russian version is scripted to be as sensationalist as possible. But unlike the American original, Russian trash talk also reinforces state propaganda. Case in point: in 2005, when the flow of immigrants and drugs from Tajikistan into Russia was quite high, a segment of the popular talk show *Five Evenings* staged a Jerry Springer–style confrontation between a pregnant eleven-year-old girl and the eighteen-year-old boy accused of being the father. At one point the host shouted, "I don't have time for political correctness here! . . . Let's say it: the boy is not Russian, the boy came from Tajikistan!" This was followed by loud applause and an outburst from another guest: "These people come to Moscow like locusts and abuse our women and girls!"[36]

The Russian journalist Arkady Ostrovsky makes the important point that trash-talk shows in the West "coexist with serious TV journalism, including news and analysis, while in Russia, they have simply replaced it and, worse, create an impression of free television where in fact there is none."[37] Russian TV critic Irina Petrovskaya agrees: "What we have in Russia is not a freedom of speech but a freedom of yelling and shouting."[38]

AMERICAN REALITY SHOWS

To American audiences, the talk show seems a little passé compared with the so-called reality show, which has come to dominate the twenty-first-century TV screen. In this section I trace the history and global spread of the American reality show, which emerged in the 1990s and has since become a staple in many other countries.

When asked about reality shows, some of my foreign interlocutors drew a sharp distinction between shows based on competitions of skill and talent, and shows based on a kind of exhibitionism. Some of the most popular TV shows in the world are amateur talent contests; there's a version of the hit singing contest *American Idol* in nearly every country. Also popular are contests in other skilled activities, such as dancing, cooking, fashion design, and reciting poetry. Because these competition shows feature "real" people, not professional performers, they are typically lumped with other reality shows such as *Survivor, Big Brother, Fear Factor,* and *The Apprentice.* But there is an important distinction between rooting for ordinary individuals doing admirable things, and voyeuristically watching them make spectacles of themselves. That is why I devote the rest of this chapter to the exhibitionist type of reality show, and take up the talent-competition type in Chapter 4.

In America, the exhibitionist reality show has two main precedents: *An American Family,* a twelve-part documentary airing on PBS in 1971, which chronicled the disintegration of a California family;[39] and *The Real World,* an MTV series debuting in 1991, which followed the spontaneous interaction of a group of young people living together. During its first few seasons *The Real World* was criticized for its juvenile tone but credited with encouraging participants to overcome racial and political differences. But the juvenile tone has long since taken over, as evidenced by the 2010 season, which began with one participant accusing another of urinating on his toothbrush and using it to scrub a toilet bowl. After a scuffle ensued, a police officer was asked whether he thought the incident had actually occurred, and he replied, "This is a reality show, so who's to say this wasn't done just for some publicity?"[40]

Because they focus on the lives of ordinary individuals, reality shows have been touted as more authentic than scripted sitcoms or dramas. Yet like the talk show, the reality show is not really about authenticity. It's about the bottom line.[41] During the 1980s, the major networks—ABC, CBS, NBC, and newcomer Fox—lost considerable audience share to cable television. So they pressured Congress to repeal the "fin-syn" (finance and syndication) rule forbidding them to produce their own shows. With repeal, the networks began to compete aggressively with cable through such low-budget offerings as *America's Funniest Home Videos* (ABC), *Rescue 911* (CBS), and *Cops* (Fox).

Featuring the rough-hewn look of the documentary but not its ethical scruples, the reality genre took off with the success of CBS's *Survivor* in 2000, and today it dominates prime time with a bewildering array of formats: dating shows, makeover shows, indoor game shows, outdoor game shows, "social experiment" shows, "hidden camera" shows, and more.[42] The cable channels retaliated by flaunting their relative freedom from regulation, and the result has been another race to the bottom. A prime example would be the MTV program *Girls Gone Wild*, which consisted entirely of video clips of women taking off their clothes and simulating sex for the camera. In 2004 the journalist Ariel Levy offered this account:

> It is 3 a.m., and I am with the *Girls Gone Wild* crew at a bar in Miami Beach . . . watching the "Sexy Positions Contest." . . . Two chunky women . . . are pretending to hump each other on a raised platform. . . . "Girls! This is not a wet T-shirt contest!" the MC bellows over the mike. "Pretend you're fucking! Let me emphasize, pretend you are really fucking! I want you to pretend like you're fucking the shit out of her doggy style." But the women are too inebriated to achieve sufficient verisimilitude, and the crowd hollers them off the stage.[43]

Network shows were a bit more decorous, but the most successful, such as the ABC dating show *Bachelor Pad* and its Fox counterpart, *Joe Millionaire*, encouraged female contestants to humiliate themselves in the hope of catching a wealthy husband. The show also pitted love against greed in ways that made greed look more compelling. Another Fox show, *Temptation Island*, tried to lure married individuals into adultery. Cable came back with "docusoap" programs such as *The Osbournes* (MTV), *Keeping Up with the Kardashians* (E!), *The Real Housewives of Orange County* (Bravo), and *Jersey Shore* (MTV), in which the materialism, vulgarity, and selfishness of ordinary people are highlighted in such a way as to turn them into celebrities.[44]

Not all reality shows are this obnoxious, but the majority exploit the all-too-human craving for attention. There was a time when the genre aroused a sense of shame. In 1997, a participant on the Swedish reality show *Expedition Robinson* threw himself under a train rather than face the public humiliation of being seen on the show. Today, by contrast, would-be participants on *Survivor* happily sign a contract agreeing not to sue the production company for subjecting them to "public ridicule, humiliation or condemnation," or for airing "factual and/or fictional" information about them that is "personal, private, intimate, surprising, defamatory, disparaging, embarrassing or unfavorable."[45]

At this point the reader may be wondering if there's anything redeeming about American reality shows. Do they ever present American life and values in a favorable light? The answer is yes. A whole subgenre—*Deadliest Catch*, about Alaskan crab fishermen, or *Whale Wars*, about efforts to curtail whale hunting—follow rugged Americans engaged in hard, challenging work.[46] In an article about similar programs on various cable channels,[47] journalist James Poniewozik makes the telling point that they are practically the only glimpses of honest blue-collar work left on American television.[48]

WHAT THE OVERSEAS MARKET WILL BEAR

One person who drew a distinction between talent-competition shows and the exhibitionist kind was a top-level media executive I met in India. When he was asked about the latter, his immediate response was, "It's important to tread carefully." An Indian himself, this executive cited the example of a reality show, created by a Western media company, that followed a family through the process of arranging their daughter's wedding, from the preliminary encounters with potential suitors through the ceremony (which the company offered to finance). It is hard to imagine a concept further removed from the typical American reality show. But as the executive explained, this program still did not find favor with Indian audiences. Indeed, it was derided as "a mockery of tradition," because while most Indians believe in arranged marriage, viewers were upset at the program's making a public display of the process. Especially "unconscionable" were the segments showing the rejection of would-be suitors.

Yet as television in India has become more competitive, reality shows have become more exhibitionistic. For example, a show called *Bigg Boss* follows the same format as *Big Brother*, a Dutch reality show licensed to dozens of countries.[49] Based very loosely on the all-seeing telescreen in George Orwell's novel *1984*, the *Big Brother* format places a group of volunteers under surveillance in a controlled environment, orders them to perform distasteful tasks, and requires them at regular intervals to nominate one of their number to be voted off the show by the viewing audience. The last participant left standing wins a cash prize and a fleeting taste of celebrity. In many countries, ordinary people flock to auditions for such shows, but in India they still hesitate. Thus, the first season of *Bigg Boss* had to rely on such minor celebrities as a female convict, a seven-foot-tall wrestler, a Pakistani transvestite TV host, and a pair of failed Bollywood actresses given to tantrums.

By contrast, Indian dating shows have no trouble recruiting guests. To be sure, one young man allegedly committed suicide after being sexually humili-ated. But another managed to persuade a women's rights activist, who was hop-ing to attract a wealthy suitor, to perform a cage dance.[50]

In Turkey, the reality show has been around since 1997, when a producer named Pelin Akat created *Will You Be My Bride?*, a program in which the choice of a bride was made not by the potential groom but by his mother. Unlike Indian viewers, who were upset by the airing of negative judgments of potential marriage partners, Turkish viewers reveled in the acid comments of mothers sizing up potential brides. Indeed, one woman's "hectoring tone" became so famous it was incorporated into a hit record. The show's 2005 finale attracted 74 percent of all viewers.[51]

As noted in Chapter 1, Arab audiences have embraced Turkish soap opera as a model of how to balance entertainment with Islamic tradition. No such balance is found in Turkish dating shows, which by 2010 had proliferated to the point of dominating fifty hours of the weekly schedule of three major channels (Star TV, FOX, and ATV). According to Turkish scholar Gozde Demirel, these programs, which originally "aimed to show the importance of family decisions in the marriage of children," have degenerated to the point where "none of them aim to marry the candidates; they want to use them as an element of en-tertainment."[52]

Demirel writes that the weakening of traditional family life in Turkey has made many young men and women feel "really alone" and "at the end of their tether." Distressingly, these lonely singles vie for a spot on dating shows (some of which have waiting lists as long as two thousand people). And when they do participate, they are ogled by total strangers who then amuse the audience with their reactions, answering questions such as, "Did you feel any electricity?" As Demirel suggests, these programs encourage matches "taken in haste, without knowing each other or each other's families and being influenced by the com-ments of others."[53]

Not surprisingly, the exhibitionist reality show has been thriving in Russia. The first, *Behind the Glass* (*Za steklom*), debuted in 2001 and quickly became a hit. An unlicensed copy of *Big Brother* (the Dutch show that films cohabiting volunteers with surveillance cameras), *Behind the Glass* placed six young contestants in an apartment with one-way glass walls in Moscow's Hotel Rossiya, where they lived for several weeks while being continually watched, not only by passersby paying twenty rubles to peep, but also (via twenty-six cameras) by a TV audience extending throughout Russia, Ukraine, the Baltics, and Central Asia. Unlike the participants in Western reality shows, who for all their shamelessness rarely disrobe, the participants in *Behind the Glass* frequently stripped, the better to soap each other in the shower and lie in bed kissing. Still, it took them a while to have actual intercourse, and when they did, the tabloid *Komsomolskaya Pravda* crowed, "Max and Margo Finally Did IT."[54]

Komsomolskaya Pravda is, of course, today's incarnation of the official newspaper of the Soviet-era youth organization, the Young Communist League. How ironic, then, to see it celebrating the portrayal of Russian youth found in *Behind the Glass*. The Maxes and Margos in that show are lazy, untidy, indifferent to books and culture, and lacking any goals beyond immediate pleasure and the hope of winning the coveted prize: a year-long lease to an upscale Moscow apartment. Hence the comment, by veteran pundit Vladimir Pozner, that the show reveals "a very big difference between people of that age today and their parents or grandparents. . . . Rightly or wrongly, their grandparents had a belief; the vast majority believed in the Soviet state, believed in the Soviet ideals. . . . These young people have nothing to believe in. . . . And when there is nothing there—no moral fiber, no ideals, really, left—then what is it that can in any way limit your conduct?"[55]

Behind the Glass was a production of TV6, an independent channel whose main shareholder, the outspoken oligarch Boris Berezovsky, criticized Putin and was forced out of business in 2002.[56] At the time, the crackdown on TV6 was taken as evidence that, in the words of its director, Yevgeny Kiselyov, "Russia is heading towards an authoritarian and totalitarian regime."[57]

Little noticed was the curious fact that this authoritarian regime encouraged the continued production of such crass and degrading entertainment. Presiding over the next wave of reality shows was Valery Komissarov, a Putin loyalist and former parliamentarian who launched his TV career as "Russia's Jerry Springer," hosting a talk show best known for its rotating cast of prostitutes.[58] In 2003 Komissarov produced his first reality show on TNT, an entertainment channel owned by Gazprom and thus deeply connected with the Putin regime. Called *House* (*Dom*), the show invited married couples with no construction skills to compete in building a house. But after a successful first season, the married couples were dispensed with, because, in the sardonic view of TNT's chief executive, "married people don't talk enough."[59]

House's successor, *House-2*, featured a cast of nubile singles whose assignment was less to build a house than to "fall in love."[60] By 2011 *House-2* was the world's longest-running reality show, airing three and a half hours a day, 365 days a year, on Gazprom's TNT. But its status as the hottest reality show was being challenged by another Komissarov production, a localized version of Turkey's *Will You Be My Bride?*

In countries like India and Turkey, localization means cleaning up the Western original. In Russia, it means the opposite. Here is a highlight from *Mother-in-Law*, described by *Financial Times* correspondent Courtney Weaver:

> With a crazy glint in her eye, [65-year-old] Yelena Bogatyreva is lunging full force at fellow contestant [52-year-old] Varvara Rade. It is an early November afternoon on the set of the Russian reality show *Mama v zakone*. Clutching a heavy object, Bogatyreva gives Rade two good whacks on the head but fails to land a third blow, for her opponent fights back, clawing at Bogatyreva's breasts and screeching like a hyena. Hair-pulling (Bogatyreva) and finger-biting (Rade) ensue, until Bogatyreva is on the floor, kicking Rade in the crotch, exposing both Rade's cleavage and her own knickers in the process.[61]

With stunning cynicism, one Russian media executive has defended such fare as expressing the true Russian soul, describing reality television as "a new Russian art form, celebrating real-life proletarian characters."[62] Komissarov, the producer of *House-2*, compares the "issues" raised in that program with the conflict of love and duty in Tolstoy's *Anna Karenina*. "These kinds of situations come up every day," he says, then winkingly adds, "Thank God, no one is throwing themselves under a train."[63] To be sure, one participant did threaten suicide after being exposed as a porn star during her on-screen wedding. But unlike Anna Karenina, most of the participants on Russian reality shows feel neither shame nor remorse.

It will be a long time before such trashy programs receive the blessing of the Indian or Turkish government—or, for that matter, of public television in the United States (imagine PBS filling its schedule with *Jersey Shore*). Putin and his allies permit such fare because they want to make money from advertisers and appear cool and hip in the eyes of Russian youth. But there is another reason: vulgar, offensive fare reinforces the power of authoritarian governments in countries where ordinary men and women are already cynical and distrustful of their fellow citizens. When the tendrils of civil society are new and fragile, pushing up through cracks in the pavement of chronic distrust, trashy entertainment can be an effective weed killer. Consider this comment by the producer Komissarov: "When people ask me, 'Why do you pick so many idiots?,' I know that I have done my job correctly."[64]

"LOW-END ENTERTAINMENT" IN CHINA

In China the story is different, for the obvious reason that its Communist regime has not collapsed. To be sure, Maoist ideology is no longer the organizing principle of the Chinese economy. But selected Maoist teachings remain the preferred filler for what my interlocutors there called "the Chinese values vacuum." In September 1989, Deng Xiaoping made a speech laying the blame for the Tiananmen Square protests on "certain comrades" who had "attached no importance to ideological work."[65] The West was engaged in a propaganda war against China, Deng warned, so countermeasures were needed. One such was a two-pronged directive from the Chinese Communist Party (CCP) to the media, especially the rapidly growing TV industry: first, to fortify the values of "socialism with Chinese characteristics"; and second, to become profitable.

The struggle to meet both directives is still unfolding, but one clear pattern can be discerned. While news and movies have always been strictly controlled (the former for political reasons and the latter because Lenin saw cinema as the key "public medium"), TV entertainment has enjoyed great latitude—until recently. In Beijing I interviewed a high official at the National Center for Radio & TV Studies at the Communication University of China, who told me that when television was first made widely available, station managers were given free rein to "marketize" entertainment, on the theory that it was "a frivolous matter, just singing and dancing and reality shows." Most of the major media companies are regionally based and receive only 10 percent of their operating expenses from Beijing; they are expected to earn the other 90 percent through advertising revenue. So as this official explained, they began filling their schedules with cheaply produced talk and reality shows—which in turn led to a "tug-of-war" with the central government, which gradually came to the realization that "low-end entertainment" was not as innocuous as originally thought.

The result was a series of disciplinary actions, the most recent occurring in 2010, when the State Administration of Radio, Film and Television (SARFT) announced its displeasure with *If You Are the One*, a phenomenally popular dating show produced by Jiangsu TV, a major channel in China's most densely populated, wealthy province. Between January, when the show debuted, and

May, when SARFT denounced it for vulgarity and materialism, *If You Are the One* regaled viewers with a lineup of twenty-four attractive young women vetting a parade of would-be suitors.

Against the (unspoken) backdrop of gender imbalance created by China's one-child policy and the traditional preference for sons, the women clearly had the upper hand—and were encouraged to use it. According to one report, they were told "not to spare the dignity of the male contestants."[66] In the entertaining display of female cockiness that followed, one woman told a suitor requesting a handshake, "Only my boyfriend gets to hold my hand. Everyone else pays 200,000 renminbi [about $30,000]." The most shocking putdown came from a model, Ma Nuo, who, when invited by a jobless bachelor to take a ride on his bicycle, replied, "I'd rather cry in a BMW than laugh on a bicycle."[67]

This was too much for the Central Propaganda Department, which promptly ordered a chorus of indignation to be sounded by the Xinhua news agency, *People's Daily*, China Central Television (CCTV), and numerous state-run websites. Then, in a grand gesture of responsiveness, SARFT directed the producers to eliminate all "overly depressing, dark or decadent topics" and retool the show to "maintain core Socialist values."[68] Out went the cynical references to fast cars, luxury apartments, and designer clothes in exchange for sexual favors. In came the wisdom of a CCP-approved psychologist and misty-eyed accounts of having volunteered for the Olympics and cared for disabled orphans. As the ratings declined, one viewer commented in disbelief, "Who *doesn't* ask about houses and cars these days when looking for someone to marry?"[69]

This oft-repeated pattern reflects what Chinese media scholar Yin Hong describes as a "conflict" between the government's support "for the building of a commercial industry" and its worry that "this commercialization has led to an overall decline in cultural quality and moral cultivation."[70] A resolution of sorts was reached in October 2011, when President Hu Jintao addressed the Sixth Plenary Session of the 17th Central Committee on the topic of "cultural security."[71] In remarks published later as an essay, Hu warned that "international hostile forces are intensifying the strategic plot of Westernizing and dividing China," especially in the "ideological and cultural fields." Noting that "the overall strength of Chinese culture and its international influence is not commensurate with China's international status," Hu urged the development of cultural products better suited to meeting the "growing spiritual and cultural demands of the people."[72]

While the experts renewed their study of what shape those cultural products would take, SARFT launched a purge of "excessive entertainment," in which dozens of talk and reality shows were either eliminated or relegated to late evening hours. It was hard to gauge the public reaction to this purge, but I doubt it was high on anyone's list of human rights violations in China. If there were any demonstrations calling for the reinstatement of *If You Are The One*, they haven't been reported in the West. Doubtless many Chinese share the government's aversion to these programs and do not feel as outraged by the censorship of provocative entertainment as the average American would.

Unfortunately, the censorship was not confined to the low end of TV entertainment. Timed to coincide with a major transition in the country's top leadership (along with Hu, six other members of the nine-member Standing Committee of the Politburo were scheduled to step down in 2012), the proposed "cultural reforms" promised to be quite sweeping.[73] Included were not just a television housecleaning but also closer supervision of filmmakers, scholars, writers, artists, and netizens, as well as a stepped-up "soft power" initiative to accompany the buildup of Chinese hard power in the region.[74]

The whole point of trash television is to titillate and shock the public, so it is hard to criticize it without sounding titillated or shocked. To splutter with outrage is to play into the hands of those who produce such programs, whether they are American, Russian, Indian, or Chinese.[75] But to defend trash television as a "new kind of public forum" in which a "diversity of voices" may be heard—a perspective that has migrated from the academic field of cultural studies into entertainment journalism—is to give it far more credit than it deserves.[76]

When faced with the downward spiral of our popular culture, most Americans neither splutter nor theorize. We shrug, laugh, or change the subject. It is only when we travel to a country very different from America that we develop a more critical attitude.

Case in point: Matt Cool (not a pseudonym) is a young American living in China who has written about the experience of appearing on a dating show produced by a Henan Province TV channel. "Having no concern about my reputation, humiliation, or face, I agreed to do it," he confesses. Partway through his six-day stint, Cool realized that "many of the competitions . . . were rigged" and "about half the cast . . . were actors or spies from other networks." He soldiered on, agreeing to stage a "romantic date" with a female participant: "I was instructed to tell her . . . that she was my one true love, and we should run away together." Then, after the show ended, he learned that the young woman had "apparently thought the whole thing was real." Hoping to apologize for "lying to the girl," and "to expose the show for being fake," he agreed to be interviewed by a local tabloid. But then he realized his "big mistake":

When the article came out, next to a picture of me the headline read: "I'm very naughty, I just came to play." The newspaper published all sorts of interesting facts I never knew about myself . . . like I "came to China because the job market was tough in America." . . . I didn't mind some of the inaccuracies. . . . But falsities that play into stereotypes Chinese people have about Americans bothered me. They portrayed me as a playboy and called me a typical American.[77]

Matt Cool may have learned his lesson, but most Americans have not. Without much reflection, we repeat the cliché that a steady diet of degrading talk shows and reality shows is "the price we pay for freedom." This may be true in America. But in authoritarian regimes like Russia and China, people pay the same price and get nothing for it. That is, they are free to wallow in degrading entertainment; indeed, they may be encouraged to do so by up-to-date autocrats like Vladimir Putin. But they are not free to change the channel and watch something better and more truthful.

4

◆

FROM POP IDOL TO VOX POPULI

The most popular TV format in the world is the amateur singing contest, currently sold as a format by the British company Fremantle Media. The format consists of open auditions held throughout a country or region, followed by a tournament-style competition in which singers are eliminated by both a panel of no-nonsense music industry professionals and the viewing public, voting by text message. Created in 2001 by the UK entrepreneur Simon Fuller and dubbed *Pop Idol* in Britain, the format is now sold in over forty markets worldwide, including the United States, where *American Idol* (Fox) has consistently topped the ratings.[1] It has also been endlessly cloned and copied. What makes it different from the reality shows discussed in Chapter 3 is that it is based on talent, not exhibitionism.

Why include a British TV format in a book about America's cultural footprint? Because its roots are American. Back in the 1930s, a CBS radio show called *Major Bowes Amateur Hour* hosted aspiring performers, and when their performances were substandard the master of ceremonies, Edward "Major" Bowes, cut them off with a loud bell. In 1948 the show moved to television, where it ran until 1970. The host of that show, Ted Mack, came up with the idea of having the audience vote for the winners by sending postcards or calling a telephone number shown on the screen.

There were no such programs on British or European television at the time, because as government-controlled services they saw their mission as educating and uplifting the masses, not pandering to them.[2] Of course, the *Amateur Hour* didn't pander, either. Mack was a gentler soul than Bowes, but he also gave short shrift to substandard performances.[3]

Thus, the success of the show could be said to consist in its peculiar, and peculiarly American, celebration of competition as a process open to all, occurring on a level playing field, bound by clear rules, and rewarding not only talent but also hard work and respect for commonly held standards of excellence. This combination of ingredients is still taken for granted by Americans. But to many people around the world, especially the young, it comes as a breath of fresh air. A number of global satellite services carry *Pop Idol* and *American Idol*, but these are mere spectacles compared with the localized shows, which are intensely participatory events. As for the music performed on these shows, it is based on an American template but incorporates local instruments, vocal styles, and lyrical content.

After highlighting the difference between today's sexualized pop music and the pop-idol show, I will consider whether the latter does more than simply conquer markets. Some observers argue that the pop-idol show imparts a sense of democratic norms and practices to people living in undemocratic societies. Others disagree, likening the shows to Russian "managed democracy" and other forms of democratic pretense found in twenty-first-century authoritarian states.

A decade after 9/11, the debate over media and democracy began to shift toward Facebook, Twitter, YouTube, and the other Internet-based social media, as they began to play a role in organizing and reporting pro-democracy movements in Iran, Tunisia, Egypt, and other countries, including Russia and China. To those celebrating the liberating power of social media, it has been tempting to conclude that television is passé. To be sure, the number of Internet users in the world is growing. But the number of TV viewers remains high, and in many places, including several Muslim-majority countries, television remains the dominant medium.[4] Furthermore, the majority of Internet users online at any given time are not engaging in political activism. They are chatting with friends and family, playing video games, watching porn—and accessing entertainment, including TV shows.[5]

Social media, like all media, are not just tools of liberation. In the hands of tech-savvy authoritarians, they are also instruments of manipulation and repression.[6] When politically mobilized, people deploy whatever media come to hand. But when politically passive, they do not. The real question is, what mobilizes people in the first place? What lights the spark? There is no single answer, but this chapter will argue that the pop-idol show, with its ethos of open competition, free expression, and democratic participation, was—and is—at least as important as social media to the pro-democracy movements of the early twenty-first century. With due respect to Marshall McLuhan, the medium is not the message. The *message* is the message.

POP MUSIC AND HIP-HOP: CRANKING UP THE SEXUAL HEAT

This chapter will begin with a look at pop music (including MTV and hip-hop), then shift to the pop-idol show. The two are treated separately, because there is an important difference between them. Beginning in the early twentieth century, jazz, rock 'n' roll, and other forms of popular music from America have had a major impact on the rest of the world. Today, American popular music is still having an impact, but the focus of that impact has narrowed to a narrow preoccupation with sex. Popular music has always been focused on romance, eroticism, and good times. But today eroticism is an obsession, with many lyrics and images verging on soft-core porn. A striking aspect of the pop-idol show is that it does not partake of this obsession. This is probably because these shows are watched by families, and because those who compete are more focused on singing than on bumping and grinding for the camera. Whatever the reason, the pop-idol show genre stands as living proof that musical entertainment can conquer the world without racing to the bottom.

Tune in to a commercial channel on any continent and you will hear music that doesn't quite sound American (because it utilizes non-American instruments and vocal styles) but that still conforms to an American template, in the sense of being melodically catchy, rhythmically infectious, and structured into three-minute songs. To call this "pop music" is to annoy those who champion "world music" as pushback against the US cultural hegemon. But except for the rare case when an unaltered folk style makes its way into the mainstream, the music referred to as "world music" is a hybrid, and its hybridity is deeply American.

Or, more accurately, Afro-American. I borrow the term *Afro-American* from the eminent critic Henry Pleasants, who uses it to describe the dominant musical idiom of the United States. Afro-American does not refer to the race of the musicians involved, because the list of people working in this idiom now includes every race and color on the planet. As Pleasants explains, the "popular" music of America—ragtime, jazz, blues, gospel, country, rock 'n' roll, hip-hop—is all based on the Afro-American idiom, broadly construed. Perhaps the most striking characteristic of this idiom is its ability to absorb musical influences from very diverse sources.[7]

This chapter will focus on the two genres of Afro-American music that have proved most globally absorptive in the late twentieth and early twenty-first centuries: the "pop" style associated with Michael Jackson; and hip-hop, also known as rap music. (*Hip-hop* is the more inclusive term, used to describe both musical and nonmusical aspects, such as music, clothing, dance, graffiti. *Rap* originally referred only to the spoken words, but later it came to be used inter-changeably with *hip-hop*. Today *rap* tends to connote the more vulgar, com-mercialized type of music, while *hip-hop* connotes grassroots, often political, expression.)

Since the advent of MTV in the 1980s and the "concert spectacular" pioneered by Michael Jackson, American pop music shifted its priority from pleasing the ear to dazzling the eye. This created a problem, because musical talent does not always correlate with good looks. Bollywood has long solved this problem by having "playback singers" provide beautiful voices for beautiful lip-syncing actors. In America lip-syncing is considered cheating. So the American solution (in an era of media de-regulation and ferocious competition, remember) has been to crank up the sexual heat.

This is also true of hip-hop. According to one study, the percentage of US music videos containing sexual content rose from 47 to 73 percent between 1985 and 2005.[8] Most of this content was not explicit, although rapper Snoop Doggy Dogg was known to release X-rated DVDs of his already smutty videos. But the sexual images were relentless, a never-ending stream of female bodies (the point of view was consistently male), writhing and gyrating in outfits that grew ever tighter and scantier. The highest concentration of these images ap-peared in videos by black performers, including pop singers—a fact that did not go unremarked, either in African-American communities or overseas.

For example, in the mid-2000s many African Americans who had grown up embracing the grassroots, multimedia art form known as hip-hop began to ob-ject to the more exploitative forms of commercial rap, in which black women are depicted as gold-digging "bitches" and "ho's," black men as loudmouthed pimps and gangbangers. In 2005 the women's magazine *Essence* launched an online debate about the topic, and as editor in chief Diane Weathers told me, the debate drew comments from readers in African countries expressing "dis-gust at what their African-American brothers and sisters are doing in entertain-ment. They wonder if we've lost our minds."[9]

This is not to suggest that Africans dislike hip-hop. On the contrary, it is popular throughout the continent. This is hardly surprising, given that its roots lie deep in West Africa by way of the Caribbean. Indeed, its point of origin is the improvised oral poetry of the *griots*, or oral historians, who could recite clan histories, offer praise songs, and practice the fine art of ritual insult. In the Caribbean, where enslaved Africans were cut off from their clan histories and had few occasions for praise, the tradition became focused on insult. Over time, this gave rise to two broad tendencies: bragging about oneself while bad-mouthing one's rivals; and, in straitened political circumstances, giving voice to the voiceless.

In American hip-hop the first tendency was carried to an extreme by the "gangsta" rap of the 1990s, which gained commercial success with its lurid tales of gangbangers killing each other (and police) and living an outrageously he-donistic lifestyle. Criticized for its violence, rap then turned toward pure he-donism, re-creating the atmosphere of a Southern strip club where white and black meet in an orgy of pole dancing, lap dancing, and hard drinking. This "party" rap is also commercially successful, both at home and overseas. But politically, it is less influential than the second tendency, that of hip-hop giving a voice to the politically marginalized.[10]

Perhaps the most salient recent example is Hamada Ben Amor, a twenty-two-year-old Tunisian who raps under the name El Général. In November 2010 he posted a hip-hop video on Facebook lambasting then President Zine al Abidine Ben Ali. The video went viral, and in December, when the fruit vendor Mo-hamed Bouazizi immolated himself, launching the Arab Spring, the crowds filling the streets chanted El Général's lyrics.

This is not to claim, as some do, that hip-hop is the leading voice of politi-cally mobilized youth in North Africa, the Middle East, and elsewhere. On the contrary, it is one of many voices, and not nearly as powerful as that of Arab pop music. When Wael Ghonim, the Google manager whose online activism helped to spark the 2011 uprising in Egypt, posted on his Facebook page an inspirational video about the movement's early "Silent Stand" protests, he con-ducted a "long search" for "a song that expressed the current situation." His choice, "The Resurrection of Egyptians," by Haitham Said, was pure Arab pop, a song whose powerful melody "created an emotional bond between the cause and the target audience" of over fifty thousand visitors to that site.[11]

Rappers in Egypt, Morocco, Iraq, Lebanon, Iran, Senegal, Somalia, Guinea, Djibouti, and many other countries speak out against injustice and tyranny. But they can reach only so many people, owing to American hip-hop's bad reputa-tion. As noted by journalist Robin Wright, rappers in the Muslim world try hard to distance themselves from "the materialism, misogyny, vulgarity, and 'gangsta' violence" of "Western hip-hop."[12] But it's not that easy to shake those associa-tions. Even in America, the distinction between affirmative hip-hop and the ex-ploitative styles is lost on many people. Overseas, it is lost on many more. That is why young people who are serious about political change tend to choose another vehicle of expression.

Drilling Down in Indonesia

Meanwhile, in the realm of pop music, cranking up the sexual heat may keep the American music industry afloat, but it also degrades the music and sets an unfortunate example for pop musicians abroad. Arguably, this is what happened to *dangdut* music in Indonesia. A blend of Malay, Middle Eastern, Indian, and American sounds, dangdut was created in the 1970s, and while it was spurned by elites, it was extremely popular. Considered too salty in the early days, dangdut was made respectable by its biggest star, Rhoma Irama. After making the pilgrimage to Mecca in 1975, Rhoma (as he is known) began writing songs that criticized the Suharto regime and the West from a Muslim perspective. By 1998, when Suharto was unseated, the elites who had previously spurned dangdut were holding it up as an authentic expression of the nation.

Rhoma's style of dangdut is still beloved, but in the mid-2000s it was replaced by that of a female star, Inul Daratista (known as Inul). Inul, a native of East Java, was known less for her singing than for her vigorous rump-twirling. Defended by fans as part of East Javanese culture, this trademark gyration was derided in the press as *goyang ngebor* (drilling). Not surprisingly, given Inul's predominantly male audience, her fame spread not through audio recordings but through live concerts, TV appearances, and millions of pirated videos.

Indonesia is 85 percent Muslim, but as historian Azyumardi Azra explained to me, its people are "very relaxed about American popular culture," regarding it as "just another ingredient in the pluralistic essence."[13] Echoing the point, Peter Bumke, the former head of the Goethe Institute in Jakarta, described Indonesians as "pragmatic and syncretic, reacting to what is foreign by adopting it and making use of it. The whole country is a patchwork, not concerned with cultural purity."[14]

This pluralism was tested in the controversy that erupted when Rhoma, backed by an alliance of radical Islamist groups, denounced Inul's dangdut as pornographic. Soon dangdut was a target in an Islamist campaign to pass a sweeping law against *pornoaksi*, a term coined to refer not only to X-rated materials but also to every behavior, private and public, that could be construed as sexually arousing, including many traditional customs and styles of dress.

Radical Islamists are a minority in Indonesia, because, as Azra noted, their "rejection of all music and images is not popular here."[15] For a while, the pornoaksi bill was blocked by a coalition of liberals and revered religious leaders, including the former president Abdurrahman Wahid (Gus Dur), who mounted a spirited defense of Indonesia's rich diversity against the Islamists' one-size-fits-all ideology.[16] But in 2008 the bill passed, and despite court challenges and moments of comic relief (one of the bill's supporters was caught watching porn on his laptop during a legislative session), it remains on the books.[17]

Reporting on the controversy, some Western journalists took a condescending tone, in effect suggesting that the worried natives should get over it.[18] But this misses the larger context. At the time of the pornoaksi debate, Indonesians were being exposed to global satellite channels carrying raunchy US music videos. Not only that, but they were also, for the first time in history, being flooded with hardcore pornography. With no laws in place to regulate it, the flood was showing up everywhere. As one resident of Jakarta told me, it was common to see little children peddling hardcore porn in gas stations. Indonesians are not puritanical, but they did not relish this inundation.

If enforced, the pornoaksi bill would threaten to outlaw the relaxed sensuality of 238 million people inhabiting over six thousand islands. But the bill was not passed because Indonesians suddenly became upset by their own customs. It was passed because they felt threatened by cultural influences coming from the outside, including the United States. "We know that pornography is produced in many different places," I was told by Endy Bayune, a writer for the *Jakarta Post*. "But *America, the West, and MTV were often invoked in the porn bill debate*" (emphasis added).[19]

MTV Does Bollywood

As noted in Chapter 1, the sari-wrapped modesty of classic Bollywood films has in recent years given way to "items," or song-and-dance sequences that, because they also serve as music videos on MTV India, have exchanged the sari for more revealing clothing and more suggestive movements. The Indian entertainment industry may have pushed back against American cultural influences in the past, but to judge by the story of MTV India, it has recently decided to stop trying.

In 1994 MTV attempted to enter the South Asian market with the same rock and rap videos it featured on its US and European channels. But it soon found itself outpaced by Rupert Murdoch's Channel V, which specialized in song-and-dance clips from Bollywood films. So MTV decided to localize. Bill Roedy, then CEO of MTV International, claims that MTV was the first company to act on the "revolutionary" idea that "instead of having one cola, one burger, one product around the world, [you need] to have a product that changes depending on where you are."[20] This claim of being revolutionary might be disputed by Murdoch, to say nothing of McDonald's. But the idea is valid nonetheless. By switching to Bollywood music videos rather than Western ones, MTV India was soon being watched in eight million homes in over one hundred Indian cities.[21] Today it is the parent company's second most popular channel worldwide.

Some of the people I met in India cited this localization of MTV as evidence of the abiding strength of the country's traditional values. Indeed, film critic Anupama Chopra cited a market survey conducted by MTV that showed a majority of affluent young Indians preferring arranged marriages over love matches.[22] Echoing this, a top executive with the UTV Group cited market research showing that "unlike American youth culture, Indian youth culture does not focus on rebellion. Instead, it focuses on growing up, careers and work, and above all, family."

These comments suggest that MTV India is making a profit substituting romance for raunch. If so, then more power to it. However, to watch the channel is to witness something else happening: a growing obsession with sex that not only ignores the old modesty but goes out of its way to poke fun at it. As one Bollywood insider pointed out to me, "You can see the influence of MTV in the way the Hindi film songs are now edited. For example, a female dancer's skill is now less important than her physical attributes, as the camera no longer films at a distance but rather relies on close-ups of her body."

As noted in Chapter 1, the classic three-hour Bollywood film was a rich tapestry, by turns comic and tragic, of an entire social milieu. In recent years that tapestry has become threadbare, its empty places filled with what critic Rauf Ahmed called "mindless items." For Bollywood's millions of poor, tradition-minded fans, both Indian and non-Indian, the reason for this unfortunate transformation must seem obvious. To quote one Nigerian viewer, "When I was young, the Indian films we used to see were based on their tradition. But now Indian films are just like American films. They go to discos, make gangs, they'll do anything in a hotel and they play rough in romantic scenes where before you could never see things like that."[23]

MTV Does Arabia

MTV did not enter the transnational Arab market until 2007, in part because that market was already saturated with Arab-owned music video channels.[24] Occupying roughly 20 percent of airtime, those channels combine music videos ("video clips") with on-screen text messages posted by viewers. The latter are extremely lucrative, as the fees for all that texting are divided between the channels and the mobile phone companies. A harbinger of social media to come, this kind of texting (called SMS, which stands for "short message service") proved hugely popular from the outset. Often the TV screen would be covered by continuously scrolling gossip, commentary, and coded flirtation.[25]

To Islamist critics, the video clip channels are immoral, because their biggest stars are attractive unveiled women. Some of those stars, such as Lebanon's Nancy Agram, are seen by most viewers as staying within the bounds of modesty. Others, notably the Egyptian singer "Ruby" (Rania Hussein Mohammed Tawfiq), chafe against those bounds. Still others, such as the Lebanese sexpot Haifa Wehbe, deliberately flout them. Yet all of these performers appear on the dominant music channel, Rotana, which is owned by the Saudi investor Prince Al Waleed bin Talal.

Saudi Arabia is the most important advertising market in the region. It is also the most repressive with regard to female dress and customs. How do Al Waleed and other media moguls in that country reconcile these two facts? One answer is what media scholar Marwan Kraidy calls "the Saudi-Lebanese connection." Because of the Saudi royal family's accommodation with the puritanical Wahhabi sect, its efforts to modernize have long been constrained. In the early days of Saudi-owned entertainment television, this meant going outside the country—recruiting mostly Egyptian talent and locating facilities in Europe. Then the facilities relocated to Beirut and Dubai, and the talent became largely Lebanese. In Kraidy's view, this arrangement works well in the era of transnational satellite television, because Lebanese media professionals are both "adept at negotiating across cultures" and willing to serve as "reliable spokespersons for the political and economic agendas of Saudi princes." At the same time, socially liberal Lebanese content provides "a platform for 'reformist' princes' [such as Al Waleed] . . . to reach the Saudi public."[26]

All of this adds up to a certain tolerance, within Saudi society, of unveiled women singing and dancing on television—as long as they are not Saudi.[27] Hard-core Wahhabi clerics have consistently railed against the music channels, and radical Islamists throughout the region hold them up as proof that the Saudis have sold out to the decadent Americans. For example, the Islamic Action Front, an extremist branch of the Muslim Brotherhood in Jordan, denounced the channels as part of a larger "Americanization of Islamic values."[28] A popular talk show on Qatar-based Al-Jazeera debated whether "music video clips should be seen as an American-Saudi conspiracy to destroy Arab and Islamic political unity."[29]

Secular critics have joined the chorus. In a widely read 2005 critique of the singer Ruby, the prominent Egyptian scholar and activist Abdel Wahab El-Messiri equated video clips with "vulgarity and alienation—the flesh parade," and warned that "to know in which direction we are heading, one should simply watch MTV."[30]

It was not easy for MTV to gain a foothold in this environment. Its MTV Europe programming was first carried on ShowTime Arabia, a channel 80 percent owned by the Kuwait Investment Group. In Dubai I met with two Arab media executives, who described ShowTime Arabia as "a channel of aspiration" for "educated, tolerant, liberal" viewers. Yet it is not clear what this meant, because when ShowTime Arabia first launched, its programming included *Girls of Playboy Mansion* and *Naked Wild On* (an E! Entertainment series featuring topless female tourists). These programs proved a bit too "edgy," one executive told me, adding that they were cancelled after a barrage of "negative audience feedback."

Mindful of this history, MTV International CEO Bill Roedy proceeded carefully when launching MTV's Arabic-language channel in 2007. At the time, he told an Arab newspaper that the new channel, MTV Middle East, would combine the parent company's "marketing expertise" with "the cultural bonds of the local partners."[31] Here it is important to note that MTV is no longer predominantly a music channel, having shifted its focus to reality shows. It has also produced a few scripted series, the most notorious being *Skins*, based on a gritty British show about dysfunctional teens that proved sufficiently offensive, even to MTV's American audience, to have been cancelled in 2011. *Skins* has not appeared on the schedule of MTV Middle East. And neither has exploitative rap. One of the video jockeys (VJs), Farid Karam Nassar, is a Palestinian-American who once worked with the rapper Snoop Doggy Dogg, but there is nothing Doggy-style about his show. "You can't show half-naked women on TV" in the Arab market, he explains. "It's a different kind of culture."[32]

Yet here, too, American cultural influence seems to be stronger than the local pushback. In 2012, the MTV Middle East schedule included several American reality shows that, to put it mildly, were not based on talent: *The Real World* (mentioned in Chapter 3); the aptly named *Jackass*; the latest from trash celebrity Paris Hilton; and other shows dedicated to the proposition that life in America is one long binge. To cite the tamest example in the lot, the MTV Middle East website offered this description of a reality show popular with young girls:

Each week *My Super Sweet 16* will document one character's outrageous journey as they plot, plan and prep for the party to end all parties. These kids expect and will only accept the absolute best. Now, it's up to them to make sure jealous siblings, stressed out parents and school rivals don't get in the way. This series gives you an up close and very personal look at the extravagant and sometimes extreme measures teens take to ensure that this milestone in their lives is commemorated by the ultimate celebration.[33]

Reading this, I recall my conversation with Hisham, the engineering student I met at the American University of Sharjah (mentioned in Chapter 3). When asked about his goals, he replied that they were not hedonistic and materialistic: "There is more to being on earth than seeking the pleasure of the moment."[34] Hedonism and materialism we will always have with us, and there are plenty of young Arabs who lack any other goals. But there are also plenty of young *Americans* who share Hisham's broader perspective—and they rarely show up on MTV.[35]

Launched as a music channel, then converted to a reality show channel, MTV would seem a logical place for a new generation of pop-idol shows. But the company has never taken that step. Why not? The most obvious reason is the need to carve out a separate market niche. But a less obvious reason is the difference between reality shows based on exhibitionism and reality shows based on talent. MTV has opted for the former, because its guiding spirit is that of American youth culture at its most self-centered and self-indulgent. Today (if you'll pardon the expression) that youth culture is getting old. But it continues to set the tone of MTV's programming, both domestic and international.

THE POP-IDOL SHOW—ARABIC STYLE

For the majority of Arab youth, the in-your-face youth culture of MTV might as well be happening on another planet. In 2009 there were one hundred million Arabs between the ages of fifteen and twenty-nine, and the unemployment rate for this "youth bulge" (constituting 47 percent of the working-age population) was between 50 and 77 percent—and ironically, the rate was higher for college graduates.[36] These are the conditions that drove the Arab Spring of 2011, and these are the conditions under which the Arab pop-idol show became more than a talent contest.

Just as the Arab satellite television market is unique in reaching twenty-four countries, so too are Arab pop-idol shows unique in drawing their contestants from many different countries. On occasion the result has been an audience vote skewed by national rivalries. For example, the 2005–6 season of *Super Star*, a pop-idol show on Lebanon's Future TV, was riven by tension over the assassination of former Lebanese prime minister (and Future TV owner) Rafic Al-Hariri, almost certainly by agents of the Syrian government. During the finale, which pitted a twenty-seven-year-old Saudi man against a seventeen-year-old Syrian woman, the latter's father rushed onstage and wrapped his daughter in the Syrian flag. The daughter responded coolly, removing the flag and draping it over her shoulder, all without missing a note. But the incident provoked a surge of anti-Syrian feeling that cost her the victory.[37]

Super Star lost ground after 2005, when Future TV became a political mouthpiece for the Al-Hariri family's anti-Syrian legacy. But it was already being outpaced by another show, *Star Academy*, airing on the Lebanese channel LBC since 2003, whose main investor was the aforementioned Saudi Prince Al Waleed bin Talal. The success of *Star Academy* is surprising, because while it is basically a talent competition, it also borrows the *Big Brother* format of having the contestants—unmarried and unrelated men and women—live together in a large house where they practice and train for the competition. The living quarters are segregated by sex, but *Star Academy* is still a bold departure from what most Muslims would find acceptable.

But here we see the difference between reality shows based on talent and reality shows based on exhibitionism. In 2003, the same year that *Star Academy* was launched, MBC introduced another localized version of *Big Brother* called *Al Ra'is* (The Boss). Produced in Bahrain, *Al Ra'is* also segregated the participants' living quarters. But that did not save *Al Ra'is* when one participant, a Saudi man, kissed another, a Tunisian woman, on the cheek. Bahrain's minister of information called a special parliamentary session to cancel the show, even though, as the chair of the session explained, the move was "opposed by the businessmen who fear that such a decision would hurt Bahrain's reputation and undermine potential investment agreements."[38]

Star Academy has avoided any such controversy, in part by basing its production in Beirut. But between 2003 and 2005 the program was officially denounced in Saudi Arabia, where the free mingling of the sexes is strictly forbidden.[39] Similar objections were raised in other countries, among the same establishment clerics, radical Islamists, and secular anti-Western intellectuals who had lambasted video clips.[40]

But strikingly, few of these objections were shared by the Arab public, because unlike the participants on *Al Ra'is* and other shows based on the *Big Brother* format, where the participants are simply thrown together in the hope that something scandalous will occur, the contestants on *Star Academy* are selected through auditions to work with music professionals. In other words, *Star Academy* gets away with having men and women live in the same building, because it shows them spending their time and energy honing their musical skills, not pulling crazy stunts for the camera. This element of aspiration and hard work makes all the difference.

As a result, *Star Academy* has shared the longevity of *American Idol* and countless other versions of the pop-idol show. At the time of this writing it is still going strong, having weathered the events of the Arab Spring. It still holds preliminary auditions in major cities from Morocco to Kuwait, dominating the LBC schedule during its four-month season. And it is still relevant to the lives of young Arabs in the terms captured by Kraidy in this prescient 2005 observation:

> *Star Academy* is, in many ways, a political program. It is political first in the sense advanced by the "alternative future" explanation of the show's popularity, in that it stages an apparently fair competition whose participants count on their personal initiative, creativity and skills, and whose winners are determined by a popular vote. This "reality" is discordant with that of most young Arabs, who are prevented from expressing their opinions, who get their jobs because of connections and rarely because of competence, and where power is wielded arbitrarily by unelected rulers and officials.[41]

One crucial dimension of this alternative future is the tension between individual competition and group solidarity. On *Star Academy*, the effect of having the contestants live together is to build camaraderie. As on *American Idol*, no one on this show smiles more broadly than the loser, and his or her first duty when eliminated is always to congratulate the winner.

Another crucial aspect of the pop-idol show is the ability to respect and abide by the popular vote—and to step aside gracefully. Needless to say, this ability is central to any contest where the rules are fair and the outcome not rigged in advance, including elections in well functioning democracies. All human beings experience defeat more often than they do victory, so audiences everywhere tend to be fascinated by the behavior of the losers on these programs. But I daresay the fascination is even more intense in countries where fair competition, never mind well functioning democracy, is practically unheard of.

In the Persian Gulf, the pop-idol genre has been further localized to focus on a more deeply rooted form of expression: poetry. Two of the most popular talent shows on Arab television are *Million's Poet* and *Prince of Poets*, both produced for Abu Dhabi TV by Pyramedia (the company founded by talk show host Nashwa al Ruwaini, mentioned in Chapter 2). Using the pop-idol format in ways never imagined by its Anglo-American creators, *Million's Poet* became a vehicle of protest in 2010, when a Saudi woman named Hissa Hilal, wearing full *niqab* (body and face covering), galvanized the audience with a poem accusing both the radical Islamists and the Wahhabi establishment of having "hijacked our culture and our religion." Calling both groups "vicious in voice, barbaric, angry and blind, and wearing death as a robe cinched with a belt," Hilal did not win the crown. But she came in third, and her performance was widely acclaimed.[42]

There is, of course, a big difference between voting by text message for a TV performer and engaging in pro-democracy activism—for one thing, the latter can be much more dangerous. There is an even bigger difference between expressing one's opinion on a TV channel controlled by the powers-that-be, and expressing it in a genuine public sphere with duly constituted rights and liberties. As political scientist Marc Lynch has noted, Arab governments have been known to meddle in the pop-idol show voting process, hoping to improve their country's position. Such meddling includes: "mass bloc voting," "shenanigans" (such as free text-message voting offered by rulers to increase the numbers for their nation's contestants), and "open manipulation" in favor of "the wealthy advertising markets of the Gulf." This kind of manipulation bears a painful resemblance to that found in pre-2011 Arab elections. Indeed, Lynch reports that on one occasion, the complaints of vote-rigging on *Super Star* became so severe that Future TV hired a British company to monitor the process.[43]

Yet this only reinforces the idea that these programs have been teaching lessons in democracy, lessons that were later brought into play during the Arab Spring. In 2005 Lynch foresaw that "reality TV fans have been innovators in the use of technology to organize and mobilize across distances, . . . skills [that] may be more transferable to the political realm than some realize."[44] The same can be said of the pop-idol show. The alternative future it projects may be an illusion, but illusions can be instructive. In the voluminous online debate about the fairness of the voting in these shows, most of which flew under the radar of even the most repressive regimes, millions of ordinary Arabs may have taught themselves a lesson or two about what constitutes a free and democratic political system.

THE POP-IDOL SHOW—CHINESE STYLE

Unlike Arab television, which is hard to control because its six hundred satellite channels reach twenty-four different countries, Chinese television is very much under the thumb of the Chinese Communist Party (CCP). This fact is sometimes lost on Westerners, because at first glance the Chinese system resembles ours. It is dominated by a few conglomerates, such as the Golden

Eagle Broadcasting System (formerly Hunan Broadcasting) and the Shanghai Media Group (SMG), which resemble their Western counterparts in being highly profit-oriented and competitive. Indeed, they compete not only with one another but also with the official broadcaster, China Central Television (CCTV), and with foreign firms seeking a toehold in the world's most beckoning market.

The competition is especially heated in what a professor at the Communications University called "low-end entertainment," where the tension between profit and political correctness leads to a tug-of-war between headstrong media executives and ideologically minded officials from the State Administration of Radio, Television and Film (SARFT). In a similar vein, Anthony Fung, a media scholar based in Hong Kong, told me that this tug-of-war was built into the system in 2001, when the CCP decreed a new approach to China's cultural industries. At that time, a distinction was made between meaningful content (*wenhua shiye*) and profit-making entertainment (*wenhua zhenye*).[45] The latter, wenhua zhenye, was not supposed to have any political ramifications. But that is not how it turned out.

In 2004 the TV division of Hunan Broadcasting (now Golden Eagle) had the bright idea of staging a pop-idol show. Recruiting a dairy company as sponsor, the company held a regional competition called *The Mongolian Cow Sour Yogurt Super Female Voice Contest*. Better known as *Super Girl*, the program was a local hit, so the company decided to broadcast it to the rest of the country via satellite in 2005. At that point, it became a national craze. Auditions in Hunan, Guangdong, Henan, Zhejiang, and Sichuan provinces drew over 120,000 contestants, and the final segment attracted four hundred million viewers and eight million text-message votes—a number that would undoubtedly have been higher if the text-message votes had not cost money.[46]

The winner, a twenty-one-year-old music student from Sichuan named Li Yuchun, was a charismatic figure who defied convention by dressing in jeans and loose shirts, wearing no makeup, and performing songs ordinarily sung by men. Tall and slim with spiky hair, her appearance would not have raised an eyebrow in the West. But in China, the victory of this apparent tomboy set off a huge public debate, making it hard for SARFT (the national media authority) to follow its first impulse, which was to cancel the show outright.

In August a writer for *China Daily* posed the question: "How come an imitation democratic system ends up selecting the singer who has the least ability to carry a tune?"[47] This line was criticized by so many Western news outlets, the author felt compelled to publish a clarification six weeks later.[48] But that line was just a ripple on a tide of commentary within China. Apart from CCTV's

Spring Festival Evening, no TV show had ever attracted such a large national audience. And as one netizen observed, the CCTV broadcast was "an official version of celebration," where "the guests are officials with connections, and common people can only watch from home"; while *Super Girl* was "a glimpse of the future Chinese civil society."[49]

An even greater political significance was discerned by Nobel Peace Prize winner Liu Xiaobo, who commented that "the selection system based upon the expert judges, the citizen judges and the viewers' votes contains the spirit of pragmatic politics." Echoing Aristotle's praise of the mixed democratic and aristocratic regime, Liu credited the program's selection process with being not only "democratic and equal" but also "balanced among different forces." In the next breath, Liu admitted that he might be "over-rating" a mere TV show in the spirit of "wishful thinking," and that *Super Girl* was more likely "a River of Forgetting that lets people release their dissatisfactions through the joy of entertainment."[50]

To judge by a 2009 study of the show's actual fans and contestants, Liu's initial assessment of *Super Girl* was more accurate. The author of that study, Thanh Nga Duong of Lund University, weighs the alternatives and decides that rather than an escape into forgetting, the program represented a strongly imagined alternative future in which the key elements were "equality, participation, and individuality."[51]

Regarding equality, Duong reports that many fans believed "any Chinese girl, whether she was a student, a migrant worker, or even a farmer, could dream of changing her life forever. . . . There was no privilege for the elite or people with *guanxi* [connections]."[52]

About participation, Duong mentions the "thousands of debates" that occurred online and quotes one contestant: "I was eliminated in the second round, but it does not matter as I got unforgettable experience."[53] In the process of competing, young women built up their own fan bases, something that happens on *American Idol* as well. For example, one of the biggest stars to emerge from *American Idol,* the country-pop singer Clay Aiken, lost to another contestant, Ruben Studdard, in 2003. To be sure, there is only one final winner per season of a pop-idol show. But as the competition unfolds, there are many smaller victories, giving rise to a general attitude of "You win some, you lose some," and the feeling—illusory, perhaps, but also inspiring—that one is living in a world where opportunities abound and the game is not fatally rigged.

Regarding individuality, Duong shares the poignant testimony of one short-lived contestant: "My parents always think that I am too ugly and can not do anything special. Whenever I sang, they felt annoyed and forced me to shut up. You should know how upset I was. I failed immediately at the first round of *Super Girl*, as you should imagine. But 30 seconds of me on television made my parents change their attitudes. Now I can freely sing any time I want in my house without their interruption."[54]

Duong admits that some have dismissed *Super Girl* as "a consumer fantasy of democracy . . . a substitute or palliate [that] . . . lulled people into thinking they have freedom although in reality they did not." Yet based on her interviews with those most affected, she concludes that, in fact, this seemingly frivolous entertainment managed to "show Chinese people new ways to be, think, look and feel, and sow seeds of democracy in people's minds."[55]

The authorities must have agreed, because as I learned from an official in the Central Committee Global Communications Office, Li's gender-bending appearance prompted "an urgent debate in the higher circles of government." The expectation at SARFT had been that this type of "low-end entertainment" would distract youth from the painful contrast between their expanding horizons and the narrow paths laid out for them. But now *Super Girl* was drawing attention to that same contrast.

While this drama was unfolding, I interviewed a Shanghai TV producer working on a pop-idol show featuring boy bands. In her view, the problem with pop-idol shows was a lack of "responsible judgment." At first I took her to mean they needed someone like Simon Cowell, the acid-tongued judge on *American Idol*, to liven things up. But then I realized she was not talking like an American TV producer, she was talking like a Chinese policy maker. What was needed, she said, was a better message, one that emphasized the work ethic, not fantasies of instant celebrity. "Americans get to choose their lives," she confided. "Chinese people find this appealing, but we cannot choose the same way."

Eventually, it was determined that the best way to deal with the problem of *Super Girl* was to hold a press conference denying rumors that Li was a lesbian. Chinese society is still not hospitable to gays, so some of the rumors were doubtless real. But a couple of my interlocutors speculated that the more likely purpose of the press conference was to *stoke* the rumors, in an effort to divert public attention from the alternative future being imagined by millions of *Super Girl* fans and contestants. Supporting this speculation was the flood of anti-Li messages suddenly on the Internet, most from thinly veiled Party sources.[56]

In 2008 all talent shows were canceled to make room for the Beijing Olympics, but shortly afterward they were restored, including a version of *Super Girl*. But it was no longer the same program. Indeed, it was no longer a bona fide pop-idol show. Even the normally compliant state newspaper, *China Daily*, griped that "the public SMS voting system was dropped in favor of professional musicians and star-makers from entertainment companies acting as judges." The same article quoted an online fan: "It was the least interesting competition of the three years, because we all knew the answer."[57]

There was another media crackdown in 2011, as part of a major cultural reform initiative leading up to the 18th National Congress in late 2012. Perhaps another version of *Super Girl* will appear after that. But if it does, it will bear little resemblance to the program that galvanized China during that fabled 2005 season, when fans held mass demonstrations in the streets and shopping malls,[58] and millions of Chinese were (in the words of one Chinese cultural critic) "swept . . . into a euphoria of voting that became a testament to a society opening up."[59]

Sun Jin, the professor of "media axiology" whom I met in Beijing (see Chapter 1), was not proficient in English, so when I asked him to explain his field, he turned to his translator, a young student who told me it was "the study of how the media construct the social values." Then, smiling sweetly as if to illustrate the point, she added: "Dr. Sun is expert in how to make the Chinese people happy about the changes."[60]

If any regime can use media to construct social values and induce happiness among its people, China's can. Its universities are full of experts in communications, social psychology, and media studies, all focused on the task of using entertainment to legitimize and preserve the supreme powers of the Chinese Communist Party. To achieve this aim, a key tactic is to form partnerships with global media conglomerates.

To the casual Western observer, such an arrangement looks like a welcome opening up. But as noted by media scholar Anthony Fung, it is part of a long-range strategy to build a global Chinese entertainment industry more powerful than America's. As Fung writes, the Chinese government welcomes "global moguls," with their "high communication technologies, advanced production, proven content, strong experience, and huge capital." But then the Chinese authorities erect "formidable barriers" to these moguls' penetration of the Chinese market. The goal, "under strong direction from above," is to make use of foreign expertise to set in motion "a reverse cultural flow" from China to the rest of the world, "ready for the day when the state is well equipped with the national power to globalize."[61]

The chief characteristic of this reverse cultural flow is excessive ideological oversight. As we've seen, such oversight may already have affected the content of blockbuster films co-produced by US and Chinese companies. In a different way, it has also affected the pop-idol show. Like the irreverent humor of the original *Kung Fu Panda*, the runaway stardom of Li Yuchun was not engineered by media axiologists or manufactured by Hunan TV. It was created by Li herself, and by devoted fans who saw in her a spark of their own craving for self-definition.

Today Li Yunchun is a successful recording artist and poster girl for the status quo. In 2008 she released an album called *Youth of China*, touted as a "gift blessing" to the Beijing Olympics. And on the numerous websites devoted to her, there is little or no mention of how *Super Girl* went from being harmless entertainment to being threatening enough to be canceled by the highest authorities.

Yet the fact remains that Li's rise to stardom went beyond both profit and propaganda. Precisely because her spark of free individual expression was recognized by millions of ordinary Chinese, the authorities will not find it easy to create an ideologically acceptable replacement. The CCP would love to create a popular culture capable of riveting the attention of young people in China and the rest of the world. But in Fung's wry understatement, "It is difficult for state media to create popular culture on their own. They have the money and the resources, but they do it in a way that exists only in the imagination of the state."[62]

SOCIAL MEDIA ARE NOT THE MESSAGE

"You cannot stop people any more. You cannot control them any longer. They can bypass your established media; they can broadcast to one another; they can organize as never before." So wrote blogger Andrew Sullivan during the 2009 green protests in Iran. Hailing "the next generation" of "Millennials" who "want freedom," are "sick of lies," and "enjoy life and know hope," Sullivan predicted a "Twitter Revolution" that would overthrow all "tyrants" and "fear-ridden establishments."[63]

Such zeal was typical of the time. Weary of taking body blows to our global reputation, Americans were groping for something to be optimistic about, and social media came readily to hand. Between 2008 (when the Colombian activist Oscar Morales used Facebook to organize antiterrorist demonstrations) and 2011 (when Facebook, Twitter, and YouTube played a key role in the Arab Spring), starry-eyed optimism about social media became the latest update on the old postmillennial dream of a perfected America going forth to perfect the world. As emphasized throughout these pages, postmillennialism lost its religious meaning a century ago, and became a secular vision of progress, reappearing with each technological breakthrough. In the early days of the Internet, the vision was of a liberated society both open and communal. With the rise of social media, it became what critics call "cyber-utopianism."[64]

Like all utopianism, cyber-utopianism has proved illusory. By 2009, when the Iranian authorities cracked down on the green movement, it became clear that pro-democracy activists were not the only ones deploying social media. The more sophisticated authoritarian governments were quickly learning how to use the same technology for censorship, propaganda, and surveillance.

To begin with censorship: back in 1993, open-source activist John Gilmore wrote approvingly that "the Internet interprets censorship as damage and routes around it."[65] This made sense at the time—one of the original purposes of the Internet was to create a communication system strong and flexible enough to resist many strains, including enemy attacks.[66] By 2000, analysts were crediting the Internet with creating "the dictator's dilemma," a situation in which an authoritarian regime would have to choose between having no connection with the modern world, and having one that, because it involved being connected to the Internet, would inevitably undermine their power.[67] This view is still out there. Indeed, in the era of WiFi, the Internet can seem a species of mental telepathy, leaping across vast distances and passing through all physical barriers. This is mistaken, of course. The Internet relies on a physical infrastructure, and the world's authoritarians have become quite adept at controlling that infrastructure. For example, in 2010 the Chinese authorities did such a thorough job of blocking the flow of messages into China, only a handful of people heard the news of dissident writer Liu Xiaobo winning the Nobel Peace Prize.[68] In January 2011 the Mubarak regime blocked all international traffic flowing through Egypt's one fiber-optic "pipeline"—a move that also came close to shutting down the domestic Internet, because so many of its support services were located outside the country.[69]

Yet the Internet still retains the fluid character described by Gilmore, finding the leaks in every dam erected to stop its flow. That is why censorship is only one of the ways that authoritarian regimes use social media. Another is to spread propaganda into every nook and cranny of their citizens' lives. For example, during the Maoist era, the Chinese people were constantly subjected to broadcast media, loudspeakers, banners, and speeches repeating the wisdom of the Chairman. In 2009 a single text message was sent from an unidentified source to thirteen million mobile phone users in Chongqing, who then forwarded it to sixteen million other phones throughout China. The words of the message were as follows: "I really like these words of Chairman Mao: 'The world is ours, we should unite for achievements. Responsibility and seriousness can conquer the world and the Chinese Communist Party members represent these qualities.'"[70]

The most important part of this message is the beginning: "I really like." This mimicry of Facebook "liking" reveals a key difference between older forms of propaganda and propaganda in the era of social media. This particular message may not have made a big difference to the twenty-nine million people who received it. But the same personalized approach can be quite effective when used by the thousands of *wu mao*, or "50 Cent" workers (so called because of their low pay), who at any one time throng the Chinese "intranet," not only "joining the conversation" (as Americans like to say) but also nudging it toward CCP-approved messages. "We don't control things," explained one 50 Center, "but we really don't want bad or wrong things to appear on the Web sites. . . . I need to play a pioneer role among other students, to express my opinion, to make stronger my belief in Communism."[71]

Even more troubling is the use of the Internet, and especially social media, to conduct ever more sophisticated forms of surveillance. For example, crowd-sourcing is a method of sharing a task with an unspecified group of people online, developed in America and Europe to enlist the public in tracking child pornographers. Today it is used by authoritarian rulers to enlist the public in tracking political dissidents. Another technique is the Distributed Denial of Service attack, in which thousands of personal computers are hijacked without their owners' knowledge. This technique is frequently used to drown dissident websites in spam.[72] And finally, keyboard-based filtering, developed by Western companies like Facebook to fine-tune the flow of advertising to individual consumers, is now used to fine-tune the flow of information to individual citizens in authoritarian regimes.[73]

Americans have criticized this aspect of Facebook, but chiefly in the domestic context, where the company sells the personal data of users to advertising companies that use that data to target potential customers with commercials that, depending on how much time an individual spends online, can be unnervingly accurate. Even more unnerving is the use of such data to profile applicants for loans, mortgages, even jobs.[74]

Less scrutinized is the sale of social media technology to authoritarian regimes that use that technology to spy on their own people. But this will likely change in the wake of the 2013 exposure, by National Security Agency contractor Edward Snowden, of US government surveillance of Americans' cell phone and Internet communications. Snowden's revelations provided fodder to authoritarian regimes claiming that US democracy is a sham (especially in Russia, where he was granted temporary asylum). And it didn't help when, rather than emphasize the self-corrective capacity of democratic institutions such as press freedom, separation of powers, and the right of the citizens to hold their government accountable, the Obama administration simply promised to do better in the future.[75] Such a promise would not have been out of place in Russia or China.

Social media are a marvelous invention, but that does not mean they have the power to reinvent human nature. Every generation of media has the potential to serve liberty or repression, depending on how it is used. In this connection, it is worth pondering the observation made by media scholars that, by encouraging exhibitionism, unscripted reality TV shows have encouraged ordinary people to accept—even to welcome—being spied upon.[76] This suggests a troubling trajectory: talk shows encourage us to spill our intimate secrets to millions of viewers; reality shows (including the aptly named *Big Brother*) normalize the act of opening our homes and exposing our daily lives to phalanxes of hidden cameras; free-form websites such as MySpace and YouTube invite each of us to broadcast our own reality show; and finally, Facebook standardizes the process, making our all-too-human craving for attention into a fungible commodity. It's only logical that authoritarian regimes should take advantage of this trajectory.

Sourish Battischaryya, a journalist I met in Delhi, told me that social media have "created a huge interface, where Indians form real bonds with Americans, seeing them as people, not characters in Hollywood films." This suggests that Facebook, YouTube, and Twitter have the capacity to correct some of the distorted views of America conveyed by our popular culture. A similar view is taken by US government officials hoping to use social media to connect with foreign audiences, especially youth. But before we wax too optimistic once again, it is worth recalling the rest of Battischaryya's comment—that this "huge interface" is enriched by innumerable real-life, face-to-face interactions between Indians and Americans through education, work, and immigration.[77]

Absent such real-life interactions, it is not clear how corrective social media can be, especially given that most people do not use the Internet to interact seriously with foreigners, any more than they use it to discuss politics or organize protests. Instead, they use it to socialize with friends and relatives—and (this is important) to access entertainment. For example, it is reported that the majority of China's 420 million Internet users barely notice the controls on their favorite sites, because they spend most of their time chatting and watching films and TV shows—including the many American films and TV shows that at any given moment are being illegally downloaded, subtitled, and file-shared.[78]

It therefore makes little sense to expect social media to correct the fun-house-mirror images of America projected by our popular culture. Indeed, it appears that their main role is to magnify, amplify, and multiply those images. The point is underscored by Bill Roedy, the CEO of MTV International, quoted earlier in this chapter. Asked in 2011 whether he thought YouTube would put MTV out of business, Roedy commented that "the most-often viewed videos on YouTube . . . *are highly produced materials that either are pirated or licensed, a trend that I believe will continue*" (emphasis added).[79]

Does America have a duty to assist foreign populations who are struggling to attain political liberty? Some would say no, on the ground that the American ideal of ordered liberty is unique to American culture, having arisen from a unique history. There is some truth to this answer. It would be folly for Americans to think we could graft the exact blueprint of our Constitution and political arrangements onto very different societies. But a greater truth is that we can, and should, share with others our distinctive ethos and the hard-won political wisdom that goes with it. Fundamentally, that ethos and wisdom are about human nature: tyranny cannot be *cured*, because human beings will always abuse power. But it can be *curbed* by institutions designed to address this reality.

For most of the past century, the task of sharing this wisdom, and the ethos that supports it, has been assumed by the government. Sometimes the government has enlisted the help of popular culture, and sometimes popular culture has played a significant role by itself.

But only recently has the entire task been shifted onto the commercial entertainment industry. As argued in the preceding chapters, this is a serious mistake. In its current form, American popular culture projects countless images of personal freedom, but it says next to nothing about political liberty. Whether conveyed by old media or new, American movies, pop music, and TV shows highlight in vivid detail the human propensity to abuse freedom and power, but they rarely show how the country's institutions were designed to mitigate that propensity. The commercial media are simply not set up to convey a rounded understanding of America and its ideals. And of late, they seem all too happy to trade some of those ideals for access to lucrative but unfree markets.

Part Two

GOODWILL HUNTING

Prologue to Part Two:
The Lesson of Odysseus

When I'm teaching Homer's *Odyssey* to college freshmen, one of the concepts I try to get across is *sophrosune*, an ancient Greek word meaning shrewdness, gutsiness, persistence, and grace. Mostly it means knowing what to do in any given situation. Not just in the sense of following the rules; anyone can do that. Sophrosune means doing the right thing, the smart thing, without consciously applying the rules. Above all, it means alertness: the capacity to read the situation, fathom the other guy's motives, grasp the moral imperative at work, and act. The personification of sophrosune is Odysseus: "the great tactician," "expert in adversity."[1]

But here the students hit a snag. Odysseus is trying to get home after the Trojan War, and in striving toward that goal he displays not just alertness but also cunning and deception—"famous for guile," Homer calls him.[2] In other words, Odysseus does not always tell the truth. So my students ask, How can a liar be a hero? Well, I tell them, it depends on your view of the world. If you see the world as a nice place, where right action means being nice to other nice people, then deception is plainly wrong. But if you see the world as a high-stakes poker game, where every card is played in deadly earnest, then right action will often mean bluffing, or at least not tipping your hand.

This combination of alertness, guile, and deception pervades the US government's peacetime relations with other nations. Woodrow Wilson famously thought the results of diplomacy should be "open covenants, openly arrived at."[3] But the United States government uses diplomacy in concert with other instruments of national power, in more or less friendly ways, depending on the circumstances. The friendlier ways include listening to others, fostering cultural and educational exchange, and reporting accurate news to people in countries where the media are censored. The less friendly ways include espionage, using culture and education to sway opinion in favor of unpopular policies, and (in situations of life and death) resorting to the deceptions of psychological warfare.

Hanging over any such discussion is *propaganda*, a charged word that acquired a bad odor during the two world wars, when the blatant falsehoods spread by governments contributed to millions of deaths. That is why, when the US Information Agency (USIA) was created in 1953, its first director vowed to avoid "a propagandistic tone."[4] In the stilted language of its charter, USIA's primary goal was "to submit evidence to peoples of other nations by means of communication techniques that the objectives and policies of the United States are in harmony with and will advance their own legitimate aspirations for freedom, progress, and peace."[5] The euphemism *public diplomacy* was coined in 1965 for the same purpose: to make sure that America would not resort to propaganda. The USIA was eliminated in 1999, and most public diplomacy tasks were transferred to the State Department. But public diplomats past and present are quick to insist, with sincerity and conviction, that they do not do propaganda.

Borrowing loosely from historian Nicholas Cull, I offer here a list of the four goals of the USIA and, by extension, every other US government agency involved in public diplomacy:[6]

1) *Listening*. Closely related to the Homeric virtue of sophrosune, listening has two sides: the respectful, considerate side, which matters when you and your interlocutors disagree; and the shrewd, calculating side, which matters when you need to know what the other guy is thinking. (For this reason Cull includes espionage under this heading.)

2) *Advocacy*. This is Cull's suggestion for a better and more accurate term than *propaganda*. It means explaining, defending, and gaining support for your government's policies and principles. As Cull notes, advocacy is not necessarily untruthful. Indeed, persuasion based on truth is the lifeblood of democratic governance. When Americans do advocacy well, we make freedom and democracy look good. When we do it badly, we discredit our ideals.

3) *Culture and exchange*. This goal encompasses both the sharing of expressive culture (literature and the arts) and the conducting of "people-to-people" programs between Americans and others. Prominent among these is educational exchange, for both students and mature scholars. The flagship here is the Fulbright Program, founded in 1946 and (uniquely at the time) structured not just to bring foreigners to the United States but also to send Americans abroad.

4) *News reporting.* In America, news reporting is performed mainly by the commercial media, but also by government-sponsored media outlets such as National Public Radio (NPR) and the Public Broadcasting Service (PBS). Less familiar to Americans are the international broadcasting efforts sponsored by the government, such as the Voice of America and Radio Free Europe/Radio Liberty. Using radio, television, and now the Internet, these outlets address overseas audiences in their own languages, and a major emphasis in all of them is the reporting of truthful and accurate news, especially local and regional news, to people in countries where the media are censored or otherwise compromised. This type of broadcasting is called "surrogate," meaning substitute.[7]

Cull mentions a fifth goal, *psychological warfare,* or the manipulation of information to defeat an enemy. This goal is defined as belonging to the military, and civilian agencies give it the widest possible berth. Notably, Cull argues for the strongest possible firewall between public diplomacy and psychological warfare, because the latter's reliance on deception, cunning, and outright disinformation quickly poisons the atmosphere of trust which public diplomats seek to cultivate.[8]

It is normal for a government agency to have more than one goal. Indeed, because government agencies are subject to diverse pressures from different constituencies, their goals are usually multiple, overlapping, and conflicting. This was certainly true of the USIA, and it is still true of any agency involved in public diplomacy. Setting psychological warfare aside, advocacy is the most difficult to reconcile with the other three goals. To advocate is to explain, defend, and seek support for the government's policy agenda as forcefully as possible without resorting to manipulation or dishonesty. There is no getting around this goal—indeed, no government would pay for public diplomacy if it did not involve advocacy. But as we shall see, it can be hard to find the right balance between advocacy and the other goals.

For example, advocacy overlaps quite naturally with listening, because people in democratic societies are accustomed to letting the other side have its say while also having theirs. But advocacy mixes less well with artistic and educational exchange, where most practitioners see it as their mission to share artistic expression, scholarship, and learning for their own sake, and not use them to further the government's ends. Nor does advocacy combine easily with news reporting, because the credibility of any news organization, especially a government-sponsored one, is hard to build up and easy to tear down at the first hint of ideological bias.

Practitioners often draw a line between "fast" and "slow" public diplomacy. The fast kind, they explain, has tactical, short-term aims: to keep track of events and continually fine-tune the position of the US government in a manner not unlike that of the "rapid response" team in a domestic political campaign. Fast public diplomacy aspires to "move the needle" of foreign opinion. But since this is rarely possible, fast public diplomacy settles for stating the US perspective as clearly as possible, and pushing back against those who mischaracterize it. Slow public diplomacy, by contrast, has strategic, long-term aims: to build relationships that will withstand crises, and to open channels of communication that will stay open even if more high-profile channels shut down.

In its heyday, USIA had the knack of keeping fast and slow separate. This knack was lost in 1999, when the agency was dismantled and its tasks scattered throughout the much larger bureaucracy of the State Department. David Firestein, a former foreign service officer and member of the US Advisory Board on Public Diplomacy, explained to me what happened:

> The problem is that PD [public diplomacy] officers have a dual role. They work in the fast wheel of advocacy, staying on top of events and crafting responses. But they also work in the slow wheel of culture and exchange, where the time horizon is much longer. This second role looks *so* irrelevant at the 8:30 AM staff meeting, where people are talking about what's happening in fifty countries where US interests are at stake. The last thing those people care about is how many Fulbrights are going to Oman this year! It's not that they don't care in a larger sense, it's just that they have no time to care *right now*. So the slow-wheel part of public diplomacy gets relegated to marginality.[9]

This insight harkens back to Odysseus, whose big mistake is to lose sight of the long term. Trapped in the cave of the Cyclops, where the greedy monster gobbles several of his crew and washes them down with wine, Odysseus plans a clever escape. After driving a burning stake into the Cyclops's single eye, he and his men cling to the bellies of the monster's sheep as they are herded out of the cave, then board their ship and start rowing out to sea. But then Odysseus trades sophrosune for the overconfidence known as hubris. Looking back, he can't help taunting the raging Cyclops: "If ever mortal man inquire how you were put to shame and blinded, tell him / Odysseus, raider of cities, took your eye!"[10] This is a mistake, because the Cyclops complains to his father, the sea god Poseidon, who sends a mighty tempest to blow Odysseus off course and delay his homecoming for ten years.

America made a similar mistake at the end of the Cold War, when it assumed the mantle of "unchallenged superpower" in a "unipolar world."[11] Looking back, we can see quite clearly that Americans, too, traded sophrosune for hu-bris. Or, to use my terms, we lost track of our distinctive ethos and succumbed to reckless optimism. When the tempest of 9/11 hit, Americans, too, were blown off course. And some would argue that, more than ten years later, we have still not found our way home.

FAILURE TO RELAUNCH

Since 9/11 every think tank, commission, task force, and advisory board in Washington has published a report on how to relaunch public diplomacy for the twenty-first century.[12] Several of these reports offer cogent recommenda-tions, but remarkably few of these have been translated into action. Why is it so hard to bring back a robust public diplomacy, when the need is so pressing? I suggest four reasons: 1) the lack of a suitable coordinating agency; 2) the lack of a significant domestic constituency; 3) heightened concern for security in American facilities overseas; and 4) intellectual paralysis caused by thirty years of culture war.

Put another way, the first reason is that no substitute has been found for the USIA. Many scattered efforts have been made to improve public diplomacy, some quite promising. But the entity that is generally assumed to be planning and coordinating these efforts—the office of the Under Secretary of State for Public Diplomacy and Public Affairs—can do neither, because unlike the USIA, it has no independent budgetary or programmatic authority. At best, this unhappily-named office is a bully pulpit. At worst, it is a place where good ideas go to die.

The second reason for public diplomacy's failure to relaunch is that this function of the government has practically no domestic constituency.[13] A major factor here is the 1948 Information and Educational Exchange Act (also known as Smith-Mundt), which authorized the creation of USIA and most of the other public diplomacy machinery still in operation today.[14] Until recently, that leg-islation contained a provision making it a crime to share public diplomacy ma-terials with Americans—a striking reflection of the nation's postwar fear of pro-paganda. Of course, this ban on domestic dissemination of public diplomacy materials has been rendered largely moot by the Internet. And the provision was repealed in January 2013, as part of the National Defense Authorization Act.[15] Nonetheless, it seems unlikely, given the American people's chronic indiffer-ence to the rest of the world, that public diplomacy will become a salient policy issue any time soon.

Third, public diplomacy has remained captive to heightened security concerns. Long before 9/11, American embassies and consulates were targeted by terrorists, especially in the conflict-ridden Middle East. But during the Cold War these threats did not stop these outposts from attracting countless visitors, drawn to their open-stack libraries, where people could read, study, and check out books, and to their cultural centers, which hosted performances, exhibitions, film series, and lectures. In many countries these facilities offered an atmosphere of openness and free expression that existed in few other public settings.

For example, the US embassy in Cairo once occupied a pleasant villa that welcomed five hundred visitors a day to its open-air café and library, described by one public diplomat as "an oasis of magazines, books, and no censorship, where people could read about their own country as well as the world." After 9/11 the villa was closed, and the embassy relocated to an imposing office block that I can personally attest is not welcoming. Even though I was an invited speaker, I could not enter that edifice without several police checks and searches. When I did, I was not surprised to learn that the number of daily visitors was about sixty.

A similar tale can be told of the US consulate in Istanbul. Before 9/11 it occupied a grand building on the city's main thoroughfare, İstiklal Caddesi, near the Çırağan Palace (formerly a residence of the Ottoman sultans, now a five-star hotel). Its programs were varied, including at one point a training program for English teachers from Central Asia, which, as I learned from Eugene Kopp, deputy chief of USIA under three different presidents, "covered a wide range of subjects, including Islam and politics, under the rubric of language instruction."[16] Of course, that location was "a security nightmare," as another public diplomat explained, adding that when an Al-Qaeda group blew up the British consulate in 2003, "that would have been us, if we were still there."

Yet this same public diplomat admitted that the new consulate, in the İstinye district well north of the city center, is "about as user-friendly as the Arizona State Prison at Yuma." I can confirm this point, having been taken to see the consulate by an American friend living in Istanbul. My attempt to snap a few photos was thwarted by a pair of Turkish guards, who demanded to see our passports and threatened to confiscate my camera. Fortunately my friend, a young blonde Californian, knew enough to play dumb. Batting her eyelashes, she gushed, "But the building is so *impressive!* It's almost like a *castle!*" Amused, the guards backed off, and I got to keep my camera. But based on that incident, I can understand why so many foreigners look at America's target-hardened outposts and wonder, *What are they doing in there?*[17]

What they are *not* doing is much slow public diplomacy. "If we're going to spend $100 million on a fortress," quipped one informant, "then why not spend another $3 million on an enhanced public presence somewhere else in the city?" Cairo and Istanbul are sophisticated cities, full of people eager to connect with Americans in a context other than debating terrorism or arguing about US foreign policy (not that this occurs very often, either). There is still a saving remnant of public diplomats and "foreign nationals" (local employees) out there who know how to make such connections. But their numbers are dwindling and their morale is low, because for the past several years they have had precious few champions in Washington. Indeed, by one estimate today's "fortress embassies" host 85 percent fewer visitors than did their pre-9/11 predecessors.[18]

This brings us to the last reason why it is so difficult to revive public diplomacy. Even before the Cold War ended, America's culture war made it all the more difficult to reconcile public diplomacy's four goals. Indeed, one of the unnoted casualties of today's ideological polarization is the nation's ability to conduct effective public diplomacy.

THE CULTURE WAR AND PUBLIC DIPLOMACY

American history is full of cultural conflict; only the naive would suggest otherwise. But today's conflict is especially virulent, for reasons that date back to the late 1960s. The counterculture that arose in the 1960s was not just an outbreak of hedonism, as charged by its conservative critics. On the contrary, it was originally allied with the Southern civil rights movement, which rescued the word *freedom* from the droning repetition of Cold War rhetoric and reminded the children of affluence that there were still such things as racism and poverty.[19] This was the counterculture's inspirational side, and it made a deep impression on the rest of the world, including many of the dissidents who eventually overthrew Soviet communism.

But there was another side to the 1960s counterculture, anticipated by the poet Allan Ginsberg in his 1955 poem *Howl*. In that beat epic, every conceivable form of intoxication, ecstasy, and madness is pitted against every conceivable form of sobriety, discipline, and reason. In a letter to his former teacher, the literary critic Lionel Trilling, Ginsberg characterized *Howl* as "a reassertion of naked personal subjective truth."[20] This side, too, made a deep impression on the rest of the world. But as we shall see, that impression was not always inspirational.

At its most radical, the 1960s counterculture assaulted not only the racial and sexual prejudices of ordinary Americans but also their most cherished values: family, faith, and country. The resulting backlash swept Richard Nixon into office in 1968 and 1972, and helped Ronald Reagan to beat Jimmy Carter in 1980. Beginning in the 1970s and continuing through the 1980s and 1990s, Americans have fought bitterly over such volatile cultural issues as abortion, no-fault divorce, busing, welfare reform, affirmative action, "political correctness," and gay marriage. In expressive culture, the quarrels have pitted conservative politicians and religious leaders against transgressive artists, angry film stars and rappers, and provocateurs of every school and stripe.

September 11 brought a hiatus, but it was brief, and the new millennium has seen an escalation of the culture war, at least among elites. Unsettled by the nation's seeming loss of global hegemony, America's political and media elites have succumbed to a classic case of "creedal passion,"[21] in which the two sides battle over the meaning of freedom. In its most extreme form, the blue-state definition of freedom is liberation from all external constraints and the eleva-tion of individual choice to an absolute value, brooking no compromise with religion, law, or custom. The red-state counterpart to this extreme definition is freedom as the unshackling of economic players from all government controls, whether of taxation or of regulation, and the elevation of predatory rent-seeking to the same moral level as productive entrepreneurship.

Observers disagree about the depth of this polarization among the popula-tion as a whole. The two political parties are more ideologically consistent than ever before, with the Democratic base deep-dyed blue and the Republican deep-dyed red. Yet large numbers of Americans refuse to identify with either party. Indeed, there is sometimes a striking disconnect between the culture war waged by the few and the problems weighing on the many. This disconnect is troubling but also strangely reassuring, because it suggests that many Americans still hold to the prudent side of our ethos. If asked, most of us will immediately affirm the need to balance freedom with a corresponding sense of duty and responsibility. But who is asking?

The main argument of Part Two is that the culture war played a significant role in the decline of US public diplomacy, even before the end of the Cold War, and that it continues to hamper our intermittent efforts to revive public diplomacy for the twenty-first century. This is related to the argument of Part One, which is that the entertainment industry is not an adequate substitute for a robust and effective public diplomacy, and that its present offerings may in fact be deleterious.

Of course, the entertainment industry is not the only actor out there. The four goals of public diplomacy are being pursued, willy-nilly, by nonstate ac-tors of every kind: corporations, foundations, nongovernment organizations (NGOs), and countless businesses and nonprofits—some working in partnership with government agencies such as the US Agency for International Development (USAID), the State Department, or the Pentagon; and some simply operating on their own. Most of these actors, including those partnering with government agencies, proceed with little or no oversight or accountability.[22]

Because it is impossible to control and direct all these different activities, critics have argued that government-sponsored public diplomacy is obsolete.[23] Indeed, some have proposed that the concept of "public diplomacy" should be expanded to include every effort by Americans to communicate with the rest of the world. For example, Geoffrey Wiseman, director of the University of Southern California's Center for Public Diplomacy, defines the "*new* public diplomacy" as encompassing every "amalgam of activities by which a transnational socio-political actor with standing in world politics openly and purposefully advances policy goals by seeking to influence, and engage with, foreign publics."[24]

This is not a workable definition of US public diplomacy. Writing this book has made me aware of the fact that the government is only one of many actors crowding the stage. But this is not news. When it comes to reaching out to the people of other nations, America is the one country where private associations and individuals have never hesitated to pursue foreign policy objectives on their own, often in the belief that the government is not competent to do so. For example, when the Carnegie Endowment for International Peace was founded in 1910, it was on the stated principle that "government, although representing the will of the people in a mechanical sense, could not possibly give expression to a nation's soul."[25]

The fast goals of public diplomacy, advocacy and psychological warfare, are clearly government functions. But what about the slow goals of listening, exchange, and news reporting? To those steeped in the American tradition of private outreach to other nations, it is vitally important to keep these slow goals as far away from advocacy and (especially) psychological warfare as possible. This is important, but that does not mean that the government should make no attempt to listen, to sponsor programs of cultural and educational exchange, or to support international broadcasting. If the past several years have taught us anything, it is that these goals matter greatly and cannot be left to the private sector.[26]

5

THE WASHINGTON-HOLLYWOOD PACT

In the post-war period, the Department desires to co-operate fully in the protection of American motion pictures abroad. It expects in return that the industry will co-operate wholeheartedly with the government with a view to ensuring that the pictures distributed abroad will reflect credit on the good name and reputation of this country and its institutions. (emphasis added)
— Memo from State Department to Motion Picture
Association of America (MPAA), 1944

It was a lovefest. Lobbyists, actors, directors, film industry CEOs, Capitol Hill staff, members of Congress, and senators all gathered in Washington in 2007 to celebrate what Michael Lynton, chairman and CEO of Sony Pictures Entertainment, called "America's most wanted export."[1] Hosted by the MPAA,[2] the meeting was kicked off by Rep. Charles Rangel (D-NY), who won applause by saying, "No matter where we go, movies create love for us!" Then, alluding to his younger days on the mean streets of Harlem, Rangel added, "One thing I learned was, don't let anyone push you around. They're pushing our country around, stealing our talent, our creations in all industries. We won't let them!"[3]

This line won even greater applause, because the whole point of the meeting was to enlist the aid of Congress in combating piracy—or "movie theft," to use the preferred term of an industry making billions of dollars on a franchise called *Pirates of the Caribbean*. A report commissioned for the meeting claimed that in 2006 MPAA members lost $6.1 billion to film piracy, 80 percent of it overseas.[4] Since then the issue of intellectual property theft has only heated up: an attempt in 2012 by the copyright industries (publishing, entertainment, computer software) to persuade Congress to pass the Stop Online Piracy Act (SOPA) and the Protect Intellectual Property Act (PIPA) ran afoul of a new political consensus putting the freedom of the "new" media over the self-interest of the "old." Yet the effort to curb piracy continues, on the part of both the Office of the US Trade Representative and the Department of Commerce.

Has America's dream factory ever relied on the government before? Most Americans would say no, because compared with the film industries of most other nations, America's has always been privately owned, competitive, and devoted more to profit than to other goals, such as preserving the nation's cultural heritage. Not only that, for most of living memory, Hollywood and Washington have been at odds. Candidates for national office sometimes confront the industry, as Barack Obama did in 2008, when he complained before an audience of show business luminaries in Los Angeles about seeing ads for torture porn movies on television while his daughters were watching *American Idol.*[5] On the other side, Hollywood routinely depicts politicians in an unfavorable light.

Yet when it comes to the rest of the world, Washington and Hollywood are like an old married couple who quarrel at home but are deeply united in public. The fact that America exports more than ten times the number of films it imports is not simply the result of the free market. On the contrary, it is the fruit of what film historian Thomas Doherty calls "a distinctly American and democratic arrangement, a mesh of public policy and private initiative, state need and business enterprise."[6] Foreign demand has always been strong, to be sure. But so have the carrots and sticks applied to foreign governments by Hollywood's friends in Washington. This is done not only because of the obvious trade benefit but also because over time, there has developed a consensus that the export of US entertainment is both good business and good diplomacy.

This chapter will trace the history of this arrangement, which I call the Washington-Hollywood Pact, and show how tirelessly Washington has worked to uphold its side of the bargain. As for Hollywood, it has delivered in terms of film export being good business. But what about its being good diplomacy?

THE FIRST HALF-CENTURY

Before World War I, America was only one player in a bumptious, marginal business operating in a manner cultural historian Victoria de Grazia calls "practically anational." Because films were silent, they could be produced by "dispersed industries whose patents and copyrights on inventions were little respected," and "marketed in pirated or dubbed versions through jobbers and middlemen." In 1910 the leading film exporter was not the United States but France, followed closely by Italy and Denmark.[7] This began to change during World War I, when southern California's sunshine, varied terrain, and low labor costs attracted film moguls such as Carl Laemmle, Adolph Zukor, William Fox, Jesse Lasky, and Sam Goldwyn to Los Angeles. By 1917, the classic studio system was on track to dominate the world, in part because the war had knocked out the European competition, and in part because the newly opened Panama Canal made it easy to ship films to Europe from the West Coast.[8]

But there was another reason for the studios' ascendancy. When America entered the war in 1917, President Wilson set up the Committee on Public Information (CPI, known as the Creel Committee after its chair, journalist George Creel). One of the first things the CPI did was ask the studios to help with the war effort. They obliged by making several aggressively anti-German movies with titles like *Escaping the Hun* and *The Kaiser, the Beast of Berlin*. Similar to the British propaganda of the time, which railed against "the Hun" for committing mostly invented atrocities, these films were intended to rally isolationist Americans to the cause.[9] But over time, Creel came to see film as the ideal vehicle for "carrying the gospel of Americanism to every corner of the globe."[10]

Hollywood's efforts were rewarded in 1918, when Congress passed the Webb-Pomerene Export Trade Act, which exempted the studios from antitrust prosecution while operating overseas, basically allowing them to form cartels to break into foreign markets. The studios took full advantage of this legislation, forming the Motion Picture Producers and Distributors Association (MPPDA) in 1922 and proceeding to sideline the previously dominant French studios, Pathé Frères and Gaumont.[11] By 1925 there were very few French films being shown in the United States, and overall, America was producing 577 films to France's 68.[12]

It must be noted that this conquest would not have occurred had Hollywood films not been immensely appealing in their own right. To quote Sol Hurok, "When people don't want to come, nothing will stop them." But without Washington's help, it would have been a lot harder to make the world safe for Mary Pickford and Douglas Fairbanks.

More help came in 1926, when the Motion Picture Division of the US Bureau of Foreign and Domestic Commerce was asked to collect information about foreign film markets from US embassies and consulates and share it with the MPPDA. The British director and former Columbia Pictures studio chief David Puttnam has contrasted this "aggressive and outward-looking" strategy with the "defensive and inward-looking" one of European governments seeking only to protect their home markets.[13]

Yet this outward-looking strategy was also a form of public diplomacy. According to its first president, former US Postmaster General Will H. Hays, the MPPDA's side of the bargain was "to make certain that every picture which is made here shall correctly portray American life, opportunities and aspirations to the world, and, too, that we correctly portray to America the life of other peoples. We are going to sell America to the world with American pictures."[14]

Between the wars, the MPPDA managed its own public diplomacy. Consequently, as long as the studios made money in Germany and Italy, American films contained no anti-fascist messages. Only in the late 1930s, when Hitler and Mussolini blocked the import of foreign films, did movies such as *Confessions of a Nazi Spy* (1939) appear.[15] And when it came to persuading a reluctant American public to enter the war, the two most effective films were not updated versions of *The Beast of Berlin*, produced under government auspices; they were *The Great Dictator* (1940), Charlie Chaplin's satirical portrait of Hitler, and *Sergeant York* (1941), a film biography of a World War I hero who had originally refused to fight on religious grounds.

This autonomy did not last. With America's entry into the war, the studios began to work closely with at least four government agencies: the Bureau of Motion Pictures (part of FDR's Office of War Information, or OWI); the Office of the Coordinator of Inter-American Affairs; the armed forces; and the emerging intelligence services. Each of these had its own agenda, and the history of their byplay with the colorful personalities of Hollywood makes fascinating reading.[16] But overall, the politicians and bureaucrats learned quickly not to meddle unduly in the creative process, and the creative types grew adept in divining what the government wanted at any given moment. The result was a steady stream of wartime productions that ranged from *Why We Fight*, Frank Capra's series of "Troop Information and Education" films, to countless features that, more often than not, managed to support the war effort without sacrificing entertainment value.

With victory came unprecedented power for America and its films. The MPPDA became the Motion Picture Association of America (MPAA) and formed an overseas arm, the Motion Picture Export Association (MPEA), also known as the "little State Department."[17] According to historian Reinhold Wagnleitner, the MPEA's goal was to reconquer the world, and its methods were those of a "classic cartel." It divided overseas revenue among its members according to their domestic box-office receipts; it "avoided competition by never placing expensive films at the same place at the same time"; and it coordinated "talent and market research" to flood foreign markets not only with new productions but also with a wartime backlog of over two thousand films. As Wagnleitner concludes, "No foreign government and no foreign film industry was a real match."[18]

There was resistance. Faced with a shortage of hard currency and forced to ration food and other essentials, the British government looked at the number of US films on British screens in 1947 (80 percent) and the amount of money flowing out of the country ($70 million), and imposed a 75 percent customs duty. The MPEA responded by declaring an embargo, forcing British theater owners to choose between going dark or endlessly repeating the same (American) films. Recalls Wagnleitner: "His Majesty's Government had not reckoned on . . . the taste of the majority of British audiences, which demanded Hollywood products."[19] London lifted the duty, and Hollywood regained its ascendancy.[20]

In wartime France, the Nazi-controlled Vichy government had banned all foreign films. So after liberation, the French public welcomed the latest Hollywood fare. So did the theater owners, who immediately began to profit from it. But Charles de Gaulle's government was not amused. Sharing the same economic worries as London, and deploring Hollywood films as an attack on French culture (it didn't help that they were transported by the US Army's Division of Psychological Warfare), Paris imposed a quota. This pleased French film producers, but unfortunately France's only source of debt relief and cash was the United States. So under the Blum-Byrnes Agreement of 1946, France was relieved of its war debt and granted $650 million in US aid—in exchange for yielding to the wishes of the MPEA. Within the year, French film production was halved.[21]

If this was America's policy toward its allies, how did it treat its vanquished enemies? Not that differently. On all fronts, Washington was engaged in a battle not just for markets but also for hearts and minds. In Britain and France, the battle was against the power and influence of the Soviet Union. In Japan, Italy, and Germany, it was against both Communism and resurgent fascism. Hence the State Department memo quoted above, in which Washington agreed to help Hollywood pry open foreign markets—on the condition that the films flowing into those markets would "reflect credit on the good name and reputation of this country and its institutions." Rarely had the terms of the pact been spelled out so clearly.

The process unfolded differently in each country. In Japan, the US occupation forces under General Douglas MacArthur ordered the Japanese film industry to avoid imperial themes such as feudal loyalty and military honor, and to emphasize American values such as individual rights, freedom of speech, and free enterprise. To reinforce the point, the occupation authorities oversaw the free distribution of over five hundred Hollywood films throughout the country.[22] In Tokyo, the Marunouchi Subaruza theater obtained exclusive rights to such high-quality films as *Rhapsody in Blue* (1945) and *The Best Years of Our Lives* (1946) and showcased them as elite culture: patrons were expected to dress up and to refrain from smoking, cursing, and wandering in and out of the theater. Each high-priced ticket came with a handsome program full of information about "American Society and Life."[23]

Like the British government, the postwar Italian government looked at the influx of American films (six hundred in 1946 alone) and passed a law to protect its own industry. But the law was a clever one: instead of limiting the import of foreign films, the Andreotti Act of 1949 charged a hefty fee to have them dubbed into Italian. The money was then used to subsidize the Italian film industry. This maneuver might have worked if Italian directors had not been devoted to the stark neorealist style, which despite its artistic and political cachet proved incapable of competing with Hollywood. So the Italian government began setting quotas, setting off several bouts of arm-twisting by the MPEA.[24]

West Germany was a special case, due to the massive clout of its film industry under National Socialism. Here the tale is one of intramural conflict on the American side, between the occupation authority and the MPEA. Initially, both parties agreed that rather than allow the German cinema to revive, the occupation should "reorient" the population by exposing them to Hollywood films.[25] Accordingly, the studios were asked to donate films that would, in the wording of the request, help to convey "to the people of the occupied areas an understanding of American life and democratic institutions."[26]

But loath to donate films capable of making money in the German market, the studios sent duds such as *Action in the North Atlantic* (1943), a war flick that understandably did not thrill the defeated enemy; and *Tom, Dick and Harry* (1941), a fluffy prewar comedy. After witnessing the German reaction to these films, a US intelligence officer filed a report pointing out the obvious: that Germans were "homesick to hear their own language in films" and preferred "backgrounds and themes as well as actors" that were "familiar"; and that "the carefree and superficial escapism of many pre-war American films" only "irritated" people "faced with bitter realities."[27]

What to do? These reactions were confined to the older generation, not the young, who already "had America in the marrow of their bones" (to quote a German colleague). So the solution was to authorize the production of a small body of films calculated to placate the older generation while also paving the way for Hollywood's eventual conquest of the young. That short-lived genre, called the *Heimatfilm* (homeland film), consisted largely of sentimental musicals that were set in Alpine villages untouched by war or Nazism, and that affirmed traditional values in ways that, ever so subtly, reconciled them with US-style consumer society.[28]

Scorned as reactionary kitsch by the postwar generation, the Heimatfilm faded in the early 1960s, leaving the field to the New German Cinema, which was too bleak to attract a mass audience. Yet even if the New German directors had been Spielbergs, the deck would have been stacked against them, because US dominance of European film markets was built into the Marshall Plan. Launched in 1948 by President Harry Truman and named after General George Marshall, the Marshall Plan is remembered by most Americans as a generous aid package to help war-ravaged European nations, including Germany, get back on their feet. Yet to many Europeans it was also the leading edge of "US cultural imperialism," because a major condition of the aid was the removal, by nations with proud cultural traditions, of all limitations on the import of Hollywood films and other American "information" products.

Reflecting on the Marshall Plan in 1969, historian Thomas H. Guback observed that while it was intended "to strengthen faltering economies against risings from the left," it was also "used as a lever to open and maintain markets for American films." Indeed, "American films were seen as propaganda vehicles for strengthening western European minds against pleas from the left."[29] That may have been the assumption in 1948. But in a few short years, the terms of the pact would change. By 1969, when Guback presented his analysis, a covenant based on patriotism and profit had been transformed into a contract based solely on profit.

THE RISE AND SLOW COLLAPSE OF THE PRODUCTION CODE

Another aspect of the Washington-Hollywood Pact, mentioned in the Introduction, was the self-censorship practiced by the film studios. That self-censorship dated back to the 1915 Supreme Court decision *Mutual Film. v. Ohio*, which defined film as "a business, pure and simple."[30] By defining the new medium as a commodity, as opposed to a form of speech protected by the First Amendment, the *Mutual* decision opened the door to government censorship. And indeed, during the 1910s and 1920s, theaters were often raided and films confiscated by local and state authorities.[31] In reaction to this threat, the MPPDA (as it was still called) began to work out a set of guidelines, eventually known as the Production Code, designed to keep the government at bay. In 1934 the Production Code Authority (better known as the Hays Office, after its first director, former MPPDA head Will Hays) was established. And the Production Code dictated the content of movies until the mid-1960s, when it was set aside in favor of the MPAA ratings system still in place today.

The Production Code helped to foster trust between the partners in the pact. Washington did not worry about the moral content of the films being sent overseas by Hollywood; and Hollywood did not worry about Washington seeking to censor the movies itself. But this mutual trust began to decay in 1947, when the House Un-American Activities Committee (HUAC) began a series of hearings intended to root out Communists and fellow travelers in Hollywood. These were not the first such hearings. Between 1937 and 1940 the committee's predecessor, the House Committee on Un-American Activities, probed the political loyalties of the film industry. But because those earlier hearings were focused on Nazism, they did little damage to the pact.[32] The same cannot be said of the anti-Communist rounds. Indeed, the HUAC hearings of 1947–51 left a bitter legacy of distrust between the nation's government and its dream factory.

There can be no doubt that Communists existed in the movie colony. Beginning in the 1930s and continuing through the war, there were a significant number of active Party members and sympathizers, just as in other walks of American life. The real question was not whether these people existed but how dangerous they were. And herein lurks an irony: during World War II, the Hollywood figures most willing to take direction from Washington were Party members. And the pro-Soviet films they produced — *The North Star, Song of Russia,* and *Three Russian Girls* — were box-office flops.[33] (Even Stalin disliked the 1943 Warner Bros. release *Mission to Moscow.*)[34] But to HUAC the actual impact of such films mattered less than the intentions of those who created them. The studio heads agreed, and in November 1947 ten people who refused to testify — the "Hollywood Ten" — were fired, and many others blacklisted.[35]

It could be argued that the studios' response to HUAC was in keeping with the tradition of self-regulation. But there is a big difference between abiding by a self-imposed Production Code aimed at violence and sex, and yielding to government pressure to purge artists with disfavored political views. By doing the latter, the studios helped to undermine their tradition of self-regulation as embodied in the Production Code.

While this was happening, the Production Code was being undermined from a different direction, as the Supreme Court ruled, in *United States v. Paramount Pictures, Inc.,* that the studios had to divest themselves of their theater chains. As part of that ruling, Justice William O. Douglas suggested that perhaps the movies should receive the same First Amendment protection as the press.[36] This was the first of several Supreme Court decisions challenging the 1915 *Mutual* decision. To repeat, that earlier decision had defined the movies as a "business, pure and simple"—a commodity, as opposed to speech or expression. As such, the movies were subject to government regulation, meaning censorship. And for the next several years, the movies were occasionally censored, mostly by state governments. It was in response to this threat that the studios created the MPPDA Production Code in 1934. Far better, they reasoned, to censor their own product than to let the government do it.

But with the *Paramount* decision it began to look as though the threat of government censorship might be lifted. If that happened, then the need for self-censorship might also disappear. And that is effectively what happened over the next twenty years.

The next step came in 1950, when the Paris Theater in Manhattan opened a trilogy of films by the Italian director Roberto Rossellini, already a scandalous figure in America because of his adulterous affair with Swedish actress Ingrid Bergman. One of the films, *Il Miracolo* (The Miracle), about a mentally unstable peasant girl who believes she's the Virgin Mary, had raised hackles in Rome but was not banned.[37] New York was less tolerant. The film was banned first by the city license commissioner, and then, on the urging of Francis Cardinal Spellman, by the New York State Board of Regents. The distributor filed suit, and eventually the case made it to the US Supreme Court, which ruled in *Joseph Burstyn, Inc. v. Wilson, Commissioner of Education of New York, et al.* (1952) that "sacrilege" was not an acceptable basis for censorship in a religiously pluralistic society.[38]

Il Miracolo did not break any box-office records, but, building on the earlier *Paramount* decision, *Burstyn* made it easier for other unconventional foreign films to enter the United States. By the 1960s, a younger and more sophisticated American audience was flocking to such imports as *Look Back in Anger* (1959), *Tom Jones* (1963), *A Fistful of Dollars* (1964), *The Good, the Bad, and the Ugly* (1966), *Persona* (1966), *The Bride Wore Black* (1968), *Stolen Kisses* (1968), and *The Passion of Anna* (1969). None of these films would shock audiences today, but most contained scenes of sex or violence that definitely pushed the envelope of the Production Code.

GIMME (TAX) SHELTER

It is an enduring myth of cinema history that the unexpected popularity of these foreign films prompted sleepy old Hollywood to wake up, get rid of the stultifying Production Code, and give free rein to a new generation of directors in the liberated 1970s. But that myth is not quite true. Far from sleeping, Hollywood had been wide awake the whole time, and busy investing significant capital in foreign film production. Indeed, every one of the foreign films just mentioned were financed and distributed by Hollywood—with Washington's help.

Here's how it worked. After the war, the economies of Europe experienced shortages of hard currency, leading to policies prohibiting the conversion by Hollywood studios of their overseas earnings to US dollars that could then be repatriated.[39] Fortunately for the studios, Congress rode to the rescue by passing the 1948 Informational Media Guaranty (IMG). Under that law, Washington promised to pay dollars for the nonconvertible currencies earned by US companies marketing "informational media" overseas.[40] What the government expected in return, according to former studio chief David Puttnam, was that the films in question would present "a favorable picture of American life."[41]

It is not clear how seriously this expectation was taken by the studios, whose main focus was on gaining control of European film markets. Even before the passage of the IMG, several studios had begun to plow their nonconvertible earnings back into overseas productions (called "runaway productions" in Hollywood). The studios also strove to make those runaway productions eligible for foreign government film subsidies. This was ironic, considering that the original purpose of those subsidies had been to keep Hollywood out of those same markets. But the studios made the system work for them. For example, by forming a subsidiary called Highland Films, Columbia Pictures was able to collect a grant from the British government to produce A Man for All Seasons (1966), based on Robert Bolt's play about St. Thomas More. The film was a hit, earning $20 million and winning top awards.[42]

One reason for the success of this and other runaway productions was the participation of British and European directors, actors, and other film talent. To their credit, the studios granted these individuals autonomy in their filmmaking. And for the most part, the foreign talent didn't complain. Their own industries were in such bad shape that most of them faced a choice between working for the Americans or not working at all.[43]

It is hard to separate this history of runaway production from what most Americans remember as the golden age of "foreign films." During the 1950s and 1960s, Hollywood underwrote several Technicolor epics made in Italy (both the "swords and sandals" type based on Roman themes, and the "beards and bathrobes" type based on the Bible); the "spaghetti westerns" of Sergio Leone; the sexy comedies of Vittorio de Sica (starring Sophia Loren); much of the British New Wave; and the long-lived James Bond franchise. Sweden and France proved more resistant, but by the mid-1960s Hollywood was helping to finance films by the Swedish director Ingmar Bergman and such French New

Wave icons as François Truffaut, Claude Lelouch, Louis Malle, and Philippe de Broca.[44]

This influx of Hollywood-financed foreign films whetted the American public's appetite for unconventional movies.[45] So it is hardly surprising that the film that finally toppled the MPAA Production Code was a runaway production: *Blow-Up*, a controversial 1968 film about a jaded photographer who finds meaning in capturing a murder on camera. Directed by an Italian, Michelangelo Antonioni, and filmed in London with British talent, *Blow-Up* was produced by a Hollywood studio, MGM. When it became evident that the film would not be allowed in the United States under the Production Code, MGM devised a clever solution. It distributed *Blow-Up* through a shell corporation created for that purpose, which, mirabile dictu, did not belong to the MPAA.

Blow-Up was a hit, and its reputation lives on as the film that, in the words of critic Richard Corliss, "helped liberate Hollywood from its puritanical prurience."[46] In the late 1960s there was still a fair amount of public pressure to keep the Production Code. But the import of cutting-edge foreign films had proved an effective form of market research. The studios were now confident that grittier, more realistic treatments of sex, violence, drug use, crime, and other such topics would resonate with the new, youthful audience. Thus, in 1968 the MPAA replaced the Production Code with a ratings system.[47] Today MPAA ratings are still enforced in most theaters. But as noted in the introduction, theaters are only one media platform among many, and for most others—video on demand, DVDs, the Internet—the ratings barrier has become virtually nonexistent.

Despite the success of the aforementioned foreign films, by the end of the 1960s Hollywood was in trouble. Most of the major studios were either losing money on extravagant attempts to replicate the box-office success of *The Sound of Music*, or they were turning out old-fashioned comedies, thrillers, and historical epics that failed to resonate with the emergent youth audience. Five MPAA members were heading toward bankruptcy when once again Washington rode to the rescue.

In 1969, with the support of the Nixon administration, Congress enacted tax credits for film industry losses that created lucrative profit shelters for individual investors. As Alan Hirschfield, then president of Columbia Pictures, subsequently testified to Congress, "The availability of this kind of financing is the single most important occurrence in the recent history of the industry."[48] Additional tax credits were created by a provision in the 1971 Revenue Act that allowed 7 percent (subsequently increased to 10 percent) of production investment to be deducted from the studios' overall corporate tax up to a 50 percent limit, with carry-forward provisions for seven years. Further sweetening the deal was the outcome of a lawsuit, brought by Disney, that made the measure retroactive to 1962.[49] As historian David Cook concludes, "Tax shelters and other tax-leveraged investment became the key mode of production finance for the rest of the decade."[50]

Such policies were "not without a touch of irony," notes former studio chief Puttnam, because "for years the studios had fulminated against the preferential tax incentives for film production offered by foreign governments." The irony is compounded by the link between these legislative favors and the "American New Wave" of the 1970s. When film buffs celebrate such "bold and adventurous" films as *Five Easy Pieces* (1970), *One Flew over the Cuckoo's Nest* (1975), and *Taxi Driver* (1976), Puttnam adds, only a few insiders recall that they "were financed using tax shelter money."[51]

"A BUSINESS, PURE AND SIMPLE"

Throughout this tale, we see Washington upholding its side of the pact. (Indeed, the aforementioned tax breaks seem above and beyond the call of duty.) But what about Hollywood? Did it continue to produce films that, in the words of the 1948 State Department memo, "reflect credit on the good name and reputation of this country and its institutions?" Or did it renege on the deal? The short answer is that Hollywood has reneged, producing films that offer at best an amusing fun-house-mirror view of America and its institutions, and at worst a distorting caricature. But there is more. Hollywood has also distorted its own self-definition in ways that, quite apart from content, serve to alienate many other countries.

We have seen how the US Supreme Court began, at mid-century, to move away from its own 1915 definition of film as "a business, pure and simple," meaning a commodity subject to government regulation (including censorship), and began to define it as cultural expression deserving of First Amendment protection. Here we encounter the greatest irony so far: the fact that when it comes to the export of film to the rest of the world, the American government and film industry still define movies as "a business, pure and simple." Touting the benefits of free trade, both Washington and Hollywood deny that there is any difference between trade in commodities and trade in cultural expression. This stance may help America to push back against foreign governments seeking to mitigate or end US dominance of their film markets. But it also fosters a troubling disconnect between the priorities of business and those of diplomacy.

This disconnect first emerged in the 1970s, when the Non-Aligned Movement, a loose affiliation of Third World nations founded in 1955 and pledged to neutrality in the Cold War, became sufficiently pro-Soviet to submit two proposals to the United Nations Educational, Scientific and Cultural Organization (UNESCO), one for a "new world international economic order" and one for a "new world information and communication order." Since their target was "US imperialism" and "US cultural imperialism," these proposals met with stiff opposition from Washington. In 1985, the Reagan administration withdrew US support from UNESCO, and America's reply to the charge of cultural imperialism became couched in the familiar language of free speech, free enterprise, and free trade. As the president told the UN General Assembly in 1987, "We cannot permit attempts to control the media and promote censorship under the ruse of a so-called 'New World Information Order.'"[52]

This focus on freedom resonated even more in the giddy atmosphere of the 1990s, when UNESCO became more pro-American and negotiated an agreement in which the phrase "free flow of information" was repeated so often it became a mantra. Yet this mantra proved unacceptable to certain ministries of culture, notably in France. Beginning in the 1980s and continuing through 2005, the French tried to carve out a "cultural exception" to the free trade ethos of the World Trade Organization (WTO).

A negotiator with the Office of the US Trade Representative, Carol Balassa was long involved in WTO audiovisual negotiations. And while she acknowledges that the US position reflected a "core belief in the social and political, as well as the economic, benefits of trade, unfettered by government regulation," she also recalls the atmosphere at the negotiations being "acrimonious and hostile," owing in part to perceived American indifference to the cultural concerns of many countries, including France.[53]

In 2005 the conflict resumed at UNESCO, when Canada and France urged the adoption of a proposal called the Convention on the Protection and Promotion of the Diversity of Cultural Expressions. The Diversity Convention (no one wants to say CPPDCE) was a mixture of economic protectionism and cultural concerns which garnered 148 votes, with four countries abstaining and only two voting against it: Israel and the United States. Some non-Western nations voted in favor of the proposal because Canada and France promised them film subsidies. But others expressed honest concern about the moral content of US films.[54]

The Diversity Convention is not binding, and to date none of the signatories has taken any action based on it. So today it might seem a mere footnote to the history of US trade relations in the mid-2000s. But the virulently anti-American narrative that drove the Diversity Convention is still out there. Indeed, in spring 2013 the French government renewed its call for *l'exception culturelle*, releasing a five-hundred-page report seeking to protect not only its domestic film, television, and music industries but also its Internet-related businesses and products.[55] Justified or not, resentment of American arrogance in the cultural dimension of trade constitutes an ongoing political fact highly relevant to US public diplomacy.

Yet this political fact continues to be ignored by both Hollywood and Washington. Indeed, it remains a cliché of free trade rhetoric that cultural concerns are sheer hypocrisy, their real goal being to protect coddled foreign film industries from the robust competition of Hollywood. For example, in 2008 the head of the MPAA, former congressman Dan Glickman (D-KS), jokingly recalled that when he was secretary of agriculture in the Clinton administration, his EU counterpart had tried to block the import of US agricultural products on the grounds that "genetically modified food was cultural." Drawing a parallel with the export of US entertainment, Glickman chuckled, "We have to be careful, because there are a lot of self-interested people out there saying, 'This is important to me, therefore it's culture.'"[56]

It is unsettling to see the world's most powerful film lobbyist credit the idea that film should not be treated as culture—that in international trade negotiations it should be regarded as no different than any other commodity. But this is how the culture-commodity debate has twisted and turned, leaving the domestic view and the overseas view at odds. Precisely because US law has come to recognize the movies as artistic expression deserving of constitutional protection, American filmmakers today have more freedom than that enjoyed by any of their predecessors, not to mention their peers in other countries. When they use that freedom to make films which flout social norms still respected in most of the world, many foreigners—not just ministers of culture but also ordinary men and women—raise objections. Those objections deserve a better response than they have been getting.

6

---◆---

"The World's Worst Propagandists"

Americans are the world's worst propagandists.
—Ambassador George V. Allen, director of the United States
Information Agency, 1957–60

When Benjamin Franklin traveled to Paris in December 1776, his main task was to gain the support of King Louis XVI for the American side in the War of Independence. This he did by playing the balance-of-power game with as much guile as any European diplomat—or, to put it another way, with as much *sophrosune* as Odysseus. Among other maneuvers, Franklin leaked intelligence about France's intentions to the British, sowing just enough suspicion between the two to advance his cause. Franklin also impressed the French nobility with his high degree of cultivation. Renowned for his scientific experiments, he was also celebrated for his wit, intellect, and refined taste in art, music, wine, and food. Not for a moment did he allow his hosts to dismiss him as a crude bumpkin, as the French were inclined to do.[1]

Yet neither did Franklin ape the nobility. On the contrary, he appealed to the philosophes' fascination with the state of nature by playing the noble savage —moving among the powdered wigs, elaborate silks, and gilded ornaments of the French court adorned in a fur cap, dowdy suit, and plain wooden walking stick. In essence, he turned his dumpy figure into a symbol of enlightened democracy. As Franklin's fame spread, his physical likeness appeared in a wide range of consumer items, from expensive oil paintings, marble busts, and Sèvres china to terra cotta medallions, cheap engravings, and wooden dolls.[2] It was an extraordinary performance, and it helped to persuade, even seduce, France into expending blood and treasure for the American cause.

This chapter focuses on the relationship between the persuasive and the se-
ductive sides of US public diplomacy. With the emergence of the mass media
in the twentieth century, the need to communicate with foreign publics, not
just governments, became more salient than ever, and that salience has only
increased in the twenty-first-century era of WikiLeaks, the Internet, and social media. It could be argued that public diplomacy comes more naturally
to America than to nations with a history of monarchy and empire, because,
unlike the narrowly focused, highly ritualized diplomacy of unelected rulers,
American diplomacy has always been self-consciously democratic. Ever since
Thomas Jefferson justified the Declaration of Independence as proof of "a decent respect to the opinions of mankind," Americans have sought, whenever
possible, to persuade and seduce commoners as well as courtiers. Following
Franklin's shrewd example, we have succeeded best when convincing others
that it is possible to be democratic while also being reasonable and cultivated.

THE EARLY COLD WAR: SKIRMISHES
ON THE FIELD OF CULTURE

America's Cold War public diplomacy was conducted largely by the United
States Information Agency (known as USIA at home and USIS, for United
States Information Service, overseas). The USIA was established in 1953 as part
of a comprehensive bill outlining the American response to the aggressive and
well financed propaganda machine being built by the Soviet Union.[3] Generally
speaking, the USIA was responsible for the four public-diplomacy goals outlined in the prologue to Part Two: listening, advocacy, cultural and educational
exchange, and news reporting (while keeping its distance from psychological
warfare). The USIA also, for bureaucratic and political reasons, shared responsibility for cultural and educational exchanges with the State Department's Division of Cultural Relations.[4]

Having lost many more of its citizens than any other country in World War
II, the Soviet Union felt entitled to bring all of postwar Europe, including the
West, under its control. To that end, Stalin spent $1.5 billion in 1950—sixty
times more than America—trying to persuade Europeans that the true protec-
tors of Western civilization were not the barbaric Americans but the refined
Soviets.[5] In 1955 the American diplomat George F. Kennan warned that these
efforts were exploiting the perennial European prejudice that Americans are
"vulgar, materialistic *nouveaux riches*, lacking in manners and sensitivity, interested only in making money, contemptuous of every refinement of esthetic
feeling."[6]

It's important not to underestimate the power of Soviet seduction. Throughout the 1950s and early 1960s, the USSR sponsored international tours by some of its finest performing artists. The repertory was strictly traditional, originality being unwelcome in the Soviet cultural sphere. Still, on its chosen battleground the USSR's culture machine was formidable. America, writes historian David Caute, "could not present a playwright better than Brecht [who moved to Soviet-dominated East Berlin in 1949], a composer as popular as Prokofiev or Shostakovich, a ballet company superior to the Bolshoi, instrumentalists more skilled than Richter, Oistrakh, or Rostropovich, ensemble acting more subtle than the Moscow Art Theater's."[7]

Yet the United States found effective ways to respond. One of the most celebrated was the transplantation of what was then a uniquely American institution: the free circulating public library. The first overseas version of this institution, appropriately named the Benjamin Franklin Library, was built in Mexico City in 1942. After World War II, the idea was introduced into the Federal Republic of Germany, and by 1951 there were twenty-seven such libraries in America Houses (Amerika Haüser) throughout West Germany and in West Berlin. Hans N. Tuch, a German-born veteran of the US Army paratroopers who directed the Wiesbaden and Frankfurt America Houses, recalls the "democratizing effect" of these institutions, "the first such libraries that the Germans had ever seen." Indeed, the directors of several major German libraries soon adopted the same practice of letting ordinary citizens "go into the library and pick out their own book, check it out, read it there, or take it home."[8]

America also made use of an indigenous art form that, for many, expressed both a cultivated aesthetic sense and the spirit of freedom and democracy. The European (and Russian) taste for jazz first developed in the 1920s. During World War II, the US Armed Forces Network won many more converts. In 1955 the Voice of America (VOA) began to beam "the music of freedom," as host Willis Conover called it, to a regular audience of one hundred million worldwide, including thirty million behind the Iron Curtain. In the early 1960s, the State Department sponsored tours by such jazz masters as Louis Armstrong, Duke Ellington, Benny Goodman, and Dizzy Gillespie.

A clear purpose of these tours, all of which included African-American musicians, was to blunt Soviet criticism of American racism. Historian Penny Von Eschen notes that there was "a glaring contradiction" in using "black artists as goodwill ambassadors . . . when America was still a Jim Crow nation."[9] She has a point. But the tours succeeded—not least because the musicians were allowed to speak freely about racial discrimination in America. Even Gillespie, whose acerbic comments on the topic upset his State Department sponsors, admitted that "our interracial group was powerfully effective against Red propaganda."[10]

And the music transcended politics. The Russian novelist Vassily Aksyonov recalls thinking of these broadcasts as "America's secret weapon number one . . . a kind of golden glow over the horizon."[11] Another young Russian wrote to Conover that jazz was "a source of strength when I am overwhelmed by pessimism."[12] Recalling his youthful days as an underground jazz musician, Czech novelist Josef Škvorecký writes that "our sweet, wild music was a sharp thorn in the side of the power-hungry men, from Hitler to Brezhnev, who successively ruled in my native land."[13]

One might ask why it took the VOA so long to begin broadcasting jazz. How could anyone object to such a compelling cultural export? The answer is that some congressmen objected, for reasons reflecting two powerful currents of opinion in 1950s America. The first was a narrow and conventional view of high culture, which saw jazz not as serious art but as vulgar commercial entertainment (this view also contained more than a whiff of racism). The second current was the zealous anti-Communism of the time, which saw jazz as suspicious because some of the individuals who played it held unorthodox political views. That these currents found a voice in Congress is a reflection of the democratic nature of American politics—in a more aristocratic regime, such populist views would have been summarily stifled.

Often what makes the difference is the ability of a leader to overcome his own artistic prejudices. One who failed to do so was President Harry Truman. In the crucial year 1947 the State Department put together an art exhibition called *Advancing American Art*, to be shown in Latin America and Europe. None of the painters included—Romare Beardon, Stuart Davis, Yasuo Kinuyoshi, Jacob Lawrence, John Marin, Georgia O'Keeffe, Ben Shahn—were pure abstractionists. That is, their works contained recognizable images. But they were modernists in the sense of departing from the realistic style of the nineteenth century (still the most popular style of art in the Western world). But that was the point of the exhibition: artists in the Soviet sphere were forced to work in a debased version of nineteenth-century realism known as Socialist Realism. *Advancing American Art* was designed to highlight the contrast between the stilted conformity of Socialist Realism and the creative freedom enjoyed in the United States.

It didn't work out that way. The American Artists' Professional League, a group devoted to nineteenth-century realism, denounced the exhibition for featuring artistic styles "not indigenous to our soil." *Look* magazine lambasted the State Department for wasting the taxpayers' money on art that didn't appeal to taxpayers. On Capitol Hill, this cultural populism fused with anti-Communism, as several politicians denounced the art as "Communistic." The final blow was delivered by the president, himself an amateur painter of distinctly nonmodernist bent. Looking at a work by Kinuyoshi, Truman said, "If that's art, I'm a Hottentot."[14] The exhibition never opened, and all seventy-nine works were auctioned off as army surplus.[15]

Eleven years later, President Dwight D. Eisenhower made a better judgment call. In 1958 the United States signed a major cultural agreement with the Soviet Union, and the following summer the USIA mounted a spectacular event, the American National Exhibition, in Moscow's Sokolniki Park.[16] All told, 2.7 million Soviet citizens attended the exhibition, with its shiny cars and boats, Kodak cameras, free Pepsi, seventy-eight-foot-high geodesic dome, Edward Steichen's *Family of Man* photographs, Disney movie-in-the-round ("Circarama"), color television, computer, young Americans fielding questions in fluent Russian, and, of course, the model American kitchen where Premier Nikita Khrushchev and Vice President Richard M. Nixon squared off on the merits of their two systems.[17]

There was also an art exhibit, which, like its predecessor, had been denounced on both cultural-populist and anti-Communist grounds. Indeed, three weeks before the fair was scheduled to open, Representative Francis E. Walter (D-PA) of the House Committee on Un-American Activities accused the exhibition of featuring Communist artists who engaged in modernist "doodling" instead of genuine (i.e., realistic) painting. As it happened, Eisenhower, also an amateur painter who cared little for modernism, understood that the purpose of the show was to showcase American freedom, not foster good relations between middlebrows on both sides of the Iron Curtain. He urged that the exhibition be included, and Nixon backed him up, declaring that "the worst thing we could do would be to withdraw any of the art at this point," because doing so "would run the risk of creating an American Pasternak."[18]

So the art exhibit went to Moscow, with one modification. In a conciliatory gesture to their critics in Congress, the organizers added twenty-six additional paintings: realistic landscapes, portraits, and genre works by such nineteenth- and early-twentieth-century masters as George Catlin, Frederic Remington, and John Singer Sargent.[19] But no one pointed out to Congressman Walter that his taste coincided perfectly with that of Premier Khrushchev, who on his second visit to the fair remarked that John Marin's *Sea and Sky* "looks as though someone had peed on the canvas."[20]

THE CIA-FUNDED "BATTLE OF IDEAS"

In 2005, at the low point of the Iraq war, Alan Riding wrote a piece for the *New York Times* titled "Rerun Our Cold War Cultural Diplomacy." In that piece, Riding praised not only the art exhibitions and jazz tours but also a variety of programs aimed at waging a "battle of ideas" with the Soviets. "Intellectuals from the former Soviet bloc have often underlined the importance of these programs," he concluded.[21]

The main arena for this battle of ideas was western Europe, where Soviet influence was especially strong. The main audience was the so-called non-Communist left: trade unionists, social democrats, and disillusioned former Stalinists. This audience was crucial, because it was deeply conversant with Soviet Communism and knew the most powerful arguments against it.[22] The programs praised by Riding began in 1947 and were active in thirty-five countries around the world—publishing intellectual journals, translating books, running an international news service, and holding star-studded intellectual conferences.[23]

But all this raises a question. The political outlook dominating these programs was anti-Soviet but also quite leftist. How did they ever get this through Congress? The answer is, they didn't. This battle of ideas was funded by private donors, including foundations like Carnegie, Rockefeller, Ford, and Guggenheim, and by ordinary Americans sympathetic to the anti-Communist cause.

Of course, if you believe that, then there's a bridge in London I would like to sell to you!

These programs were not funded by Congress, but neither were they funded privately. Under the rubric of an ostensibly private organization called the Congress for Cultural Freedom (CCF), they were funded covertly by the CIA, which funneled money through a variety of channels, including the foundations just mentioned and several others set up for that sole purpose.

The era of covertly funded cultural programs ended in 1967, when the New Left magazine *Ramparts* ran an article exposing the CIA funding behind an array of Cold War activities, including the Congress for Cultural Freedom. This article, followed by another in the *New York Times*, served to discredit the whole CCF effort. Defenders argued, correctly, that covert arts were hardly in the same category as covert ops. But at the time, this was a losing battle. By 1967 most Americans knew about the CIA's overthrow of left-leaning governments in Iran (1953) and Guatemala (1954), and public anger was rising against the duplicity of President Lyndon Johnson's administration about the war in Vietnam.

Against this backdrop many were shocked to learn that reputable artists, writers, and intellectuals had accepted CIA funding.[24]

The shock was largely justified. Secret government subvention of free citizens' groups is a violation of bedrock American principle. And the CIA's covert funding scheme bore an uncomfortable resemblance to the Communist Party's longtime strategy of using "front organizations" to infiltrate social and political institutions. In the 1920s, when the German Communist Willi Münzenberg set up the first front organizations in Europe, his pet name for them was "Innocents' Clubs." Münzenberg's comment about them will send shivers down the spine of anyone who shares Tocqueville's regard for the American voluntarist tradition: "These people have the belief that they are actually doing this themselves. This belief must be preserved at any price."[25]

Yet it's important to ask: how closely were the CIA's "innocents" controlled? In most Soviet fronts, the members were closely monitored and any deviation from the Party line severely admonished. In the CIA fronts, not so much. As historian David Caute writes, it is tempting to concoct a "grim story of covert dollar (or ruble) subsidies, epistolary whispers, and phantom foundations," and from there leap to the "false conclusion" that "he who paid the piper wrote the tune," but most CIA grantees were headstrong characters disinclined to take orders from any government.[26] "The CIA might have tried to call the tune," says historian Hugh Wilford, "but the piper did not always play it, nor the audience dance to it."[27]

Today, most historians agree that the Congress for Cultural Freedom made a difference, especially during the crucial first decade of the Cold War, when it helped to carve out a small but crucial advantage for liberal democracy at a time when its future was in peril. In retrospect, George Kennan defended the organization with stark clarity: "This country has no ministry of culture, and the CIA was obliged to do what it could to try to fill the gap."[28]

THE YEARS OF GETTING IT RIGHT

Kennan was correct: there is no United States ministry of culture. Yet in an important way, the whole idea of a ministry of culture is out of date. Historically, the salient fact about ministries of culture in Europe and in many other parts of the world is that they were rooted in aristocratic traditions in which hereditary elites were expected to preserve their nation's heritage and, when necessary, use it to impress (and intimidate) others.

In Europe, this aristocratic stance is no longer politically acceptable. Steve Green is a British cultural expert who has worked in both the British Council and the European Union National Institutes for Culture (EUNIC).[29] From where he sits, "The classic model of cultural diplomacy as an activity of a nation state, conducted bilaterally," is a thing of the past; and twenty-first-century cultural diplomacy is "developing in two very active directions. The first involves the arrival of new players; the second, the development of a multilateral approach."[30] Green could also have said "two very *different* directions," because the cultural diplomacy of some new players—Russia, China, Iran, the Persian Gulf kingdoms—is decidedly nationalistic. But perhaps this is a tacit reason why the Europeans wrestle with the new challenge of being inclusive, multicultural, and democratic.

This is not a new challenge for America, though. Since the days of Benjamin Franklin, American cultural diplomacy has sought to balance artistic cultivation with democratic and inclusive values. Kennan is right to observe that a meddling Congress makes this harder to do. But as noted above, a meddling Congress is part of what Americans mean by democracy. European cultural officials speak frequently about "arm's-length" programs, by which they mean exchanges, festivals, and other activities immunized against political oversight. It is, of course, crucial to protect cultural programs from the self-interested meddling of domestic political factions. But the expectation that nations will engage in cultural programs for purely disinterested reasons is utopian. The shadow of propaganda hovers over all public diplomacy, including cultural programs, because no government can afford to pay for open-ended interaction with every other nation. When a government ponies up for a library, exhibition, or performing arts tour, it does so for a reason.

The best cultural diplomats of the early Cold War understood this. But they also understood that cultural programs work best at arm's length from advocacy. The veterans I interviewed said that the best thing about working for the USIA and the State Department's Division of Cultural Relations in the 1950s and 1960s was that they were given free rein to discover the right balance, in any given setting, between "pure" cultural and educational exchange and advocacy on behalf of freedom and democracy.

For example, Yale Richmond was the first cultural diplomat in Poland after the US-USSR cultural agreement of 1958, and the first thing he noticed upon his arrival in Warsaw was "how tired the Poles were of being hammered by propaganda, first by the Nazis and then by the Communists." So as he explained to me, Richmond and his colleagues "decided the best approach would be not to hammer them with more propaganda." In 1959, Richmond began an exchange of US and Polish graduate students and university lecturers that later evolved into the Fulbright Program for Poland. He also reestablished the American library in Warsaw, which had been closed by the Polish Communist government in 1950, and launched a program of Polish-language publications.[31]

Transferred to Moscow in 1967, Richmond helped to organize tours by the New York Philharmonic, the Alvin Ailey Dance Theater, and other US performers, and to distribute the popular Russian-language magazine *Amerika*. He also continued to do what he had done in Poland, which was to spend endless hours talking with others in their own language about nonideological topics. "People get tired of politics," he told me. "It's important to change the subject." About universities, ballet, or the previous evening's play or concert, "people felt they could speak freely. I never had to say *freedom* or *democracy*. They got the point."[32]

Sometimes those conversations were with government officials. "My major achievement in Moscow," Richmond told me, "was to get out of the office every day and call on some Russian office where no American had ever visited before and discuss Soviet-American relations. I was always received correctly, if not cordially."[33] In a similar vein, Iain Elliot, a Scots-born Russia specialist who traveled widely in the USSR, recalled that the cultural affairs diplomats usually got further with Russian officials than did the senior public diplomacy officers: "The public-affairs officers felt obliged to promote US policy, often in the face of strong ideological resistance, while the cultural affairs diplomats could usually discuss a wider range of subjects in comprehensible Russian."[34]

There is also a great deal to be learned from writers and artists themselves. As noted by the distinguished Arabist and diplomat Hume Horan, creative people are often more intuitive and insightful than government officials:

> It's the embassy cultural officers who get the real internist's-eye view of a difficult country. They have fewer restrictions placed on their movements. Since Arab writers and artists are in a terrible financial situation and nobody cares about their work, they come cheap: for the price of a meal and a bit of appreciation, they'll pour their souls out to you, providing the kind of psychological clues to the workings of a system that a political officer will never get from his Foreign Ministry contacts.[35]

This is not to suggest that cultural diplomacy is easy. As any good politician can attest, it takes more skill to shoot the breeze with constituents than to lecture them on policy. It's the same in public diplomacy. The better you are at interacting with others on a social level, the more receptive they will be to your political perspective. As Elliot put it, "People think: if you've bothered to learn our language and understand our culture, we have more in common and we trust you more."[36]

COUNTERCULTURE AND CULTURE WAR

One reason why US cultural diplomats in the 1950s and early 1960s had so much freedom was that the higher-ups in Washington trusted them to serve both the nation's interests and its ideals. In other words, both the home office and the practitioners in the field had a shared sense of mission, not only about what their goals were but also about the proper way to pursue those goals. With the upheavals of the late 1960s, this shared sense of mission began to erode. Those upheavals have been analyzed by social scientists, cultural historians, and literary scholars. But they have rarely been scrutinized by the chroniclers of US public diplomacy, who tend to focus on political change. By focusing on cultural change, I may seem to be further tangling an already tangled history. But that is not my intention. Rather, I hope to clarify the impact of the late-1960s counterculture on US public diplomacy, because that impact is still being felt.

The most striking fact about the late 1960s and 1970s was that the American counterculture, in particular rock music, played a significant role in winning the hearts and minds of Russian and Eastern European youth. The story is entwined with that of jazz, which remained popular in the Soviet bloc longer than it did in the United States. But beginning in the 1950s, many younger listeners in the East began to acquire a taste for rock 'n' roll, taping shows off the US Armed Forces Network and, in an ingenious procedure known as *roentgenizdat*, copying smuggled records onto discarded X-ray plates and selling them through a network that at one point reached to Siberia.[37] In the early 1960s, the VOA took the hint and began to include rock 'n' roll in its music programs.[38]

By the late 1960s rock 'n' roll had become rock, a harder music with edgier lyrics. But rock proved even more influential. Indeed, a stunning example of its influence occurred in Czechoslovakia, where shortly after the 1968 Prague Spring was crushed by Soviet tanks, a band calling itself Plastic People of the Universe (PPU) became a potent symbol of resistance. About the PPU's music, the less said the better. (In the early days their performances were more like "happenings" than concerts.) But their defiant attitude toward the Communist authorities attracted a large following, and in 1976, when the band members were subjected to a Kafkaesque trial, Vaclev Havel spoke out in their defense, and the trial became a rallying point for many different groups incensed at Soviet-imposed repression.[39]

The PPU admired such cutting-edge American bands as the Velvet Underground and the Mothers of Invention, whose blackly satirical lyrics were matched by their bleakly absurdist performance style. Indeed, the name "Plastic People" was taken from a song by Frank Zappa, the leader of the Mothers of Invention. Because these American bands drew on a tradition of avant-garde performance harking back to earlier European art movements such as futurism and Dada,[40] they found a receptive audience among not only the youth but also the intellectuals of Eastern Europe and Russia.[41]

Needless to say, neither the Velvet Underground nor the Mothers of Invention were promoted by the USIA or the State Department. Indeed, many cultural affairs officers living overseas found themselves mystified by the whole counterculture. As one commented wryly to me, "We missed the 1960s." But when the Cold War ended and information began to flow from East to West, it became apparent that avant-garde rock had been an important vehicle of protest against repressive Communist rule.

The 1960s counterculture also affected the visual arts. Early in the decade, the International Art Program—an organization set up by the State Department and the USIA to oversee America's participation in the world's most prestigious contemporary art exhibitions, the Venice Biennale and the São Paolo Bienal—mounted two award-winning shows. In 1965 the National Endowment for the Arts (NEA) was established, and for a brief moment it seemed as though the art world and the US Congress were working in tandem. But the moment passed all too quickly. That same year, when President Johnson agreed to celebrate the founding of the NEA with a White House Festival of the Arts, a number of prominent artists, led by the poet Robert Lowell, announced a boycott, intended to express their "dismay and distrust" over the escalating war in Vietnam.[42]

Three years later, America took a beating from the international arts community when, at the 1968 Venice Biennale, angry demonstrators shouted "Yankee Go Home" and, according to one witness, blamed the United States not just for Vietnam but for "whatever was wrong with the Biennale," which they denounced as "a fascist, capitalist, commercial art show."[43] The following year, the blows began to come from the American arts community. Of the twenty-three artists chosen for the US exhibit at São Paolo, nine refused to participate, stating that "the American Government pursues an immoral war in Vietnam and vigorously supports fascist regimes in Brazil and other areas of the world."[44] In historian Michael Krenn's apt summary, US cultural diplomacy was now "threatened not so much by domestic critics of modern art or congressmen searching for Communist artists but by a foreign audience and American artists who were increasingly at odds with U.S. foreign policy."[45]

Officials struggled to cope. For the 1970 Venice Biennale, International Art Program director Lois Bingham decided to send not a conventional collection but a group of "artist-professors" who, by bonding with students and peers, would achieve "that international understanding and respect which are essential to any semblance of world peace."[46] The result was as painful as it was predictable. Urged by Bingham to create "an entirely freewheeling, expressive atmosphere," in which art would be made "pertinent to today's world," printmaker William Weege created a poster saying, "Impeach Nixon." This did not please Bingham, who later fumed that "once an American goes abroad, especially if he is on an official government project, he is an American first and always."[47] Weege was ordered to stop, an outcome that underscores Krenn's quip that "the line between being pertinent and impertinent was very thin indeed."[48]

As American artists and intellectuals continued to lambaste the government through the 1970s, it became difficult to run cultural programs relying on those same people. The balance was partly restored when a low-key midwesterner named James Keogh was named USIA director. Like his predecessor, the hard-charging anti-Communist Frank Shakespeare, Keogh scrutinized every work of art and publication that went out under the agency's name. But unlike Shakespeare, he also dealt respectfully with his critics. According to Eugene Kopp, deputy chief of USIA under Presidents Nixon, Ford, and George H. W. Bush, Keogh's response whenever he got "letters calling him a Neanderthal and a censor" was to write "nice letters back, explaining that certain items were not appropriate for an art show funded by the taxpayers. His tone was never combative or strident."[49]

THE CULTURE WAR AND THE TRIUMPH OF ADVOCACY

In 1980 America elected a president, Ronald Reagan, whose tone was likewise never combative or strident. But Reagan's election occurred in the midst of a culture war whose bitterness and persistence harked back to the 1930s feud between two Appalachian clans, the Hatfields and the McCoys. Some battles were about social issues, such as school prayer, feminism, divorce, abortion, and homosexuality; others were about proposed remedies for racial discrimination, such as school busing and affirmative action; still others were about artistic and intellectual issues, such as offensive rock and rap lyrics, federal funding for the arts, and political correctness on campus.

The impact of the culture war on public diplomacy was to make it harder to balance advocacy with the other three goals of listening, cultural and educational exchange, and news reporting. During the 1970s, cautious diplomats began to edge away from culture in particular, says retired public diplomat Donald Bishop. In an oral history of his years in USIA, Bishop recalls that when he began his career in 1979, "Culture was the fluff, policy was the freight. A seminar on the need to reduce non-tariff barriers during the Uruguay Round, according to the doctrine, was worth more than programming visiting clog dancers."[50] Predictably, this attitude deepened the reluctance of artists, academics, and other cultural figures to participate in USIA programs.

The USIA thrived nonetheless. During the 1980s, the last decade of the Cold War, Presidents Reagan and George H. W. Bush made sure the agency had the resources it needed to lead the final charge against the Soviet Union. It is important to recall that the Soviet propaganda machine was still up and running at the time—indeed, when Reagan took office in 1981, the Soviet Union was spending $2.2 billion on overseas propaganda, as opposed to America's $480 million.[51] Under Charles Z. Wick, the USIA director appointed by Reagan, the agency received a massive infusion of cash, peaking at $881 million in 1986.[52]

Wick was a close friend of Reagan's, a fellow Californian who had worked as a band leader, talent agent, attorney, venture capitalist, and political fundraiser. So his communication skills (like those of his boss) had been shaped in show business and polished in the many venues where wealth and power meet. But he rubbed many in the State Department the wrong way, both culturally and ideologically. The cultural friction arose from Wick's show business background. "There was some snobbery when he arrived," I was told by one former USIA officer. "The guardians of programs in high culture looked askance at his piano-playing." This particular officer felt that "anyone who had written arrangements for Fred Waring while still in college should be taken seriously," but this was not the view of "Washington program officers who assumed they were the true custodians of art, culture, American studies, and so on, distanced from grubby politics."[53]

There's an old aviator's joke that a helicopter is just forty thousand nuts and bolts flying in close formation. Echoing his predecessors, Wick proposed the bureaucratic equivalent: "The administration's best speakers and thinkers should assemble to urgently shape a coordinated strategy to enable the United States *to speak with one voice.*"[54] In theory, this was an attempt to restore a sense of shared mission to the USIA. But in practice, it had the effect of defining advocacy as the agency's single, overriding goal—to the detriment of listening, cultural and educational exchange, and reporting the news. At least, this was the opinion of those USIA officials whose sympathies lay on the other side of the deepening culture war.

Reagan did not feel any particular animus against the arts and humanities. Rather his early 1981 proposals to slash funding for the NEA and the National Endowment for the Humanities (NEH) by half, and to terminate most federal grants to museums, were an expression of his small-government philosophy. But those cuts stirred outrage in the arts community—and among academics. Unfortunately, this was answered by equal outrage on the part of Reagan's more zealous lieutenants. According to Cull, USIA began a blacklist of prominent Americans deemed "insufficiently supportive of White House policy." Along with such avowed leftists as James Baldwin, Allen Ginsberg, Betty Friedan, and Ralph Nader, the list included Walter Cronkite, Coretta Scott King, John Kenneth Galbraith, McGeorge Bundy, Madeleine Albright, and others. When the news of this list broke in 1984, writes Cull, Wick was "outraged," and during a subsequent congressional hearing a candidate for USIA deputy director, Leslie Lenkowsky, "served as the necessary blood sacrifice."[55]

This was hardly the last such episode. Throughout the 1980s, both sides in the culture war struggled to shape the content of public diplomacy. For example, the Reagan administration pressured the Fulbright Program to require foreign scholars to begin their American sojourn with week-long "orientation" sessions intended to inoculate them against the left-wing views they would encounter at US universities.[56] On the liberal side, cultural affairs officers sought unsuccessfully to arrange speaking tours for such outspoken liberals as Daniel Ellsberg and Gloria Steinem.[57] A decade later, these struggles would take their toll.

"BIPARTISAN BAD JUDGMENT"

We now turn to the post–Cold War decision to turn public diplomacy over to the private sector, in particular the commercial media. In the decade after the collapse of the Soviet Union, drastic cuts were made to cultural and educational exchange programs: between 1993 and 2001, funding for such programs dropped by more than one third, from $349 million to $232 million (adjusted for inflation). Between 1995 and 2001, the annual number of participants in such programs fell from forty-five thousand to twenty-nine thousand. Then in 1999 the USIA was dismantled and absorbed into the State Department, a move that deprived it of its independence and flexibility, not to mention its operating budget. By the end of the 1990s, many American libraries and cultural centers—from Vienna to Belgrade, Ankara to Islamabad—had closed their doors.[58]

Clearly, some of this destruction can be chalked up to the culture war. After the 1994 election brought a conservative Republican majority to the House of Representatives, Senator Jesse Helms (R-NC) vowed to slash funding for a number of agencies seen as dominated by people whose sensibility reflected that of the 1960s counterculture. These included the NEA, the NEH, public broadcasting, and the Fulbright Program. Helms had been on this warpath since 1987, when a photograph of a plastic crucifix submerged in urine (Andres Serrano's *Piss Christ*) won a regional art contest sponsored by the NEA, and his campaign had gained momentum in 1989, when the explicit sadomasochistic photographs of Robert Mapplethorpe were included in an NEA-funded exhibition in the (very public) Corcoran Gallery in Washington.[59]

In a painful irony, the USIA was not one of Helms's original targets—and certainly, none of its cultural programs included anything like Serrano's *Piss Christ* or Mapplethorpe's *X Portfolio*. But five years later, after a series of battles to save these various agencies, the USIA became the only one to take a fatal hit. In the opinion of Cynthia Schneider, former ambassador to the Netherlands and a champion of arts diplomacy, "Jesse Helms's attitude toward USIA was linked to Mapplethorpe."[60]

Yet the culture war was not the whole story. In the recollection of former deputy chief Eugene Kopp, "Closing USIA was bad judgment, but it was *bipartisan* bad judgment."[61] In other words, Jesse Helms did not act alone. Supporting him in the decision to close the USIA were three prominent Democrats: Senator Joe Biden (D-DE), Secretary of State Madeleine Albright, and Vice President Albert Gore, whose campaign for leaner government and fascination with "the information superhighway" made the USIA look cumbersome and obsolete. Feeling pressure to reap a "peace dividend" from America's victory, these leaders saw USIA as a Cold War relic that could now be dispensed with.[62]

During the 1990s, a few stalwarts argued that public diplomacy had other aims and served other regions. Some even went so far as to suggest that part of the peace dividend should be spent on renewed cultural and educational programs, to provide ballast in a world set adrift. But the bipartisan consensus was otherwise, because both Republicans and Democrats shared a triumphalist view of free enterprise. Watching people in the former Soviet bloc flock to American consumer goods, all concerned could easily feel enthusiastic about America's reputation being safely entrusted to the market.[63]

One indication of that sentiment was a change that occurred during the late-1980s US-USSR Bilateral Information Talks. Leading the 1988 delegation to Moscow was USIA director Wick, accompanied by several other government officials and business leaders, including publishers, media moguls, and Jack Valenti of the MPAA.[64] Just one year later, as the Communist regimes of Poland and East Germany were crumbling, the US delegation included no government officials, just business leaders. And while Wick still headed the delegation, he did so as a former government official now working as a representative of Rupert Murdoch's News Corporation. In Cull's pithy summation: "The private sector now seemed poised to move into the territory opened by the public diplomacy of the Reagan years."[65]

From the perspective of a senior foreign service officer whom I met in China, the result was all too clear: "We dropped off the cultural stage after the Cold War ended. The argument in Washington was, 'America is out there.' But we tried to explain, 'We don't get any benefit from what is out there!'"

THE ECLIPSE OF AMERICAN HIGH CULTURE

This situation remains basically unchanged in the second decade of the twenty-first century. America does get some benefit from what is out there, as argued in Chapter 4. But the nation gets no benefit from the fact that its rich artistic and literary heritage is now all but unknown, even in countries where the public still has a favorable opinion of the United States.

In Poland, for example, the memory of Yale Richmond's cultural center has long since faded, and the vast majority of Poles associate America with blockbuster films and hard rock bands. In Warsaw I spoke with a professor of American studies (one of a handful at Polish universities) who recalled with wry amusement having been stopped for a minor traffic violation and asked what she did for a living. (Polish police are evidently more inquisitive than their American counterparts.) "When I told him I taught American literature," the professor told me, "the officer burst out laughing and said, 'That's impossible, there's no such thing!'"[66] On the other side of the globe, an American diplomat studying Mandarin in Beijing expressed a desire to discuss *meiguo wenming,* or American civilization, only to be told by his Chinese teacher that such a discussion was not possible, because "those two words don't go together."[67]

Further evidence of the current invisibility of American high culture comes from Simon Anholt, co-publisher of the Anholt-GfK Roper Index, an annual survey that asks a thousand respondents in each of twenty countries to rank fifty nations by such criteria as "governance," "people," "tourism," and "investments." In this index, the United States consistently ranks near the top for "popular culture" but near the bottom for "culture and heritage." Asked about this disparity, Anholt replied that "the old idea that the US is only good for popular culture and commerce has now hardened into a very negative perception."[68]

American cultural diplomacy has long sought to offset such negative perceptions. In 1998, when the USIA was about to be closed down, its director, Joseph Duffey, warned against leaving "the portrayal of American culture . . . exclusively to the mainstream media." With remarkable prescience, he continued:

While the United States enjoys a dominant position in the production and exportation of entertainment products, it remains debatable whether these products best serve America's broader interests and ultimately democracy itself. . . . [If] morally questionable programming is viewed as destructive to the moral fiber of American citizens, then what can be said of such programming when it is given wider airing on the international stage? On the one hand, it can have the same corrosive effect in countries that embrace American entertainment. . . . On the other hand, in countries that are repelled by American and Western values, such as those in the Pacific Rim, espousing a new "neo-Confucianism," or Islamic countries that reject Western secularism, such programming only confirms the worst suspicions that the West, and America in particular, is morally corrupt and intellectually devoid.[69]

However prescient, this analysis had zero political traction in 1998—three years before September 11, 2001.

MEANWHILE, IN THE MIDDLE EAST

One reason why political Islam succeeded in the 1970s was because it represented the West not in terms of its economic, political and scientific achievements, but in terms of what was perceived as its libertine lifestyle.
—Nabil Khatib, executive editor, Al Arabiya News Channel[70]

In the spring of 2008 I hosted a panel discussion on public diplomacy at Boston College. The key speakers, Yale Richmond and William Rugh, were both veterans of USIA and the State Department who are highly respected for their service and writings (Rugh also served as US ambassador to Yemen and the United Arab Emirates). Because the two men had so much in common, I was surprised to learn that they had never met before. They were not surprised, however, because as they pointed out, their careers unfolded in different worlds.

Richmond's career unfolded in the Soviet sphere, where, as noted above, America's counterculture fueled youthful protest. But it's important to remember that rock music was hardly the whole picture. In Poland, for example, a quite different force was at work. Pope John Paul II (born Karol Józef Wojtyła in Wadowice) was the first pontiff to visit a Communist country. When he arrived in Poland in 1979, his motorcade from the Warsaw airport was greeted by two million Poles shouting, "We want God!"[71] At an open-air mass the pope blessed a group of visiting Czech Catholics, whose banner made no reference to the Plastic People of the Universe.[72]

The conclusion to be drawn here is that not all those who revolt against tyranny are fired by the spirit of anarchy. It can be liberating to engage in outrageous behavior to violate the norms of a repressive regime. But when a regime is seen as vicious and corrupt, the revolutionary is more likely to be cast as an upright, god-fearing figure, fired by the need to restore virtue to the realm. Historically, this second scenario is much more common, and it is certainly the way millions of Muslims, not just terrorists, have conceived of their struggle against the repressive regimes that, with US support, have until recently held sway in the Arab and Muslim Middle East. This is hard for Americans to accept, because we are accustomed to seeing ourselves as virtuous liberators, not vicious oppressors.

Such is the arena where William Rugh's career unfolded. As he and his fellow "Arabists" are well aware, there was a time in the Middle East when America was seen in a quite favorable light. After World War II, the USIA opened three cultural centers in Egypt, and they flourished through the 1950s. Indeed, in 1955 the agency persuaded President Gamal Abdel Nasser to write a preface to *The Truth About Communism*, a book published by the USIA, and to require all high school students to visit an American library.[73] Of course, 1955 was also when mounting tensions with Israel, and an American refusal to sell weapons to Egypt, led Nasser to pivot toward the Soviet Union.[74] But as evidenced by the careers of both Richmond and Rugh, the more volatile the political situation, the more vital the cultivation of long-term relationships. When a foreign population is adamantly opposed to US policy, no amount of advocacy can win them over. That is precisely when the smart cultural affairs officer changes the subject.

For example, Rugh writes that when Nasser began to tighten restrictions on US officials in the late 1950s, an exception was made for Bill Lovegrove, the cultural affairs officer in Cairo. Not only did Lovegrove bring in "artists and performers people wanted to see," he also gave the impression he "was not interested in politics," which made Egyptians "more comfortable with him." The upshot was that Lovegrove "was able to have more discussions than others about American society and culture with important Egyptians, which under the circumstances was very worthwhile."[75] Equally worthwhile were the one-month tours of the United States arranged for emerging leaders—including Anwar Sadat.[76]

These efforts came to an abrupt halt in 1967, when Egypt, Jordan, Syria, and their Arab supporters suffered a painful defeat in the Six-Day War against Israel. Believing Nasser's widely broadcast claim that America had directly aided Israel, several Arab countries broke diplomatic relations with Washington. Not

surprisingly, this break caused a decline in the number of aspiring foreign service officers taking up the study of Arabic language and culture. And as sympathy for Israel swelled in the United States, many seasoned Arabists in the
diplomatic corps found their influence withering—unless they tried mightily,
as some did, to distance themselves from Israel's Arab enemies.[77]

The timing of this rupture could not have been worse. In 1966 Nasser's
government executed Sayyid Qutb, the writer and activist who, together with
Mawlana Mawdudi in Pakistan and Ruhollah Khomeini in Iran, developed the
main tenets of political Islamism—a call to Muslims to join together in a global
Umma (community of the faithful), overthrow their secular, postindependence
governments, and build a new caliphate to stand as a bulwark against the materialism and moral degeneracy of the West. The eminent French scholar Gilles
Kepel considers Qutb "the greatest ideological influence on the contemporary
Islamist movement."[78]

In the United States Qutb is best known for having paid a Tocquevillian visit
in 1948 but not having responded with Tocquevillian impartiality. Sent by the
Egyptian government to study US educational methods, Qutb spent six months
in Greeley, Colorado, a community founded in 1870 as a self-conscious exercise
in postmillennial perfectionism, whose devout Christian settlers were vetted
for temperance, literacy, and civic-mindedness. In the vision of the town's promoter and supporter, *New York Tribune* editor Horace Greeley, the town would
stand as a bulwark against the moral degeneracy of the *American* West.

By all accounts, these virtues were still evident in 1948. But they were lost on
Qutb, who described Greeley as a garish Babylon whose residents had "reached
the peak of growth and elevation in the world of science and productivity, while
remaining abysmally primitive in the world of the senses, feelings, and behavior." His best-known observation is of a church social where "the dance floor
was replete with tapping feet, enticing legs, arms wrapped around waists, lips
pressed to lips, and chests pressed to chests."[79] Making matters worse for the
Egyptian visitor, the pastor himself dimmed the lights and played the hit record
"Baby It's Cold Outside."[80]

This incident is usually played for laughs, as in a 2003 National Public Radio
piece comparing Qutb's memories with those of elderly Greeley residents who
had attended church socials in the 1940s. About the dance, one gentleman remarked, "Boy, I must have missed something. I'd be interested in knowing what
church that was. Couldn't have been the Baptist." About Qutb's image of "the
American Temptress" whose "seductiveness lies in the round breasts, the full
buttocks, and in the shapely thighs," and whose dress seeks to "awaken primal

sensations," two ladies recalled wearing "skirts and blouses," "bobby socks rolled down," and "saddle shoes."[81]

Clearly, Qutb had some hang-ups. But before some Hollywood producer green-lights a comedy called *The 42-Year-Old-Virgin Goes to the Rockies*, consider this comment by another Greeley senior: "If he described it that way last year, I would buy into it."[82] It's one thing to laugh at the prudishness of Qutb, who never married (it is said) because the women in his village were too backward and those in Cairo too forward.[83] It is quite another to laugh at the offense taken by millions of devout Muslims in the 1970s, when large numbers of them had their first encounters with American culture. In deeply conservative societies such as Iran and Egypt, this encounter reinforced existing views of the West as godless, decadent, and dangerous. Needless to say, the 1970s were also a time of rising opposition to US policies in the Middle East. But hated policies are more hated when the people shaping them appear morally repugnant.

Mardo Soghom, an Iranian journalist working for Radio Free Europe/Radio Liberty in Prague,[84] is not a religious man. But he recalled the culture shock brought by Americans to his home city of Esfahan. Between 1973 and 1977, he told me, after the price of oil went up and the Shah could afford to buy fighter jets and other US arms, "there was a big service center in Esfahan, so they brought in mechanics, weapons systems experts, instructors, language teachers. They came in the thousands, very suddenly." These were not the first Americans in Esfahan, but the earlier visitors were teachers, missionaries, or experts in various fields who were far fewer in numbers and kept mostly to themselves. The new wave of Americans "mingled with the population, and many people were shocked by their behavior—especially that of younger Americans. Alcohol was legal then, and teenagers would hang around liquor stores wearing shorts and carousing. They weren't tourists passing through. They stayed and partied, at a time when Iranians were supersensitive to the fast social changes and worried about their kids."[85]

A similar situation arose in Egypt in 1973, when Nasser's successor as president, Anwar Sadat, broke with the Soviet Union and embarked on an *Infitah* (Open Door) policy toward the United States. In 1974 President Nixon visited Cairo and received what Thomas Lippman, a veteran Middle East correspondent for the *Washington Post*, calls "a tumultuous welcome" that "revealed a reservoir of pro-American sentiment that had survived years of official hostility."[86] Soon Egypt was attracting US aid, military cooperation, and business investment, and Sadat was hosting lavish visits by Hollywood celebrities such as Elizabeth Taylor and Frank Sinatra.[87]

Yet as Lippman adds, the same "policies that gave the Egyptians more access to Western ideas, films and publications" also made them mindful of the dangers of "extramarital sex or drugs for their children or free choice in vocation or marriage or pornography on the newsstands." Most Americans would draw a line between "free choice in vocation and marriage" on the one hand, and the rest of these items, especially drugs and pornography, on the other. But for Egyptians the line was harder to draw, as a segment of elite youth in Cairo began to wear blue jeans, play rock music, and experiment with alcohol and drugs. Lippman gives the example of a young man named Ismail Hakim, the son of a well-known playwright and a great fan of the American rock musician Jimi Hendrix. Unfortunately, Hakim did not imitate just his idol's guitar playing. He also imitated his addictions, dying of substance abuse in 1978.[88]

Strikingly, an even larger segment of Egyptian youth rejected these American influences as a form of "Westoxification."[89] And as Lippman reports, this larger segment did not consist solely of the poor, the rural, and the uneducated. On the contrary, rejection of American and Western cultural influences was the dominant view among the educated sons and daughters of the striving middle class:

> The gap between university students who wear traditional Islamic dress and go to religious meetings and those who wear jeans and spend their time at expensive watering holes was visible and volatile. Egyptians of every shade of political opinion were at least uncomfortable with the sudden emergence of Cairo as an international playground. . . . The story of Ismail Hakim was upsetting even to the Westernized bourgeoisie; to the religious activists, it was just more evidence of what they already knew.[90]

AN OPPORTUNITY MISSED

During the 1970s the American counterculture inspired youth and dissidents in Europe and the USSR. But its celebration of personal liberation had the opposite effect in the Arab and Muslim world. With the notable exception of the Gulf kingdoms, this celebration was, if not embraced, then tolerated by Westernized elites seeking to modernize their nations. At the time, Western and Western-educated intellectual elites assumed that religion was a residue of the past that would inevitably fade away as traditional societies advanced into the modern world.[91] Based on this assumption, the forward-looking leaders of Turkey, Egypt, and Iran waged aggressive campaigns against customs and beliefs considered "backward," especially those of Islam.

This provoked a powerful backlash, which would not have surprised Tocqueville, whose far-reaching critique of the French Revolution included a harsh judgment of its aggressive antireligious stance. Because belief in a transcendent reality "is as natural to the human heart as hope itself," he wrote, "men detach themselves from religious belief by a sort of intellectual aberration." Thus, Tocqueville predicted that any regime which tries to suppress religion in the name of liberty will end up suppressing liberty itself.[92]

At the same time, Tocqueville shared with the American founders the conviction that religious fanaticism is a critical source of faction and civil strife. But he also appreciated the argument, set forth in the writings of Jefferson, Madison, and others, that the fault lies not with religion but with the conjoining of religion and political power. As Tocqueville wrote, "Religion cannot share the material strength of the rulers without being burdened with some of the animosity roused against them."[93]

This is why American religious institutions have flourished: they are not conjoined with political power, so they are not ordinarily burdened with the animosity it arouses. But at the same time, the Free Exercise Clause of the First Amendment ensures that religiously based opinions can be freely expressed in the public square.[94] This is why, in the second decade of the twenty-first century, a small number of Muslims, including some Islamists, believe that rather than being destructive to faith, the American regime of religious liberty actually helps it to survive—and thrive. The source of this insight is the American political tradition. But Americans did not try to share it with the Islamists of the 1970s. If they had, it might have made all the difference.

7

US INTERNATIONAL BROADCASTING

Beginning in the 1920s, the world's governments turned to the new medium of radio as a way to influence public opinion in other countries. The Netherlands in 1927 was first, followed in the 1930s by the Soviet Union, fascist Italy, Britain (with the "Empire Service"), France, Nazi Germany, and imperial Japan. America was slow to enter the fray, owing to its tradition of press freedom, private ownership, and aversion to state-sponsored media. But in 1941 President Roosevelt became alarmed at the amount of Nazi propaganda flowing into Latin America and initiated anti-Nazi broadcasts into that region.

Since then, the US government has continually used a range of media, from radio to satellite television to the Internet, to broadcast a variety of messages to the rest of the world. I say *broadcast* because, despite occasional ventures into "dialogue" and the current fascination with social media, the overwhelming thrust of this communication effort has been "one to many," with the "one" being the US government and the "many" being the particular audiences it deems relevant at any given time.

The history of US international broadcasting is confusing, because unlike similar efforts in other nations, it was not built on the foundation of an existing media organization. The obvious contrast is with British international broadcasting, which emerged from an older government-owned radio service, the British Broadcasting Corporation (BBC). Founded in 1922, the domestic BBC had been in existence for a decade before the Empire Service (as it was then called) was launched in 1932. Today the renamed World Service is connected with, and shares a brand name with, the domestic BBC. There is no American equivalent to this. On the contrary, our brand-name broadcaster, the Voice of America (VOA) did not emerge from any domestic broadcasting service, public or private.

Even more confusing is the fact that the VOA is one of several entities constituting US international broadcasting (*entity* is the term of art used for the various broadcast services). Each of these entities has a different history. The VOA
began life in 1942 as a German-language channel intended to penetrate Nazi
Germany, then grew into a worldwide service operating in dozens of languages.
Radio Free Europe (RFE) began in 1949 as a CIA-funded service, based in
Munich and providing news and information to East Germany and the other
satellite nations that had come under Soviet domination. Radio Liberty (RL),
also CIA-funded, provided the same service to the Soviet Union. Like the VOA,
RFE and RL broadcast in dozens of languages and were typically staffed by
émigrés under American supervision. In 1972 the CIA ceased funding these
entities, and in 1974 they were joined together as RFE/RL and became a direct
grantee of Congress. When the Cold War ended, RFE/RL moved its headquarters from Munich to Prague. While RL continues to broadcast to Russia, RFE
has shifted its focus to the former Soviet republics of Central Asia and (more
recently) to Iraq, Iran, Afghanistan, and the border region between Afghanistan
and Pakistan, causing insiders to joke that it should now be called "Europe-Free
Radio."

Three more entities have appeared over the years. In 1983, the Office of
Cuba Broadcasting (OCB) began broadcasting into Fidel Castro's Cuba. In
1996, Radio Free Asia (RFA) began transmitting to China and eight other East
Asian countries. And in 2002 and 2004, two Arabic-language services, Radio
Sawa and Al-Hurra television, entered the transnational Arab market.

This landscape would be easier to survey if these entities all fit together as
neatly as do the various branches of the BBC. Since 1999 they have been under
the purview of a single oversight body, the Broadcasting Board of Governors
(BBG), answerable to the State Department. But this has not created coher-
ence, in part because the nine members of the BBG are part-time appointees,
most of whom lack the skills and background necessary for effective oversight of
such a complex undertaking. The BBG includes the secretary of state as an ex
officio member, but as one observer has noted, "State Department interest and
involvement [in the BBG] has dwindled to the vanishing point."[1] In Washington, there is a near consensus that the BBG was badly conceived, and that it has
created more problems than it has solved. Some call for greater centralization
along the lines of the British system, but this idea meets resistance because each
of the entities has a distinct history, organizational culture, and constituency.

These bureaucratic issues are important, because they hamper the ability
of US international broadcasting to work as well as it should. But this chapter
focuses less on the organizational challenges than on the conceptual ones. As

discussed in Chapter 6, much has changed since the early Cold War, when the point of US public diplomacy was to send messages of freedom through the Iron Curtain. These changes include the rise of a disruptive counterculture in the 1960s; the conservative backlash and culture war that followed; and the fateful decision, during the triumphalist 1990s, to entrust America's reputation to the commercial media. Owing to these changes, quite a few Americans now find the whole idea of government-sponsored broadcasting to foreign countries obsolete or repellent. This sentiment is at times justified, but as I argue below, there are still compelling reasons to retain most of the entities that constitute US international broadcasting.

Like the rest of public diplomacy, US international broadcasting requires the balancing of multiple, overlapping, sometimes conflicting goals. The entities differ in how they achieve, or fail to achieve, the appropriate balance. But all of them must give some weight to each of three goals:

1) *Reporting the news.* This goal is to broadcast news about America, other countries, and the world in a way that upholds the norms of professional journalism. These norms include truthfulness, accuracy, thoroughness, and fairness. These norms have changed over time, as the scrupulously objective stance taken by the mainstream US media during the first half of the twentieth century was challenged in the 1960s by a new generation of journalists who, rather than claim objectivity, reported from an openly acknowledged political perspective. Since then, "advocacy journalists" have insisted that reporting from an explicit perspective is not the same as indulging in bias or engaging in propaganda. Indeed, they claim to respect the facts and opposing perspectives as much as, or more than, the mainstream media do. (Note: Because I am already using *advocacy* to describe one of the four goals of public diplomacy, I do not use the term *advocacy journalism* in this chapter. Not surprisingly, advocacy is also one of the goals of US international broadcasting [see below]. To refer to the type of journalism that appeared in the 1960s, I will use the term *perspective-based journalism.*)

As noted in the prologue to Part Two, a major emphasis in US broadcasting is the provision of "surrogate" (substitute) news reporting to countries where the media are tightly controlled by the government. More than any other task undertaken by US international broadcasters, surrogate news reporting is the most suffused with a sense of mission and high purpose.

2) *Conveying a "full and fair picture of American life."* The phrase is President Harry Truman's, part of a speech justifying the continuation of

public diplomacy after World War II. Expressing the hope that "private organizations and individuals in such fields as news, motion pictures and communications will, as in the past, be the primary means of informing foreign peoples about this country," Truman suggested that the government's role was to make sure the picture received by "other peoples" was "full and fair."[2] In the context of international broadcasting, this goal is most closely associated with the Voice of America. But it is never wholly absent from the other broadcast entities. And while this goal is admittedly amorphous, it is critically important, not least as a counterweight to the fun-house-mirror images conveyed by popular culture.

3) *Advocating for US government policy.* This goal—to explain, defend, and seek support for US government policy—is identical to the public-diplomacy goal by the same name. And just as advocacy often conflicts with the other goals of public diplomacy, so too does it conflict with the other goals of international broadcasting. Many journalists involved in US international broadcasting would like to eliminate this tension by getting rid of advocacy. But that is not likely to happen. Advocacy is an inescapable part of any government's communication with the world. As such, it is worth doing—and doing well.

The focus of this chapter is on how successfully these goals have been balanced by the various entities constituting US international broadcasting. I begin with the VOA, whose formal charter reflects the three goals listed above, and consider the reasons why it has come to emphasize the first, news reporting, at the expense of the other two. I then consider the main challenge now facing the VOA and all the other broadcast entities: the adoption, by twenty-first-century authoritarian regimes, of the worst formulas of America's commercial news media; and the rejection, by those same regimes, of America's best tradition of press freedom.

Next my analysis turns to Radio Free Europe/Radio Liberty (RFE/RL), the Office of Cuba Broadcasting (OCB), and Radio Free Asia (RFA). Historically, these entities have focused on surrogate news reporting. And for them, the main challenge has always been working with émigrés who know the countries and languages but have yet to learn the difference between professional journalism and oppositional propaganda.

Finally, this chapter looks at the latest addition to US international broadcasting: two commercial-style channels aimed at the Arabic-language market, Radio Sawa and Al-Hurra television. Created by the BBG shortly after 9/11, these entities reflect both the shortcomings of the BBG and the view, prevalent at the time, that America's commercial media are uniquely skilled at communicating with the world. Today, after a decade of war and upheaval in the Arab Middle East, the limitations of that view are evident. And so is its corrosive impact on all three goals of US international broadcasting. Thus, I end this chapter with some suggestions (continued in the conclusion) for how to renew the three goals for today's very different political and media environment.

THE VOICE OF AMERICA

The VOA is associated with the Cold War, but as noted above, it actually began in February 1942, with the first US-sponsored radio broadcast that went into Nazi Germany. That broadcast opened with the words: *Heir spricht eine Stimme aus Amerika* (Here speaks a voice from America). The name stuck, and by war's end the VOA was broadcasting in twenty-seven languages. After the war, the VOA was cut back, then rebuilt amid mounting tension with the Soviet Union. In 1953 it was incorporated into the US Information Agency, where it remained until the USIA was dissolved in 1999, at which point it became a stand-alone federal agency under the purview of the BBG. In 2012 the VOA celebrated its seventieth birthday as America's official international broadcaster, every week sending 1,500 hours of programming in forty-three languages to an estimated global audience of 123 million. And like the other entities, the VOA now communicates via radio and every other existing media platform, from satellite television to the Internet and social media.[3]

From the start, the VOA's main challenge has been to balance the goals of news reporting and advocacy. But for the first several years, this balance was fairly easy to achieve, owing to a shared sense of mission regarding the need to be truthful and to avoid engaging in blatant propaganda. This part of the story begins with a principled rejection of propaganda rooted in lessons learned by the British and Americans after the First World War.

In 1915 the British government disseminated a "report" detailing atrocities committed by German soldiers in Belgium. Some of the stories were true, but many were not. Indeed, the most lurid accounts—of mass rape, mutilation, and child murder—had been fabricated to stir public hatred against the "Hun." In 1917 America followed suit, with the newly formed Committee on Public Information enlisting the fledgling film industry to help rally isolationist Americans to the cause. As noted in Chapter 5, the studios obliged by making films that amounted to little more than hate-mongering against Germany.

Only later, during the 1930s, did Britain and America realize how much damage their hate propaganda had done. For one thing, Adolf Hitler and Joseph Goebbels began to imitate it. For another, millions of people outside Germany refused to believe the early reports of Nazi atrocities, assuming that these stories, too, had been fabricated.[4] This realization prompted a change of heart going into World War II. Both the British and the American governments used psychological warfare in that conflict, needless to say. But when it came to communicating with large foreign populations, they took the relative high ground of refusing to spread blatant falsehoods. Hence the promise set forth in that first VOA broadcast: "The news may be good for us. The news may be bad. But we will tell you the truth."[5]

It is, of course, problematic for any government to characterize its wartime communication as *the truth*. But the VOA was facing an enemy whose stock in trade was "the big lie," as Hitler called it in *Mein Kampf*.[6] As noted by the VOA's first director, the actor and film producer John Houseman, it was only by being truthful about Allied setbacks in the early years of the war that the VOA's news reporting could "establish a reputation for honesty which we hoped would pay off on that distant but inevitable day when we would start reporting our own invasions and victories."[7] This same rejection of propaganda carried over into the VOA's other goal of advocacy for the Allied cause. Indeed, for the duration of World War II there was very little daylight between the VOA's two goals of truth-based advocacy and truthful reporting of the war (within the bounds of military security).

At war's end, the VOA was scheduled for termination. But as the Soviet Union tightened its grip on Eastern Europe and stepped up its propaganda efforts elsewhere, the VOA was given a new lease on life as part of the 1948 Information and Educational Act.[8] In 1951 it received a boost in funding as part of President Truman's "Campaign of Truth," only to run into trouble the following year, when Senator Joseph McCarthy (R-WI) and several other members of Congress accused it of harboring Communist spies.

As noted by former VOA director Alan Heil, the agency responded to "the McCarthy debacle" by enlisting its most dedicated journalists in the drafting of a charter outlining the agency's commitment to both truth-based advocacy and truthful reporting.[9] In 1976 this commitment was signed into law as the VOA Charter. The reader will note that the three goals of the charter replicate those of US international broadcasting more generally:

1) "VOA will serve as a consistently reliable and authoritative source of news. VOA news will be accurate, objective, and comprehensive."

2) "VOA will represent America, not any single segment of American

society, and will therefore present a balanced and comprehensive projection of significant American thought and institutions."

3) "VOA will present the policies of the United States clearly and effectively, and will also present responsible discussions and opinion on these policies."[10]

In the VOA as in other government agencies, it is up to the practitioner to balance these goals when they conflict. One who did so was Edward R. Murrow, the eminent journalist appointed USIA director by President Kennedy. Celebrated for his brave reporting from London during the Nazi blitzkrieg, and for testing the limits at CBS News with uncompromising documentaries such as *Harvest of Shame* (a 1960 film about the mistreatment of migrant farmworkers), Murrow uttered the oft-quoted dictum: "To be persuasive we must be believable; to be believable we must be credible; to be credible we must be truthful."[11]

Yet shortly after taking office at USIA, Murrow attempted to stop the British Broadcasting Corporation from airing *Harvest of Shame*, because the Kennedy administration feared the film would reflect badly on US agricultural interests. As reported by historian Nicholas Cull, "the BBC refused to pull the film and Murrow's attempt to censor his own journalism became a brief scandal. The slip was symptomatic of the degree to which Murrow had traded in his old journalistic hat for a new role in government."[12] Many VOA journalists saw this incident in the same light. For example, the VOA's veteran news director Bernie Kamenske dubbed Murrow "the man who invented truth," implying that the principled journalist had become an unprincipled propagandist.[13] But this accusation overlooks what Murrow was really trying to do, which was strike the proper balance between reporting the news and advocacy—as called for in the VOA Charter.

That balance became more elusive in the late 1960s. In 1965 the US authorities in Vietnam formed a Joint US Public Affairs Office (JUSPAO) to shape coverage of the war. This worked for a while, with reporters doing their job while also accepting the limits imposed by the military. But as the conflict grew, so did the number of journalists—from 20 in 1963 to 637 in 1968. And some began reporting on the differences between what they were hearing in JUSPAO's official press briefings (also known as the "Five O'Clock Follies") and what they were seeing on the ground.[14] The resulting "credibility gap" fueled protest back home and fostered distrust between American journalists and their government.

That distrust deepened in 1972–74, when the nation's leading news organizations—the *Washington Post*, the *New York Times*, *Time*, and the major broadcast networks—pushed for full exposure of President Nixon's involvement in the Watergate scandal. After his resignation in August 1974, Nixon reportedly told supporters that without the mainstream media's relentless pursuit of the story, "Watergate would have been a blip."[15] That same year, *Time* reported that applications to journalism schools reached a record high.[16]

Clearly, a new generation of journalists was abandoning the mainstream media's time-honored stance of objectivity, and embracing the new mode of reporting from an openly declared political perspective. In the domestic context, there's nothing wrong with perspective-based journalism; on many occasions it has served as democracy's safeguard. But in the context of international broadcasting, perspective-based journalism has a way of increasing the friction between the goal of news reporting and that of advocacy.

"A MAJOR SCOOP"

Friction became conflict on September 12, 2001. On that day, while the fires were still burning in the rubble of the World Trade Center and the Pentagon, the VOA aired an interview with a member of the Egyptian organization Al-Gama'a al-Islamiyya ("the Islamist Group"). By their own account, the producers wanted to include an Arab Islamist perspective on the terrorist attacks that had occurred the previous day. But while some members of Al-Gama'a al-Islamiyya had renounced violence, the organization was still associated in the public mind with the 1997 attack on tourists in Luxor, in which fifty-eight foreigners and four Egyptians were machine-gunned and hacked to death. So the interview outraged Congress and embarrassed the State Department. And later that same month, it came back to haunt the VOA when its news department scheduled an interview with Taliban leader Mullah Mohammed Omar.

Acting VOA director Myrna Whitworth later defended this second interview as "a major scoop," noting that "all the major news organizations had been clamoring to get an interview with Mullah Omar, but we got it."[17] But what Whitworth's comment overlooks is that the VOA is not a commercial news outfit chasing a scoop, it is an agency of the US government. The VOA was swiftly reminded of this fact when the State Department, still smarting from the political backlash against the Al-Gama'a al-Islamiyya interview, asserted its authority and scotched the Mullah Omar interview.

At a press conference announcing this decision, State Department official Richard Boucher did not accuse the VOA staff of providing "equal time for Hitler," as Senator Jesse Helms had recently done.[18] Instead, Boucher invoked the advocacy goal of US international broadcasting, as stated in the VOA Charter. Quoting the charter's call for "responsible discussions" on policy issues, Boucher stated, "We don't consider Mullah Omar to be a responsible discussant."[19] Just weeks after terrorists harbored by the Taliban had killed three thousand Americans, this seems a reasonable statement. But it was not taken as such by the 150 VOA employees who threatened to quit. Nor was it seen as reasonable by the many American and foreign reporters who joined with the Society of Professional Journalists in denouncing "any attempt by the US government to curb or sway free and fair news reporting and discussion."[20]

Ironically, many of those denouncing the VOA quoted Murrow—without acknowledging that if Murrow had been in Boucher's shoes, he would almost certainly have made the same call.

NEGLECTING THE SECOND AND THIRD GOALS

These incidents reflect the degree to which professional journalistic standards have changed, leading many VOA staff to see themselves as journalists first, government broadcasters second. Predictably, this self-definition causes them to neglect the second and third goals of the VOA Charter—and of US international broadcasting more generally. As outlined earlier, the charter's second goal is to "represent America, not any single segment of American society, . . . [through] a balanced and comprehensive projection of significant American thought and institutions." In other words, US international broadcasting should convey a full and fair picture of American life.

Does the VOA do this? A glance at the "USA" page of its English-language website suggests that this second goal is basically ignored. The page carries the same news headlines as any other domestic news site, the only difference being the addition of a little more context than would be needed by American readers. The coverage of American society, culture, and institutions is spotty and superficial. And the only element that came close to fulfilling this second goal, a folksy blog about America's highways and byways, was removed in 2012.[21] The visitor seeking a full and fair picture of American life will be disappointed.

The third goal of the VOA Charter is advocacy: to "present the policies of the United States clearly and effectively," along with "responsible discussions and opinion on these policies." Today this goal is not ignored so much as marginalized, as the VOA's advocacy is confined to the production of "editorials" set apart from the news. This policy was initiated by the Carter administration as a way to draw a bright line between opinion and news, thereby affirming the VOA's journalistic independence. But in 1982 the editorials, written by Reagan appointees, became harder-hitting, provoking resentment on the part of the VOA staffers obliged to put them on the air.[22]

Today, the VOA's editorials are the opposite of hard-hitting. Composed by cautious bureaucrats and massaged sometimes by as many as eight State Department offices, they have been reduced to what one VOA editor calls "a weird, bland thing that nobody wants to read, let alone translate and include in their broadcast." The VOA English-language website places the link for "Editorials" at the very bottom of the page, where few visitors will notice it. And when the link is opened, it becomes immediately apparent from the anodyne materials presented there that effective advocacy is no longer a VOA priority.[23]

SHARING THE MISSION OF SURROGATE NEWS

In recent years the VOA has become intensely focused on surrogate news reporting. This is not a new departure for the VOA—after all, the agency began life as a surrogate news service into Nazi Germany. But this shift has been viewed by some of the other entities as an encroachment into their territory. Joan Mower, an Africa expert and VOA veteran, told me that the VOA turned to surrogate broadcasting in 1999, when the USIA was dismantled and the VOA, which had been part of the USIA, was reorganized as a stand-alone federal agency under the oversight of the BBG. "A lot of people welcomed that change," Mower explained, "because they saw it as an opportunity to do less advocacy and more journalism."[24] A news director at one of the other broadcast entities commented that "VOA wants to do surrogate news because that's what the people in their service areas want."

For example, the VOA now operates a Pashto-language news channel in the Afghan-Pakistani border region. To some degree this channel duplicates the efforts of RFE/RL (indeed, the two services share the same regional transmission facility).[25] According to Tayyeb Afridi, a Pakistani journalist who has worked for Pakistani state radio in the region, these "American Radios" are basically the same: valuable because "they talk about security, politics, human rights and freedom," but limited because (in Afridi's opinion) "they can't criticize US policy toward Pakistan."[26]

A more visible example of VOA surrogate broadcasting is the Persian News Network (PNN), a satellite TV service to Iran. Owing to that nation's strategic importance, both the PNN and Radio Farda (RFE/RL's Persian-language service) are better funded than most comparable entities. But to judge by two internal reviews, one in 2009 and another in 2011, the production values and, more important, editorial standards of the PNN are inferior not only to those of the Persian service of the BBC World Service, but also (in some ways) to those of Iranian state television.[27] Not surprisingly, the PNN also neglects the second and third goals of the VOA Charter (representing America and advocacy).

Yet the PNN can boast one success. Many Iranians, especially urban youth, are interested in American popular culture, so in 2008 the PNN's flagship program became a version of *The Daily Show with Jon Stewart,* called *Parazit.*[28] Hosted by two Iranian Americans based in Washington, *Parazit* reached a significant audience, despite heavy jamming by the Iranian government (*Parazit* means "static" in Farsi). It also circulated widely on social media.[29] *Parazit* ended in 2012, reportedly because of disagreements between its two hosts. But as other entities contemplate similar efforts to reach urban youth in their target countries, a question arises: Did this program, modeled on an American show with a mocking attitude toward serious journalism, represent the best use of the VOA's limited resources?

Highly relevant to this question is the decision of the Iranian authorities to produce a clone of *Parazit* on state television. To some Western observers, this is evidence of *Parazit*'s success.[30] But surely this is the wrong measure. In commercial entertainment, being copied is proof of popularity, and popularity is the sole measure of success. In surrogate broadcasting, by contrast, the point is to provide foreign audiences with news and information that their government does not want them to receive. In that context, being copied should be interpreted as evidence of failure. This is not to suggest that the VOA should have dropped *Parazit.* Political satire has often played a role in surrogate broadcasting, and if *Parazit*'s barbs were sharper than those of the state-authorized show, then by all means it should have continued. But just as *The Daily Show with Jon Stewart* is not a substitute for real political news and debate in America, neither is *Parazit* a substitute for serious news reporting.

"THE WORST FORMULAS OF AMERICAN BROADCAST JOURNALISM"

A seasoned editor in both the private-sector media and at RFE/RL, Jay Tolson was working for the BBG in Washington when I asked him about the challenges facing US international broadcasting. His reply was straightforward: "One of the biggest challenges is that the worst formulas of American broadcast journalism are now being repeated in authoritarian countries. The rulers of Russia, China, Iran, and other closed societies now realize you can let people chatter about nothing all day, and nothing will come of it. What they don't allow is the model of Western print journalism, with its in-depth reporting and analysis."[31]

Chapters 3 and 4 discussed the wide range of entertainment media permitted in contemporary authoritarian regimes. A similar permissiveness is found in their news media, which can appear free to the casual observer, but are not free in the ways that matter most. Apart from a few pockets of serious journalism, typically intended to have a high profile in the West, news organizations in these countries are not expected to be truthful, accurate, thorough, or fair. Instead, as noted by Tolson, they are encouraged to attract audiences—and advertising revenue—by whatever means necessary. So they recycle the worst formulas of American broadcast journalism.

These formulas are three. First is "soft news," or "infotainment," which mimics the trappings of news broadcasts but focuses on celebrity gossip, tabloid-style coverage of scandal and crime, and confessional interviews in the style pioneered by ABC's Barbara Walters. Second is the polemical talk show, featuring heavily biased reporting and personal attacks against political opponents. And third is the "headline news" format pioneered by CNN and now imitated by several other countries, including Russia, Iran, and China.

The first two formulas began to flourish in America after the repeal of the Fairness Doctrine in 1987. Here we see the importance of government regulation in sustaining the norms of professional journalism in the broadcast media, as opposed to the print media. America's major newspapers and news magazines still maintain fairly strict standards of truthfulness, accuracy, thoroughness, and fairness. But they do so as a matter of pride and tradition, not because of government regulation. And there are plenty of other print media that do not maintain these standards.

The broadcast media are different. From the beginning, the government has had an interest in regulating the airwaves, and in 1949 the Fairness Doctrine was established by the Federal Communications Commission (FCC) to require the holders of broadcast licenses to devote a certain amount of airtime to controversial public affairs, and to do so in a manner that included opposing views. This regulation was repealed in 1987 as part of the Reagan administration's push to deregulate the telecommunications industry.

It is no accident that Rush Limbaugh launched his influential radio talk show in 1988. For while the spirit of the Fairness Doctrine still presides over the "big three" networks (CBS, NBC, and ABC) and the Public Broadcasting Service (PBS), it has disappeared from talk radio, the Fox network, and cable TV channels such as MSNBC. Indeed, in all of these outlets (and much of the Internet), one-sided reporting, ad hominem attacks on perceived ideological opponents, and a glib, sarcastic tone have become the norm.

Needless to say, neither infotainment nor the polemical talk show is appropriate for US international broadcasting. If they were forbidden by authoritarian regimes, then there might be some reason to include them in a mix of programming that also included serious news reporting. But as suggested by the example of *Parazit*, neither infotainment nor the polemical talk show are forbidden. On the contrary, both formulas have been adopted by Russia, Iran, China, and other authoritarian regimes to earn advertising revenue and to try and convince viewers that their media are as free as those in the West.

The third formula, "headline news," is not so clearly a departure from serious journalism. The pioneer here was CNN International, with its reliance on short, rotating news segments, delivered in English and enlivened with on-the-ground video from the world's hot spots. This formula is very attractive to advertisers because it works well in airports, upscale hotels, offices, and other settings where busy, affluent people congregate. For this reason, its various clones now include Fox World News, BBC World News, DW-TV (Germany), France 24, NHK World (Japan), and two entries from the relatively free and open Arab media: Al-Jazeera English (Qatar) and Al-Arabiya English (on the Saudi-owned MBC network).

In recent years a number of authoritarian countries have created their own versions of CNN International. These include Russia Today, Iran's Press TV, and China's CCTV News. These channels embrace the headline news formula not only because it makes money, but because it lets them present an "open," modern face to the rest of the world, while at the same time slanting coverage in an ideologically approved manner. It might be objected that this is what all these headline news channels do. But there is a difference between the first group of channels listed above (including the two Arab channels) with their fairly consistent commitment to the norms of professional journalism, and the glaring omissions and pro-regime puffery found on Russia Today, Iran's Press TV, and CCTV News.

Just to cite one example, the British journalist Oliver Bullough offers this account of the journalistic practices of Russia Today (RT):

> RT does not lie, but it is selective about what facts it uses. . . . Russia is aggressively capitalist, with astonishing inequalities of wealth and rampant corruption. Male life expectancy lags behind that of countries such as Bangladesh. The state prosecutes opposition activists such as Pussy Riot, and 30 journalists have been murdered with impunity in the country since 1992. . . . And yet, RT campaigns on all these issues in *other* countries. . . . It reported on the Moscow protests in the winter of 2011–2012—but [editor in chief Magarita] Simonyan tweeted that the organizers would "burn in hell" and the reports lacked the detail of [RT's] work on Occupy [Wall Street]. That is a pattern that holds true for almost all matters that affect both Russia and the west.[32]

In a striking contrast with surrogate broadcasting, the CNN formula provides little of substance to audiences seeking accurate news about what is happening in their own backyard. The difference was made clear to me by Nabil Khatib, executive news director for Al-Arabiya: "The CNN-type channels . . . offer a very limited menu—the same 'short list' of stories, all given basically the same treatment. This may be fine for Westerners and others accustomed to having other sources of in-depth news. But it doesn't speak to the locals in many countries. The Sudanese laborer who is hungry and angry needs to have better information about what is going on in Sudan. But his concerns are not included."[33]

Twenty-first-century authoritarian countries do not allow serious professional journalism, political analysis, and debate, but they do allow nearly everything else. The audiences in these countries are no longer captive. Yet they are distracted, amused, and unlikely to gravitate automatically toward US-government-sponsored channels. Nearly everyone involved in US international broadcasting is aware of this changed environment. But there are sharp disagreements about how best to maintain a robust American presence within it. To some BBG members and staff, the best strategy is to emulate the commercial media: seek to maximize audience size (especially among the critical youth demographic) by playing down serious news and public affairs in favor of lighter fare, and by shifting from traditional media platforms such as radio and television toward the Internet and social media.

Others judge this commercial strategy to be self-defeating, and argue that US international broadcasting, instead of seeking to attract the largest possible audience, rather should seek to fulfill its three goals in such a way as to impact relevant elites. Yet it is also true that most of those now involved in US international broadcasting favor the first goal (news reporting) over both the second (conveying a full and fair picture of American life) and the third (advocating on behalf of US government policy). Later I will make some suggestions about how to remedy this neglect. But for now, let me endorse international broadcasters' sense of mission about surrogate news reporting in closed media environments. The vital importance of this kind of journalism is reinforced by the fact that while audience numbers for surrogate channels tend to be low during periods of calm, those numbers skyrocket during times of crisis or conflict, when listeners, viewers, and netizens realize that their own media are not telling them the truth.

RADIO FREE EUROPE/RADIO LIBERTY

This disagreement over how best to maintain a robust presence in today's changed media environment came into high relief in the winter of 2012–13, when a crisis erupted at Radio Liberty over its radio and Internet service to Russia. Promising to win a larger audience share in the crowded Russian market, a newly appointed RFE/RL director, a former CNN executive named Steve Korn, ordered a decrease in the amount of hard news and a corresponding increase in the amount of infotainment. Out went over forty Russian-language journalists, including some of Russia's most respected political reporters, and in came proposals for material that one Russian commentator likened to "in-flight magazines."

Korn's actions provoked a hue and cry at RFE/RL and rare scrutiny back in Washington. Yielding to political pressure, the BBG dismissed Korn and replaced him with Kevin Klose, a former RFE/RL director and more seasoned figure familiar with the goals of US international broadcasting. In May 2013 Klose accompanied two BBG members to Russia, and after meeting with "Russian media experts and champions of human rights and civil society," the BBG members called for the reinstatement of the fired Russian journalists and a redoubling of "US international media efforts in that country."[34] For the champions of the commercial model, this outcome was a defeat. For its opponents, it was a victory. Unfortunately, it did little to resolve the differences between the two sides.

TURNING EMIGRÉS INTO JOURNALISTS

Surrogate broadcasting got its start in 1946, when the US occupation authority in Berlin created a German-language service, called Radio in the American Sector (RIAS), to push back against Soviet-sector propaganda. In 1948, when the Soviets blockaded West Berlin, RIAS gained thousands of new listeners in East Berlin. This development inspired the German staff of RIAS to call for a more powerful short-wave transmitter to reach all of East Germany. The idea was not to speak on behalf of the United States, but to provide East Germans with accurate news about what was going on in both parts of Germany—something the Soviets forbade.

The Americans took to the idea, and soon similar broadcasts were reaching every Communist-ruled country in Eastern Europe—and a sister service, Radio Liberty, was penetrating the Soviet Union. These surrogate services were covertly funded by the CIA, just as the Congress for Cultural Freedom had been. But unlike the Congress for Cultural Freedom, RFE/RL survived the 1967 exposé and continued broadcasting from its base in Munich through the end of the Cold War. Then, amid debate over whether to eliminate RFE/RL, President Havel of the Czech Republic invited it to move to Prague and, in an ironic flourish, take up residence in the former Communist Party headquarters in Wenceslas Square. In 2009 RFE/RL moved again, to a new building, two subway stops away, that is better equipped to communicate via short-wave radio, medium-wave radio, local FM affiliates, satellite, Internet, and social media to audiences in twenty-two countries and regions.

RFE/RL still bears the taint of its CIA origins, in the sense that many people, not just critics but mainstream journalists, routinely refer to it as a propaganda outlet, implying that it focuses more on advocacy than on news reporting. This is hardly the case. RFE/RL has always focused on surrogate news reporting into closed societies lacking free media. But this presents a challenge, because while surrogate broadcasting cannot succeed without the language skills and fine-grained regional knowledge of émigrés, many of those émigrés are strangers to the journalistic norms of truthfulness, accuracy, thoroughness, and fairness. Indeed, some are so passionately opposed to the repressive rulers of their homelands that they are willing to broadcast anything that might weaken those rulers, including blatant propaganda.

This challenge was driven home during the Hungarian uprising of 1956, when some of the émigrés working for RFE's Hungarian service hinted in their broadcasts that if more people joined the uprising, the United States would come to their aid. Of the thousands killed by Soviet troops, it is impossible to say how many went into the streets having been influenced by RFE. But the bloodbath prompted the State Department to draft a set of guidelines for RFE/RL employees similar to those of the VOA Charter.[35]

Despite such excesses, surrogate broadcasting would not be possible without its émigré employees. During the Cold War, the staff contributed greatly to RFE/RL's extraordinary archive of information about the Soviet bloc, known as the "research unit." Sonia Winter, a former Czech national who worked in the research unit for several years, spoke to me in Prague about the grueling routine of staying on top of events while overseeing a team of analysts writing detailed reports: "Our research unit was legendary. Day by day, for years and years in the same regions, we built up a knowledge base that had no peer anywhere else."[36] Significantly, two primary subscribers of the RFE/RL research unit were the CIA and the BBC World Service.[37]

Russia expert Iain Elliot, who worked at Radio Liberty from 1987 to 1993, offered a concurring opinion: "Lofty-minded State Department types often failed to understand the USSR, with its layers upon layers of motives and priorities based on internal politics. Americans tend to assume that other actors are rational. Time and again, they would take some Soviet news item straight, without asking, 'Why was this reported now?' For the Russian editors at RFE/RL that question was second nature. So they were invaluable."[38]

The émigré staff was also crucial to RFE/RL's cultural programming. For example, two émigré intellectuals, Ruslan Gelischanow and Alexei Tsvetkov, recalled for me some of the programs carried on Radio Liberty. *Broadway 1776* highlighted Russian culture in New York. Another show featured Russian speakers reading literary works banned in the Soviet Union. *Atlantic Diary*, hosted by Tsvetkov, sought to interpret US politics, culture, and society for an intelligent Russian audience. "We admit our audience was small," Gelischanow remarked. "But it was also educated, influential, sympathetic to America." And as Tsvetkov added, "The idea was to correct the Mickey Mouse image Russians had of Americans as stupid and lowbrow."[39]

Radio Liberty underwent a transformation in the 1990s, for reasons practical and political. The practical reason was that fewer Russians were relying on short-wave receivers. During the Soviet era, the short-wave signal, which can travel great distances, was the dominant medium for broadcasting across Russia. It was also the only medium that US broadcasters could use to penetrate such a vast continental nation. (America's short-wave signals were jammed, but as the Soviet authorities knew all too well, jamming was extremely expensive.) After the Soviet collapse and the rise of independent media in the 1990s, Russian listeners began to abandon short-wave in favor of the FM signal, which cannot travel the same distances but has better sound quality.

It was during that heady decade, when Russia seemed to be moving in the direction of a wide-open media environment, that Radio Liberty adapted to this change by signing contracts with FM affiliates across Russia to carry its programming. But a few years later the political problem appeared. As part of his crackdown on private and independent media, Putin forced the cancellation of most of those contracts.

NEW SURROGATE SERVICES AT RFE/RL

Since 2001 three new surrogate services have been added to RFE/RL: Radio Azadi (serving Afghanistan), Radio Mashaal (serving Afghan-Pakistani border region), and Radio Farda (serving Iran). All of these channels carry programs produced in Prague, but they transmit from a variety of geographical locations, as well as via the Internet. In the case of Radio Azadi and Radio Mashaal, it has been possible to produce some programs in Kabul, Afghanistan. Throughout these broadcast regions, these surrogate services are under continual attack— by the Taliban, by Al-Qaeda and its offshoots, and by the Iranian government. So they, too, must struggle to teach their émigré staff the difference between responsible journalism and propaganda.

The most successful is Radio Azadi, which provides round-the-clock programming to roughly half of Afghanistan's adult population. Azadi uses a variety of media, but the most important is short-wave radio, which is widely used in Afghanistan because, in addition to covering long distances, it is also the most effective medium for reaching into remote mountain areas.[40] Wisely, Radio Azadi also relies on its émigré staff to shape programming for a region where religious and moral sensibilities are easily inflamed against America. Ahmedullah Takal, an Afghan journalist whom I spoke with in Prague, shared these observations about what it had taken to launch the service in Kabul:

> Afghan listeners do not like to hear voice-over translations. Even if they know that a professor from a certain university can talk about an issue, they prefer to hear it in their own language, not translated from a second language. Afghans also listen together in families, because family is so important. That is why one of our most popular shows is called *In Search of Loved Ones*, devoted to reuniting family separated during the war.[41]

As suggested by Takal's remarks, Radio Azadi includes non-news programming. Indeed, he had this to say about a comedy show, called *Pepper Jam*, that he developed: "Even in Afghanistan, people need to laugh. There's more to life than bombs and terrorism." Asked how he is able to judge what is in good taste and what is not, he smiled: "That's easy. I just remember my mother is listening. I keep her in my mind, because she is the kind of listener I hope our programs will reach."[42]

Radio Mashaal, which transmits into the Afghan-Pakistani border region, uses on-the-ground reporters to provide a more accurate account of local events than is given by the Taliban's virulently anti-American "mullah radios."[43] This kind of reporting is dangerous, as evidenced by the fate of a local radio journalist not connected with RFE/RL; he offended the Taliban by playing a song requested by both male and female listeners. The man was stabbed to death and beheaded in early 2012.[44] Yet in spite of the danger, some of these local reporters have learned how to make Radio Mashaal's surrogate mission a success. According to a Pakistani journalist familiar with the region, "Radio Mashaal does a good job of telling people what is going on in their surroundings."[45]

Finally, there is Radio Farda, which began broadcasting into Iran in 2002. Unlike Afghanistan, which allows Azadi and Mashaal to transmit within its borders, Iran is actively hostile to Farda. Consequently, its programs are produced in Prague and transmitted from locations outside Iran, notably Dubai. Launched shortly after 9/11, Farda was pressured from the beginning to reach as many young Iranians as possible. So it devoted 80 percent of its airtime to pop music. This caused a stir in Iran, where only state-approved religious music was permitted on the air. But as concerns mounted in Washington over Iran's support for terrorism and program to build a nuclear weapon, Farda was also pressured to provide high-quality surrogate news.[46]

Farda's response to this pressure has been to hire additional staff in Prague, but also to enlist the aid of reporters, bloggers, and citizen-journalists inside Iran. Some of these have indulged their anti-regime passions. But others have proved a rich source of fine-grained local news in a country where a large proportion of the population are heavy users of the Internet and social media.[47] As recalled by Jeffrey Gedmin, RFE/RL president between 2007 and 2011, "Farda has gone after corruption stories in ways others don't. We had something on the sad, bizarre story of dog prisons. Pets were being confiscated by authorities, ostensibly because pet dogs do not conform to the mullahs' vision of Islam. We've done hard-hitting reporting on fuel rationing. . . . If the leader of a bus drivers' union is arrested in Tehran and nobody else covers it, then that's our story. About 80 percent of what we do is domestic."[48]

These local reporters have been acclaimed for their courage. And courage is needed, because the Iranian government actively persecutes all independent journalists, including Farda's. Perhaps the most famous case is that of Parnaz Azima, a Farda reporter based in Prague, who traveled to Iran in 2007 to visit her ailing ninety-five-year-old mother. Immediately upon her arrival Azima was placed under house arrest for eight months, and when she was finally released, the authorities warned her that if she continued to work for Farda they would take away the deed to her mother's house. (Today Azima works for the VOA's PNN, and the situation with her mother's house is still unresolved.)[49]

Farda reporters and staff are also harassed in their Prague headquarters. According to Gedmin, "The Iranian government will summon one of our journalists to come home to face charges before a revolutionary court, and if they refuse to go, the government requires bail. If the journalists decline to pay that—a figure ranging from $50,000 to $100,000—then the government will often threaten to confiscate the property of a relative."[50]

THE OFFICE OF CUBA BROADCASTING AND RADIO FREE ASIA

RFE/RL is not the only broadcast entity focused on surrogate news. Two others have appeared since the 1980s—the Office of Cuba Broadcasting (OCB) and Radio Free Asia (RFA). The OCB began in 1983 with Radio Martí, named for the poet-patriot José Julián Martí Pérez and established at the behest of influential Cuban Americans. In 2010 the Office of the Inspector General for the BBG estimated the daily audience for Radio Martí at around 30 percent of the Cuban population.[51] TV Martí was added in 1990, but its audience size has been hotly disputed. For example, a 2011 congressional report estimated it at less than 2 percent of the population, while other reports based on refugee interviews produce higher figures.[52]

The most salient aspect of the OCB is its generous funding. Indeed, it could be argued that even if the OCB's audience were 100 percent of the Cuban population, its budget would still be disproportionate to those of its fellow surrogates.[53] For example, in 2012 the budget for the OCB, which broadcasts in one language to one small island, was $28 million. The comparable figure for RFE/RL, which broadcasts in twenty-eight languages to twenty-one countries (including Russia), was $93.2 million. For Radio Free Asia, which broadcasts in nine languages to six countries (including China), the figure was almost $41 million.[54]

Why the disparity? Like the émigrés at the other surrogates, the Cuban Americans who support the OCB are passionate about bringing freedom to their homeland. But unlike the others, these émigrés are US citizens who constitute a powerful domestic lobby. Owing to the proximity of Cuba, the OCB is unique among US international broadcasters in being able to transmit its signal from domestic US radio and TV stations. And as it happens, those stations belong to wealthy Cuban Americans who also contribute generously to both Republican and Democratic political campaigns.

Radio Free Asia (RFA) has no comparable domestic lobby. On the contrary, when it was launched in 1996, it had the support of human rights groups but not of the larger US business community, whose main concern (then as now) was to stay on Beijing's good side. The only previous effort to penetrate China had been in 1951, when a CIA-funded service (very different from today's RFA) had to be abandoned because its supporters came to realize that, unlike the Russians at the time, the Chinese did not own short-wave receivers. Today RFA faces the same challenge as Radio Liberty did in the 1990s: that of penetrating a large continent without being able to use the long-distance short-wave signal. But unlike Radio Liberty, which after the fall of Communism signed contracts with the Russian government to broadcast on local FM affiliates, RFA has never made any deals with the Chinese government. Instead, its Mandarin, Cantonese, Tibetan, and Uyghur programs are produced in Washington and transmitted from various locations outside China. These services also maintain a steady presence on the Internet, despite ongoing efforts by the Chinese government to block access to their sites.

Serving six countries (China, Burma/Myanmar, Cambodia, North Korea, Laos, and Vietnam) in nine languages (Mandarin, Cantonese, Burmese, Khmer, Korean, Lao, Tibetan, Uyghur, and Vietnamese), RFA reaches some of the least open societies on earth.[55] Yet its émigré journalists have managed to win numerous awards. Some of those awards have been for on-the-ground report-ing; others have been for advocacy—specifically, advocacy in favor of human rights. In 2011, the inspector general for the BBG found RFA "dedicated to its mission," blessed with "strong direction," and "creative" in meeting the chal-lenge of "providing accurate and timely news and information to Asian coun-tries whose governments prohibit access to a free press."[56]

THE BBG AND THE POST-9/11 ARABIC SERVICES

In 2002 the Broadcasting Board of Governors responded to the events of 9/11 by embarking on a new kind of international broadcasting in the Arab Middle East. This new model was presumed to be more effective because, instead of following the old charters and guidelines, it would emulate the methods of the commercial media. This did not turn out to be a prudent decision. But before tracing its consequences, let us step back and consider the BBG.

As noted above, the BBG has a poor reputation in Washington. Indeed, in federal workplace surveys its own employees have for the past several years ranked it near the bottom. For example, a 2011 survey of thirty-seven federal agencies found the BBG ranked thirty-third in job satisfaction, thirty-fifth in "results-oriented performance culture," thirty-sixth in "talent management," and dead last in "leadership and knowledgeable management."[57] In the pithy summary of Carnes Lord, a former staffer at the National Security Council who teaches military strategy at the Naval War College, the BBG is "a highly dysfunctional organization."[58]

The problem is partly structural. The eight members of the BBG are ap-pointed by the president on a bipartisan basis, with four from each party and the secretary of state serving as the ninth, ex officio member. One member serves as chairman, though the secretary of state has never served in that role. In theory, the BBG functions as a "collective CEO," with all nine individuals working together, sharing power, and making decisions based on consensus.[59] But in practice, the BBG has become an awkward blend of too much power and too little accountability. "With no one individual really in charge," writes Lord, "members have become accustomed to freelancing according to their own particular interests, setting up personal fiefs, and meddling in personnel and other operational issues, while not providing coherent overall direction or discipline to the enterprise as a whole."[60]

"We used to resent the USIA's dabbling," former VOA director Alan Heil told me, "but compared with the BBG, that would be paradise!"[61] There's a fine line between oversight and micro-management, and for many observers the BBG oversteps that line by making ill-informed decisions about such matters as hiring and firing and the expansion and contraction of various language services.

I have already mentioned the crisis that ensued when Radio Liberty was ordered by a new BBG-appointed director to cut back on serious political coverage in the winter of 2012–13. Earlier in 2012, around the time the Obama administration was declaring its intention to "pivot" toward East Asia, the BBG decided to cut three of the VOA's East Asian language services. And not just any three. The proposed cuts were to the Tibetan service, at a time when Tibetan Buddhist monks were immolating themselves in protest against Chinese rule; to the Cantonese service, at a time when Beijing was shutting down all Cantonese media in Guangdong Province (fifty million people) and possibly Hong Kong (another seven million) with the intention of replacing them with Mandarin media; and to the Burmese service, at a time when Burma/Myanmar was taking its first tentative steps toward democratic reform.[62]

To be sure, there was a bureaucratic rationale for each of these cuts, having to do with cost and efficiency.[63] But the citizen who seeks the long-term strategic justification for these decisions will unfortunately come up empty.

RADIO SAWA

Returning to 2002: the BBG's first response to the shock of 9/11 was to eliminate the VOA's Arabic service, on the ground that it was not reaching a sufficiently large youth audience. At the time, the VOA had been lobbying for funds to expand and improve that service, but its requests had been denied, in part because of its aforementioned blunders in offering airtime to known terrorists.

Meanwhile, the BBG board's most forceful member at that time—Norman J. Pattiz, founder and CEO of the giant Westwood One radio network—persuaded his fellow board members that he had a better idea. Based on the then-prevailing assumption that the private sector was immeasurably better than the US government at communicating, Pattiz proposed giving US international broadcasting a shot of commercial adrenalin. Media scholar Monroe Price summarizes the rationale:

Pattiz foresaw his innovation as breaking through the traditional distinctions between the Voice of America and the so-called surrogate radios. . . . Pattiz's vision transcends this divide by relying on a new model, one that would draw on commercial counterparts to overcome any ideological obstacle. This would be "a global, research-driven U.S. government broadcasting network" that fulfills the missions of both the surrogate radios and the Voice of America by broadening the distribution mechanisms and bringing them under one mode of control.[64]

Given the sense of urgency following 9/11, it is understandable that the BBG and Congress should have seized upon Pattiz's idea. His proposal was little more than an update on the prepackaged music format he had pioneered in US commercial radio, but he was an impressive entrepreneur, well positioned to make a persuasive case. During the 1970s and '80s, Pattiz had built a successful business distributing radio programs throughout the United States via satellite. He had also acquired a number of new properties, such as the Mutual Broadcasting System and the NBC Radio Network. That was why in 1988 he was invited to join the trade delegation to Moscow led by USIA director Charles Z. Wick.[65] During that trip (mentioned in Chapter 6), Pattiz signed an agreement to launch a commercial-style pop music channel in the Soviet Union. At the time, this agreement was understood as part of a new US-USSR trade initiative having no connection with US international broadcasting.

Pattiz's agreement fell apart when the Soviet regime collapsed three years later. But in early 2001 he and BBG consultant Bert Kleinman were in Qatar, proposing the creation of a similar channel for the transnational Arab market. "That was before September 11," Kleinman told me. "After September 11, the idea of reaching out to Arab youth with radio was clearly a thing the US needed to do. The idea received strong support from the Bush administration and approval by Congress." In other words, the same idea that had been part of a trade initiative back in 1988 was now being interpreted as a "new model" of US international broadcasting. As Kleinman commented to me, neither he nor Pattiz expected any return on this new channel: "We could have stayed in commercial radio, but this was service to our country."[66]

In 2002, Congress appropriated $36 million to launch Radio Sawa ("together"), a channel playing a mixture of American and Arabic pop music, interspersed with brief news segments. If Pattiz and Kleinman had expected to make a profit on this deal, that would not have been so bad. As shown in Chapter 5, there have been many occasions in the past when Hollywood film studios made a profit furthering the aims of the US government. Of course, Radio Sawa was different in being taxpayer-funded. But precisely for that reason, this "new model" of international broadcasting deserved more scrutiny than it was given by the BBG and Congress.

Indeed, someone should have asked whether an infusion of American and Arab pop music was an adequate response to the Islamist radicalization of Arab youth. As noted by former VOA director Robert Reilly, when the VOA used jazz and popular music during the Cold War, it did so "within a format devoted mainly to substance—news, editorials, and features." By adopting the format of commercial radio in the United States, Radio Sawa effectively reversed this ratio–and in the process reinforced "the image of America created by the popular media, [which] . . . often repels much of the world."[67]

Radio Sawa responded to this criticism by adding more news. But according to independent outside monitors, the kind of news it added had little nutritional value. Indeed, it consisted of short news segments that rarely went beyond the headlines disseminated by the Associated Press and other global news agencies.[68] This was because, as Kleinman explained to me in 2005, Radio Sawa's market research showed that young people "want news to be relatively short and up to the minute."[69] I am sure that Kleinman's research was correct, and such a finding would have been highly relevant to a commercial radio channel seeking to maximize audience size. But again, should this be a priority of US international broadcasting? As Reilly concludes, "Numbers of listeners certainly matter, but not as much as who is listening—and to what."[70]

In the wake of the Arab Spring, the most cogent criticism of Radio Sawa is that it fosters the impression among Arab youth that the US government neither understands nor respects their deeper concerns. In an interview prior to the uprising in Egypt, an American diplomat who spent many years in that country shared with me this prescient remark: "Young Egyptians feel disappointed when Americans reach out to them only as consumers. They don't crave iPods, they crave serious contact." To illustrate, the diplomat recalled attending a rock concert in Cairo and striking up a conversation with some audience members. Asked whether they were enjoying the concert, they replied, "It's OK, but we would much rather continue this conversation!"

AL-HURRA TELEVISION

Radio Sawa is one of two entities created in the immediate aftermath of 9/11. The other, joined with Radio Sawa in the Middle East Broadcasting Network (MBN), is Al-Hurra ("the free one"), a satellite TV service launched in 2004 at a start-up cost of $67 million. According to BBG staff director Jeffrey Trimble, Al-Hurra was conceived "in the grand tradition of Jim Lehrer [the veteran anchor of *PBS NewsHour*]: news, current affairs, and information."[71] But this comparison is misleading. The *NewsHour* is a single program, airing sixty minutes a day, five days a week; Al-Hurrah is a channel, broadcasting around the clock in the manner of other all-news channels in the transnational Arab market. Still, if the quality of Al-Hurra's programming were comparable to that of the *NewsHour*, then its hefty annual price tag ($32.2 million in fiscal 2012) might be justified.[72] But most observers agree that Al-Hurra got off to a rocky start and has yet to achieve its original goal of winning audiences away from such leading Arab news channels as Qatar's Al-Jazeera and Saudi Arabia's Al-Arabiya.

It makes sense for America to try to establish a presence in the Arab satellite TV market. As noted in Chapter 4, that twenty-four-nation market is more open and free than the Russian, Iranian, or Chinese markets. And while anti-American feeling runs high, that is all the more reason to present smart, state-of-the-art broadcasting that presents the US perspective in an accessible language and style. The problem with Al-Hurra is that it has never come close to doing this. On the contrary, its first few years were spent lurching from misstep to misstep while absorbing resources that the BBG might better have spent elsewhere.

The first misstep occurred in March 2004, when Al-Hurra chose not to cover the Israeli assassination of Hamas founder Ahmed Yassin. While the other Arab news channels were reporting live from Gaza City, Al-Hurra aired a cooking show featuring a dish—pork with red wine—that violated Islamic dietary laws. The next misstep occurred the following month, when amid the furor over prisoner abuse at Abu Ghraib prison, Al-Hurra aired an interview with President Bush that ended with him patting news director Mouafac Harb on the back, saying, "Good job!"[73] These blunders offended Arabs and many liberal Americans, but in 2006 Al-Hurra also managed to outrage many conservative Americans. First it broadcast a lengthy speech by Hezbollah leader Hassan Nasrallah, with no backgrounder describing his support for terrorism. Then, while covering a Holocaust deniers' conference in Iran, one of its reporters asserted, uncritically, that the Jews had "provided no scientific evidence of the Holocaust."[74]

Barraged with criticism, the BBG commissioned a study by the Center for Public Diplomacy at the University of Southern California. Completed in 2008, that study concluded that Al-Hurra was "not performing at the level that it needs to reach in order to be successful," and that its failures were "related to the fundamentals of journalism, not the exigencies of politics." Among the problems cited were "a lack of news and topical programming tailored to the interests of the Arab audience," "perceived bias," and "a lack of connection to the Arab street."[75] The BBG embargoed this report for several months, perhaps because its conclusions were so negative. Yet in practical terms, the most damning judgment was that of newly elected President Obama, who in January 2009 chose to give his first interview before the Arab TV audience not on Al-Hurra but on the Saudi-owned Al-Arabiya.[76]

Today, Al-Hurra is the go-to channel for speeches and press conferences by US decision makers, and for coverage of US policy debates pertaining to the Arab world. It also airs Arabic-subtitled versions of such US programs as PBS's *NewsHour*, *Frontline*, and *Nova*; CBS's *60 Minutes*; and A&E's *Biography* and *Modern Marvels*. Further, it carries a wide variety of talk shows and interview shows covering topics from women's rights to health, sports to entertainment, technology to business. Finally, it offers documentaries about life in America and certain chapters of US history, such as the civil rights movement of the 1960s.

This array of programming is definitely an improvement on the early days of Al-Hurra. And likewise the programming on Radio Sawa has also improved. According to Deirdre Kline, a long-term spokeswoman for both services, Radio Sawa now carries "more news per day (more than 7 hours) than VOA Arabic did, and more news than any other youth-oriented radio station in the Middle East."[77] Clearly, both services are trying to fill an important niche in the complex, crowded, transnational Arab market. The trouble is, it is the same niche that was emptied back in 2002, when the VOA's Arabic service was abolished to make room for Pattiz's "new model." Radio Sawa and Al-Hurra now strive to achieve three goals—presenting an American perspective on the news, offering a glimpse of American life beyond the clichés, and advocating responsibly for US foreign policy—that bear a strong resemblance to the original three goals of US international broadcasting. Could it be that, far from creating a "new model," these new services have been struggling to live up to the old one?[78]

RENEWING THE THREE GOALS

I stated earlier that US international broadcasters are mindful of the challenge posed by twenty-first-century authoritarian regimes adopting the worst formulas of America's commercial news media while rejecting its best traditions of press freedom. But as I also noted, US international broadcasters are divided about the best way to grapple with this challenge. Some decision makers, including some BBG members and staff, believe that the best solution is to have the various entities adopt the methods of the deregulated commercial media. But others understand that those media are not hospitable to serious journalism. The resulting dilemma is well expressed by Al-Arabiya's Nabil Khatib: "If you're interested in news, you need to be independent of governments. But news isn't profitable, and that is a challenge that many in our region resolved by relying on government help."[79]

The only way to resolve this dilemma is to revisit the three goals of US international broadcasting. First and foremost, this would mean reporting the news in a truthful, accurate, thorough, and fair manner, even when it reflects badly on America. For surrogate reporting that relies on the knowledge and talents of émigrés, renewing the first goal would also mean teaching the norms of professional journalism to colleagues who have had only limited exposure to them. Noteworthy here is the testimony of Sonia Winter, the former Czech national quoted earlier, who began her career at RFE/RL as an émigré reporter:

> It is totally unrealistic to think that just because we are relying on local reporters, we are fostering good journalism. They have to learn how to do it! This is what I had to do. As a Czech reporter under Communism, I wrote everything according to one official truth. I broke that mindset after three years at a British university, but then working for the RFE in Washington, for a long time I simply accepted the US government view. It took me two years on the job to understand that we are doing something different here. *We are serving America's interest, yes, but we are also doing honest reporting.* We walk a fine line, and you can't teach that to people in just two or three weeks. [emphasis added][80]

As for the second goal—conveying a full and fair picture of American life— renewing it would mean doing justice to this country's history, culture, and institutions, while also contesting the distorted picture of American life conveyed by our popular culture. I will say more about this in the conclusion.

Finally, there is an urgent need to renew the third goal of US international broadcasting—advocacy. By now it should be clear that this is the most vexed of the three, and that many individuals involved in US international broadcasting would be happy to dispense with it. As noted in Chapter 6, foreign service officers often take a similar view, dismissing the advocacy part of public diplomacy as a hindrance to other, more congenial, goals. This view is mistaken—and dangerous, because without the capacity to advocate forcefully and persuasively for its policies, the United States will be reduced to playing defense in a world full of offense-playing propagandists.

HUMAN COMMUNICATION, NOT STRATEGIC COMMUNICATION

What would forceful, persuasive advocacy look like in the twenty-first century? Let me say first what it would *not* look like. In the wake of 9/11, the lion's share of the funding for public diplomacy went to the Department of Defense, for an array of initiatives described as "strategic communication." Over the subsequent decade, the term *strategic communication* came to be used interchangeably with *public diplomacy*. That era ended in 2011, when Admiral Michael Mullen admitted (while stepping down from the chairmanship of the Joint Chiefs of Staff) that by engaging in such efforts the military had encroached on civilian territory and unnecessarily duplicated the work of foreign service officers engaged in public diplomacy. A year later, the Pentagon announced that it would no longer engage in strategic communication and that the term would be dropped.[81]

This was welcome news, because the military's venture into this realm was both wasteful and fruitless. It was wasteful, because as one senior diplomat quipped to me, "Instead of giving the resources to the agency with the mission, they gave the mission to the agency with the resources." Because the relevant congressional committees have different budget categories, it is hard to evaluate the overall disparity in appropriations between military strategic communication and civilian public diplomacy.[82] But given that the entire annual budget for the foreign affairs establishment is roughly equivalent to what the Pentagon spends in a day, no serious observer doubts that expenditures on military strategic communication far exceeded those on civilian public diplomacy.[83]

Unfortunately most of those tasked with strategic communication had little or no relevant experience. For example, in October 2001 the Pentagon recruited Air Force Brigadier General Simon "Pete" Worden to head a new $161-million agency called the Office of Strategic Influence (OSI). An outside-the-box thinker on space technology, Worden's mission was to contest radical Islamist ideology on what the military defined as the "new information battle space" of the Internet.[84] His solution was "to provide direct, unfettered access to global information" through the distribution of free digital radios and laptops to young people in the Arab Middle East and South Asia, regions he characterized as living in the twelfth century. "The target is the kids," he declared, "and information is the atomic bomb."[85]

This strategy was ill-informed, to say the least. As we've seen, both the Middle East and South Asia had by 2001 become well saturated by satellite television, and the information bomb imagined by Worden had long since exploded, provoking the complex array of responses discussed in these pages. At any rate, the OSI lasted only four months, because it was rumored to be planning a global disinformation campaign that included such deceptive practices as planting false stories in foreign news media. True or not, those rumors raised a hue and cry, not just among journalists but among public-affairs officers at the Pentagon.[86]

Judging from a document Worden produced later that year, that outrage was at least partially justified. While conceding that "the truth and unlimited access to it" is still the best form of propaganda, the document went on to suggest that "outright lies can be effective, particularly when the promulgator has a long history of apparent 'truth telling.'"[87] That document was never published, so I am quoting from a journalist's account. But if Worden's statement is quoted correctly, then the OSI was pondering a course of action profoundly disquieting to anyone who believes in the hard-earned British and American tradition of truth-based advocacy.

With strategic communication now in mothballs, how should advocacy proceed? We cannot turn back the clock, but it is helpful to consider the agency that in addition to housing the VOA conducted most of America's public diplomacy around the world. In its heyday, the USIA was small, nimble, and virtually independent of the State Department. According to one veteran of both agencies, "The State Department is like General Motors; USIA was like Harley Davidson. State attracted cautious generalists well suited to transferability between posts; the USIA attracted deep area specialists with strong language skills and a nonconformist streak." Another USIA veteran, Eugene Kopp, quoted Henry Loomis, the legendary VOA director between 1958 and 1965, describing the USIA as "the largest aviary in the world."[88]

Loomis meant this as a compliment—an acknowledgment, by a seasoned practitioner, that advocacy is best conducted by rare birds. This was true during the Cold War, and it was still true during the US occupation of Iraq, when US troops faced a ruthless insurgency and incipient civil war. At that time, the Bush administration asked a foreign service officer named Alberto Fernandez to become, quite literally, the voice of America on Arab satellite television.[89]

A fluent Arabic speaker, Fernandez made over five hundred appearances, some lasting minutes but many lasting an hour or more, in which he mixed it up with all kinds of people, including celebrity hosts on Al-Jazeera, Al-Arabiya, and other top-rated channels. As noted by Arab media expert Marc Lynch, this "one-man show" was not conducted in the usual State Department style of "grim diplomat reading from a script," but rather by a down-to-earth, flesh-and-blood individual "willing to argue, to get angry, to make jokes—in short, to offer a real human face."[90]

In 2006 a media tempest erupted over a comment that Fernandez made on Al-Jazeera, about the early days of the US occupation: "We tried to do our best but I think there is much room for criticism because, undoubtedly, there was arrogance and there was stupidity from the United States in Iraq."[91] Brandished by Glenn Beck and other red-state pundits as proof that the State Department was soft on terrorism, the comment was quickly retracted by Fernandez and did not harm his career, although it could have hurt that of a younger foreign service officer with a less sterling track record.[92]

From a source inside the State Department I learned that the disputed comment was part of a longer speech intended to reach out to Sunni insurgents opposed to Al-Qaeda, a strategy that eventually led to the cessation of violence known as the "Arab Awakening." Clearly, advocacy performed at this level is a high-wire act, fraught with risk not only from enemies overseas but also from attention-seeking pundits and politicians at home.[93] But sometimes a high wire is the only possible path across an abyss of distrust.

8

BEARERS OF GLAD TIDINGS

A few years ago I went sightseeing in Washington with a friend, a German born after World War II who, like many of her countrymen, wrestles continually with the legacy of Nazism. On an earlier visit to Berlin, she had shown me the Topography of Terror, an exhibit about the Third Reich then located outdoors on the ruins of the headquarters buildings of the Gestapo and SS. Now, after a sweltering tour of the Washington Mall, we stopped at the Lincoln Memorial, where my friend asked me to read aloud the inscribed words of the Second Inaugural Address. Doing so, I found myself moved almost to tears. Walking down the steps, my friend asked, "Do you love your country?" Unthinkingly, I said, "Yes." Her next comment has stayed with me ever since: "I cannot imagine what that would be like."

Most Americans are not about to stop loving our country, and because of that, we rarely go abroad without attempting to share its glad tidings, however we interpret them.[1] As argued throughout these pages, the true glad tidings of America are expressed in our national ethos of hope for human flourishing under conditions of liberty, combined with prudence toward the waywardness of human nature. These true glad tidings are also expressed in the political wisdom of the American Framers, which upholds the virtues of liberal institutions but warns of the dangers of concentrated power. In the words of James Madison, "If men were angels, no government would be necessary. If angels were to govern men, neither external nor internal controls on government would be necessary."[2]

Unfortunately, these true glad tidings are often neglected in favor of good causes pursued in a spirit of reckless optimism. Some of these good causes come from the blue-state side in the culture war. Others come from the red-state side.

A few come from both. What they have in common is a dream of remaking the world in the image of an idealized America that never really existed. As noted in the introduction, this dream is rooted in postmillennial Protestantism, which in the late nineteenth century summoned Americans to perfect their own nation, then all the others, in anticipation of the final Day of Judgment.

This chapter traces three paths by which Americans bear glad tidings to a skeptical world: those of the volunteer, the soldier, and the missionary.[3] The goal is not to treat these three paths exhaustively—they are far too large and complex for that. Rather it is to consider how effectively they bear America's distinctive combination of love of liberty, skepticism about human weakness, and distrust of concentrated power.

Each path has a different history, but all were forged at times when the majority of foreigners had little exposure to this country and were eager to learn about it from American visitors, whether volunteers, soldiers, or missionaries. Today the situation is different. America is out there, depicted through our omnipresent popular culture, and billions of people view us through that lens. In addition, twenty-first-century transportation and information technology make it easier for Americans to visit other countries. But this enhanced mobility and connectedness also make it easier for Americans to remain inside our American bubble. It is widely agreed that the best form of public diplomacy is what President Eisenhower called "people-to-people" contacts. Globalization has increased the quantity of such contacts. But has it increased their quality?

VOLUNTEERS

The Ugly American, the best-selling novel published in 1958 by political scientist Eugene Burdick and career naval officer William Lederer, is not great literature. But it does sound a powerful polemic against the insularity of Americans overseas. Indeed, while the book is set in Southeast Asia during the lead-up to the Vietnam War, it could, with minor adjustments, be just as well set in any of today's trouble spots.

In the epilogue, the authors urge US diplomats and aid workers to quit their "golden ghettos" and go "off into the countryside and show the idea of America to the people." One American who fails to do this is Senator Jonathan Brown, the "incorruptible" chair of the Foreign Relations Committee, who travels to Southeast Asia not to engage in a "whiskey-drinking, social-butterflying" junket but "to dig into everything." Despite the senator's good intentions, he is thwarted by the staff of the US embassy in Saigon, who conspire to prevent him from seeing or hearing anything that might raise doubts about the effectiveness of the generous aid flowing to the French as they struggle to contain the Communist insurgency. Back on the Senate floor, Senator Brown silences a much better informed critic with the words, "Gentlemen, I was there."[4]

The Ugly American is an ironic title, because the most beautiful American in the book is physically ugly, a Pittsburgh engineer named Homer Atkins, who despite his homeliness embodies the American ethos.[5] Ill-dressed and awkward next to the smooth diplomats he meets at the US embassy in Saigon, Homer nevertheless knows what kind of aid is needed: not big projects, "T.V.A.'s scattered all over the country," but small enterprises, like brick factories and canning plants, "that the Vietnamese can do themselves." But the "princes of bureaucracy" are unmoved, especially when Homer tells them "to get off their asses and out into the boondocks."[6]

Eventually Homer acts on his convictions. Reassigned to a remote village in the fictional country of Sarkhan (modeled on Burma), he bonds with a local mechanic who shares his practical bent, and in defiance of the village headman develops a system to irrigate terraced rice paddies without hauling the water by hand. Meanwhile, Homer's down-to-earth wife Emma settles in, learning the language and ways of the Sarkhanese. The most revealing moment comes when, flushed with pride at having invented a cheap, effective pump using a bicycle drive mechanism, Homer is tempted to foist it on the local people without considering how they are likely to respond. Wisely, Emma tells him: "You've a good machine there. I'm proud of you. But don't think that just because it's good the Sarkhanese are going to start using it right away. . . . You have to let them use the machine themselves in their own way. If you try to jam it down their throats, they'll never use it."[7]

THE PEACE CORPS

The Ugly American is often credited with having inspired the founding of the Peace Corps in 1961. But that program was not initially designed to attract sober, practical folk like the Atkinses. Instead, caught up in the heady idealism of President Kennedy's first year in office, the Peace Corps summoned recent college graduates with no particular skills to take up residence among the Third World poor. Writing about those early days, historian Elizabeth Cobbs Hoffman states that "the Peace Corps leadership tended to place more faith in the idealism of its volunteers than in the content of specific projects." Indeed, the leadership "felt it a betrayal to develop programs on the assumption that most people are not extraordinary." So the leaders approved vague goals such as "community development," which placed "far too many neophyte organizers in positions where they could hardly help but fail."[8]

The best volunteers soon learned that the Third World poor can be just as ornery as the folks back home. As Emma says to Homer, "Whenever you give a man something for nothing, the first person he comes to dislike is you."[9] Hoffman traces how the volunteers gradually "developed a more realistic understanding of the limits of US influence," causing the Peace Corps to place more emphasis on skills and maturity than on starry-eyed idealism.[10] Thus, the organization that celebrated its fiftieth anniversary in 2011 was quite different from the one envisioned in 1961. Having dispatched over 210,000 Americans to 139 countries in the past half-century,[11] today's Peace Corps no longer sees its mission in terms of what Hoffman calls "the innate goodness of Americans and the innate goodness of their power."[12]

The Peace Corps also imposes quite stringent demands on its volunteers. In addition to studying the language and culture of the host country, each volunteer "must make a commitment to serve abroad for a full term of 27 months"; go "where the Peace Corps asks you to go, under conditions of hardship, if necessary"; and be "responsible, 24 hours a day, 7 days a week for your personal conduct and professional performance."[13]

Yet the eight thousand Americans now serving in seventy-seven countries stay more connected to the outside world than their predecessors did. Many have Internet connections and cell phones; and the rules have been relaxed to permit on-site visits by family members, a three-week trip home, and (perhaps most significant) regular monthly breaks with fellow volunteers.[14] Indeed, a perusal of online journals kept by Peace Corps volunteers suggests that, for many, their friendships with fellow volunteers matter as much, or more, than their ties with local people. Do these changes make it harder for Peace Corps volunteers to cross the cultural divide between themselves and their hosts? One recent incident suggests that the answer is yes.

In 2009 a Peace Corps volunteer named Kate Puzey, posted to the village of Badjoude, Benin, was murdered in her sleep. While working as a teacher, Puzey had formed a girls' club where her pupils could talk about their problems —because, in the words of a family member who visited Puzey on-site, "It's hard to be a girl in that part of the world."[15] When some of the girls reported being molested by a local man employed by the Peace Corps, Puzey sent an e-mail to Peace Corps headquarters in the capital, Cotonou, asking that he be fired. He was, but as it happened, his brother was also a Peace Corps employee, working in the Cotonou office. The case has not been proven, but many suspect that the molester's brother intercepted the e-mail, because shortly after the firing, Puzey was found with her throat cut.

According to reports aired on the ABC News program 20/20 in January 2011, the response of the Peace Corps to this incident was distressing. First, it rebuffed the inquiries of Puzey's parents; then it stonewalled the press, on the ground that it could not comment on an investigation pending in Benin.[16] But equally distressing was the way Puzey went about trying to protect her pupils. Without questioning her motives or her courage, I wonder why, after spending almost two years in Badjoude, this young American could not find a way to deal with the problem locally. The sexual molestation of schoolgirls is not an accepted custom in West Africa, any more than in America. Was there no one in Badjoude to whom Puzey could appeal? Why did she resort to an e-mail asking a US official in a distant city to fire the offender?

Instead of focusing on these questions, the ABC reporters focused on a topic that was easier for their American viewers to digest: the charge, brought by a group of former volunteers, that over the previous decade one thousand of them had been sexually assaulted by men from their host communities, and that the Peace Corps had failed to protect them and sought to cover up the incidents that did occur. In November 2011 Congress responded to these charges by unanimously passing a law requiring the Peace Corps to respond to sexual assaults in a more timely, responsible, and transparent manner.[17] When President Obama signed the bill into law, its Republican co-sponsor, Representative Ted Poe of Texas, remarked: "The time has come to stand up and protect America's angels abroad."[18]

Poe's word choice is revealing. Peace Corps volunteers are not angels, they are human beings. And so are the people among whom they work. It follows, therefore, that any serious effort to curb sexual assault must include an honest reckoning with certain obdurate realities: first, that American women tend to dress and behave in ways considered provocative in many countries where the Peace Corps sends volunteers; second, that the world is flooded with US entertainment depicting American women as sexually voracious; and third, that most cultures still place the burden of sexual propriety on the female—a view that is, needless to say, diametrically opposed to the American insistence (once feminist, now mainstream) that no woman ever, under any circumstances, invites sexual assault.

To judge by the language of the Peace Corps bill, no such reckoning with reality occurred. The bill mentions briefly the need for "cultural training relating to gender relations."[19] But its overwhelming focus, and that of the surrounding debate, was on the organization's failure to "protect America's angels."

THE GENDER AGENDA

Of all the glad tidings being borne abroad by Americans today, gender equality is high on the list. Shortly after taking office, Secretary of State Hillary Clinton called "the oppression of women . . . the last great impediment to universal progress," adding that "so-called women's issues are stability issues, security issues, equity issues."[20] *New York Times* columnist Nicholas Kristof declares "the global struggle for gender equality . . . the paramount moral struggle of this century, equivalent to the campaigns against slavery in the nineteenth century and against totalitarianism in the twentieth."[21] During the 2012 presidential campaign, both candidates cited gender equality as a top priority for US foreign policy makers. And at the grassroots, millions of Americans now support a "gender agenda" that includes efforts to stop female genital cutting, honor-killing, child marriage, sex trafficking, war rape, and myriad other harms inflicted on girls and women.[22]

Wanting to heal the brutalized, free the enslaved, aid the resourceful, and educate the deprived is admirable. But to do these things effectively, we need to consider some hard questions. For example, how well does the American gender agenda export to other, very different societies? When Americans preach to others about women's rights, do the others see the images we see—of mothers, sisters, wives, daughters, and friends being safe and healthy, educated and respected, free and responsible for their own lives? Or do they see the images purveyed by our ubiquitous popular culture—of American women being rampantly materialistic, promiscuous, contemptuous of men, and indifferent to such family duties as caring for children and the old? Does our preoccupation with individual freedom, including sexual freedom, over other, more communal claims make our gender agenda seem a promise or a threat?

This last point is the key to understanding why so many of our efforts to improve the condition of women fail. Some of the practices Americans find abhorrent—female genital cutting, child marriage, honor-killing—are customs. We associate them with Islam, but they are neither unique to Muslim societies nor found in all of them. Other harms, such as sex trafficking and war rape, are unfortunately common in some parts of the world, but they are hardly customs. On the contrary, they are universally seen as crimes. This distinction is not always clear, needless to say. What one culture accepts as a custom may be rejected as a crime by another culture. But the distinction is important nonetheless, because it is always counterproductive to treat the customs of others as though they were crimes—and vice versa.

Consider female genital cutting, the practice of "purifying" girls by excising some portion of their external genitalia. For years, NGOs, the UN, and various governments have sought to discourage the practice by defining it as a crime—female genital *mutilation*. This has led to the passage of many resolutions and laws, including imposing fines on the midwives who perform it. To be fair, governments have also made attempts to treat the practice as a custom, paying families to spare their daughters, trying to introduce "alternative initiation rites," and "medicalizing" the procedure by bringing it into hospitals.[23] But none of these methods has worked, because all have been aimed at individuals, not communities.

The method that has worked was midwived by a former Peace Corps volunteer. Posted to Senegal in 1974, Molly Melching remained in West Africa for the next thirty-five years, learning several regional languages and working with Senegalese colleagues to develop a grassroots model of informal education that used traditional storytelling to impart information about agriculture, health and hygiene, microenterprise, and other topics of practical concern to rural villagers.[24] In 1991 Melching founded Tostan,[25] an NGO designed to spread this model to other countries in Africa. Along the way, female genital cutting became one of the topics discussed. But as one participant recalled, "The goal of the Tostan program is not and never has been to impose opinions . . . the Tostan teacher [typically a member of the same ethnic group as the participants] never told us to abandon 'the tradition.' Rather, the methods used allowed us to meet together, learn information . . . and then discuss openly and truthfully."[26]

When the village of Malicounda Bambara announced its decision to abandon female genital cutting in 1998, it was not because Melching or some other outsider had preached to them about women's rights. It was because the villagers, armed with medical facts learned in Tostan and reassured by their imam that the practice is not required by Islam, made a communal decision to stop. A communal decision was necessary, because as Tostan well understood, female genital cutting was considered necessary for marriage and respectability. Soon other villages and ethnic groups that intermarried with one another took the same pledge, and by 2012 over six thousand villages in eight African countries had followed suit.[27]

Melching is not as well known in America as another opponent of female genital cutting, the performance artist Eve Ensler, whose one-woman play, *The Vagina Monologues*, began as an off-Broadway polemic in 1996 and is now the centerpiece of "V-Day," a regular event on US college campuses in which students and faculty call for an end to "violence against women." (According to the V-Day website, in 2011–12 there were 5,850 such events in 1,800 locations, including all fifty states, Puerto Rico, and sixty-one countries.)[28] Needless to say, "female genital mutilation" is routinely listed as an example of such violence.

Created during the culture war of the 1990s, *The Vagina Monologues* is based on the premise that the best way to dispel the ignorance, shame, and anger surrounding female sexuality is to speak loudly and graphically about such topics as pubic hair, vaginal secretions, menstruation, masturbation, orgasm, and rape. In 1998 Ensler added a sketch about war rape in Bosnia, and since then the play has addressed graver topics than some of those addressed in the original, such as the discomfort of tampons or the humiliation visited upon women by speculum-wielding gynecologists.[29] For example, Ensler's NGO (also called V-Day) spent the better part of 2009 publicizing the issue of war rape in eastern Congo.

But these graver topics have not fundamentally altered the V-Day approach, which is to use "taboo-breaking" language to express "fierce, wild, unstoppable" opposition to anything deemed harmful to women, whether custom or crime.[30] Such high moral dudgeon, not to mention self-dramatization, plays well on US college campuses. But it also explains why most performances of *The Vagina Monologues* in non-Western settings are held in small venues attracting Westernized elites. Just to cite one example, a 2004 performance in Cairo was closed to all but a few selected guests.[31]

One of V-Day's proudest achievements is its support of Panzi Hospital in the Congo province of South Kivu, which specializes in the repair of vaginal fistulas.[32] And the organization has joined other Western NGOs in creating "safe houses" for victimized girls and women. Safe houses, or women's shelters, are unproblematic in America, where they are widely seen as protecting women from criminal behavior. But here again, we must distinguish between customs and crimes. In places like eastern Congo, where cultural norms have broken down and people are desperate, safe houses can be a godsend. But there are some hard questions here, too. The suffering in Congo is not gender specific — in a single news report from 2008, one woman spoke about militiamen seizing her husband and beating him to death in the street; another recalled her fifteen-year-old son being impressed as a child soldier; a third lamented the brutal killing of her son: "He was my youngest child. I don't know how I will live without him."[33] Do Americans wish to tell the Congolese that we care more about their wives and daughters than about their husbands and sons?

The questions are even harder in settings where cultural norms remain more or less intact, but people feel threatened by their possible breakdown. In such settings, I learned from one seasoned NGO leader, safe houses can be counterproductive: "When you go in and start building safe houses so girls can run away, you cut against what is most important to the people: the unity of their families and communities. It looks like you are fighting the community itself." Cruel, repressive customs are bad for women—and men. But before trying to change them from the outside, Americans would do well to remember the words of foreign policy analyst Walter Russell Mead: "Many people in the world, not all of them men, find the American approach to gender relations genuinely repugnant and frightening."[34]

SOLDIERS

Writing about the US Marine Corps in the closing days of the Vietnam War, journalist Thomas Ricks reports that morale "hit bottom," with thousands of racial incidents, a decline in the quality of volunteers, and a high rate of illegal drug use. The same demoralization affected the other services, as a generation of soldiers bore the brunt of civilian anger and bitterness over the war's conduct and outcome. As Ricks observes, the situation began to turn around in the 1980s, when, encouraged by the Reagan administration, the military began rebuilding itself technically and materially—and remoralizing itself by drawing on older strains of "honor, courage, and commitment."[35]

Today a majority of American civilians think highly of "our men and women in uniform." Indeed, a Gallup poll reports that between 1975 and 2012, the percentage of Americans expressing "a great deal" of confidence in the military rose from 27 to 43. (Forty-three percent is lower than the 52 percent recorded in 1991, but it is nevertheless higher than the level of confidence expressed in any other US institution in 2012.)[36]

Yet this confidence coexists with a more or less deep cultural divide. Ricks foresaw this divide in 1997, when he observed that the new, assertive, all-volunteer military defined itself in opposition to a civilian culture that was increasingly "fragmented, individualist, and consumerist."[37] Journalist Robert Kaplan concurs, noting that the South produces the most soldiers of any US region, and that the military is becoming "a guild in which the profession of combat-arms is passed down from father to son." To illustrate the point, Kaplan quotes a major general who realized, while attending his son's graduation from Stanford University, that theirs was the only military family present—and that "many of the other parents had never even met a member of the military before."[38]

One effect of this cultural divide is a tendency to value "hard" power over "soft."[39] As the US invasions of Afghanistan and Iraq devolved into occupations, there was very little attempt to communicate anything positive about America's intentions.[40] According to John Carman, then civilian deputy director of strategic communication for Joint Forces Command in Iraq, this failure was all too evident on the ground. There was no solid, responsible civilian backup to help consolidate the gains made by the armed forces. And there was certainly no public diplomacy presence. As Carman put it to me, "No airplanes were arriving bringing foreign service people and aid experts. There was a void, and we [the military] had to scramble to fill it."[41]

The void was not easily filled. In 2005, when the violence in Iraq was spiraling out of control, I spoke with a Marine major assigned to strategic communication who told me that he and his peers felt an urgent need for more guidance. Having been trained for combat, they did not expect to be doing what amounted to public diplomacy. As loyal marines they were willing to shoulder this unfamiliar duty. But they were also painfully aware that their training had not included any lessons in the craft of imparting American goals and ideals to foreign audiences—especially in a war zone.

The logical solution would have been an increase in funding for existing public diplomacy in the State Department. But as noted in Chapter 7, massive funds were allocated to the Defense Department to create new strategic communication programs, many of them created by private contractors with little or no relevant experience. At best, the programs they devised were not very impressive duplicates of existing State Department programs.[42]

Among the many books written about America's blunders in Afghanistan and Iraq, one of the more compelling is by a full-throated supporter of those wars. A political conservative and former president of St. John's College, John Agresto was recruited in 2003 to serve as senior adviser to the Iraqi Ministry of Higher Education. But his good intentions were "mugged by reality," to quote the title of a memoir he wrote about that year. A large part of that reality was the conduct of his fellow Americans. For example, he found it "unbearable" to ride through Baghdad with a security escort who kept pointing his weapon at "ordinary Iraqis going to work, going to market, minding their business." As Agresto recalls, those Iraqis "didn't need the slightest command of English to know they were being pushed around and cursed on their own streets."[43]

Agresto describes the occupying forces as "arrogant, scared, ignorant, and armed." He could have added crude, perverse, and insulting. "Checkpoints were a special torture for Iraqi women," he writes. "Humiliation was constant. Once, when one of my senior advisor colleagues complained that her female translator was distraught at being ridiculed by the soldiers, . . . the snickering response came from the soldier that he was commenting to his buddy on the size of her breast *pocket*, nothing more."[44]

Unfortunate though these incidents were, Agresto calls them "nothing compared with Abu Ghraib." In that shameful episode, Iraqi prisoners were forced by their American guards to strip naked and be photographed in a variety of grotesque, obscene poses. Agresto's comment on Abu Ghraib sounds a note rarely heard from most mainstream critics of the war:

> It wasn't the revelations of torture, as such, that so troubled Iraqis. Rather, it was the character and sexual nature of these abuses . . . , the willingness of American females to be photographed sexually abusing naked men, and the joy that they all seemed to display in not only degrading Iraqis but at degrading their own natures as well. . . . Abu Ghraib was a gift to our enemies and an utter disaster for America and its friends.[45]

When mentioning Abu Ghraib, it is important to note that several of the miscreants were not soldiers but private contractors, part of a massive system of outsourcing by the US government that has been faulted for its lack of accountability and oversight.[46] Indeed, the security guards escorting Agresto around Baghdad were probably contractors, too. Of the thirty-seven interrogators accused of abusing prisoners at Abu Ghraib, fully twenty-seven were private contractors. But as noted by political scientist Allison Stanger, "none of the civilians implicated in the abuses were prosecuted or punished."[47]

Of course, those on the receiving end of such behavior do not care whether their tormentors are soldiers or contractors; what matters is that they are Americans.[48] When the Abu Ghraib story broke in 2004, Secretary of Defense Donald Rumsfeld called the behavior of the interrogators "un-American."[49] He was right: the vast majority of US soldiers (and contractors) are decent people. But he was also wrong: nothing could be more American than the reckless optimism that sent thousands of callow young soldiers into Iraq on the assumption that, simply by toppling a dictator, they could turn a country ravaged by tyranny and hatred into a free, stable, and peaceful ally of the United States.

THE MAKING OF SOLDIER-DIPLOMATS

There is another side to the story, however. Some of the blunders and horrors just described were the result of the soldiers' deep ignorance about their surroundings. This ignorance stems partly from life in the major Forward Operating Bases (FOBs), which provide soldiers with fast food, air-conditioning, fitness centers, US media, broadband connection, and top-notch medical care. Known as "fobbits," these soldiers are satirized by army journalist David Abrams in comparison with the "door-kickers," or combat infantrymen, who stagger in from patrols "smelling of sweat, road dust, and occasionally, blood."[50] A similar if less vivid assessment is offered by military analyst Eliot Cohen:

> Life in the FOB poses a problem for the kind of wars the United States will face in the coming decades. It is a life generally isolated from the populations the military seeks to influence; a life that consumes enormous resources in sustaining and protecting itself abroad; and a life that does not lend itself to the broader intellectual and cultural experiences that make soldiers (or anyone else for that matter) wiser and better leaders.[51]

But not all US soldiers are fobbits and door-kickers. On the contrary, America's recent wars have also produced an extraordinary crop of tough, shrewd, soldier-diplomats, men and women toughened by combat but also sharpened by hard-won knowledge of the "human terrain" in which they are operating. Typically this knowledge is won doing counterinsurgency (COIN), a form of warfare described by military strategist David Kilcullen as "armed social work: an attempt to redress basic social and political problems while being shot at."[52]

Army Major Sean Morrow is a West Point graduate who served in the "tip of the spear" during the 2003 invasion of Iraq, then returned during the "surge" of 2007–8 to command an infantry unit conducting COIN operations in the southern Sunni Triangle. Echoing Carman, the deputy director of strategic communication in Iraq, and the Marine major I met in 2005, Morrow told me that on his second deployment, "there was no help coming from State or USAID. We had to figure it out for ourselves." What Morrow's unit figured out was that "we couldn't command the Iraqis. All we could do was settle in and let life go on around us." Their first action was to take a census, less for the purpose of counting heads than "to put an American in every house," because "meeting with everyone made it harder for Al-Qaeda to single anyone out for talking to us."[53]

Prior to the arrival of Morrow's unit, the US troops in the region had been door-kickers, patrolling the area in heavily armored vehicles and adopting a suspicious, often hostile, stance toward the population—a form of soldiering described by Kilcullen as "day-tripping like a tourist in hell."[54] Thus, when Morrow and his soldiers removed their body armor, helmets, and wraparound sunglasses, and sat down with people in their houses, they were frequently told that, after five years of war, this was the first time their hosts had ever met an American. "We showed them our faces," Morrow explained, "hoping that if they got to know us, they might hesitate the next time somebody asked them to kill us."[55]

Combined with efforts to improve security and living conditions, this strategy led to the defection of a local sheikh allied with Al-Qaeda. With the help of this defector, Morrow and his men were able to hunt down several other Al-Qaeda operatives. This is the other side of counterinsurgency. As Morrow told me, "We were always ready to kill. That sounds horrible, but it is a reality. I often made deliberate decisions to reduce our security, but it was a very calculated risk. Be assured, when we were in T-shirts playing soccer with Iraqis, we had already conducted a security sweep, inspected every player and fan inside our outer security perimeter, and put snipers on roofs. I really loved those people, but I could never trust my soldiers' safety to them."[56]

By the time Morrow's unit shipped out, the number of violent incidents had dropped from several per day to only one in four months. Kilcullen advises counterinsurgency units to depart quietly, without telling the locals.[57] Asked about this, Morrow laughed: "We didn't sneak away! We went around telling everyone how much we were going to miss them."[58]

Such stories are heartening, and not too long ago there were similar stories coming out of Afghanistan. "Scipio" is the online pseudonym of a US Marine who served in the Korengal and Pech River Valleys in 2008–9. He kept a blog as part of an Embedded Training Team (ETT) with the Afghan National Army (ANA), and to judge by postings like this one, he was going about it the right way:

> A good ETT needs to be an infantryman, operations officer, diplomat, civil affairs professional, engineer, intelligence analyst, supply officer, mechanic, linguist, and communications specialist. He must also have the patience to talk for two hours about business and yet accomplish nothing; the ability to refuse to help without alienating; the stomach to take food and drink that might not be prepared according to what you're used to . . . and the fortitude to deal with the same issues and problems week after week. Having a bad day is not allowed.[59]

Unfortunately, the American effort to train the Afghan army and national police was soon having some very bad days, as members of the ANA and national police began turning their weapons on their US and NATO trainers. By September 2012 over fifty Western soldiers had been killed in "green on blue" or "insider" attacks, and speculation was rife about their causes. The initial assumption, by US and NATO officials, was that all or most of these killings were by Taliban infiltrators. But in a report for the Center for Strategic and International Studies, security analyst Anthony Cordesman estimated that only 10 to 25 percent of the killings were by Taliban.[60] Counterinsurgency expert John Nagl suggested that the rest were committed by "disgruntled or frustrated Afghans after a decade of foreign occupation."[61] Other observers pointed to the "cultural cluelessness" of the Americans involved.[62]

This third factor is reflected in some of the comments by Afghan soldiers. For example, an ANA soldier in Khost Province told a reporter that "the real problem" behind the insider attacks was not Taliban infiltration but the fact that ordinary Afghans "cannot tolerate negligence and degradation of their country's sanctity."[63] A commanding officer in Kunar Province noted that Afghan recruits from remote villages "do not know anything else except religion and their traditional codes" and "see attitudes of foreign forces alongside themselves which are not compatible to what they understand."[64] Such comments bear out the warning delivered by a 2011 army report based on interviews with both sides. In that report, a "crisis of trust and cultural incompatibility" was said to be brewing between the Afghans, who complained of "arrogant, rude, bullying" behavior by the Americans; and the Americans, who complained of grossly unsoldierly behavior by the Afghans.[65]

Would more soldier-diplomats have helped? In that same army report, some of the Afghans said they were "especially impressed with embedded training teams (ETTs)," and "much preferred this mode of training and mentorship."[66] Perhaps a larger contingent of Morrows and Scipios could have reduced the number of killings by ordinary Afghan recruits, as opposed to Taliban infiltrators. More soldier-diplomats might also have reduced the number of Taliban attacks, because as Morrow's experience reminds us, unit commanders with the cultural savvy to build trust among the local population tend to get better intelligence than those who lack that savvy. With better intelligence, it might have been easier to tell who was a Taliban infiltrator and who was not.

There is, of course, a limit to what can be accomplished by soldier-diplomats in the field. In Morrow's view, COIN can be a useful tactic when an army is already involved in a conflict and the political tide has a chance of turning in its favor. But COIN cannot by itself turn the tide.[67] This cautionary view is shared by Douglas Ollivant, a retired army lieutenant colonel who served as a COIN adviser in Iraq and Afghanistan. In an article about the US troop surge in Iraq, Ollivant describes how the surge took advantage of the decision, then being made by a critical mass of Sunni leaders, to shift their loyalty away from Al-Qaeda (who were proving to be poor allies against the Shi'a majority) and toward the Americans (who were promising to protect Sunni lives). "A counterinsurgency is ultimately a political conflict," writes Ollivant, "and while military forces can shape politics, they cannot determine a political outcome."[68]

Without this momentum, Morrow would probably not have been able to win over his local sheikh and reduce the level of violence in his area of operations.

But as Morrow himself pointed out to me, "If we had stayed on our bases and not had the surge, the Sunnis would have simply fought to the end. Because we were out in the sector, developing relationships and practicing COIN, we created a chance for them to move away from Al-Qaeda."[69]

GAME OF DRONES

Counterinsurgency is still official doctrine, taught in military academies and basic training. But it is costly—some would say prohibitively so, even in good economic times. In an era of budget cutting and staggering national debt, not to mention war weariness on the part of the voters, many would agree with the pungent assessment of Cynthia Efird, a former ambassador well versed in military matters: "If the only way to defeat violent extremism is to help every at-risk society become free, prosperous, and well governed, then there's not enough money on God's green earth, not to mention wisdom and judgment, to do that."[70]

Obscuring the failure of COIN in Afghanistan has been the seeming success of unmanned aircraft, known as drones, and of highly trained special operations forces in locating and destroying terrorist targets. During his first term, President Obama ordered at least 239 covert drone strikes—five times as many as the number ordered by President George W. Bush—and there was a general consensus that these were instrumental in "degrading" both the Taliban and Al-Qaeda.[71] Similarly, the success of the Navy SEAL mission that killed Al-Qaeda leader Osama bin Laden in May 2011 encouraged some strategists to conclude that the United States was now capable of protecting its interests abroad without the expense and danger of large numbers of "boots on the ground."

If this conclusion is correct, then the US military has no further need of soldier-diplomats. But clearly this is not true. In the first place, drone warfare and special ops depend on accurate intelligence, and while much of that intelligence can be gathered by sophisticated surveillance technology, not all of it can. The best intelligence is still the human kind. And second, soldier-diplomats will be needed in the wars most likely to be fought over the next several years. Most analysts agree that, while it is possible that the United States could face a major war with a great power like China, it is inevitable that it will face a series of minor conflicts with the potential of becoming major threats.[72] For example, a religious or ethnic civil war could turn genocidal, prompting a US-led coalition to intervene on behalf of the vulnerable population. Or a nuclear-armed state such as North Korea could collapse, requiring a similar intervention to keep weapons of mass destruction from falling into the hands of terrorists or international criminals.

On such occasions, drone strikes and special ops will not be enough. Troops will be required. And so will the cultural savvy of America's soldier-diplomats, because as Douglas Ollivant writes, "When there is a crisis, there is no more useful tool than several thousand young Americans who are trained, organized, and equipped to resolve problems among the population in unsafe and ambiguous environments. *One silver lining of America's wars in Iraq and Afghanistan is that its land forces now understand ambiguity very, very well*" (emphasis added).[73]

MISSIONARIES

American soldiers are sometimes stereotyped as anti-Muslim, in part because many of them are observant Christians. When an incident occurs such as the 2012 burning of Qur'ans at the Bagram Air Field in Afghanistan, the global media go into overdrive, suggesting that Americans are religious fanatics just like our enemies. Lost in the shouting is the fact that hundreds of thousands of US servicemen and women routinely display an instinctive American respect and tolerance toward other faiths, including Islam.

For example, in March 2008 a sergeant in Sean Morrow's unit, a mechanic from Alabama, suggested doing what his brother used to do back in Birmingham: hold a basketball camp for the local boys, and when it was over, give each participant a new Bible. Of course, the sergeant understood that Bibles would not do. "Here," the soldier commented at the time, "we gave out Qur'ans."[74] The Qur'ans were supplied by a local sheikh, who told Morrow, "Since the people here are poor, it's good that each kid can now have his own Qur'an— something his family maybe didn't have before."[75]

Nineteenth-century Protestant missionaries did not hand out Qur'ans. But in many non-Christian settings, including the Middle East, they focused less on conversion than on founding many of the region's first modern hospitals and schools.[76] Originally intended to convert Maronite and Coptic Christians to Methodism, Presbyterianism, and other Protestant denominations, these schools gradually shifted their emphasis to serving the local population, Muslims as well as Christians.[77] And as researchers Timothy Shah and Robert Woodberry have documented, many Protestant-founded institutions, including self-supporting churches, helped to "instill habits of voluntarism" among people of other faiths.[78]

Missionaries and foreign converts often make the point that overt proselytizing is much less effective than living by the precepts of Christian charity. Bob Fu (Fu Xiu) is the founder of ChinaAid, the Texas-based group that helped blind activist Chen Guangchang escape from detention by the Chinese authorities.[79] In a recent essay, Fu recalls the American teachers who guided his conversion "in the strange, empty autumn of 1989" (after the Tiananmen Square massacre). Like many others, those teachers were American Christians defying the Chinese ban on proselytizing by smuggling the gospel into English-language classrooms.[80] For Fu, they showed "kindness and love . . . not to change China, but to offer life-giving truth in an authentic manner."[81]

In Africa, the number of US Protestant missionaries grew steadily during the nineteenth century, eventually exceeding that of European Catholics, and today there are devoted missionaries in every corner of that continent. To cite just one example: Reverend Danny McCain is an American minister who teaches religious studies at the University of Jos in northern Nigeria. Recently, after a surge of violence between Christians and Muslims in the region, McCain organized a faith-based AIDS program that reached tens of thousands of students and earned the admiration of Yorubas, Igbos, and Hausas—Christian and Muslim alike.

In the field, the work of such missionaries often meshes seamlessly with that of secular humanitarian aid organizations.[82] And like aid workers, some missionaries have proved fearless and tenacious in the face of great evils. For example, Carl Wilkens, the head of the Seventh Day Adventist relief organization in Rwanda, was the only American to remain during the 1994 genocide. Working with a network of Rwandans, Wilkens saved hundreds of lives, including an orphanage full of children.[83]

To judge by the numbers, Christian missionaries have had considerable success. Today, a majority of the world's Christians live in non-Western countries.[84] And 35 percent of the world's missionaries now serving outside their homelands come not from North America or Europe but from Asia, Africa, and Latin America.[85] Indeed, the United States is now the world's top *importer* of missionaries, with approximately 32,500 proselytizing foreigners arriving each year (more than the number arriving in any other nation).[86]

As for the number of US missionaries overseas, it is hard to calculate precisely. The Catholics and Mormons keep records, but most Protestants have not done so since the 1960s, when the traditional denominations began to be outpaced by nondenominational churches, including the so-called megachurches.[87] Still, the United States, with only 10 percent of the world's Christians, remains the world's top *exporter* of missionaries, roughly 126,650 in 2011.[88] And the sheer affluence of American Christians give them influence disproportionate to their numbers. As noted by sociologist Robert Wuthnow, US believers control "more church revenue than Latin America, Africa, and Asia combined."[89]

GOSPEL TOURISM

So far, I have made American missionaries sound like intrepid spirits venturing far outside the bubble. But that is only part of the story. In recent years a great many American Christians have jumped on the missionary bandwagon, with mixed results. Some churches still require all their missionaries to commit a significant amount of time — for example, Mormons must spend between eighteen months and two years on their overseas assignments.[90] But many others now encourage what critics call "gospel tourism," sending ever larger numbers of believers abroad for ever shorter stays.

The statistics are revealing. Between 1998 and 2001, the number of *long* mission trips (lasting one year or more) grew by 5.5 percent, to about 43,000; while the number of *short* mission trips (lasting between two weeks and one year) grew by 255 percent, to about 350,000.[91] In 2009 Wuthnow reported that this trend was accelerating, with the number of *very* short mission trips (lasting two weeks or less) topping a million.[92] And this figure does not include the skyrocketing number of "service" trips taken by students in high school and college.[93]

Few of these short-term missionaries know anything about the countries they visit.[94] For example, Bob Fu of ChinaAid deplores the "instant noodle" approach of many American Christians now traveling to China. Unlike the teachers he knew back in the 1980s, who spent "years living and interacting with the Chinese before their mission bore spiritual fruit," today's Americans tend to "visit China for a few months" and display no understanding of the fact that "after 60 years of communism and wave after wave of class struggle, . . . Chinese souls cannot be harvested like stalks of corn in a field, or iPads on an assembly line."[95]

This sentiment is shared by foreign pastors. Dave Livermore, head of the Global Learning Center at Grand Rapids Theological Seminary, asked 250 foreign pastors what they "hate about American mission projects," and several responded by saying that visiting Americans seemed more interested in feeling good about themselves than in learning about the people they were meeting. One commented that visiting Americans were "obsessed with picture taking and making videos during our evangelical programs. It's really quite embarrassing for us."[96]

Short-term missionaries are also prone to ill-considered acts of generosity. Anglican priest John Rowell defends the American habit of lavishing money on impoverished churches overseas, calling it a "Marshall Plan for Christ."[97] But more prudent observers warn against the corruption and dependency that result. Based on research conducted in Zimbabwe, where he grew up as the son of missionaries and served for twenty-one years, veteran missionary Robert Reese offers this sober assessment:

> Short-term volunteers are currently supplying pastors in Zimbabwe with all sorts of money and equipment from computers to cars, without accountability for their use. Church members become amazed that their pastor is driving a new car and has money to send his children to the best schools, or to visit foreign countries, while they remain in poverty. These members become understandably disconnected from their pastor and his ministry, since he is no longer theirs. They have become powerless through the good intentions of strangers.[98]

Another veteran missionary, Glenn Schwartz, recalls the impact of impulsive generosity on one West African church where a long-term US missionary had been working to instill "principles of self-support" in the local congregation and its African pastor. With considerable effort, the congregation had raised what to them was a lot of money, $110, and were preparing to use it to "plant" a new church when a short-term American visitor felt suddenly overcome with "pity" and wrote the congregation a check for $6,800. "The result," writes Schwartz, "was that the pastor immediately began to ask where he could find more of that kind of money," and the long-term missionary "saw his efforts go down the drain."[99]

Richard Mouw, for twenty years the president of Fuller Theological Seminary, recalled in an interview how Christians in impoverished countries used to admire US missionaries for voluntarily abandoning their comfortable lifestyle in order to propagate the faith.[100] Compare this with the impression made by Americans seeking, in the language of one Christian travel agency, "a life-changing mission trip . . . designed to be Christ-centered, affordable, safe, and hassle free!"[101] When Americans arrive with expectations like these, the local people may be forgiven for thinking that we never leave home without our affluence, and that with proper handling and a sufficient number of photo ops, we can be induced to part with some of it.[102]

EXPORTING THE CULTURE WAR

Far worse than gospel tourism is the igniting of an American-style culture war. This is what an American pastor named Scott Lively did in Uganda in 2009. Together with two American associates and an ambitious local pastor, Lively preached a series of fiery sermons describing homosexuals as satanic figures intent upon destroying the Ugandan family. The result was a virulent antigay crusade and the introduction into parliament of a bill that would not have made homosexuality a crime (it already was) but would have banned gay-rights organizing and mandated the death penalty for anyone committing a same-sex act with a minor, disabled individual, or person infected with HIV/AIDS.[103]

The bill never passed, but it stirred up even more antigay hostility than already existed in Uganda. In America, conservative Christians define homosexuality as a voluntary path of sin, proscribed by the Bible, and consider it their duty to rescue as many sinners from that path as possible. The methods used to accomplish this rescue may strike nonbelievers as ridiculous or offensive, but they are not, in the majority of cases, coercive or violent. Such has not been the case in Uganda. There, the tsunami of hatred raised by Lively and others has led to severe harassment, beatings, "therapeutic rape," and the murder of a gay-rights activist named David Kato.

Ironically, Lively now distances himself from these events. While serving as the pastor of a small church in Springfield, Massachusetts, he told a reporter from the *Boston Globe* that while he still regards gays as "the agents of America's moral decline," his current congregation have greater concerns, such as homelessness and drug addiction. "We're not fighting the culture wars here in Springfield," he said. "The issues here are more fundamental than that."[104] Evidently Massachusetts cannot afford the luxury of a culture war over homosexuality, but Uganda can!

ADVICE FOR THE SOJOURNER

The *Ugly American* ends on a gloomy note. Senator Brown, who, thanks to his diplomatic handlers, tours eight Asian countries without learning a thing, wins the ear of Congress by intoning, "Gentlemen, I was there." But several other characters, including Homer Atkins and others who hunkered down in the mud to tackle challenges with the Sarkhanese, are ignored.[105]

Half a century later, the same scenario can easily be imagined, since those who have spent a significant amount of time overseas, learning how to communicate and work with people from a foreign culture, are often distrusted by those who make decisions back in Washington. Yet what The *Ugly American* does not fully acknowledge is that there is often a good reason for the decision maker's distrust. It is hard, sometimes painful, to learn fully the ways of another country. Many of those who undertake this arduous task end up distancing themselves, in one way or another, from their own country. At the extreme, this distancing can result in conflicted loyalties—the most serious symptom of the disease known by diplomats as "clientitis."

George Shultz, secretary of state under Reagan, tells the story of how he used to meet with newly appointed US ambassadors in his office, where there was a large globe. "Ambassador," Shultz would tell each one, "you have one more test before you can go to your post. You have to go over to the globe and prove to me that you can identify your country." Without fail, the ambassadors would spin the globe and point to the countries where they were assigned to serve. The exception was former Senate Majority Leader Mike Mansfield, about to return for another term as US ambassador to Japan. Spinning the globe, Mansfield put his finger on the United States, saying *"That's* my country."[106]

It's worth noting that Mansfield is still well remembered and highly esteemed in Japan. The lesson here is that it is not necessary to "go native" to succeed with the "natives" of another land. It *is* a mistake to lose track of who you are, and to over-identify with the "Other." But it is also a mistake to be so sure of yourself that you become overbearing. For many Americans, prone as we are to parochialism, these are opposite sides of the same coin.

This lesson is especially valuable for those of us who have not spent a significant amount of time overseas. Full disclosure: I am my own best example of the parochial American. When beginning the research for this book, I was quite nervous about venturing outside the country where my ancestors have lived since the seventeenth century. But fortunately, I was given some good advice on the very first leg of my journey by an American who had been living in Turkey for several years. She offered various tips, such as "carry your own toilet tissue," that were useful if mundane. But she also said something that has proved invaluable: she told me how to behave when asking others for help.

The key, she explained, was to "let them do it." Part of our cultural baggage as parochial Americans is the conviction that our way of doing things is more efficient, sensible, and practical than anyone else's. So when we ask foreigners for help, and their actions don't seem right to us, we become impatient. And that guarantees a bad outcome.

The truth of these words was driven home when the SIM card in my cell phone refused to work, and I visited a shop in downtown Istanbul to get it fixed. Only one of the young men working in the shop spoke English, so I quickly lost track of what was happening as they all gathered around the phone and began arguing in Turkish. Without the advice of my American contact, I would have expressed impatience, perhaps even asked why they didn't just fix the damn phone. If I had, then my unfixed phone would have been returned with a shrug: "Very sorry, ma'am." The correct course of action was to do nothing, which is what I did. I stood there patiently, not saying a word, until my fixed phone was returned with a smile: "No charge, ma'am." I had won them over by simply not acting like a know-it-all American.

Such advice may also apply in the United States, needless to say. But most Americans do not need it at home. We do need it overseas, where we most conspicuously lack the special blend of humility and trust required of the sojourner in a foreign land. That humility and trust are not sufficient for bearing the true glad tidings of America, but they are necessary. Without them, we will remain trapped inside our bubble, arguing with ourselves and projecting grandiose fantasies onto the world. With them, we can relearn the fine art of hunkering down in the mud with others and sharing our knack for solving problems—and our faith that they can be solved.

"Freedom's Just Another Word"

In 1886, when the Statue of Liberty was dedicated, it was a symbol of republican self-government, a gift from freedom-loving France to freedom-loving America that faced out toward a world dominated by monarchies and empires. By the early twentieth century, the Statue became a symbol of welcome to immigrants. A little later, when the totalitarian regimes of the twentieth century upgraded their methods of coercion and control, it gained another layer of meaning as a symbol of resistance to that new and frightening form of tyranny. And throughout its history, the Statue has been neglected and mocked, closed and darkened, threatened by terrorists, and battered by storms. But it has also been renovated, rededicated, reopened, and reilluminated. If it were to wash away tomorrow, Americans would find a way to rebuild it.

Ideas are harder to restore. Most Americans believe that our country stands for freedom and democracy. But how often do we remind ourselves that freedom and democracy require both hope and prudence? That the essential skill in constructing a viable system of self-government is not the capacity to dream that human nature will be straightened out at some point in the future, but the ability to work with the crooked timber of humanity as it exists today?

This book was written against the backdrop of a global debate about the merits of freedom and democracy versus twenty-first-century authoritarianism. Today's authoritarians extol their regimes for making needed improvements on the rickety architecture of Western self-government. Their people, generally speaking, disagree. Indeed, most of the world's people, especially the young, yearn for freedom and democracy, understood in the gut sense of having a say in one's own life and in the life of one's country. But if the post–Cold War era has taught us anything, it has taught us that yearning is not enough. There must also be *learning*, because we live in a time when these political ideals carry a freight of anxious questioning: Does freedom mean license and anarchy? Does democracy mean social disharmony and mob rule? Are these ideals universal human goods, or alien Western concepts used as a cover for domination?

Other societies do not need to reproduce American history or replicate the American political system in order to realize the ideals of freedom and democracy. But they do need to grasp the political wisdom of the American founding, which says that no system of government can foster liberty without also constraining the waywardness of human nature. That wisdom, and the American ethos that goes with it, are good for all people, not because they are American but because they cut a path between naive optimism and cynical pessimism. Without them, no form of self-government can work well or last long.

It would seem logical, therefore, that Americans would strive to teach this political wisdom and ethos to others. This chapter looks at two different realms where such teaching is presumed to be occurring—government-sponsored democracy promotion and higher education—and asks how the lesson is going.

DEMOCRACY PROMOTION AND RELIGION

The promotion of democracy around the world has long been a stated goal of US foreign policy. In 1983 this goal was institutionalized with the creation of a new government-supported NGO, the National Endowment for Democracy (NED).[1] For the next two decades, NED worked to support oppositional political parties, build democratic institutions, and strengthen civil society in over a hundred countries. With the collapse of Communist regimes in Eastern Europe and Russia, these efforts seemed destined for global success.

But the new millennium brought setbacks. When the attacks of 9/11 prompted the United States to invade two Muslim-majority countries, democracy promotion was highlighted as the key rationale—and given a bad name. As one sympathetic observer, Thomas Carothers of the Carnegie Endowment, wrote in 2007: "A generation of work to build consensus at home and legitimacy abroad for US democracy promotion is in disarray."[2] The democratic tide began to ebb, as the number of democracies stopped growing, and several floundering ones, including Russia and Venezuela, lapsed into dictatorships.

More recently, the political drama that began with the Arab Spring has acquired tragic overtones. And although the much-vaunted "Chinese model" has lost much of its luster, there are still many places in the world where the prospect of relief from grinding poverty seems worth the price of political liberty. Everywhere, America's enemies repeat the charge that democracy promotion is an imperialist plot to bring other nations to heel.[3] And words lead to actions, as democracy promotion has begun suffering what Carothers calls "a punishing backlash." Citing Russia's 2012 closing of the USAID mission in Moscow, and the expulsion or legal prosecution of NED-supported NGOs in Egypt, he warns that "a growing number of governments, especially in the former Soviet Union, Latin America, and the Middle East, have taken actions to block international elections assistance, restrict international funding for civil society organizations, or reject Western democracy support altogether."[4]

Given this discouraging picture, some Americans advise caution, even re-treat. But others recommend seizing the moment and steering democracy promotion in a whole new direction. In this view, Americans should stop promoting democracy as a purely secular ideal and start promoting it as an ideal for what scholars call "faith-saturated societies."[5] In other words, America should become actively involved in a global debate over whether freedom and democracy can be made compatible with public expressions of strong religious faith.

At the end of Chapter 6, I expressed my regret that American public diplomats failed to engage with the fledgling Islamist movements of the 1970s. In particular, the US government made no attempt to highlight the difference between the American tradition of religious liberty and the French tradition of *laïcité*, or radical secularism. This was unfortunate, because the French tradition has always been stronger, informing the modernization campaigns of such powerful leaders as Mustafa Kemal Atatürk in Turkey, Gamal Abdel Nasser in Egypt, and Shah Mohammad Reza Pahlavi in Iran. America stands for something different, but at no point in this history has that difference been part of America's message to the Muslims of the world.

This failure, or refusal, to highlight the American tradition of religious liberty is more troubling today than in the 1970s, when the consensus of educated opinion, in the West and elsewhere, was that religion was a backward phenomenon gradually yielding to science and modernity. Today, religion is resurgent, and the only part of the world that is not faith-saturated is western Europe. And even there, public life is marked by conflict between radical secularists who condemn any form of public religious observance as the death knell of "Enlightenment values," and restive Muslim communities whose leaders condemn secular government as the enemy of faith.[6]

The *Economist* wrote a few years ago that "America's church-state divide has the same advantage as democracy under Winston Churchill's definition: it is the worst way for a modern society to deal with religion, 'except for all those other forms that have been tried from time to time.'"[7] This assertion is based on a recognition that America's church-state divide is not, as many now suggest, a total separation of the two, with religion strictly relegated to the private sphere. On the contrary, churches and other religious organizations in America have always been able to express themselves politically, even as they have remained separate from the state.

There is, of course, no established church in the United States. During the colonial period, most of the thirteen colonies did have established churches, and some persisted after the Revolution (for example, the Congregational Church in Massachusetts was not disestablished until 1833). But there was no official Church of America, and in 1789 the Bill of Rights prohibited the creation of one. In the words of the First Amendment: "Congress shall make no law respecting an establishment of religion, or prohibiting the free exercise thereof."

But the Establishment Clause is not antireligious. On the contrary, by sparing religion the encumbrance of being part of the government, the Clause makes room for religion to flourish. In Chapter 6 I quoted Tocqueville's assertion that "religion cannot share the material strength of the rulers without being burdened with some of the animosity roused against them."[8] Tocqueville made this assertion while comparing the French and American revolutions. As he saw clearly, the French revolutionaries fought against *both* the Bourbon monarchy *and* the Catholic Church, giving their revolution a bitter aftertaste of anticlericalism. The Americans, by contrast, fought *with their churches* against the British king, marking their revolution with what historian Sydney Ahlstrom calls a "complete absence of anticlericalism."[9] In Tocqueville's cogent summary: "In France, I had seen the spirits of religion and freedom almost always marching in different directions. In America, I found them intimately linked together in joint reign."[10]

In practice, this "joint reign" of religion and freedom has meant a robust public role for religious opinion on public issues. In recent decades, many of the believers entering the American public square have been conservatives defending traditional moral values. This has prompted some liberals to sound a *laïcist* note, denying the right of religious citizens to "impose their values" on the society as a whole. But as a prominent American stated in 2006:

> Secularists are wrong when they ask believers to leave their religion at the door before coming into the public square. Frederick Douglass, Abraham Lincoln, William Jennings Bryan, Dorothy Day, Martin Luther King—indeed, the majority of great reformers in American history—were not only motivated by faith but repeatedly used religious language to argue for their cause. So to say that men and women should not inject their "personal morality" into public-

policy debates is a practical absurdity. Our law is by definition a codification of morality, much of it grounded in the Judeo-Christian tradition.[11]

That prominent American was not the born-again Republican president, George W. Bush. It was his successor, Barack Obama, who at the time appeared to understand that if devout citizens were truly forbidden by the Constitution to express themselves politically, the United States might still have laws on the books prohibiting persons of African descent from running for public office, and he might not have been elected president.[12] To deny the longstanding public role of religion in America is not only historically inaccurate, it is also highly misleading to millions of people around the world who would like to reconcile their faith with their yearning for freedom and democracy.

AVOIDING THE FIRST FREEDOM

Thomas Farr, a former diplomat who now teaches at Georgetown University, is a prominent advocate of helping religious believers in faith-saturated countries work out "a democratic accommodation between religion and state."[13] In language redolent of the American ethos, Farr writes that America must "learn how to encourage religious actors who can lead their communities toward democratic norms by making arguments embedded within [their faith] . . . Ordered liberty demands realism about human nature. If democracies are to succeed in highly religious societies, they must be grounded in religious freedom." But Farr is right to call this "a tall order."[14] Despite the large numbers of Americans going abroad as missionaries, the official stance of the US government toward faith-saturated societies, including many that welcome large numbers of American missionaries, is relentlessly secular.

There are three main reasons for this secular stance. The first is a narrow interpretation of the Establishment Clause as forbidding US government officials to have any contact with religion. This interpretation has been relaxed on the home front—indeed, as Frederick Barton and two colleagues from the Center for Strategic and International Studies report, the Establishment Clause has been contravened by forty years of jurisprudence, clearing space for government support of "faith-based" charitable activities. Regrettably, Barton and his colleagues find no comparable precedent on the international front. So while "a few practitioners" are willing to "take the necessary risks," the majority of "diplomats, soldiers, and aid workers" stick to "a risk-avoidance strategy," even when "working in a faith-saturated society."[15]

The second reason is lack of capacity. American diplomats, soldiers, and aid workers are not trained to debate the place of religion in their own political order, let alone overseas. Farr believes that a necessary qualification for representing America overseas should be an educated awareness that its "model of liberty, in combination with its thriving religious culture, is unique in the world," and that "these features characterize the American order as much as its democratic political system or market economy."[16] But as he adds, this is not a sufficient qualification. Precisely because our model is unique, Americans often fail to understand the relationship between religion and politics in other countries, especially Muslim-majority ones.

Francis Ricciardone, former ambassador to Egypt and current ambassador to Turkey, does understand this relationship. But when I asked him about the role of American diplomats in the intra-Islam democracy debate, he counseled caution: "We don't want to enter the debate if that means choosing statements we like and trumpeting them everywhere. That would make us unwelcome intruders into a deep and serious family dispute. All we can do is facilitate the debate, ask questions, and *listen*. There are a lot of people out there in the Islamic world saying sensible things. But when they ask for our opinion, we should refrain from giving it until they have asked seven times."[17]

Such caution is well advised. But let us imagine that Muslim leaders in a certain country *did* ask seven times for our opinion. What would we say? Here we encounter the third reason for the US government's relentlessly secular stance: the culture war that has already done so much to thwart America's ability to communicate effectively with the world.

The impact of the culture war on democracy promotion can be seen in the story of the International Religious Freedom Act (IRFA), passed by a majority-Republican Congress in 1998 amid the polarization of President Clinton's second term.[18] The next several years saw IRFA achieve two of its original goals: the naming of an ambassador-at-large for international religious freedom, and the creation of a monitoring operation similar to that of Freedom House, to keep a list of "countries of particular concern."[19] But IRFA has failed to achieve its most important goal, which was to place religious freedom at the center of democracy promotion.[20]

The main cause of this failure was resistance by the State Department. Instead of answering directly to the secretary of state, as outlined in the bill, the ambassador-at-large was relegated to the Bureau of Democracy, Human Rights, and Labor, where, as Farr recalls, his "bureaucratic and functional isolation . . . communicated to officials inside the department in Washington, and to foreign capitals that the issue [of religious freedom] was unconnected to the broader imperatives of US foreign policy."[21]

Adding to IRFA's isolation was a critical mass of opinion within the State Department that, echoing the entrenched secularism of Europe, regards religion as a dangerous aspect of human nature that is best kept under control by a rigidly enforced policy of "toleration" and banishment from the public square. From this perspective, faith is an interloper in politics, and the Establishment Clause is best interpreted as permitting private observances only.

But culture wars have two sides, and IRFA's political fortunes were not aided by the strain of American Christianity for which the purpose of US foreign policy is to fulfill the premillennialist prophecy of securing the Holy Land and converting the Jews in preparation for the Second Coming. And while the vast majority of IRFA's Christian supporters harbor no such doctrinal agenda, a significant number of American Christians—and Jews—do harbor a belief in the "otherness" of Islam as a religion implacably opposed to "our values." This belief is grounded in a hyper-awareness of the threat posed by radical Islamists who (in the words of anthropologist Robert Hefner) "reject democracy as un-Islamic [and] are so passionate in their opposition that their presence in a society can present a serious challenge to civic peace and the realization of democratic ideals."[22]

Yet as Hefner and others have noted, this view of democracy is not typical of the world's Muslims. On the contrary, the 2003–4 World Values Survey (the most comprehensive to date) found levels of support for "democratic ideals" and "how democracy works in practice" to be just as high in Muslim-majority countries as in the West.[23]

This does not mean most Muslims favor what Hefner refers to as "the Atlantic-liberal variety [of democracy] familiar and favored in the United States and Western Europe."[24] On the contrary, the World Values Survey also showed "greater support for a strong societal role by religious authorities" in Muslim-majority countries than in the West.[25] A majority of the world's Muslims may support democracy, writes Hefner, but a significant proportion also have "'un-liberal' views on women, non-Muslims, and matters of religious freedom." Thus, the form of democracy most likely to take hold in Muslim-majority countries is "'civil Islamic or 'Muslim' democracy."[26]

Yet such "un-liberal" views are hardly unique to Muslims. On the contrary, the World Values Survey found similarly high levels of support for religious authority among most non-Western populations, including many that are not Muslim.[27] What's needed is what political scientist Alfred Stepan calls "the twin tolerations"—a willingness on the part of the state to tolerate the prerogatives of religious authority, and a corresponding willingness on the part of religious groups to tolerate the prerogatives of the state.[28] Each democracy must achieve its own accommodation about where to draw these lines and make sure they are peacefully and equitably enforced.

In America, these lines are in dispute, with some citizens calling for a stronger religious presence in the public square and others roundly condemning any such presence. At the moment, the latter have the upper hand, with Americans, especially elites, defining *freedom* very expansively, to include a degree of individual choice that violates many religiously sanctioned norms. This could change, but for now this is the accommodation that Americans have reached. The point is that other religious societies, if they are to become democratic, must be allowed to reach their own, possibly quite different, accommodations.

The American culture war is not as severe as those of some other countries, but it is severe enough to hamper our ability to help others achieve what Hefner calls "a third way between theocracy and secular democracy, in which 'religious principles and democratic values coexist.'"[29] Watching events cascade in the turbulent wake of the Arab Spring, it is hard to avoid the dispiriting conclusion that, despite America's deep involvement in the region, which has cost thousands of lives and billions of dollars, we have failed to convey the most vital lesson of our own history.

HIGHER EDUCATION

Father Franz Magnis-Suseno is a Catholic priest born in Germany who has lived in Indonesia since the early 1960s. A respected, even revered figure, Fr. Suseno has not converted many Muslims. But then, he hasn't tried to. What he has done is persuade large numbers of Indonesians that their country's customary tolerance for religious and cultural diversity is a better guardian of Islam than the Wahhabi alternative. In Jakarta Suseno shared with me his views on higher education.

Reflecting on the fact that several Islamist terrorists had studied in the West, Fr. Suseno noted that almost all of them studied the so-called STEM subjects (science, technology, engineering, and mathematics). Just to cite one example: Khalid Sheikh Mohammed, one of the masterminds behind the attacks of 9/11, received a Bachelor of Science degree in mechanical engineering from North Carolina Agricultural and Technical State University.

This is part of a larger pattern of non-Western students concentrating in the STEM subjects. And while technical knowledge can facilitate the terrorists' deadly work, Fr. Suseno offered a more compelling reason for the pattern: "Among the Muslims of my acquaintance, those who study science and technology often feel humiliated by the superiority of the West. This can cause them to retreat into a simplified and defensive version of Islam. But those who study humanities, especially religion and philosophy, are able to bring their own heritage to the table. It seems paradoxical, but exposure to Western views both strengthens their own faith and makes them more receptive to the beliefs of others."[30]

Words to ponder when considering the increasingly global reach of US higher education. In the late 2000s, two distinguished institutions, New York University and Yale University, announced plans to plant new, American-style liberal arts colleges—four-year, residential schools offering a well-rounded undergraduate education in the sciences, social sciences, and humanities—in the unliberal soil of the United Arab Emirates, China, and Singapore. These new colleges have the potential of providing foreign students with the enriching experience described by Fr. Suseno. But the most noteworthy thing about these new colleges is how drastically they depart from what most people in the world think of as US higher education—namely, technical training in business, the STEM fields, and the health professions.

Consider, for example, the 764,495 foreign students enrolled in US colleges and universities during the 2011–12 academic year. Forty-one percent of those students were in the STEM fields, 22 percent in business management. Only 8.8 percent were in the social sciences, and a mere 2.2 percent in the humanities.[31]

Or consider the hundreds of "branch campuses" run by US institutions in countries from the Persian Gulf kingdoms to Singapore, Malaysia, and China. Just to cite one example: Qatar's Education City hosts degree programs bearing the names of Carnegie Mellon, Cornell Medical School, Georgetown School of Foreign Studies, Northwestern, Texas A&M, and Virginia Commonwealth. A few of these branch campuses collapsed in the wake of the 2008 financial crisis, but the trend continues. In 2012 there were seventy-eight up and running and thirteen on the drawing board. Despite the name, these branch campuses bear scant resemblance to US liberal college campuses. They are more like job-training institutes.[32]

Finally, these and other wealthy countries are recruiting American academic talent to help create new, state-of-the-art research facilities. Almost without exception, these new "centers" and "institutes" are focused on scientific and technical fields of interest to the host governments.

THE APPEAL OF THE TECHNOCRATIC UNIVERSITY

There is nothing new about foreign governments being drawn to the science and technology aspects of US higher education. The sociologist James Coleman once described the typical American university as an agglomeration of three different components:

1) The liberal arts college, devoted to traditional learning and character formation. This component is the oldest, dating back to 1636, when Harvard College was founded to train the Puritan clergy of Massachusetts.

2) The research university, devoted to "pure," disinterested scientific inquiry directed by the individual researcher. This type of institution emerged in Germany during the nineteenth century, and was introduced into America in 1876, with the founding of Johns Hopkins University.

3) The "technocratic university," serving the interests of agriculture, industry, and government through applied research and workforce training.[33] Here the starting date is 1862, when Congress mandated grants of federal land to all the states, on the condition that they create colleges for the study and teaching, not only of traditional academic subjects, but also of subjects related to "agriculture and the mechanic arts."[34]

Not surprisingly, the component most attractive to foreign governments has been the technocratic university, with its focus on applied research directed not by the individual researcher but by external funders interested in particular problems. This is especially true of authoritarian governments. Indeed, there is a clear history of such governments doing their best to avoid both the liberal arts college and the "pure" research university, seeing them as repositories of unwanted American ideas about society and (especially) politics. Thus, authoritarian governments have consistently sought to steer their students toward the technocratic university, and away from the other two components.

For example, Saudi Arabia began in the late 1930s to send students to the University of Southern California (USC), with strict instructions to focus on technical subjects related to the petroleum industry. That posed no problem for USC because, as one American geologist recalls, USC in those days was "basically a nuts and bolts university as far as the oil patch was concerned."[35]

The story was similar with the Soviet Union. After the cultural agreement of 1958, Soviet students began arriving on US campuses. But as noted by veteran diplomat Yale Richmond, who spent many years overseeing these exchanges, these students tended to be mature individuals narrowly focused on applied science and technology. The "fields of study were determined by an interagency governmental committee according to the needs of the Soviet economy," Richmond writes, and "the Soviet participants were simply told, without prior consultation, that they were being sent to the United States." This changed over time, but as Richmond adds, it was not until the late 1980s that Soviet students were allowed to enroll in degree programs in the social sciences and humanities.[36] One obvious difference with today is that the Soviet Union did not encourage its students to pursue business degrees!

Authoritarian governments are still trying to control the process of educational exchange. For example, the generous scholarship program launched by King Abdullah in 2005 sends tens of thousands of Saudi students to the United States each year (thirty-four thousand in 2011–12).[37] But these students are almost always slotted into business courses and STEM fields, causing some to complain that they are being made to study things that do not interest them.[38] Other governments, such as the United Arab Emirates, Singapore, and China, exert similar controls.

The example of China is particularly striking, because in 2011–12 China sent the world's largest contingent of foreign students to US colleges and universities—over 25 percent.[39] Many Chinese students are mid-career professionals with a track record of loyalty to the Party. All are monitored by their government. The methods are more subtle than in the old Soviet days, but the degree of control can be impressive. For example, a diplomat I met in China shared his frustration that several students chosen by the US embassy for a Fulbright program in America had suddenly dropped out. As the diplomat explained, Party officials are not supposed to vet Fulbright candidates, but they do vet them. And in this case, the students who failed to meet with Party approval were pressured not to participate.

SOWING THE SEEDS

When confronted with such efforts to control the process, the default position of most US educators is to look the other way. At times this reflects naiveté, but more often it reflects a deeply ingrained faith that any exposure to US higher education, no matter how circumscribed by a foreign government, will automatically sow the seeds of freedom and democracy. Sharing this faith is the Institute of International Education (IIE), an organization that was founded in 1919 and that has long partnered with the State Department in overseeing US educational exchange. The IIE officials I interviewed were not unaware of the challenge of working with authoritarian governments, but they clearly had faith in the liberalizing power of American higher education.

In some ways, this faith is well grounded. Even today, when skyrocketing tuition is making higher education less affordable for Americans,[40] most people in the world agree with John Waters, former president of the American University in Beirut, that "the word 'American' is to education what 'Swiss' is to watches."[41] I heard such sentiments in every country I visited, including those with histories of anti-Americanism. In Jakarta, the prominent intellectual Azyumardi Azra told me that "even those Indonesians who oppose US foreign policy have America as their first choice for higher education."[42] In Dubai, a media marketer noted that "even when Arabs have negative stereotypes of Americans, we dream of sending our kids to an American university."

For many of the individuals I interviewed, the proven virtues of US higher education include institutional variety, the American style of teaching, and academic freedom.[43] Regarding the first, I heard continual praise of the system's wide range of choice, ease of access, and openness to second chances. In Mumbai, for example, Khozem Merchant, the president of Pearson India, an educational publishing company, told me that in his experience, "there's all the difference in the world between the UK system and the US system. In the UK, only the door at the back is open. In the US, all the doors are open. Education is an incredibly farsighted form of public diplomacy for America."[44]

Another virtue is the American teaching style, which contrasts sharply with the global norm of professors lecturing to students as though pouring knowledge into empty vessels. The seminal figure here is John Dewey, whose argument for active as opposed to passive learning has shaped generations of American educators.[45] In Egypt, China, Poland, even Britain, colleagues confided that they would love to adopt this style but cannot, owing to various factors such as class size and ingrained habits of deference. An American diplomat in Shanghai told me that "the Chinese greatly admire our universities, especially the fact that the students can *speak*." Michael Driessen, an American political scientist who has taught in Italy and Qatar, shared his impression that "exposure to the small classrooms, and the interaction between students and teachers . . . energizes everyone in a good way."[46] Casual, approachable, soliciting and not suppressing questions, and encouraging vigorous debate, this teaching style is at the heart of the liberal arts college.

The final virtue is America's now cherished ideal of academic freedom. I say "now" because it was not until the late nineteenth century that US universities declared their independence from external authorities, whether religious or political. Before then, their mission had been to transmit the moral and cultural heritage of Christianity, both by training clergy and by molding the character of the social elite. That is why Johns Hopkins, the nation's first research university, began life without an undergraduate college: its stated goal was not to transmit heritage but to push back the frontiers of scientific knowledge.[47] By the early twentieth century, the American research university was asserting the principle that research was not "pure" unless it was under the exclusive control of the researcher.[48]

This commitment to academic freedom, combined with the Dewey-inspired vision of learning as a cooperative venture, account for the widespread view of US higher education as a seedbed of freedom and democracy. Even the editors the *Wall Street Journal*, not known for their love of academe, wrote recently that study in the United States is "a useful myth-dispelling exercise," in which foreign students are exposed to "American life and values in action."[49] But is this still the case on American campuses? And more broadly, does the rapidly growing global market for US degrees carry with it any meaningful exposure to America's distinctive ethos and political wisdom?

THREE TRANSFORMATIONS

To address these questions, it is necessary to consider the ways in which US higher education has changed over the last half century. The student protests of the late 1960s seem like ancient history to today's university students, but their legacy persists. Indeed, that legacy has wrought three lasting transformations that have significantly affected the tone and character of US higher education.

The first of these transformations is the permissive culture of the undergraduate campus, which, in the words of one US education official, "turns liberty into license." Ironically, this greater permissiveness has been accompanied by a greater parochialism toward the rest of the world, as American students focused on the enjoyment of their personal freedoms retain that focus even when studying abroad. The second transformation is a wavering commitment to academic freedom in the technocratic university, whose reliance on the largess of outside entities such as the US government, foundations, and corporations in recent years has been extended to the deep-pocketed governments of wealthy authoritarian countries. The third is a curriculum, especially in the humanities and social sciences, which is heavily skewed toward a harsh, one-sided critique of American ideals and institutions.

I will describe each transformation in turn, beginning with its emergence on US soil and continuing with its various impacts on foreign perceptions of American-style freedom and democracy. Then I will consider the topic introduced above: the bold attempt, by New York University and Yale, to plant American-style liberal arts colleges in the un-liberal soil of United Arab Emirates, China, and Singapore. Will these new ventures impart the ethos and political wisdom of their homeland? Or will they adapt all too well to the seemingly benign climate of twenty-first-century authoritarianism?

The Permissive Campus Culture

For most of their history, American undergraduate colleges assumed the role of in loco parentis, taking responsibility for the conduct of their students. But in 1961 this role came under challenge, when the US Court of Appeals for the Fifth Circuit ruled in *Dixon v. Alabama* that colleges could not deny undergraduates the right to free speech. At issue was the expulsion, by Alabama State College, of six black students for taking part in a civil rights protest.[50] Subsequent rulings redefined undergraduates as "non-minors" with full constitutional rights, making it difficult to impose any restrictions beyond state and local laws. "Today the very concept of discipline is a relic," writes one legal scholar. "We are in a contractual relationship with students."[51]

This relaxation of adult authority has had far-reaching consequences, most notably a growing epidemic of alcohol abuse. A two-year study published in 2012 by researchers at the University of Wisconsin called "binge drinking," or the rapid consumption of excessive amounts of alcohol, "a pervasive public health problem." Noting that "fifty percent of college students who drink report alcohol-induced blackouts," the researchers report that, among these, one in eight ends up in a hospital emergency room.[52]

Closely related to binge drinking is the practice of "hooking up," or sex with casual acquaintances, which is frequently said to have replaced dating and long-term relationships. Hooking up is purported to turn sex into a hassle-free stress reliever, but some studies find that it leaves students, both male and female, unhappy and dissatisfied.[53]

It is important not to exaggerate the extent of these behaviors. A 2008 survey by the National College Health Assessment found that students overestimated the amount of binge drinking and hooking up occurring on campus. For example, the respondents consistently reported a low number of sex partners in their own case, but estimated a much larger number in the case of fellow students.[54] It is hardly surprising that perceptions of the campus "party scene" should outrun the reality. But while American undergraduates have the opportunity to correct those perceptions as they mature, foreign students may not. Indeed, a good many foreign students carry those perceptions home with them.

Equally troubling is the degree to which American students bring the campus party scene to other countries. Commenting on the "American-student-dominated parts of Florence, Bologna, and Rome," an American professor teaching in Italy reports "numerous empty beer bottles left in the piazza that 10 years ago weren't there," and "disparaging articles in Italian papers chronicling the new phenomenon of binge drinking." Noting that "people always drank wine" in Italy, this witness deplores the way in which "the idea of going out to get hammered" is now "reinforcing stereotypes about the ugly American."[55]

In an assignment to write a new chapter for *The Ugly American*,[56] a former student of mine offered this thinly veiled account of a classmate preparing for a semester in Paris: "Learning the language, tasting the local fare, and experiencing the abundance of high culture that France has to offer was probably the farthest thing from his mind. On the contrary, the student envisioned his semester as an opportunity to kick his feet up and have a good time. Since he was in a program of fifteen other Americans . . . who all felt similarly about their abroad experiences, his semester of relaxation and partying was readily attainable."

The student described in this essay was planning to stay in Paris for a semester, so perhaps he had time to notice his surroundings. But semester-long programs are becoming increasingly rare—indeed, American study abroad programs are beginning to resemble the "gospel tourism" discussed in Chapter 6. In 2012 the IIE reported that between 2005 and 2011 the number of "short-term" study abroad programs (eight weeks or less) rose from 51.2 to 58.1 percent, while "mid-length" programs (one to two quarters or one semester) fell from 42.1 to 38 percent. As for "long-term" programs (academic or calendar year), they fell from 6.7 to 3.9 percent, making the legendary junior year abroad practically extinct.[57]

Given the tendency of American students to carouse their way through foreign cities, it may be a blessing in disguise that the percentage studying abroad is rather low. According to the IIE, the number of American undergraduates venturing overseas reached a record high of 236,470 in 2011. But this figure represented only 9.1 percent of the total college enrollment that year.[58] And not surprisingly, elite universities send many more students abroad than do working-class community colleges.

Further, most American students go abroad in ways that can only be described as parochial. For example, the range of their destinations is considerably narrower than that of the missionaries examined in Chapter 8. Of the 150,000 US students who studied in Europe in 2011, roughly 40,000 went to English-speaking countries. To be sure, another 55,000 went to Italy and Spain.[59] But the majority of these students traveled in groups, perhaps learning something of the culture but rarely becoming immersed in the language. Indeed, according to one expert, most American students who brave non-English-speaking countries tend to remain in English-speaking enclaves, including "'transplanted' American college environments."[60]

What is the impact of America's permissive yet parochial undergraduate culture on foreign students? For the hundreds of thousands who study in the

United States each year, the impact can be quite negative. Just to cite one prominent example, deposed Egyptian president Mohamed Morsi recalls that, while earning a PhD in engineering from the University of Southern California, he admired America's scientific and technical achievements but was repelled by its cultural decadence.[61] Morsi is an Islamist, so many Americans may not sympathize with his reactions. Yet such reactions are not uncommon. According to Jerrold Keilson, an expert in the field of international education, "There's a lot of culture shock, and the way most foreign students cope with it is by withdrawing into foreign student ghettos."[62]

Reinforcing these foreign student ghettos is the technocratic focus mentioned above. In 2011–12, 43 percent of all foreign students on US campuses were in the STEM fields, and over half were graduate students. Most of these were employed as research or teaching assistants.[63] Often struggling with English and spending long hours in the laboratory or library, these students have little time for any meaningful engagement with their surroundings. According to one US foreign service officer who worked on educational exchange in Shanghai, Chinese students "wear paths between their dorm rooms, the classrooms, and the library. They don't even eat, much less socialize, in the dining halls, because they save money by having a rice cooker in their room."

Foreign students can be further constrained by family pressures. If American parents have qualms about sending their offspring to "party schools," foreign parents have greater fears about sending their sons and (especially) daughters to unsupervised US campuses.[64] Indeed, one reason for the popularity of overseas branch campuses run by US universities is that they are perceived to have a less-permissive environment than the home campuses of those same universities. The reasons why foreign families prefer branch campuses include cost, distance, and the difficulty of obtaining a US visa.[65] But some families also echo the reason given by a young Qatari woman interviewed in a 2008 PBS documentary, who volunteered that she was studying at a US branch campus in Qatar's Education City because "it is a little taboo to send your daughters abroad. Although more people are opening up to it now, people are still uncomfortable. . . . There's kind of that fear of just being either swept up in the culture or even destroyed by the culture."[66]

Joel Harrington served for seven years as associate provost for global strategy at Vanderbilt University. When I asked him to describe the advantages and disadvantages of having large numbers of foreign students attend American universities, his response was more measured than that of some boosters of international education. The advantages included: 1) many foreign students "decide to stay and enrich American society in various ways"; 2) some of those who "do go back to their home countries maintain strong personal and professional ties with Americans"; and 3) "some of the values of civil society and economic competition are taken back and become rooted in the home country."[67]

But Harrington was also mindful of two disadvantages: 1) foreign students often "leave with superficial knowledge of the US and few or no personal friends—or even have negative personal experiences and therefore negative associations with the US"; and 2) "the returning scientists and other experts make their home institutions, especially universities, so strong that students stop coming to the US." Harrington concluded that "it is up to all of us in the US to make sure that foreign graduate students have a broad and positive experience, and not a narrow or negative one."[68] To do that, administrators, faculty, and students at American colleges and universities need to think long and hard about the impression that today's permissive campus culture is making on hundreds of thousands of young foreign visitors, many of whom will go on to become leaders in their own countries. But there is very little evidence that the topic is ever considered.

Academic Freedom and Applied Research

The second transformation wrought by the 1960s is a wavering commitment to academic freedom in the technocratic university. As noted above, the technocratic university dates back to the Civil War era, when Congress mandated the creation of land-grant colleges. But it did not really become "a brain for society" until World War II and especially the Cold War, when federal agencies such as the Defense Department and the CIA began to tap academic expertise.[69] At first this state of affairs was not seen as subverting the missions of the liberal arts college and the research university. But this changed in the late 1960s, when New Left students and faculty rose in protest against the university's "complicity" with the "war machine."

In response, the more controversial defense- and intelligence-related research moved off the campuses and into independent think tanks and R&D firms. But this did not mean an end to the technocratic university. In both the natural and the social sciences, federal money has continued to fuel the growth of massive research facilities, and as government money has been supplemented by research grants offered by external actors such as foundations, corporations, and foreign governments, the line between pure and applied research has become blurred.

Whenever an externally funded project raises suspicion among students and faculty, the solution is to house it in an "institute" or "center" separated to varying degrees from the rest of the university. But the separation is rarely a *cordon sanitaire*. On the contrary, many American academics go back and forth between pure research, with its spirit of open-ended inquiry, and applied research, with its willingness to be directed by generous sponsors. This wavering commitment to academic freedom is problematic enough at home, where biased results can be openly challenged by competing researchers. It is more problematic in countries such as Russia, China, Singapore, and the Persian Gulf kingdoms, where American universities have been recruited to help develop state-of-the-art research facilities.[70]

Much of the research undertaken in these new facilities seems benign. For example, the Masdar Institute in Abu Dhabi, developed with the help of the Massachusetts Institute of Technology (MIT), is dedicated to finding new sources of sustainable energy.[71] For American academics accustomed to having their work ignored by domestic politicians, it is doubtless rewarding to have it appreciated by seemingly enlightened foreign rulers. Furthermore, twenty-first-century authoritarians can sound a lot like American businessmen when singing the praises of innovation and creativity in fueling a dynamic and growing economy. But make no mistake. Such rulers may praise the spirit of free inquiry, but in in their countries free inquiry is a privilege, not a right. And these new research facilities may be touted as a home for independent researchers eager to follow their own instincts, but their real purpose is to nurture homegrown technocratic elites capable of managing and directing successful versions of "authoritarian capitalism."[72]

The Radical Critique

Turning now to the social sciences and humanities, the main transformation which has occurred since the 1960s is that these disciplines have come to be dominated by a radical critique of the United States as a country driven by racism, sexism, militarism, religious bigotry, and corporate greed. This critique has had favorable impacts, most notably a more inclusive attitude toward women and ethnic minorities. But it has also encouraged the predictable and sometimes stifling uniformity of opinion known as political correctness.

The downside of political correctness is reflected in Peter Hessler's 2001 memoir of teaching English in China with the Peace Corps. What Hessler vowed *not* to do in his Sichuan Province classroom was emulate certain professors he had known at Princeton and Oxford, who "wielded their theories like molds, forcing books inside and squeezing out a neatly-shaped product. Marxists turned out Marxism; Feminists turned out Feminism; Post-Colonialists turned out Post-Colonialism. It was like reading the same senseless book over and over again." So in the privacy of a provincial college classroom, Hessler encouraged his students to read novels, poems, and plays in their own way, at a safe remove from both the restrictiveness of the Chinese cultural authorities and the narrowness of post-1960s literary theory.[73]

In a similar vein, an Australian professor of cultural studies I met in Hong Kong regaled me with a description of American academics as "self-enclosed," "obsessed with race and gender," and inclined, even at international gatherings, to "hold conferences with themselves." The only way for a foreigner to "fit in," this woman said, was "to become like an American academic." Otherwise, "the Americans will listen to you for a moment, but when you don't strike the right politically correct note, they will say, 'I am stunned that you are not addressing X!'"

The political correctness of the American campus has aroused many conservative critics.[74] But in the present context, it is more helpful to quote a liberal one. In December 2001, the historian Elizabeth Cobbs Hoffman wrote an op-ed piece for the *Los Angeles Times* in which she described herself as coming "from the activist left" and being "proud of that heritage." But she also suggested that when American college students returned to their classrooms on September 12, 2001, "they found minimal guidance if they were looking for an intellectual bridge between love of country and a sophisticated understanding of the nation's place in the world." The reason for this lack of guidance, Hoffman continued, was that, "as teachers, we urge youth to learn from the country's errors, but offer few lessons in what it has done right."[75]

PLANTING LIBERAL ARTS COLLEGES IN UNLIBERAL SOIL

Now let us turn to the latest phase in the export of US higher education—namely, the four-year liberal arts college, established in countries with no tradition of liberal arts education. At the moment these are three: the college created by New York University for Abu Dhabi (NYU-Abu Dhabi); the college being developed by NYU in cooperation with East China Normal University (NYU-Shanghai); and Yale University's ambitious partnership with the National University of Singapore (Yale-NUS). All three of these bold new ventures intend to go beyond the usual confines of the STEM subjects, business degrees, and applied research. Indeed, they all boast cutting-edge curricula in the social sciences and humanities. The question is, will they also try to impart something of America's distinctive ethos and political wisdom? Or will they focus exclusively on the country's faults, thereby reinforcing the authoritarian party line that freedom and democracy have failed in America and should not be attempted elsewhere?

It is too soon to tell, because at the time of this writing, only one of these new liberal arts colleges is up and running: NYU-Abu Dhabi. But that is all the more reason to consider them in the light of the three transformations discussed above.

The first transformation, a permissive campus culture that offends foreign mores, is not likely to become an issue at NYU-Abu Dhabi, because that institution is designed to stay aloof from its surroundings.[76] Located in a $28-billion cultural complex on Saadiyat Island,[77] NYU-Abu Dhabi draws 30 percent of its students from America, and the other 70 percent from thirty-eight other countries.[78] Only a handful of students, and no faculty, are from the UAE.[79]

One reason for these numbers is that Emiratis are a minority within their own country—only about 15 percent. Another is that Emiratis are very conservative socially.[80] "Emiratis are not fundamentalist," I was told by Abdulakhaleq Abdullah, a professor at Emirates University and member of the Dubai Cultural Council, "but they are very proud and guarded about their language, customs, and families."[81] Thus, Emiratis prefer their own sex-segregated, religiously observant universities to NYU-Abu Dhabi, where the students are permitted to live in co-ed dorms and have easy access to liquor.[82] "It works just like it does in America," one student told a reporter. "The drinking age is 21, but you can get around that."[83]

Asked about the possibility of scandal at NYU-Abu Dhabi, NYU president John Sexton gave a surprisingly blasé reply: "A couple of years ago, I had two students who wanted to copulate on a desk as an art project. So something will happen, I'm sure."[84] I daresay Sexton's reply would have been less nonchalant if the majority of students at NYU-Abu Dhabi were actually from the Emirates. But they are not, and this "global university" floats apart from its surroundings as decisively as any upscale hotel full of expats.

As for NYU-Shanghai and Yale-NUS, they seem unlikely to develop a campus party scene. One reason is that they will not float apart from their surroundings in the sense of not serving the local population. On the contrary, their partnership with local universities means that they will draw the majority of their students from the host nation and from neighboring Asian countries. NYU-Shanghai and Yale-NUS also hope to attract American students, but while the legalities are somewhat vague at the moment, both of these colleges seem likely to wield some sort of in loco parentis authority over undergraduate life.

A larger challenge looms when we consider the second transformation: the wavering commitment to academic freedom in the American technocratic university. Because these new liberal arts colleges plan to go beyond the technocratic offerings of the past (business, the STEM subjects, the health professions), their claim to academic freedom is correspondingly greater. Will that claim be honored by their authoritarian hosts?

Bryan Garsten is a political theorist at Yale who served as the chair of the Yale-NUS curriculum committee. The document produced by that committee is impressive and deserves to be read by every educator seeking to bring the American ideal of the liberal arts college into the twenty-first century. But as Garsten explained to me, "Singaporean policy and rhetoric have sometimes tried to distinguish academic freedom from political freedom, suggesting that a university needs only the former."[85] This suggests that the overseas partner in this venture may not share the American partner's ingrained assumption that a liberal arts education is the foundation of democratic citizenship.

Yet Garsten also told me that after a "year of intense work on this project," he was cautiously optimistic. "Some leaders in Singapore's government see the link between academic freedom and political freedom. They think that at least some degree of liberalization and democratization [is] inevitably in Singapore's future, and they hope that institutions such as Yale-NUS can help to create an elite set of leaders and citizens who will be in a position to play wise and responsible roles in these developments."[86]

This cautious optimism is reflected in the curriculum report for Yale-NUS. Rather than confront the issue of a connection between academic and political freedom, the report finesses the topic by assuming, without argument, that Singapore is headed for a democratic opening. For example, the section on critical reading and listening skills predicts that these skills will become more important "as civil society in Singapore and elsewhere continues to grow more vibrant online and on the ground." Another section predicts that the "cosmopolitan education for a rooted and responsible citizenship" being offered at Yale-NUS will prove vital at "this moment of generational change, [when] many of our students will find themselves faced with new opportunities for participation in civil society and politics."[87]

But what if these predictions do not come true? According to the 2012 report of Human Rights Watch, Singapore has made some improvements in recent years. But it still "resorts to charges of contempt of court, criminal and civil defamation, and sedition to rein in its critics"; permits the "arrest and virtually unlimited detention of suspects without charge or judicial review," including up to three years of involuntary "rehabilitation" for suspected drug users; and punishes numerous offenses by caning and death. As for "human rights defenders," they "risk being fined, jailed, bankrupted, and forbidden from traveling outside the country without government approval."[88]

The Yale-NUS document includes a highly principled "core statement on freedom of expression."[89] But it does not tie this statement to any particular course of action, should Singapore not experience a democratic opening. Singapore is a tiny country, and some of its leaders may well wish to educate a liberal elite disposed toward political reform. But prudence suggests that other, equally powerful leaders may have the quite different goal of nurturing a home-grown technocratic elite capable of managing and directing a successful version of authoritarian capitalism.

This brings us to the third transformation: the radical critique of America that has narrowed the vision of the humanities and social sciences. A central theme of this book has been the cynical manipulations of twenty-first-century authoritarians who use US-style media to keep their populations amused and distracted, while crushing any political speech that might threaten their power. Some Americans are fooled by these manipulations, because they unthinkingly equate freedom of nonpolitical expression with the liberty to criticize one's government. That is, they assume that a government that allows individuals to watch nude Paris Hilton videos will also allow liberty of political speech.

In a similar way, American academics are sometimes fooled by seemingly enlightened authoritarians who echo their own debunking views of the United States. There are three steps to this process. The first is when American academics share their one-sided critique of US history, society, and institutions with foreign colleagues. This critique is taken very seriously, because, as noted by historian Elizabeth Cobbs Hoffman, "Our academic communities produce most of the world's scholarship on the United States. Too often they implicitly encourage critics in other countries to assume that America is culpable for all that goes wrong." The second step is when foreign scholars and pundits "parrot the very things we have said about ourselves."[90] And finally, the third step is when the most corrosively critical Americans are welcomed as truth tellers by foreign governments that have no interest in the truth.

What's needed here is some pushback, a critical mass of American academics willing to offer a more rounded vision of their country, one that shows its successes as well as its failures. This is especially true in the study of American politics. Rare indeed is the foreign student who has access to a reasonable course on this subject. In 2007 I heard about such a course from a group of recent Cairo University graduates I interviewed in that city. It was called "Model US Congress," and it was clearly the highlight of their undergraduate career.

By their own testimony, the students had enrolled in the course not because they admired American politics but because they wanted to "learn how the enemy thinks." As one woman explained, "We started out expecting to learn how George Bush runs America, thinking that it was pretty much the same as how Mubarak runs Egypt." The students discovered quickly that the US president was not as powerful as his Egyptian counterpart. Then, after adopting the identities of various US senators and assembling for a committee session on the war in Iraq, they learned even more. "We didn't understand how the process works until we were made to discuss the real situation," said one. Another added: "The whole tone changed, because we were being asked, 'What would you do?' Suddenly we were forced to find common ground, hammer out a compromise, and figure out what was really in the public interest." The sentiment of the group was summed up by the comment "Learning how decisions are actually made in the US overcame our conspiracy theories. It moved us from the hatred square to the criticism square."

Perhaps a similar course should be required of the more recalcitrant members of Congress. In any case, it is worth noting that the sponsor of this course was the US embassy, not an American university.

In recent years Americans have begun to feel uneasy about the cost, accessibility, relevance, and quality of a college education. Indeed, a few critics are predicting that US higher education may soon collapse under its own weight.[91] But this is definitely not the view from abroad, a fact driven home to me when, before giving a lecture at China's elite Tsinghua University, I was introduced as a Harvard graduate. At the mere mention of the name the audience gasped, and several people leaned forward as though expecting a blessing. All they got was a lecture, and all I felt was embarrassed. But it's easy to see how a steady diet of such kudos might persuade American academics that they can do no wrong.

Are America's colleges and universities pulling off the neat trick of being all things to all people, while not offending anyone on the planet? Perhaps. But if that is so, then we need to ask why our system of higher education, once regarded as a bulwark of democracy and freedom, no longer gives offense to the enemies of those ideals.

CONCLUSION

The world's nation-states are creaking under the strain of global problems, but they are far from disintegrating. Rivals, notably China, are challenging America's political and economic power, but they are far from challenging its cultural influence. Nor has any other country come close to assuming the mantle of world leadership that still rests uncomfortably on the shoulders of the United States. In short, America is not about to exit the world stage. Therefore, foreign opinion remains important to Americans. Indeed, in this era of globally connected media, it may be more important than ever.

Why, then, does US public diplomacy remain feeble? I have argued that it was a serious mistake to cut back on government-sponsored public diplomacy and entrust America's reputation to the entertainment industry (and to the various nonprofits analyzed in Chapters 8 and 9). But what is the appropriate role for government? America speaks to the world with a multiplicity of voices, including foundations, NGOs, arts organizations, universities, businesses, religious groups, and so on. Why not keep the government out of it? This idea appeals to Americans, with our penchant for private initiative and limited government. But the result is a cacophony that can be confusing, even insulting to others. What's needed is a more focused and authoritative voice.

It is not enough to affirm the role of government, however. We must also affirm the need for a proper balance among the four goals of public diplomacy: listening, cultural and educational exchange, reporting the news, and advocacy. Further, we must insist on a firewall between these goals, which rely on trust, and psychological warfare, which relies on deception.[1] These themes have been sounded time and again in the post-9/11 debate over public diplomacy. Yet too often the next step is not serious reform but a quick fix or faddish enthusiasm that fails to give new focus and substance to US public diplomacy.

To find that focus and substance, Americans need to do two things. The first is to find some common ground upon which to stand while speaking to others in the name of America. This cannot wait until we resolve our cultural and political differences, because those differences will never be adequately resolved. Indeed, the genius of our institutions and way of life is precisely that they recognize this fact, and make it possible for us to live together in spite of it. If America is still admired as a city upon a hill, it is not because other powerful regimes and global elites see it as an arsenal of hard power or an engine of material progress, but because ordinary men and women look up to it as a fragile but lasting experiment in setting the better angels of our nature against the worse.

The second thing we must do is reckon with what our pervasive popular culture is telling the world about us. Freed from regulation and restraint, America's entertainment media now revel in portraying all the vulgarity, violence, and vitriol they were once forbidden to portray. This is unfortunate, because every society has a golden mean between repression and license, and American popular culture once occupied that mean, pleasing large and diverse audiences while respecting widely held norms of decency and propriety.[2] This was true of Afro-American music when it "crossed over" to the white audience, and of vaudeville when it "cleaned up its act before taking it on the road."[3] Respecting shared norms never cramped the style of musical geniuses like Louis Armstrong or brilliant comedians like the Marx Brothers.[4]

As noted in Chapter 2, it is ironic that the major Hollywood studios, normally bitter enemies of censorship, quietly self-censor their most profitable exports: special-effects blockbusters. Imposed neither by the government nor by the MPAA, the restrictions on sex and violence in blockbusters are a straightforward response to a multibillion-dollar global market that, contrary to the conventional wisdom of the past forty years, does not automatically demand ever greater doses of raunch and gore. On the contrary, that market includes many societies, notably India and China, where families still go to the movies together. So in essence, the studios *are* cleaning up their act before taking it on the road.

There's a lesson here for public diplomacy. No one ever accused Afro-American music or vaudeville of being timid, pious, or dull. On the contrary, the earthy exuberance of blues, gospel, and jazz provided a meeting place for black and white in times of slavery and segregation; and the irreverent humor of vaudeville, trading freely in ethnic stereotypes, offered comic relief from group frictions arising from mass immigration. The special gift of American popular culture is not to "shock the bourgeois"—any amateur can do that. Rather it is to address human difference while respecting human dignity. This gift is worth preserving, because, like the spotless facilities and friendly smiles at McDonald's, it is both universally appealing and universally beneficial.

What follows are three sets of suggestions for reviving US public diplomacy against the distorting backdrop of globalized popular culture. The first pertains to public diplomacy and international broadcasting as presently conducted, and grows out of conversations with seasoned practitioners, including US public diplomats and international broadcasters, and their foreign colleagues.

The second set of suggestions pertains to *cultural diplomacy*, the traditional term for the use of culture in public diplomacy. Historically, cultural diplomacy has meant exchanges and other programs focused on literature, the visual and performing arts, and heritage in the sense of antiquities and monuments. Condemned as elitist, such high-cultural diplomacy has been downplayed by the US government. But that is all the more reason to revive it—not in an elitist spirit but in the best American tradition of making high culture accessible to all.

The third set of suggestions pertains to the elephant in the living room: the massive, ongoing export, legal and illegal, of US entertainment. Owing to cultural and technological change, censorship of these exports is not an option. So what can public diplomacy do about entertainment that offends foreigners or distorts their understanding of America? My answer is straightforward: *contest the picture.* Export the American debate over popular culture, and create forums in other countries for public discussion of popular culture content, ours and theirs. What better way to demonstrate the power of free speech, including criticism and censure, as opposed to repression and censorship?

PUBLIC DIPLOMACY AND INTERNATIONAL BROADCASTING

Since 9/11 over forty reports and studies have been published recommending changes in US public diplomacy. Most of these affirm the primary role of government, but they disagree about other matters, most notably the 1999 decision to close the USIA and shift the primary responsibility for public diplomacy to the State Department.

Those who regret this decision make some important points based on the way the USIA worked in its prime. These are as follows:

1) Public diplomacy should be conducted as independently as possible of the cautious and cumbersome State Department bureaucracy.

2) Public diplomats in the field should be able, as far as is feasible, to design their own programs, and to have direct access to resources. They must also have strong language skills, a deep knowledge of the societies

where they are posted, and—above all—the judgment and freedom to take calculated risks.

3) Finally, there should be no stigma attached to sharing with others America's distinctive ethos and political wisdom.

I hasten to add that the USIA did not have a consistent record of success. Its programs varied in quality, and in the 1980s and 1990s it became a house divided, with one side regarding advocacy as the sole goal worth pursuing, and the other rejecting any taint of advocacy as unacceptably propagandistic. This division rendered the agency vulnerable, and as we've seen, the decision to dismantle the USIA was bipartisan and not strongly resisted.

As mentioned in Chapter 7, the Pentagon spent the post-9/11 decade creating a parallel universe called strategic communication, in which many of the activities of public diplomacy were duplicated, not very successfully, by defense contractors with no previous experience in diplomacy, cultural and educational affairs, or journalism.[5] By 2006 this effort was judged a failure by Defense Secretary Donald Rumsfeld; a year later, his successor, Robert Gates, called for a transfer of public diplomacy resources from Defense back to civilian agencies;[6] and in 2012 the Pentagon announced the termination of the strategic communication initiative.

Since then, the record has been mixed. A trickle of resources has flowed to the State Department to do public diplomacy, and as one senior diplomat explained to me, "Everybody at State has to check the PD [public diplomacy] box now. In the old days there *was* no PD box!" But according to another diplomat whose career had focused on public diplomacy, "All this loose talk about everyone in State becoming a public diplomacy officer is just wind, because most junior officers are too inexperienced to do real public diplomacy. All they can talk about is what they know, which is the visa process. So they get a day off from the visa line and go speak to university students about how to get a visa to study in the US. And those events have to be arranged by the experienced officers, taking time away from more important things."

Based on the conviction that public diplomacy is a necessary government function but that it does not belong in the State Department, one school of thought would reconstitute the USIA. But that is unlikely to occur, because as Nicholas Cull observes, public diplomacy "has burst the banks of the Department of State and flooded into other areas of international life."[7] Other parties to the debate see nothing wrong with the status quo—that is, with letting the private sector, especially the commercial entertainment industry, continue to represent America to the world. As shown throughout this book, this laissez-faire solution is actually part of the problem. Another school of thought, arising within the national security establishment, continues to call for a centralized, highly disciplined office of strategic communication to coordinate and monitor all US government messaging to the world. As we have seen, there are several problems with this hard-line view, ranging from the poor quality of the work done by inexperienced contractors to the fact that it makes no room for the long-term, trust-building activities of "slow" public diplomacy.

The most promising approach is to reconstitute public diplomacy as a joint activity, or set of activities, undertaken by the government in partnership with the private sector. Once again, dozens of commissions and study groups since 9/11 have proposed some version of this arrangement. The main justification is well expressed by the Los Angeles–based Center for Global Engagement: "For all the strengths of government, experienced and qualified nongovernmental organizations can often act more quickly, more nimbly, more widely and in ways government never could in order to engage foreign publics."[8]

In broad terms, I endorse this sentiment. But it is not enough to reorganize the bureaucracy and enlist the help of nonprofits. What's needed is a major rethinking of the overall mission of US public diplomacy. I am not suggesting that we need to redefine the four basic goals—they are enduring, as is the challenge of finding the appropriate balance among them. Instead, we need to reflect soberly and prudently about how best to attain those goals in the changed environment of the twenty-first century.

Suggestions for Public Diplomacy

• *Stop using* public diplomacy *as a synonym for* advocacy.
Advocacy is important, but to repeat, it is only one of four public diplomacy goals (the others being listening, cultural and educational exchange, and reporting the news). As shown in Chapter 6, the political divisions of the 1960s caused many liberal academics, artists, and journalists to become alienated from the government and averse to participating in public diplomacy. Their aversion led public diplomats even further in the direction of treating advocacy as "the freight" and the other three goals (especially culture) as "the fluff." As the culture war heated up during the 1980s, conservatives began to focus even more exclusively on the freight, and soon the term *public diplomacy* was narrowed to mean advocacy only. Today this narrow definition persists on one side of the ideological divide but not on the other, a difference in language that makes it hard to think clearly about the relation of advocacy to the other three goals.

• *Evaluate public diplomacy efforts by appropriate standards.*
Public diplomacy needs to be evaluated, but the same techniques cannot be used to gauge its "fast" and "slow" activities. For instance, the activities associated with

advocacy are fast, because they seek to "move the needle" of foreign opinion or, failing that, to keep foreign opinion from deteriorating by cogently articulating the US position. A good example is the "rapid response" team put together by Karen Hughes, Undersecretary of State for Public Diplomacy and Public Affairs under President George W. Bush, which monitored the Arab media in the mid-2000s and responded to falsehoods and disinformation in a way that was tough but truthful.[9]

Such activities are typically assessed by tracking them against short-term fluctuations in foreign opinion polls. Ted Kniker, an expert in the evaluation of government programs, dismisses such techniques on the ground that "there are too many external variables involved." But as he also concludes, "People use them anyway."[10]

These same techniques can be disastrous when used to evaluate the slow activities related to listening, cultural and educational exchange, and news reporting. One senior public diplomat compared their use to "potting a tender young plant, watering and feeding it, and then pulling it up by the roots every week to see how it's doing." The best way to evaluate these slow activities, says Kniker, is to elicit the candid assessment of the practitioners themselves: "When the people doing the work buy into the evaluation process, we can tell a lot about how well their programs are succeeding. We don't have to wait thirty or forty years for some Fulbrighter to become prime minister."[11]

• *Restore autonomy to public diplomats in the field. If recruited and trained right, they will make mistakes (that is inevitable), but they will also work wonders.*
As noted at the end of Chapter 8, the foreign service worries about "clientitis," an ailment that develops when officers in the field "go native" and begin to develop biased judgment and perhaps even conflicted loyalties. During the Cold War, this diagnosis was applied to Soviet experts regarded as soft on Communism. Today, it is applied to Arabists judged soft on Islamism. Unfortunately, Washington's response is to quarantine the patient and ignore his or her voice. This treatment is worse than the disease, because as David Newton, a respected Arabist who served as President Reagan's ambassador to Iraq and President Clinton's to Yemen, remarked to me, "The most serious problem we face in the Middle East is the feeling that America does not listen."[12]

How to recruit good listeners? Here again, we confront the legacy of the culture war. On the blue-state side, the talent pool includes the Peace Corps, NGOs, and international visitors programs, whose volunteers can become quite adept at interpreting America to visitors.[13] Another source is academia, although some observers argue that the abstruse theories currently taught in the field of international relations are irrelevant at best. More promising are academic recruits who have a background in regional studies and languages and who have also studied or worked with seasoned practitioners.[14]

To these I would add a red-state source: the growing number of military veterans who resemble USIA old hands in having considerable cultural and linguistic savvy about the world's trouble spots. These soldiers did not gain their savvy in academia, but then neither did most of the old hands. For example, Yale Richmond began his public diplomacy career in 1948 as a twenty-five-year-old military government officer of a small town in Bavaria, where he arrived "completely on my own" and wondering "how would Germans react to me as a Jew?"[15] Only a rare bird would succeed in such an assignment (Richmond did). But as argued in Chapter 7, public diplomacy is a vocation for the kind of rare birds who feel a commitment to their country (and are not likely to fly the coop).

• *Recruit "purple" public diplomacy teams made up of blue-state and red-state officers, train them together, and require them to serve together in the field.*
Creating "purple" public diplomacy teams is risky, but not as risky as what we are currently doing, which is exporting our culture war. For example, in the recent conflict over a draconian antigay law in Uganda, American citizens stoked the flames on both sides. As noted in Chapter 8, American preachers delivered sermons demonizing homosexuality in a society where the overwhelming majority of the population, Christian as well as Muslim, disapprove of it. When these preachers gained a hearing by joining forces with Ugandan ministers accusing the gay-rights movement of being a Western conspiracy, violence broke out, and one well known gay activist, David Kato, was killed.[16]

What was the US embassy's response to this furor? It took sides, sending its senior officer to join a march protesting the murder of Kato. Some Americans would applaud this decision, others would deplore it. But that is precisely the point. When Americans are divided on an issue, our public diplomats should try to explain that division, while also affirming our country's basic principles—in this case, the respect for the will of the majority, weighed against protection for minority rights.[17]

What the embassy in Kampala should have done is speak forcefully about the history of gay rights in America and stress that while some Americans oppose homosexuality on religious grounds, our society does not countenance hate-mongering and violence. But to do this, we need public diplomats who can look past their own ideological blinders and see that the job is not simply to explain what divides Americans but also to impart what we cherish in common—for example, the capacity to disagree vehemently but not violently.

• *Organize public diplomacy along regional rather than country lines.*
Instead of mirroring the State Department's country-based missions, the structure of public diplomacy might work better if it mirrored the Defense Department's regional commands. This structure, suggested to me by foreign-service and military officers involved in liaison efforts between State and Defense, has the advantage of bringing the oversight of public diplomacy closer to the field, while insulating

both overseer and field officer from the demands and whims of Washington. In other words, rather than having to report to a dozen different offices in the State Department, a public diplomat in Kigali, Rwanda, would report only to his or her immediate superior in, say, Johannesburg, South Africa. The hope is that the superior, being based in the region, would focus more on events in Rwanda than on the op-ed page of the *Washington Post*.

This suggestion also recognizes that the flow of twenty-first-century media is no longer confined within national borders. The twenty-four-nation market for Arab satellite television is the most obvious example. But other regions, from sub-Saharan Africa to East Asia, also share regional media influences. The Pentagon's strategic communication efforts were directed at these regional audiences, and while most of those efforts were not worth emulating, their regional structure might well be.

Suggestions for International Broadcasting

• *Appoint public diplomacy professionals and foreign policy experts to the eight-member Broadcasting Board of Governors (BBG); return managerial authority and budgetary discretion to the directors of the various entities (Voice of America, Radio Free Europe/Radio Liberty, etc.); and create a strong professional CEO to oversee and broker between them.*

This simple three-step change would accomplish a lot. First, a more sophisticated BBG board would have a better understanding of what international broadcasting is all about. A step in the right direction was taken in August 2013, when strategist Matthew Armstrong and Ambassador Ryan Crocker joined the BBG board.[18] Second, having a real CEO would put an end to the "collective CEO" arrangement that at present allows individual governors to meddle in management decisions that should not concern them. This meddling grew worse during President Obama's first term, when the BBG decided to make individual governors "chairs" of the various entities, all but usurping the authority of the directors.[19] The precise status and powers of the CEO are still being debated. But unlike some of the sweeping transformations being proposed, these three steps seem doable.

• *Do not sacrifice journalistic standards to audience share.*

The three goals of US international broadcasting are related to those of public diplomacy more generally, but they differ in emphasis. Two of these goals—conveying "a full and fair picture of American life," and advocacy—have been neglected in recent years, which is unfortunate because, as argued in Chapter 7, both are vital.

At the same time, it cannot be denied that the remaining goal of US international broadcasting is the primary one: to report the news, especially surrogate local and regional news, to countries where the media are censored or compromised. With good reason, this goal is suffused with a greater sense of mission than the others.

It is all the more surprising, then, to see the BBG compromise this goal in an effort to reach the largest possible audience. The BBG does not do this out of disrespect for surrogate news reporting. On the contrary, several board members and staff are motivated by a concern that America's surrogate news is not reaching as many listeners, viewers, and netizens as it should. The solution, in their view, is to adopt a more commercial approach.

But as illustrated by the crisis that erupted at Radio Liberty in early 2012, such an approach is misguided. Indeed, it plays into the hands of twenty-first-century authoritarians who no longer bludgeon their people with tendentious propaganda but rather amuse and distract them not only with entertainment but also with imitations of American infotainment, polemical talk shows, and glitzy "headline news." In other words, today's authoritarians copy America's worst commercial broadcast formulas, while forbidding its best journalistic traditions of truthfulness, accuracy, thoroughness, and fairness. The only suitable response is to uphold those traditions and endeavor to teach them to others.

• *In free and partly free markets, produce good programs in cooperation with established foreign channels, rather than maintain expensive US channels that struggle to attract audiences.*

For the past several years this has been done by two Washington-based nonprofits, America Abroad Media (AAM) and Layalina Productions. AAM specializes in co-producing public affairs programs with such widely watched channels as Turkey's CNN Turk, Indonesia's Metro TV, Pakistan's Express News TV, and Afghanistan's Tolo TV. In 2012 AAM produced four 90-minute "town meeting" dialogues between audiences in Pakistan and Afghanistan, shown on Express News and Tolo. and a popular twelve-part series called Reema Khan's America, which followed the famous Pakistani actress as she married a Pakistani-American and adjusted to life in the United States.[20]

Layalina's first success was a reality series called *On the Road in America*, which accompanied a group of young Arabs on a cross-country trip across the United States. The series attracted a large audience on MBC, the number one transnational network in the Arab world, and was followed by another show called *American Caravan*, which accompanied a group of Americans across the Arab Middle East. Most recently Layalina worked with INJAZ Al-Arab (the Middle Eastern–North African branch of the American-based NGO Junior Achievement) to produce a program called *Generation Entrepreneur*, which chronicles the ups and downs of young Arabs starting their own businesses.[21]

At the time of this writing, neither AAM nor Layalina receives significant or sustained government support. But perhaps they should. According to executives from both companies, their overseas partners are eager for high-quality material from America tailored to the interests and concerns of their audiences. But because their partners' ability to pay for such programs is limited, AAM and Layalina must produce them at a loss. This is where the government could step in—and, by underwriting these efforts on a sustained and consistent basis, reach many more viewers than Al-Hurra reaches, at a much lower cost.

• *In unfree markets, open both the Voice of America (VOA) and the surrogate entities to programs produced by independent nonprofits; and in addition, encourage the surrogate entities to carry programs about America.*

As noted above, US international broadcasters tend to focus on news reporting and neglect the secondary goals of conveying a full and fair picture of American life, and advocating for the policies of the US government. Many would argue that these secondary goals are irrelevant to surrogate news reporting, which after all is not "about us" but "about them." This argument harks back to the days when the VOA was presumed to be exclusively "about us," and the surrogate entities—Radio Free Europe/Radio Liberty, the Office of Cuba Broadcasting, and Radio Free Asia—were presumed to be exclusively "about them." But as noted by two veterans of US international broadcasting, Ross Johnson and Eugene Parta, this distinction is no longer meaningful in a world of globalized media.[22] The great merit of the programs being produced by AAM and Layalina is that they focus on both "us" and "them." Co-produced with media companies in other countries, such programs—not just "town meetings" but also talk shows, reality shows, and performance-based shows—have the potential to bring Americans and others together in new and unprecedented ways. I will say more about this in the sections that follow.

THE CHALLENGE OF HIGH CULTURE: "LEVELING UP"

The traditional use of high culture in diplomacy is to foster goodwill between elites, with rulers and diplomats dazzling one another with their glorious heritages. When one nation conquers and subjugates another, high culture is used in a different way, to assert the superiority of the conqueror. This was true of Britain, France, and the other Western colonial powers, even after their former possessions achieved independence. Today, by contrast, British and European cultural diplomats prefer to downplay any sense of a glorious heritage in favor of a multilateral approach that keeps the interests of any one government at arm's length.

America is different. Lacking an aristocratic past, this country has long endeavored to prove itself both civilized and democratic. Thus, its cultural diplomacy has been guided by the same ideal as our domestic cultural philanthropy:

giving people of all backgrounds, including the most humble, access to humanity's highest achievements. This ideal was expressed with great clarity in 1905 by the dean of Worcester Academy, the Massachusetts prep school attended by songwriter Cole Porter: "Democracy is not a leveling down, but a leveling up."[23] The ideal of "leveling up" motivated the wealthy founders of America's great public libraries and museums.[24] And on many occasions it has motivated its cultural diplomats.

That ideal seems forgotten today, as US public diplomats seem to regard the export of high culture as a snobbish activity that is irrelevant, even antithetical to the national interest. This neglect of high culture is mistaken on three counts.

First, it is foolish to ignore foreign elites, especially in countries where the capital is the center of both politics and culture. In this regard, America is the exception: Washington is more cultured today than in the past, but no one has ever accused it of being the nation's cultural capital. If Washington's cultural bigwigs react negatively to an event at the German embassy, their reaction will make nary a ripple on Capitol Hill. But if Berlin's cultural bigwigs attend a Fourth of July celebration at the US embassy, where the only cuisine offered is Kentucky Fried Chicken and Burger King (as I witnessed a few years ago), the wave of their amused contempt will travel further.

Second, America's heritage is inherently less elitist than that of the Old World. Every civilization worth its salt has both a "cultivated" and a "vernacular" arts tradition.[25] But in America the two are intertwined, with major artists drawing on popular genres (Herman Melville on explorer's journals, Mark Twain on Afro-American folktales, Aaron Copland on Shaker hymns); commercial entertainers rising to the level of celebrated artists (Duke Ellington, Charlie Chaplin, John Ford); and cultivated and vernacular figures engaging in fruitful collaborations (Leopold Stokowski and Walt Disney, Stuart Davis and Earl Hines, Twyla Tharp and Billy Joel).

Third, the open, accessible teaching style that makes American universities so appealing is also part of the way we present high culture. Leonard Bernstein's televised *Young People's Concerts* are an obvious example from the past. But there are countless others, from the "Favorite Poem Project" of former poet laureate Robert Pinsky to the "Shakespeare in the Park" program pioneered by the Public Theater in New York (and more recently the Public Theater's "Mobile Unit," which performs live Shakespeare in prisons, nursing homes, and homeless shelters). To present America's heritage in a user-friendly way, as opposed to doing so in a snobbish way that condescends to ordinary men and women, is an excellent use of resources.

Suggestions for High Culture

• *Use the mass media to share what is finest and highest, including classic popular culture, and do so in the best American tradition of "leveling up."*
As shown in Chapter 6, the hopes of America's cultural diplomats have often been thwarted by the political suspicions and middlebrow sensibilities of our elected officials. This, too, is a sign of the democratic cast of American culture. Rather than being directed by an aristocratic, politically insulated establishment, cultural policy in the United States gets disputed in the political arena. This is why a major battlefield of America's culture war is Congress; why America's cultural steward-ship is weak and divided; and why its political class is sometimes allergic to any talk of arts funding. How many major political figures today have the chutzpah to say, "This is America's finest cultural expression. Share it with the world and send the taxpayers the bill"?

Yet this is exactly what the nation's publicly funded cultural agencies—the National Endowment for the Arts (NEA), National Endowment for the Humanities (NEH), Public Broadcasting Service (PBS), National Public Radio (NPR), and American Public Media (APM)—have been doing for years. Sometimes used as political footballs, attacked for elitism and political bias, these agencies are also cultural stewards, and together they have produced an impressive body of attrac-tive, accessible material devoted to the country's heritage.[26] The public's esteem for this material is revealed every time a budget-cutting politician calls for the elimination of these agencies, only to run into a solid wall of bipartisan public resistance.

What the public has not supported, but could perhaps be induced to support, is the use of this material in public diplomacy. Whenever this idea has been pro-posed in the past, it has quickly run into a legal and financial obstacle—namely, that it would cost too much to clear the rights, because they are typically held not by the agencies producing the programs but by a wide array of private parties, from collectors to institutional archives to performers' unions. For example, a segment of the PBS series *American Masters* about Ella Fitzgerald might contain images, sounds, and film clips from dozens of proprietors whose permission was granted for limited use only. It would be daunting and expensive to clear all those rights, even for limited use overseas—and for public diplomacy purposes, unlimited use is much preferable.[27]

Is this obstacle insurmountable? Chapter 5's account of the Washington-Holly-wood Pact suggests it is not. And so does the fact, reported in Chapter 7, that the much-maligned Al-Hurra television channel now rebroadcasts such PBS programs as *The Newshour*, *Frontline*, and *Nova* to its Arabic-speaking audiences. Where there's a political will, apparently, there's a way.

Such a project would probably have to start small, perhaps dubbing selected programs and offering them to appropriate foreign channels for a small fee.[28] In countries where the media are not free to make such deals, the programs could be carried on the various media platforms of the VOA or surrogate services. One could also anticipate further dissemination through illegal downloading and knockoff DVDs. While not officially approved by the US government, such pirated distribution would likely reach a broad audience—and perhaps the lawyers would be mollified knowing that versions dubbed in foreign languages would have little resale value in English-speaking markets.

Another gold mine of material lies in the "vaults" of the entertainment industry: films, recordings, and radio and TV shows dating back several decades. Much of this material deserves to gather dust, but some deserves to be preserved. But these "heritage assets," as former NEA chief Bill Ivey calls them, are often neglected and even destroyed, because "to these media industries, heritage will always play second fiddle to the core mission—creating shareholder values by selling new product."[29] For Ivey the solution is to establish a federal department of cultural affairs, empowered to curate this scattered and eroding heritage. He may be right, but given America's entrenched antielitism, that is unlikely to happen. A better approach might be to enlist the aid of more preservationist-minded commercial firms, such as Turner Classic Movies, Rounder Records, and the like; and to summon the political will to make this heritage part of a more eloquent public diplomacy.

- *Export the high culture of Europe in a distinctively American way.*
It would be wrong to suggest that Europeans no longer share their cultural riches. As Steve Green, the British cultural official quoted in Chapter 6, explained to me, "Nowadays, cultural diplomacy is undertaken by a massive range of players and not just the old style cultural institutes. The UK's leading orchestras, opera, ballet, theatre companies, and museums all have their own extensive international programs. They don't need the British Council's support anymore."[30]

Nevertheless, it is true that cultural diplomats from the former colonial powers are more comfortable pursuing many-sided "conversations" and programs of economic aid and capacity building rather than touting their own cultural heritage. Indeed, postcolonialist political correctness makes it hard to imagine non-Westerners actually being interested in the high cultural heritage of their former oppressors. Yet very often non-Westerners *are* interested, and this interest creates an opening for America. If our cultural stewards can bring Shakespeare to "underserved" communities at home, why not overseas? Why not work with overseas partners to bring European classics to non-Western audiences? For example, a skillfully translated and adapted version of the *Oresteia*, Aeschylus's trilogy about the cycle of blood vengeance finally arrested by Athena's call for a jury trial, might resonate powerfully in a country riven by tribal or sectarian violence.

It may be objected that producing a play is a lot of hard work, and that bringing the requisite number of theater professionals from America would be too costly. But what if the play were produced and performed locally? In 2004 the US embassy in Cairo sponsored a very successful all-Egyptian production of Thornton Wilder's *Our Town*, according to Nimet Naguib, the Egyptian cultural affairs officer quoted in Chapter 3.

Our Town is not the *Oresteia*, needless to say, and when Naguib first mentioned this production to me, I was skeptical, because Wilder's play is now regarded as old-fashioned and trite—and in cultural diplomacy circles, remembered as a cliché of Cold War cultural exchange second only to *Porgy and Bess*. But my skepticism faded as I heard more. First, the play was translated into colloquial Egyptian Arabic, giving a vivid local color to its humor, family sentiment, and poignant evocation of life's brevity. Second, the only American involved was the director, Seth Gordon, whose unpretentious style made a favorable impression on the cast and crew, a group that included some of Egypt's most prominent actors and theater artists.

Further, this production was a success not just in Cairo but also in the cities of Minia, Fayoum, and Ismailia, where, as Naguib recalled, "People were still talking about it three years later."[31] Most tellingly, its run coincided with the news of prisoner abuse in Abu Ghraib. But as Naguib also told me, "There were some protests in the theater lobby, but because the cast was Egyptian and it is so much an 'everyman's' play, they couldn't find anything to attack about it."[32]

• *Assist others in preserving their own cultural heritage.*
Google "Baghdad" and "cultural heritage," and you will see thousands of references to the 2003 looting of the National Museum of Iraq while US troops were otherwise engaged. Add the acronym "ICHP," and you will see maybe a hundred references to a more positive American contribution: the Iraq Cultural Heritage Project, launched in 2008 by the Educational and Cultural Affairs division of the State Department. Founded to help repair the museum and recover looted treasures, ICHP now works in museum development, conservation training, professional development, and scholarly collaboration. Iraq is obviously a high priority for such efforts, but the Educational and Cultural Affairs division of the State Department runs similar projects in other countries.

Preservation of foreign antiquities, and efforts to stem their illegal trafficking, may seem the slowest possible form of public diplomacy. But these forms of assistance can create deep reservoirs of good feeling, if done in the right spirit—that of serious collaboration, not unilateral action.

• *Help others to make their cultural riches more democratically accessible.*
Hans-Ulrich Seidt, the director of culture and communications for the German Foreign Office, told me that when working as his country's cultural attaché in

Washington, he spent most of his time "taking visitors to the gift shop in the National Gallery." In Europe there is still strong resistance to adding profit-making entities to venerable cultural institutions. That's why Seidt wanted German cultural officials to see the National Gallery, a glorious space where serious exhibitions exist quite happily beside bustling commerce. As he reported, some of his countrymen were offended by the Rembrandt coffee mugs and Monet mouse pads. (Who wouldn't be? Apart from the people who buy them, of course.) But others were quite taken with the possibility of helping Germany's struggling cultural sector in this way.[33]

This type of assistance would be especially meaningful in non-Western countries. When Francis Ricciardone was ambassador to Egypt in the mid-2000s, he discovered a collection of VOA tapes from the 1970s and 1980s containing interviews with hundreds of cultural luminaries, such as the Nobel Prize-winning author Naguib Mahfouz, the classical composer Mohamed Abdul Wahab, and the eminent actor Yehia Shaheen. Using a $10,000 grant from the Educational and Cultural Affairs division of the State Department, the Cairo embassy produced a three-CD compilation of the best interviews and distributed about two thousand copies. The full contents of the CDs were also made available on the embassy website, along with transcripts in Arabic and English.

To judge by the ambassador's comments in the liner notes, an even wider distribution would have been justified: "Most people around the world are aware of ancient Egypt's rich bequests to human civilization. These recordings are a small sample of the less well known but equally rich cultural and intellectual heritage that modern Egypt has given to the world. . . . It is our pleasure to offer it back with the same respect, interest and admiration with which it was originally recorded."[34]

• *Adopt the Radio Sawa ("together") approach of presenting US and foreign cultural expression side by side.*
If it works for pop music, why not try it with high culture? In a 2008 report for the Saban Center at the Brookings Institution, former ambassador Cynthia Schneider and public diplomacy scholar Kristin Nelson proposed an Arabic-English version of the aforementioned "Favorite Poem Project."[35] This is an excellent idea that could conceivably reach a large popular audience, in Iran as well as in the Arab countries, through Sawa-style radio programs of spoken poetry. It is hard for Americans to appreciate the central position of poetry in Arab and Persian culture, but perhaps we could find common ground in former US Poet Laureate Robert Pinsky's insistence that to read a poem aloud for pleasure is more important than to dissect one in a classroom.

The Sawa approach could also be taken to classical music, with *classical* defined as Duke Ellington defined it: "There are only two kinds of music, good and bad." Just as Radio Sawa tailors its mix of Arabic and Western pop music to different

Arab markets, so, too, could American musical presenters, working with foreign colleagues, tailor radio broadcasts to make both Western and non-Western classics comprehensible to ordinary listeners. Here, too, the idea would be to "level up" the music with respectful but down-to-earth commentary that appeals to the curious as well as to the cognoscenti.

CONTESTING THE ELEPHANT

The fun-house-mirror images of America conveyed by our popular culture are out there, giving aid and comfort to those who would like to see the nation discredited. This is not going to change any time soon. But what could change, with sufficient self-awareness, is the capacity of individual Americans to counter these distortions. The first step would be to listen to what others have to say about our popular culture.

By "others" I mean not extremists but ordinary men and women. Some of what they would say would sound intolerant, but that would not mean they "hate our freedoms."[36] Dictators and fanatics may revile America's political liberties, but most people do not. On the contrary, what I found in my interviews, and what emerges from a careful reading of global opinion, is that most people admire America's political liberties but recoil at the image of excessive personal freedom held up to them by American popular culture: an image of the isolated individual, detached from family and community, whose life is consumed by the ruthless pursuit of sex, money, or power. In societies where people have good reason to believe that the ties of family and community are all that stand between the individual and chaos, this image is unnerving.

In Chapter 1 I described the American social fabric as both loose-weave and cohesive, in the sense that the bright threads of our cooperative, civic spirit are interwoven with the dark strands of our ambivalence toward the demands of family and community. The trouble with today's popular culture is that it fails to weave these strands together. Either the image is too bright, portraying American communities as a version of Disneyland's Main Street and promising victory to all who strive; or it is too dark, portraying daily life as a nightmare of disconnection, hedonism, selfishness, and dysfunction. In sum, popular culture fails to reflect the American ethos.

This is why foreign visitors to the United States are frequently surprised to meet Americans whose lives reflect that ethos, in the sense of taking responsibility both for their own individual lives and for the well-being of their families and communities. It is also why Americans need to listen to foreign criticism of our popular culture. Very often, that criticism sounds a lot like our own. So in that spirit, I offer the following suggestions.

Suggestions for Popular Culture

• *Stop treating American entertainment as cultural expression at home and a commodity overseas. Become mindful, at least, of other countries' legitimate concerns about content.*

In 1915 the US Supreme Court defined the movies as "a business, pure and simple," exposing the new medium to censorship by state and local authorities.[37] In the 1960s this definition was overturned, and filmmakers won the same freedoms enjoyed by other artists in America. Yet when responding to the efforts of foreign governments to protect their own cultural industries and traditions, both Washington and Hollywood revert to the 1915 definition of film (and other entertainment products) as a mere commodity. It should not be surprising that this contradiction annoys many knowledgeable foreigners. If they object to the crude and violent content of American entertainment, they are met with lectures about free speech. If they express concern for the survival of their own entertainment industries, they are met with lectures about free trade.

This situation is not likely to change any time soon, but from the standpoint of public diplomacy both Washington and Hollywood could do more than lecture. Carol Balassa, the former US trade negotiator quoted in Chapter 5, proposes a public-private partnership devoted to assisting foreign filmmakers in distributing their work, both in their own countries and internationally. Distribution is daunting enough for an independent filmmaker in America, whose best hope is to attract the attention of a major distributor at a major film festival. It is even more daunting for a foreigner, because almost all of the major distributors are American, and their primary focus is on the US market, which is notoriously unreceptive to foreign films.

Past efforts to assist foreign filmmakers have focused almost entirely on the creative process and on the practical aspects of production. This is because most foreign filmmakers are much more preoccupied with these issues than with the challenge of actually marketing their films to audiences. But as noted by British producer David Puttnam, distribution is essential: "I can make the most thrilling or challenging movie imaginable . . . , but unless I have a well-thought-out arrangement with an effective worldwide distribution resource . . . , I am, to a great extent, wasting my time."[38]

Thus, Balassa suggests a US-sponsored film distribution program aimed at helping foreign filmmakers find—or create—effective local and regional distribution companies, as well as gain better access to the global distribution system dominated by the United States. Notably, she suggests that any such program would be better "branded" as coming not from the US government but from "the US private sector, whose film production and distribution expertise is the subject of worldwide admiration."[39] In other words, Hollywood should receive the lion's share of credit for an initiative that could come only from Washington.

If Balassa's proposal were taken up by Washington, what leverage would it have to enlist the cooperation of Hollywood? The question is a sobering one, because in some ways the transnational corporations that now preside over the American entertainment industry are bigger and more muscular than any government agency, with the exception of the Pentagon. Nevertheless, those corporations still need government help—for example, in finding a way to curb global piracy. So Washington could conceivably ask for something in return.

• *Keep an eye on the military-entertainment complex.*
Until recently, Hollywood never kowtowed to the military. Even at the height of World War II, when officials from the Office of War Information attempted to dictate the content of feature films, they were firmly resisted by the studios.[40] During the McCarthy era, the studio heads cooperated with the government, but the larger filmmaking community became quite alienated from Washington. The Vietnam War reinforced this alienation, as a new generation of filmmakers grew openly hostile to American militarism.

A break in this hostility occurred with the box-office success of *An Officer and a Gentleman* in 1982. But it took another thirty years for the relationship between Hollywood and the US military to become as warm as it is today. As noted above, the Pentagon is today the only part of government with muscles as big as those of the corporations presiding over the entertainment industry. What most Americans don't realize is that the Pentagon has been flexing those muscles of late. Indeed, it has come close to dictating the content of at least some feature films and TV shows.

This situation not only compromises the entertainment industry's much-touted independence, it also produces work that often bears a disturbing resemblance to the entertainment-propaganda churned out by authoritarian regimes.

So far, this American entertainment-propaganda does not do as well in the global market as do the action-oriented films and TV series described in Chapter 2. For example, in 2012 the military-produced feature film *Act of Valor* did not do nearly as well internationally as *The Dark Knight Rises*, released at the same time. But this doesn't mean we can ignore the growth of a military-entertainment complex. What's needed is greater oversight and regulation of the relationship, but that seems unlikely, given the political clout of both the Pentagon and Hollywood.

We therefore need to do what Americans do best, which is to play the watchdog. Journalists, critics, bloggers, and consumers should keep track of these collaborations in a way that is vigilant toward the real danger, but also prudent in recognizing that not every collaboration is a sellout and not every film depicting military heroism a crypto-fascist plot.

• *Pay close, critical attention to the compromises the US entertainment industry is making to gain entry to the vast Chinese market.*

As noted in Chapter 2, the prospect of the Chinese market is so alluring, some US entertainment companies seem willing to barter away their hard-won creative freedom in order to break into it. The conventional wisdom in the American news media is that Hollywood is bargaining hard and getting what it wants. For example, shortly after DreamWorks Animation announced that it was building a new studio in China in early 2012, the Chinese government announced that it was raising its annual import quota of foreign (read: US) films from twenty to thirty-four.

Given the timing, this raising of the quota was widely reported as a victory for Hollywood (and for Vice President Joe Biden, who helped broker the deal). But I wonder. The greater the number of US films produced with an eye to the dazzling Chinese market, the greater the leverage the Chinese authorities will have over their content. At some point, it may cease to matter whether US-Chinese co-productions are actually produced in America or in China. But this will not be a neutral outcome, because while Hollywood may not consider these films part of a global contest for cultural superiority, China most certainly will.

At the same time, the manipulations of the Chinese regime should not be equated with the cultural pushback arising in foreign markets with conservative social values, such as India, Indonesia, parts of Africa, and the Arab Middle East. As argued in Part One, such cultural pushback reflects genuine popular sentiment against offensive material. Such sentiment exists in China, but responding to it is hardly the first priority of the regime. Instead, the Chinese Communist Party deliberately confounds what the public finds *morally* objectionable with what the Party finds *politically* unacceptable.

An example of this would be the elimination of the pop-idol show *Super Girl* by the State Administration for Radio, Film, and Television (SARFT). As described in Chapter 4, SARFT's opening gambit against that immensely popular show was to hold a press conference denying—and thereby intimating—that the winner, Li Yuchun, was a lesbian. Clearly, SARFT was less concerned with Li Yuchun's sexual orientation than with the fact that she had just attracted the enthusiastic votes of eight million Chinese citizens.

The prospect of US entertainment companies surrendering creative freedom to ideologically aggressive foreign governments did not arise during the Cold War, because none of the Communist powers was in a position to tempt Hollywood with a rich consumer market. Today, however, China is in that position, which is why its apparent ability to bend Hollywood to its will ought to trouble us. This is not just a matter of film markets; it is also a matter of what Joseph Nye and the State Department call smart power. And China's stated intention is not just to rival Hollywood's profit-making power; it is also to usurp America's place as the world's dominant culture. Based on what China has produced so far in the way of entertainment, this may seem beyond its reach. But remember: Hollywood is signing up to help.

• *Keep the Internet free, but curb the freedom of US Internet companies to sell rope to the hangmen of freedom.*
Americans tend to expect only good things from the latest technology, and the Internet came along just as the Cold War was ending. So it is hardly surprising that our public diplomats should have been seized by cyber-utopianism between the 1990s and the Arab Spring. Today a more prudent view has set in, owing to mounting evidence that authoritarian regimes have learned to use the Internet for censorship, propaganda, and surveillance.[41] In response, the US government has been waging a vigorous defense of "Internet freedom." But it has not yet reckoned with its own role in creating the new cyber-dystopias.

Just as Washington has long boosted the export of American entertainment, so too has it assisted the sale of US information technology to authoritarian governments. Many Americans think US-based corporations should be able to do business wherever they want, as long as they do not violate US law. So companies such as Yahoo!, Google, Microsoft, Cisco, and AOL have felt free to sell goods and services to authoritarian governments indifferent to their citizens' human rights.[42] Some of these goods and services are neutral in the sense that they could be used for a variety of purposes. But many are non-neutral, in the sense that their clear purpose is to upgrade the machinery of political surveillance and control.

At some point, it may become politically viable for the US government to forbid the sale of non-neutral information technology to authoritarian regimes. But at the moment this seems a distant prospect. In part, this is because many Americans lack a sense of proportion about the dangers involved. Comfortable in our own civil liberties, we define the issue as "Internet freedom," when for millions of others it is freedom in the original, life-and-death sense. As some astute critics have noted, Americans tend to focus too much on their own government's blocking of information in the virtual world, and not enough on the blocking by foreign authoritarian governments of political action in the physical world. Information is vital, but even the best information is worthless if people cannot use it to build and sustain real, on-the-ground political organizations.[43]

• *Fight fire with fire.*
In free and partly free markets overseas, contest the distortions of popular culture with co-produced talk and reality shows aired on mainstream channels. As noted above, two US nonprofit media companies, Layalina Productions and America

Abroad Media, produce high-quality programs for widely watched foreign channels. Some of these programs are "town meetings" and talk shows focused on public affairs; others are reality shows adapted to a constructive purpose. These strike me as formats ready-made for the discussion of popular culture.

Under the town-meeting format, a multigenerational American audience could meet with a similar audience overseas to discuss well-known entertainment genres such as soap operas, action films, or pop-idol contests. It would be critical to include the full spectrum of reasonable opinion from both countries, including the views of those, religious leaders and others, who favor censorship. Equally crucial would be the presence of knowledgeable participants who can anchor the discussion in facts, and maintain an atmosphere of civility. This may not sound terribly exciting to Americans, but we are spoiled. In many non-Western countries, there is so little serious criticism or debate about popular culture, whether imported or homegrown, that audiences, especially young audiences, would respond enthusiastically to the prospect.

I base this comment on my own experience speaking with foreign youth, both overseas and in America. Worldwide, the keen interest that young people have in popular culture is matched only by the dearth of real debate on the topic. This dearth exists even in India, with its mature entertainment industry and huge number of newspaper readers. As Rauf Ahmed, a prominent Mumbai editor, commented to me, "Stars and directors do not like to be criticized." Another well-known Indian film scholar showed me a stack of newspapers with Bollywood headlines, and noted that none contained serious reporting or criticism about films, "just celebrity gossip, scandal-mongering, and PR fluff."[44]

Using the talk show format, a suitable host could invite ordinary guests to share their reactions to popular culture, pro and con. Here the model would not be in-your-face "infotainment"—the world does not need more of that. Rather the model might be Oprah Winfrey's book club, which focused on drawing out the emotional responses of untutored readers. From a public diplomacy perspective, the purpose of such shows would be to air subjects that might otherwise fester and, while festering, fuel popular suspicion that offensive popular culture is part of an American conspiracy. For this reason, such talk shows should make no secret of being supported by the US government.

As noted in Chapter 3, the reality show format does not automatically mean crass exhibitionism. The popular Layalina series *On the Road in America* was based on an MTV program called *Road Rules*, which managed to last several seasons without sinking too deeply into the muck. When task-oriented or based on a competition of skill or talent, reality shows can be entertaining, even uplifting. This is also true of the other Layalina program mentioned above, *Generation Entrepreneur*. Filmed in several different countries, it offers something that Arab viewers rarely see: young Arabs pursuing similar ambitions in a variety of national and cultural settings. At a time of rising sectarian conflict in the Middle East, such programs might even try to bridge the Sunni-Shia divide.

As for reality shows about Hollywood itself, they typically take a tabloid approach, dwelling on the decadent behavior of a few self-destructive celebrities. Why not take the opposite approach and follow the sane, normal lives of the hardworking men and women who actually make the movies? This kind of thing is already popular as filler on movie channels and DVDs, because the public is keenly interested in the craft of filmmaking. Aimed at overseas audiences, such programming could profile mature stars and directors known for their professionalism, as well as sympathetic technicians and crew members with a flair for explaining what they do. Further, by following these individuals home to their families and communities, a more subtle message could be sent about the normal lives of Americans being different than the distortions of popular culture.

Would foreign media companies see such programs as contrary to their self-interest? For example, would MBC, which devotes an entire channel to action films, refuse to carry a public-affairs show in which screen violence is criticized? It's hard to say, but my hunch is that some companies would regard such programs as a way to answer their own critics—and perhaps find their own society's golden mean of cultural expression.

• *Use popular music to engage with foreign youth, not entertain them in a commercial format.*
Radio Sawa, the channel initiated by former BBG member and commercial radio mogul Norman Pattiz, plays a commercial-style mix of American and Arab pop music to audiences in the Middle East. The most cogent criticism of Sawa is that it reaches out to an undifferentiated youth audience, as opposed to a carefully targeted audience of thinkers, movers, and shakers.[45] Since entertaining the masses is not part of public diplomacy, many critics have concluded that Radio Sawa is not the best use of scarce public diplomacy resources.

But does this mean popular music should never be used in public diplomacy? I would say no, because I can think of two cases where, after a period of trial and error, it came to be used quite effectively.

The first is a series of presentations on country music by David Firestein, a former foreign service officer from Austin, Texas, who served several years in Russia and China and who speaks both Mandarin and Russian fluently. Firestein told me that State Department officials back in Washington were too "jazz and hip-hop oriented" to appreciate the potential appeal of country music. But officials in the field were more supportive, and the programs went over very well. "A lot of people liked the strong vocals and the melodies," Firestein explained. "They also liked the lyrics, because they emphasized a different side of America, a side they could relate to better: hard work, family, and learning the difference between right and wrong."[46]

The point is underscored by this comment by Dan Southerland, executive editor of Radio Free Asia, who told me that when one of Firestein's country music presentations was aired on an RFA Mandarin service show, "People called and said, '*Make him ambassador!*'"[47]

The other effective use of popular music has been the State Department's "hip-hop diplomacy," which, rather than beaming the music indiscriminately at listeners, aims it carefully at specific audiences. For many Americans, the term *hip-hop* (or *rap*) conjures profanity, degrading sexual references, and swaggering threats of violence.[48] This strain of rap dominates the commercial mainstream in the United States, Britain, and Europe. But it is not the type of material featured in "hip-hop diplomacy." Instead, that program focuses on the grassroots art form that arose in New York City during the 1970s and continues to give a voice to disaffected minority youth.

Today this grassroots art form is practiced everywhere in the world, including in most Muslim-majority countries. Picking up on this trend in 2005, at the low point of the Iraq war, the Bush administration began to send African-American and Muslim-American rappers to North Africa, the Arab Middle East, Pakistan, Mongolia, and Indonesia. The idea was to draw disaffected Muslim youth away from violent extremism by connecting them with "hip-hop envoys" who personified the racial and religious diversity of America, as well as its freedom of expression. In 2006 a similar program was started in Muslim immigrant neighborhoods in Britain, the Netherlands, and France (to the discomfiture of some British, Dutch, and French officials).[49]

The obvious model here is the celebrated Cold War jazz tours. But this parallel is misleading, for a couple of reasons. First, jazz from the 1950s forward was no longer popular music, so the tours in many of the countries drew only elite audiences. There were exceptions: Louis Armstrong's 1960 tour of West Africa and Duke Ellington's 1971 tour of the Soviet Union both drew huge, ecstatic crowds.[50] But according to Thomas Simons, the diplomat who in 1963 accompanied Ellington to the Near East and the Subcontinent (Turkey, Iraq, Iran, Afghanistan, and Pakistan), the audiences in those countries were made up largely of expats and westernized elites. In Kabul, for example, the US embassy gave out eight thousand free tickets for a fifteen-thousand-seat stadium, but only a handful of people showed up. One reason, Simons recalled, was that the concert was scheduled on "camel market day." But another reason, as Simon had to explain to Ellington, was that "not everyone gravitated to jazz, despite what people like to think now."[51]

Not everyone gravitates to hip-hop, either. But unlike jazz in the 1950s, hip-hop is still a viable form of popular music, embraced by millions of young men and women as a way to vent emotions, express opinions, and (on occasion) challenge regimes. This is quite in keeping with hip-hop's origins in Caribbean and West African ritual praise—and insult. But this emphasis on speech also makes hip-hop different from jazz, which is fundamentally about musical sound. This poses a challenge to public diplomats seeking to deploy hip-hop against hostile ideologies. Like all speech, the supercharged lyrics of hip-hop can be turned to any purpose. During the Arab uprisings of 2011–12, hip-hop was used to express a variety of views: anti-regime, pro-regime, anti-democracy, pro-democracy, religious sectarian, radical Islamist. In such contexts it is tricky for an American "hip-hop envoy" to connect with a particular audience without inadvertently taking sides in a local conflict.[52]

Yet in one respect, hip-hop diplomacy has been strikingly on target. According to Toni Blackman, the first and foremost hip-hop envoy, one of the program's key messages is that commercial rap—the kind where the performer "behaves like a juvenile delinquent on MTV"—is only "two percent." This two percent, she points out, is "what mainstream radio and television represent . . . Lil Wayne, or Jay-Z or 50 Cent, . . . [but] that is not what we're talking about." Instead, Blackman talks about "the other 98 percent," the part of hip-hop that "reaches across generations" to express "spirituality, religion, feelings and emotions, love songs, celebration of one's parents . . . true stories from the heart."[53]

To judge by the reaction of one Moroccan participant, Blackman's message gets across, and it is not just about hip-hop. It is also about America: "I went around saying to a lot of rappers, men and women, it's not what you see in TV and movies from US what is happening in US. It's not the same. . . . People in America, they are not so vulgar, they are just talking like us, about real topics."[54]

• *Remember that America's distinctive ethos and political wisdom are not the exclusive property of Americans. But that should cause us to cherish them all the more.*
What is the best thing about America? To judge by the rhetoric of politicians and other public figures, it is the American propensity to dream—and dream big—about the future. The products of a history shaped by Protestant postmillennialism and Enlightenment faith in science, Americans like to envision the day when we will be, if not perfect, then considerably better than we are now. Recast as a secular "religion of progress," this propensity to dream about the future is continually reinforced by our country's steady, at times spectacular, record of technological achievement.

By contrast, the American ethos (and the political wisdom associated with it) seeks the good for human beings as they are, not as we would like them to be. Yet it does seek the good, which is why I find it worrisome that this ethos is so little known beyond our water's edge. During the heated debates over the ratification of the US Constitution, James Madison wrote: "Were the pictures which have been drawn by the political jealousy of some among us faithful likenesses of the human character, the inference would be, that there is not sufficient virtue among men for self-government; and that nothing less than the chains of despotism can restrain them from destroying and devouring one another."[55] The same is true of the likenesses of America now drawn by its popular culture.

Within the United States, the American ethos has been subject to three major criticisms. The first, arising in the late nineteenth century, dismissed it as a quaint holdover from a prescientific age. The second, emerging in the mid-twentieth century, lambasted it as hypocritical, given the many injustices scarring the nation's history. The third, dominating the landscape today, discredits the ethos on cultural-relativist grounds as part of an ethnocentric worldview that may resonate with Americans but has little meaning for the rest of humanity. Rather than reject these criticisms out of hand, I would apply them to those aspects of America that are in fact outdated, hypocritical, and ethnocentric. The ethos is not among these. On the contrary, it is a cultural universal in the sense of being essential to any working definition of *freedom* and *democracy.*

Most Americans would agree. Yet too often we take this ethos for granted, not realizing how poorly it is now being conveyed to others. I blame this on the culture war, which has generated two conflicting visions of what America stands for: a blue-state vision of unfettered personal and sexual freedom infused with perfect racial and gender equality; and a red-state vision of unrestrained economic liberty resting on stainless citizen virtue. When communicated to the rest of the world, neither of these visions conveys our country's true depth and complexity.

In 1958, the authors of *The Ugly American* predicted that the struggle with Soviet communism would be won or lost "in a multitude of tiny battles" occurring "mainly . . . in the minds of men." Their words could also apply to today's struggles with authoritarianism and Islamist extremism: "The sum of these tiny battles will decide whether our way of life is to perish or to persist." Yet there is a glaring difference between then and now. Back in the 1950s, policy makers and diplomats focused on foreign public opinion but also believed, in the spirit of technocrats everywhere, that they could manage it. Indeed, the whole premise of *The Ugly American,* stated in the authors' epilogue, was that the United States could win the Cold War if the government would just send "a small force of well-trained, well-chosen, hard-working, and dedicated professionals" overseas to "show by example that America is still the America of freedom and hope and knowledge and law."[56]

Today that premise is outdated, as a continual torrent of information cascades through the global media and the Internet, and all people, not just Americans, are more mobile than ever before. Yet the metaphor of tiny battles still pertains, because there are still only a limited number of competing worldviews out there, and the United States must contend with those that are most hostile and threatening to it. That is why policy makers, diplomats, politicians, military officers, and pundits strive to track what is being said about America in the world's top news outlets, not to mention major blogs and social media sites.

This obsession with news is understandable, given the importance of press freedom in America and the fact that foreign elites share that same obsession. But the premise of this book has been that a significant number, perhaps even a preponderance, of today's tiny battles are being fought not in the news media but in the mundane realm of popular culture. The wisdom of America is clear and straightforward: political liberty can be sustained only by self-governing individuals and prudently devised institutions. Yet when our fellow human beings look at America through the screen of our entertainment, what they see most darkly is a rejection of tradition, religion, family, and every kind of institutional restraint, in favor of unseemly egotism and libertinism. Attracted and repulsed by this image, they might be forgiven for not appreciating the part about self-governance.

ACKNOWLEDGMENTS

First of all, I owe a debt of gratitude to the late James Q. Wilson for discouraging me from writing this book. Walking on a beach in Malibu, I shared with him my central argument, and he responded by saying that there is no way such an argument can be proven with social scientific evidence. Yet as it happened, I was encouraged, because as Jim also commented, the same is true of all really important questions. Second, I am grateful to Robert Asahina for his friendship and superb judgment, both in writing and in life. Without Bob's timely interventions, this book might not have been written.

Another editor friend, Jay Tolson, expanded my intellectual horizons by inviting me to serve as literary editor of the *Wilson Quarterly*. When his successor, Steve Lagerfeld, published my first attempt to relate popular culture to public diplomacy, the article struck a chord with several seasoned practitioners—Carol Balassa, Donald Bishop, John Brown, Eugene Kopp, Yale Richmond, Rick Ruth—who, after diplomatically correcting my worst errors, began opening doors for me that I would never have found on my own. Behind those doors were others too numerous to mention, and the happy result is a book nourished by the insight and experience of over three hundred men and women in eleven countries.

There isn't room to thank all those people here, but let me mention a few who offered decisive encouragement and practical assistance: Kris Brewer of MIT, who with Zen-like patience raised my IT IQ; Montgomery Brown of the Earhart Foundation, who at a crucial stage provided the funding to see the project through; Carol Huang, who with great good humor helped to lay the groundwork for my overseas research; Peter NeCastro, who with a sure hand and a sharp wit lightened the burden of final proofreading; Mark O'Connor, David Quigley, and Joseph Quinn at Boston College, who gave me leave and welcomed me back; Nadia Schadlow at the Smith Richardson Foundation, who provided me with a generous travel grant; S. Frederick Starr, who challenged me to exit the American bubble; and Enders Wimbush, who encouraged me to circumnavigate the globe solo.

In every country I visited, there were men and women whose help, hospitality, and conversation made all the difference: Clive Davis, Mohini Patel, and Patrick Spaven in the UK; Reinhard Bütikofer, Annette Goerlich, Thomas Kleine-Brockhoff, Renée Krebs, Antje Kuchenbecker, Annelie Runge, Manfred Stinnes, and Claude Weinber in Germany; Lucyna Aleksandrowicz-Pedich, Christopher Garbowski, and Franek Lyra in Poland; Daniel and Hanka Raus and Sonia Winter in the Czech Republic; Murat and Catherine Somer in Turkey; Sally Elmoez and Nimet Naguib in Egypt; Jihad Fakhreddine and Abdallah Schleifer in the UAE; Bulent Cantimur, Rakesh Chopra, Aruna Dasgupta, Raja and Anjolie Menon, and Kiran Nagarkar in India; Endy Bayuni, Zorry Coates, Moritz Kleine-Brockhoff, and Ahmad Suaedy in Indonesia; John Barrett, Jennifer Galt, Carrie Li, and Barry Simmons in China; Patrick Cheung and Meaghan Morris in Hong Kong.

Some of those I interviewed for *Through a Screen Darkly* preferred to remain anonymous; others were willing to be quoted by name and at length. For sharing key insights I would like to thank (in addition to those named above) Rauf Ahmed, Simon Anholt, Richard Arndt, Dev Benegal, Peter and Brigitte Berger, Brian Carlson, Anu Chopra, Nicholas Cull, Cynthia Efird, Iain Elliot, Emre Erdogen, Harvey Feigenbaum, David Firestein, Anthony Fung, Jeffrey Gedmin, Ruslan Gelischanow, Robert Hefner, Alan Heil, Teng Jimeng, Nasreen Munni Kabir, Nabil Khatib, Aaron Lobel, Sean Morrow, Joan Mower, Halit Refiğ, Keith Reinhard, Francis Ricciardone, Leon Shahabian, Steven Siwek, Mardiros Soghom, Dan Southerland, Franz Magnis-Suseno, and Barry Zorthian.

For reading and commenting on the manuscript at various stages, I am indebted to several of the people already mentioned, as well as to Jess Castle, Daniel Chirot, Tim Evans, Matt Keeley, Natalia Quirk, Saman Saleem, and Roberta Wilson.

While working on this book I had the privilege of testing my ideas in several public forums. For the opportunity to do so, I thank Jerzy Axer and Piotr Wilczek of the Kolegium Artes Liberales at the University of Warsaw; Peter Berger of the Institute on Culture, Religion, and World Affairs at Boston University; Karlyn Bowman of the American Enterprise Institute; the members of Broadcasting Board of Governors; Alex Carpenter of the University of Alberta; David Chappelle of the University of Oklahoma; Mary Lou DeLong of the Council for Women of Boston College; Margy Faulkner of the Chilton Club in Boston; Jeffrey Gedmin of the Legatum Institute in London; Nadia Hijab of the Cosmos Club in Washington; Peter Schuck of Humanity in Action; Jon Shields of Claremont McKenna College; the staff of Radio Free Europe/Radio Liberty in Prague; and Alan Wolfe of the Boisi Center for Religion and Public Life at Boston College.

For research assistance above and beyond the call of duty, I thank Jordan Dorney, Carol Huang, Kate Mahoney, and Katie Moulton. For swiftly grasping what this book would be about—for making the connection between her father's speaking tours for the US Information Agency and her son's taste in rap music—I thank my agent, Carol Mann. And for his extraordinary patience, warmth, and relentless scrutiny of the manuscript in its early stages, I owe a major debt of gratitude to Chris Rogers of Yale University Press.

Finally, my husband Peter Skerry. There is no way to thank Peter. He is the rock upon which my life is built.

NOTES

INTRODUCTION

1. The acronym FPI stands for Front Pembela Islam, Malay for Islamic Defenders Front.
2. Interview, Jakarta, 4/4/07.
3. Just to cite a couple of recent examples, see Tristin Hopper, "Irshad Manji Book Tour in Indonesia Runs into Trouble with Islamic 'Thugs,'" *National Post* (May 10, 2012); and "Lady Gaga 'Devastated' as Indonesia Concert Cancelled," BBC Asia (May 28, 2012).
4. Interview, Jakarta, 4/5/07.
5. Of course, the UK, western Europe, and Japan have been doing it longer. Today many newly minted TV and film producers imitate UK, West European, and Japanese models. But most of those models were derived from American originals, for the simple reason that America has the world's longest history of privately owned media and commercial popular culture.
6. Interview, Jakarta, 4/5/07; email to author, 7/15/13.
7. *Support for Tougher Indecency Measures, but Worries About Government Intrusiveness* (Washington: Pew Research Center, April 19, 2005), 2.
8. "By far the largest since 2002," this survey interviewed 45,239 respondents in forty-seven countries in April 2007. See *Global Unease with Major World Powers* (Pew Global Attitudes Project, June 27, 2007), 102.
9. Steven Kull et al., *Public Opinion in Iran and America on Key International Issues*, Program on International Policy Attitudes, University of Maryland (January 24, 2007), WorldPublicOpinion.org.
10. Pew (2007), 102.
11. "Egyptians on Obama, US Policies, and Democracy," WorldPublicOpinion.org (June 3, 2009).
12. Interview, Jakarta, 4/3/07.
13. Figures are in constant dollars. See "Services Supplied to Foreign Persons by U.S.

MNCs Through Their MOFAs," "Motion picture and video industries," Bureau of Economic Analysis, Washington, DC (2012), Tables 9A and 9c.

14. See Allen J. Scott, "Hollywood in the Era of Globalization," Yale Center for the Study of Globalization (29 November 2002); and Pamela McClintock, "Global Box Office Hit $31.6 Bil in 2011, Fueled by Exploding International Growth," *Hollywood Reporter* (March 22, 2012).

15. Stephen E. Siwek, *The True Cost of Motion Picture Piracy to the U.S. Economy*, Policy Report 186 (Washington: Institute for Policy Innovation, September 2006), 21 and 23.

16. Interview, Jakarta, 4/1/07.

17. Interview, Berlin, 9/1/06.

18. Telephone interview, 5/1/07.

19. Pew (2007), 99. Only in Israel and three African countries did a majority disagree. The question about "American ideas and customs" was not asked in the United States.

20. "Oh Wow! Some Highlights of 2011," *Wall Street Journal* (December 23, 2011).

21. Interview, Cairo, 3/11/07.

22. The visitors in this study were from Mexico, where many people have visited the United States. Conceivably the contrast between screen and reality is even greater for visitors from farther away. Jerrold Keilson, *The Impact of the International Visitor Experience in Mexico*, unpublished manuscript (2001).

23. John Keegan, *A History of Warfare* (Vintage, 1994), 46.

24. Francis Fukuyama, "The End of History?," *National Interest* (Summer 1989); and Madeleine K. Albright, interview on *Today Show* (NBC-TV, February 19, 1998), accessed at US Department of State Archive.

25. Bill Ivey and Heather Hurlburt, *Cultural Diplomacy and the National Interest*, Curb Center for the Arts, Enterprise, and Public Policy (Vanderbilt University, 2005), 18.

26. For the definitive history of that decade, see Nicholas J. Cull, *The Decline and Fall of the United States Information Agency* (Palgrave, 2012).

27. Quoted in Victoria de Grazia, *Irresistible Empire* (Harvard University Press, 2005), 299.

28. "A Model of Christian Charity," edited by John Beardsley. Accessed at: http://religiousfreedom.lib.virginia.edu/sacred/charity.html.

29. See Isaiah 42:6, 49:6-8, and 60:3. Also Matthew 5:16.

30. This distinction is cogently explained by Martin Diamond in *As Far As Republican Principles Will Admit* (American Enterprise Institute, 1992), ch. 21; and by Jerry Z. Muller, *The Mind and the Market* (Knopf, 2001).

31. *Benjamin Franklin: The Autobiography and Other Writings* (Signet Classic, 1961), 78.

32. *Democracy in America*, trans. George Lawrence, ed. J. P. Mayer (Perennial Classics, 1969), Vol. II, Part II, ch. 9, 527.

33. See Perry Miller, "Declension in a Bible Commonwealth," *Nature's Nation* (Belknap Press, Harvard University, 1967), 48.

34. The maxim is an old Latin proverb: *Religio peperit Divitias, et filia devoravit matrem.* See *Magnalia Christi Americana* (Ecclesiastical History of New England), s. 63 (1702).

35. See Gordon Wood, *The Creation of the American Republic* (Norton, 1969); and *The Radicalism of the American Revolution* (Vintage, 1993).

36. The term is from Montesquieu, who defined four political regimes: despotism, monarchy, aristocratic republic (ruled by an elite), and democratic republic (ruled by the people). See *The Spirit of the Laws,* 2.1, 2.4.

37. These conditions for democratic virtue are also from Montesquieu. See *The Spirit of the Laws,* 4.5.

38. "Remembering Adam Smith," *Wall Street Journal* (April 6, 1994).

39. Ibid.

40. *The Wealth of Nations* (Modern Library, 1965), Part I, ch. 8, 79.

41. Quoted in James Hookway and Patrick Barta, "Sun Kyi Pressed over Talk of Rift," *Wall Street Journal* (June 7, 2012).

42. See George M. Marsden, *Religion and American Culture* (Wadsworth, 2001), 33–34.

43. According to one participant, camp meetings in the South, where both races attended, would occasionally end when "great billows of sound . . . rolled over the encampment, and . . . the voices of the masters and veterans among the white people would echo back, in happy response, the jubilant shout of the rejoicing slaves." Quoted in Eileen Southern, *The Music of Black Americans* (University of Chicago Press, 1970), 99.

44. See Marsden (2001), 61–62.

45. The Great Awakenings also included *pre-millennial* sects, such as the Millerites and Adventists. Today, pre-millennialism makes headlines whenever its adherents predict the Rapture or call someone they dislike the Anti-Christ. But historically, it has not dominated in America, because its expectation of doom fails to mesh with the country's Enlightenment-bred faith in progress.

46. Charles Sheldon, *In His Steps* (1897). Accessed at Project Gutenberg: http://www .gutenberg.org/ebooks/4540, chs. 1 and 31.

47. See *The True and Only Heaven* (Norton, 1991), passim.

48. "Intellectual Autobiography," in *Reinhold Niebuhr: His Religious, Social, and Political Thought,* ed. Charles W. Kegley and Robert W. Bretall (Macmillan, 1956), 12.

49. See John Kouwenhoven, *The Arts in Modern American Civilization* (Norton, 1967, first published 1948), 13–15.

50. *Idea for a Universal History with a Cosmopolitan Intention,* Thesis 6.

51. *American Politics: The Promise of Disharmony* (Harvard University Press, 1981), 14, 4.

52. The terms *blue state* and *red state* were given their present meaning by NBC journalist Tim Russert during the 2000 presidential election and are striking for the choice of *red,* traditionally the color of the far left, to designate Republican-leaning states. The terms are hardly definitive, but they do capture the flavor of America's political and cultural divisions in the early twenty-first century. And they are less confusing than *left* and *right,* never mind *liberal* and *conservative.* The word *state* is also misleading, because these two ideological camps are not (yet?) congruent with state borders. But to drop it would be to raise again the far-left connotation of *red.*

53. *Federalist Papers*, No. 10.
54. CCP White Paper (2005), quoted in Richard McGregor, *The Party* (Harper 2010), 20.
55. Tianjian Shi and Jie Lu, "The Shadow of Confucianism," *Journal of Democracy* 21:4, 125.
56. Pew (2007), 2.
57. See Walter Berns, *The First Amendment and the Future of American Democracy* (Regnery, 1985); and Harry M. Clor, *Public Morality and Liberal Society* (University of Notre Dame Press, 1996).
58. For an incisive treatment of this topic, see Evgeny Morozov, *The Net Delusion* (Public Affairs, 2011).
59. This anecdote was related by actor Will Smith at "The Business of Show Business," MPAA-sponsored forum held at the Donald W. Reynolds Center for Art and Portraiture, Washington, DC, February 6, 2007.
60. Interview, London, 7/25/06.
61. Interview, Jakarta, 4/3/07.

PART ONE PROLOGUE. CULTURAL EXPORT — AND PUSHBACK

1. See James L. Watson, ed., *Golden Arches East* (Stanford University Press, 1997), passim, 31.
2. Defined narrowly, *Bollywood* refers to films produced in Mumbai (Bombay), which constitute only 20 percent of the total. Another 40 percent are produced in Andrha Pradesh and Chennai. But *Bollywood* also refers to Indian film more generally.
3. See Anupama Chopra, "Slumdog Comedian," in *Daily Beast* (August 4, 2009): http://www.thedailybeast.com/articles/2009/08/04/slumdog-comedian.html.
4. For an amusing look at the perils of adapting the family sitcom *Everybody Loves Raymond* for the Russian market, see *Exporting Raymond*, directed by Phil Rosenthal (Culver Entertainment et al., 2010).
5. See discussion of cultural protectionism in Chapter 5.
6. See Carol Balassa, *America's Image*, report for Curb Center for Art, Enterprise, and Public Policy (Vanderbilt University, 2008).
7. It is worth noting that US officials rarely acknowledge this fact. As one senior diplomat confided in me, "I can testify from conversations at embassies that there is no sympathy for local objections. The local folks with moral or cultural objections to American films will be thought of as prig yahoos."
8. For a lucid overview, see Marwan M. Kraidy and Joe F. Khalil, *Arab Television Industries* (British Film Institute, Palgrave MacMillan, 2009).
9. "Company Profile," McDonald's website: http://www.aboutmcdonalds.com/mcd/investors/company_profile.html. Accessed 6/21/12.
10. Watson (1997), 33.
11. Interview, Jakarta, 4/1/07.
12. At least this was true before 2008, when the company announced that it would no longer use harmful trans-fats in the oil used to cook its french fries. See "McDon-

ald's Holds Down Dollar Meal, Making Menu Healthier," *International Business Times* (May 22, 2008).

13. Interview, Beijing, 4/15/07.

14. Another nugget the Chinese showed in their theaters in the 1970s was a made-for-television film called *Nightmare in Badham County*, about two young women whose car breaks down in a small town. When they spurn the sexual advances of the local sheriff, played by Chuck Connors, the women are thrown into jail and roughed up by the guards.

15. Interview, Beijing, 4/16/07.

16. Daniel Fox, introduction to Simon N. Patten, *The New Basis of Civilization* (Harvard University Press, 1968; originally published 1907), xvi.

17. *The Decline and Rise of the Consumer* (D. Appleton-Century, 1936), 94–96.

18. *Liberty and Freedom* (Oxford, 2006), 4–8.

19. See William Safire, "Bush's 'Freedom Speech,'" *New York Times* (January 21, 2005).

CHAPTER 1. THE AMERICAN WAY OF SEX

1. See *When Marriage Disappears*, report of the National Marriage Project (University of Virginia and Institute for American Values, 2010).

2. Despite their scientific-sounding titles, Kinsey's *Sexual Behavior in the Human Male* (1948) and *Sexual Behavior in the Human Female* (1953) were based on a decidedly unscientific sample of the US population. But Kinsey had perfect timing: he persuaded Americans that they were already liberated and that the only thing standing between them and utopia were their inhibitions. This provided the opening for Hefner, the reconstructed Methodist whose brilliant rebranding of sex transformed it from a dangerous passion to a disposable product.

3. Quoted in *Changing Minds, Winning Peace*, report of the Advisory Group on Public Diplomacy for the Arab and Muslim World (2003), 21.

4. These include *Three's Company* (ABC, 1977–85), *Seinfeld* (NBC, 1990–98), *Melrose Place* (Fox, 1992–99), *Living Single* (Fox, 1993–98), *Ally McBeal* (Fox, 1997–2002), and *Sex and the City* (HBO, 1998–2004). I would also add *Desperate Housewives* (ABC, 2004–present), whose characters are married but might as well not be.

5. David Crane, Marta Kauffman, and Kevin Bright, quoted in Matt Lauer, "*Friends* Creators Share Show's Beginnings," MSNBC (May 4, 2005). Accessed at: http://www.msnbc.msn.com/id/4899445/.

6. These figures are for 1994–2005. Some of the channels that carry *Friends* are DIGITURK in Turkey; the Saudi-owned Middle East Broadcasting Center (MBC, reaching all twenty-four Arab markets); and the state-owned Dubai ONE (which airs it several times a day). Warner Brothers e-mail, 10/5/07.

7. The VCD, or video compact disc, is a cheaper version of the DVD and is overwhelmingly the format of choice among media pirates.

8. *Friends* is watched in Argentina, Australia, Belgium, Brazil, Canada, Chile, Colombia, Denmark, Finland, France, Germany, Greece, Hungary, Italy, Mexico,

Netherlands, Norway, Peru, Poland, Romania, Russia, South Africa, Spain, Sweden, United Kingdom, Venezuela. Warner Brothers e-mail to author, 10/5/07.

9. George Weyman, editor of *Arab Media & Society*, interview, Cairo, 3/11/07.

10. "The New Girl Order," *City Journal* (Autumn 2007).

11. According to the Internet Movie Database, the DVD of *Friends* was legally released in China in 2004: http://www.imdb.com/title/tt0108778/releaseinfo?ref_=tt_dt_dt. *Ally McBeal*, *Sex and the City*, and *Desperate Housewives* are all widely available on pirated VCDs, as well as on downloaded files with Mandarin subtitles added by English-speaking fans.

12. James Poniewozik, "Queer Eye for Straight TV," *Time* (March 7, 2005).

13. Hisham El Shaarani, interview, Sharjah, 3/20/07.

14. Interview, Mumbai, 3/28/07.

15. Interview, Beijing, 4/17/07.

16. Internet Movie Database.

17. CBS website: http://www.cbs.com/daytime/the_bold_and_the_beautiful/about/.

18. Javier Lizarzaburu, "How Telenovelas Conquered the World," BBC News (April 1, 2006).

19. They also have a large following on Spanish-language channels in the United States. See "Telenovela," Museum of Broadcasting Communications: http://www.museum .tv/archives/etv/T/htmlT/telenovela/telenovela.htm; and Monte Reel, "In Latin America, Teens Are Getting Soaps in Their Eyes," *Washington Post* (April 16, 2005).

20. As Kermode argues, this is true even in sophisticated narratives that refuse to end with a moral—their refusal *is* their moral. See *The Sense of an Ending* (Oxford University Press, 1968).

21. See Arvind Singh and Everett M. Rogers, *Entertainment-Education* (Lawrence Erlbaum, 1999).

22. See Alessandra Stanley, "Ramadan TV Gently Pushes Saudi Boundaries," *New York Times* (August 19, 2012).

23. Phil Sands, "Syrian Soap Operas Sidelined by Protests and Censorship," *The National* [UAE] (July 23, 2011).

24. See *Global Unease with Major World Powers* (Pew Global Attitudes Project, June 27, 2007), 102, 88.

25. See Edward Luce, *In Spite of the Gods: The Strange Rise of India* (Doubleday, 2007), 8; and Mira Kamdar, *Planet India* (Scribner, 2007), 193.

26. Nasreen Munni Kabir, *Talking Pictures: Conversations on Hindi Cinema with Javed Akhtar* (Oxford, 1999), 35.

27. Kamdar (2007), 67.

28. Manjeet Kripalani and Ron Grover, "Can New Money Create a World-Class Film Industry in India?," *Business Week Online* (December 2, 2002).

29. E-mail to author, 3/5/09.

30. Patricia Uberoi, "Imagining the Family: An Ethnography of Viewing *Hum Aapke Hain Koun . . . !*," in *Pleasure and the Nation: The History, Politics and Consumption of Popular Culture in India*, ed. Rachel Dwyer and Christopher Pinney (Oxford, 2001), 310.

31. Ironically, two Indian employees of Orion Pictures, Mukesh Talreja and Nikhil Ad-

vani, announced in 2009 that they had persuaded Warner Brothers to give them the legal right to produce an Indian remake of *Wedding Crashers*, in exchange for full presentation and distribution rights worldwide. The film has not yet been released, so it is not yet possible to gauge the degree of cultural pushback it contains.

32. Predictably, the 2000 version of *Meet the Parents* was a remake of a 1992 independent film by the same title, which *Variety* described as "a blatant attack on marriage, suburban indifference, Christian hypocrisy and the nuclear family." See Suzan Ayscough review (August 13, 1992).

33. Box Office Mojo, All Time Box Office, Worldwide Grosses: http://www.boxoffice mojo.com/alltime/world/.

34. Meena Iyer, "Hollywood Bets Big on Bollywood," *Times of India* (October 19, 2008).

35. See Hariqbal Basi, "Indianizing Hollywood: The Debate over Bollywood's Copyright Infringement" (January 2010), unpublished law review article accessed at: http://works.bepress.com/hariqbal_basi/2.

36. Anupama Chopra, interview, Mumbai, 3/27/07; Bamzai, "How India Watches movies," *India Today* (December 6, 2007).

37. This trend is further exacerbated by the growing preference of poor rural Indians for watching films at home. According to the Confederation of Indian Industries (CII), 75 percent of rural Indians now prefer to watch movies at home, typically on pirated VCDs. Quoted in Bamzai (2007).

38. Interview, Mumbai, 3/29/07.

39. Interview, Mumbai, 3/29/07.

40. Ralph Ellison, "The Little Man at Chehaw Station," in *Going to the Territory* (Random House, 1986), 21.

41. See Robert T. Michael, "An Economic Perspective on Marriage," in *Family Transformed*, ed. Steven M. Tipton and John Witte, Jr. (Georgetown University Press, 2005).

42. Linda J. Waite and William J. Doherty, "Marriage and Responsible Fatherhood," in Tipton and Witte (2005), 151–54.

43. *The State of Our Unions* 2001 (National Marriage Project, Rutgers University, 2001); cited as NMP/Gallup Survey in Barbara Dafoe Whitehead, "The Changing Pathway to Marriage," in Tipton and Witte (2005).

44. Whitehead (2005), 175.

45. Morris Dickstein, *Gates of Eden* (Basic, 1977), 81.

CHAPTER 2. EMPIRE OF SPECIAL EFFECTS

1. Most of the blockbusters mentioned in this chapter are international co-productions, but they are Hollywood products because most of their financing and all of their promotion and distribution are controlled by the "big six" members of the Motion Picture Association of America: Walt Disney Motion Pictures Group (The Walt Disney Company), Sony Pictures Entertainment (Sony), Paramount Pictures (Viacom), 20th Century Fox (News Corporation), Universal Studios (NBC Universal), and Warner Bros. (Time Warner).

2. In terms of revenue earned overseas, the top ten films are almost always Hollywood blockbusters. In May of 2013, for example, these were *Avatar*, $2 billion; *Titanic*, $1.5 billion; *Harry Potter and the Deathly Hallows Part 2*, $960 million; *Marvel's The Avengers*, $888 million; *Skyfall*, $804 million; *Pirates of the Caribbean: On Stranger Tides*, $803 million; *Transformers: Dark of the Moon*, $771 million; *Lord of the Rings: The Return of the King*, $742 million; *Ice Age: Continental Drift*, $716 million; and *The Hobbit: An Unexpected Journey*, $714 million: http://www.boxofficemojo.com/alltime/world/.

3. "The Book of the Century," Salon.com (June 4, 2001): http://www.salon.com/2001/06/04/tolkien_3/.

4. Frank Miller and Lynn Varley, 300 (Dark Horse Comics, 1998).

5. Touraj Daryaee, "Go Tell the Spartans: How 300 misrepresents Persians in History," Iranian.com (March 14, 2007).

6. Azadeh Moaveni, "300 Sparks an Outcry in Tehran," *Time* (March 13, 2007).

7. Azadeh Moaveni, "300 — Fact or Fiction?," *RealClear Politics* (March 22, 2007).

8. See Box Office Mojo: http://www.boxofficemojo.com/alltime/world/.

9. Li Chengpeng, www.sina.com, quoted in "Avatar: A Eulogy for China's 'Nail Houses'" (January 13, 2010): www.chinaview.cn.

10. Tom Long, "Fourth 'Pirates' Movie Makes Little Sense but a Lot of Noise," *Detroit News* (May 19, 2011).

11. Quoted in Li Huizi, "'Kung Fu Panda' Punches Away at Controls on Creativity" (July 4, 2008): www.xinhuanet.com.

12. See Maureen Fan, "'Kung Fu Panda' Hits a Sore Spot in China," *Washington Post* (July 12, 2008).

13. Fan Huang, *The Shanghaiist* (July 8, 2011).

14. See Wesley Jacks, "Movie Industry: Artistic Alliances," in *News China Magazine* (August 2012).

15. See Chen Jiying, "Movie Theater Deal: Silver Smokescreen," in *News China Magazine* (August 2012).

16. Quoted in "'Kong [*sic*] Fu Panda 2' Incorporates More Chinese Elements," Thinking Chinese website (May 28, 2011): http://thinkingchinese.com/index.php?page_id=291.

17. The same thing has happened with the *Iron Man* franchise. According to one report, Disney-Marvel, which is co-producing *Iron Man* 3 in China, is "rumored to have drastically altered the portrayal of its villain 'The Mandarin' and added a 'positive' Chinese character to its plot," in order "to please local authorities." See Chen Jiying (2012). After *Kung Fu Panda* 3, the next production in the Oriental DreamWorks pipeline is *The Tibet Code*, based on the best-selling novels by He Ma. The story follows a band of intrepid Chinese heroes as they seek to recover ancient Buddhist treasures hidden by the ninth-century Tibetan ruler Lang Darma, who is said to have persecuted Buddhists. To Hollywood, this promises to be a great adventure similar to the Indiana Jones series. To China, it presents a golden opportunity to rewrite a crucial episode in Tibetan history with the Han Chinese as the good guys.

18. "Kung Fu Panda Gives Food for Thought," *China Daily* (July 5, 2008).

19. "Political Humor in a Post-Totalitarian Dictatorship," in *No Enemies, No Hatred* (Harvard University Press, 2010), 187.

20. Production Code of the Motion Picture Industry, accessed at: http://productioncode .dhwritings.com/index.php.

21. Created by the novelist Owen Wister in 1902, *The Virginian* was made into a movie four times: in 1914, 1923, 1929, 1946, and (for television) 2000.

22. Bosley Crowther, "'A Fistful of Dollars' Opens," *New York Times* (February 2, 1967).

23. Edward Buscombe, "The Western," in *The Oxford History of World Cinema* (Oxford, 1996), 293.

24. For example, Cagney played a tough FBI agent in *G-Men* (1935), and Robinson played a detective in *Bullets or Ballots* (1936) and *The Amazing Dr. Clitterhouse* (1938).

25. Quoted in Brian Stelter, "Serial Killer Moves to CBS, to a Not Entirely Warm Welcome," *New York Times* (February 16, 2008).

26. I heard a similar story from a veteran foreign service officer, who described the typical US embassy program in which an American journalist speaks to local reporters in an authoritarian country: "The American dutifully explains all the techniques of diligent investigative journalism, including FOIA requests and reviews of business filings, property records, contracts, lawsuit transcripts, etc. But to the foreign journalists, this is not helpful, because for them, none of this evidence exists."

27. *First Blood* (1982), *Rambo: First Blood Part II* (1985), and *Rambo III* (1988).

28. John Mueller, "Dead and Deader," *Los Angeles Times* (January 20, 2008).

29. Interview, Hong Kong, 4/19/07.

30. See David Edelstein, "Now Playing at Your Local Multiplex: Torture Porn," *New York* (January 28, 2006).

31. Darren Bousman, interview with MTV online (June 16, 2007).

32. Eli Roth, interviewed by Elvis Mitchell, *Interview* (June 2007).

33. For a probing exploration of this theme, see Will Self, "When It's Too Violent to Watch," *Telegraph* (September 28, 1996).

34. Review of *Dark Knight* in *London Daily Telegraph* (July 26, 2008).

35. For a full exposition of this philosophical argument, see Harry M. Clor, *Public Morality and Liberal Society* (University of Notre Dame Press, 1996).

36. Concurring opinion, Brown v. Entertainment Merchants Association (July 2011), 16.

37. Opinion of the Court, in ibid., 5.

38. See ESRB website: http://www.esrb.org/ratings/ratings_guide.jsp.

39. Some games contain a grain of skepticism toward their own violence. For example, one of the games in the Japanese series Metal Gear Solid invites the gamer to consider all the bleeding corpses he has created, and ranks play according to how few enemies have died, not how many. But this was the exception that proves the rule. I am indebted to Matthew Keeley for this observation.

40. I am indebted to Matthew Keeley and Thomas Warns for this account of violence in video games.

41. Interview, Beijing, 4/16/07.

42. Press release, New Zealand Office of Film and Literature Classification, quoted at *Scoop Independent News* (July 7, 2006), http://www.scoop.co.nz/stories/PO0607/ S00059.htm.

43. As evidenced by two of my best informants on this topic, Matthew Keeley and Thomas Warns, it is clear that lifelong gamers can grow up to be sane and intelligent young men.

44. Interview, Hong Kong, 4/21/07.

45. Robert Cochran, co-creator of 24, quoted in Donna Miles, "Military, Hollywood Team Up to Create Realism, Drama on Big Screen," American Forces Press Service (June 8, 2007); http://www.defense.gov/News/NewsArticle.aspx?ID=46352.

46. Philip Strub, "The Pentagon's 'Hollywood Liaison,'" interview on *The Kojo Nnamdi Show*, WAMU 88.5 FM, Washington, DC (July 19, 2012); http://thekojonnamdishow .org/shows/2012-07-19/pentagons-hollywood-liaison/transcript.

47. Quoted in Jordan Zakarin, "Act of Valor and the Military's Long Hollywood Mission," *Huffington Post* (February 21, 2012).

48. Interview, Boston, 4/16/10.

49. Tech. Sgt. Jeremy Phillips, quoted in Matt Ford, "Real Hurt Lockers in Iraq," *Air Force Times* (March 8, 2010).

50. Of the $222 million earned by *Fahrenheit 9/11* to date, roughly 54 percent was earned in the United States and 46 percent earned overseas. Figures from Box Office Mojo.

51. Figures from Box Office Mojo, accessed 8/8/12.

52. Retired army Colonel Stuart Herrington, quoted in Tea Lulic, "TV Torture Influencing Real Life," Digital Journal.com (February 12, 2007): http://www.digitaljournal .com/article/112710.

53. For a magisterial treatment of this theme, see Darius Rejali, *Torture and Democracy* (Princeton University Press, 2007).

54. "Torture's Long Shadow," *Washington Post* (December 18, 2005).

55. See Benji Wilson, "The New Jack Bauer: Tough on Torture, Sweet on Obama," *Telegraph* (January 15, 2009).

56. This scene is pure propaganda: there is no evidence of mass executions or organ harvesting being committed by Americans in Iraq. Unfortunately, the same cannot be said for the film's reenactment of the beating and sexual humiliation of prisoners in Abu Ghraib.

57. Quoted in Constanze Letsch, "Dialog der Kulturen," *Jungle World* (February 22, 2006).

58. See interview with Bavarian Minister-President Edmund Stoiber, *Bild am Sonntag* (February 19, 2006).

59. According to one American diplomat I interviewed, the 4th Infantry Division was fully intending to travel across Turkey to Iraq when the Turkish parliament was still voting on the matter. "When the needed approval failed by three votes," this officer said, "a lot of people wondered what the embassy had been doing to assure it would pass!"

60. Interview, Istanbul, 3/6/07.

CHAPTER 3. TELEVISION BY THE PEOPLE, FOR THE PEOPLE?

1. Interview, Sharjah, 3/20/07.
2. At the time of this writing, the global market for unscripted TV formats is dominated by the United Kingdom (43 percent), followed by the United States (22 percent) and the Netherlands (11 percent). See "Entertainers to the World," *Economist* (November 5, 2011), 66–67.
3. Interview in *Reason* (November 1, 1981).
4. Ibid.
5. Chad Raphael, "The Political Economic Origins of Reali-TV," in *Reality TV*, ed. Susan Murray and Laurie Ouellette (NYU Press, 2009).
6. Andrew Tolson, "Talking About Talk," in *Television Talk Shows*, ed. Andrew Tolson (Lawrence Erlbaum, 2001), 26.
7. Mike Kappas, quoted in Joshua Gamson, *Freaks Talk Back* (University of Chicago Press, 1998), 82–83.
8. Quoted in Kathryn Lofton, *Oprah: The Gospel of an Icon* (University of California Press, 2011), 3–4.
9. Ibid., 118–19.
10. On the gnostic dimension of New Thought and New Age, see Catherine Tumber, *American Feminism and the Birth of New Age Spirituality* (Rowman and Littlefield, 2002).
11. Amy Wellborn, quoted in Lofton (2011), 71.
12. See Lasch, *The Culture of Narcissism* (W. W. Norton, 1979): Rieff, *The Triumph of the Therapeutic* (Chatto and Windus, 1966). For a more contemporary version of this critique that mentions Winfrey by name, see Christina Hoff Sommers and Sally Satel, *One Nation Under Therapy* (St. Martins, 2006).
13. *American Protestantism in the Age of Psychology* (Cambridge University Press, 2011), 2.
14. For the definitive treatment of the idea that there is no longer any place on earth where people's core values may be taken for granted, see Peter L. Berger, *The Heretical Imperative* (Doubleday, 1980).
15. Interview, Istanbul, 3/7/07.
16. See Mark Sedgwick, *Islam & Muslims* (Intercultural Press, 2006), 163–64; and Michael Cook, *Forbidding Wrong in Islam* (Cambridge University Press, 2003), ch. 5.
17. Email to author, 7/25/13.
18. I am indebted to Kambiz GhaneaBassiri for this definition.
19. Marwan Kraidy and Joe Khalil, *Arab Television Industries* (Palgrave MacMillan, 2009), 34. The estimate of six hundred channels comes from *Arab Media Outlook 2009–2013*, published by Dubai Press Club (2009), 13. For a description of the lack of oversight, see Kraidy and Khalil (2009), 142.
20. *Principles for Organizing Satellite TV in the Arab World* (2008), http://www.al-bab.com/media/charter.htm.
21. Ibid.
22. Kraidy and Khalil (2009), 52.

23. See Gayal Nkrumah and Mohamed El-Sayed, "Egyptian Press: Forget Me Not," *Al-Ahram Weekly Online* (February 22–28, 2007): http://weekly.ahram.org.eg/2007/833/pr1.htm.

24. Serhan also pulled off the stunt of seeming to comply with the wishes of a radical cleric while getting the better of him. She agreed to the demand of Abdel Maged, a leader of the extremist group Al Jamaa Al Islamiya, that she interview him from a separate room, then proceeded to place *him* in a separate room while she remained in the studio with two other (male) guests.

25. See Anna Swank, "Sexual Healing," *Arab Media & Society* (Summer 2007): http://www.arabmediasociety.com/articles/downloads/20070514233620_AMS2_Anna_Swank.pdf.

26. Rhym Gazal, "For the Middle East's Oprah, No Shortage of Taboos," *The National* (October 15, 2008).

27. See Katherine Zoepf, "Saudi Women Find an Unlikely Role Model: Oprah," *New York Times* (September 19, 2008).

28. Muhammed el-Mulhem, quoted in Kraidy and Khalil (2009), 68.

29. E-mail to author, 5/19/13.

30. Telephone interview, 8/27/12.

31. After protests erupted against the parliamentary elections of December 2011, Russian president Dmitry Medvedev made Surkov deputy prime minister in charge of economic modernization; with Putin's return to the presidency in 2012, Surkov's influence continued to wane. See Peter Pomerantsev, "Putin's Rasputin," *London Review of Books* (13 December 2011); and Charles Clover, "'Grey Cardinal' Ousted as Putin Shuns Spin-Doctors' Dark Arts," *Financial Times* (May 14, 2013).

32. Quoted in Ellen Barry and Michael Schwirtz, "Vast Rally in Moscow Is a Challenge to Putin's Power," *New York Times* (December 24, 2011).

33. Zinaida Burskaya, quoted in ibid.

34. See Tom Balforth, "Internet TV Channel Challenges Kremlin's Information Monopoly," Radio Free Europe/Radio Liberty website (December 22, 2011): http://www.rferl.org/content/hip_internet_tv_channel_challenges_the_kremlins_information_monopoly/24430547.html.

35. E-mail to author, 5/24/13.

36. Host and guest of *Five Evenings*, quoted in Arkady Ostrovsky, "Free Speech Loses the Argument to Soft Soap and Sensation," *Financial Times* (August 19, 2005).

37. Ostrovsky (2005).

38. Quoted in Arkady Ostrovsky, "From Freedom a Return to Pliant Propaganda, *Financial Times* (June 27, 2006).

39. The story of this production and its aftermath are dramatized in the 2011 HBO film *Cinema Verite* [*sic*].

40. Garry Flot, New Orleans police officer, quoted in Richard Thompson, "Toothbrush-as-Toilet Scrubber Sickens Housemate, Triggers Police Action," *Times-Picayune* (March 21, 2010).

41. See Raphael in Murray and Ouellette (2009).

42. In developing reality shows to compete with cable, the US networks were following

in the footsteps of state-subvented channels in Britain and Europe, which developed similar shows to compete with newly formed private channels.

43. "The View from the Sidelines of the 'Sexy Positions Contest,'" *Slate* (March 23, 2004).

44. In a striking display of obtuseness, the 2011 season of *Jersey Shore* took its gaggle of self-caricatured Italian Americans to Florence, where they systematically refused to acknowledge they were in a foreign country—except when insulting the locals for speaking Italian and wailing when their hair dryers and curling irons blew out the electrical current. See Alessandra Stanley, "Ciao, Jersey: Hello, Italy: No Culture Shock Here," *New York Times* (August 6, 2011).

45. Andy Dehnart, "The Curse of Reality TV," *Playboy* (August 26, 2011).

46. Both programs are produced by Discovery Channel. See Dehnart (2011).

47. *Ice Road Truckers* (History Channel), *Ax Men* (History Channel), *Black Gold* (truTV), and *Dirty Jobs* (Discovery).

48. See "Reality TV's Working Class Heroes," *Time* (May 22, 2008).

49. Here the word *format* refers to a set of instructions for adapting a copyrighted program for particular local settings. For example, the *Big Brother* format is sold to local media companies all over the world by its creator, the Netherlands-based company Endemol.

50. See Heather Timmons, "In India, Reality TV Catches On, with Some Qualms," *New York Times* (January 9, 2011).

51. Peter Conradi, "Turks Mourn Reality TV Groom," *Sunday Times* (October 23, 2005).

52. Gozde Demirel, "New Marriage Trends in Turkey: 'Screen Marriage,'" *Quaderns de la Mediterrània* 15 (2011).

53. Ibid.

54. Quoted in John Daniszewski, "Glasnost to Glass House," *Los Angeles Times* (November 24, 2001).

55. Quoted in ibid.

56. See John A. Dunn, "Where Did It All Go Wrong?," in *The Post-Soviet Russian Media*, ed. Birgit Beumers et al. (Routledge, 2009), 44.

57. Quoted in "Putin Blamed for TV Shutdown," BBC News (January 22, 2002).

58. Courtney Weaver, "Mother of All TV shows," *Financial Times* (December 16, 2011).

59. Roman Petrenko, quoted in "From Sex to Stalin," *Economist* (September 28, 2006).

60. Ibid.

61. Weaver (2011).

62. Marina Williams of Endemol Corporation, quoted in Weaver (2011).

63. Quoted in Weaver (2011).

64. Ibid.

65. "We Are Confident That We Can Handle China's Affairs Well," quoted in Anne-Marie Brady, *Marketing Dictatorship* (Rowman and Littlefield, 2008), 45.

66. Ma Nuo, quoted in Edward Wong, "China TV Grows Racy, and Gets a Chaperon," *New York Times* (December 31, 2011).

67. Quoted in Xiyun Yang, "China's Censors Rein in 'Vulgar' Reality TV Show," *New York Times* (July 18, 2010).

68. SARFT directive, June 2010, quoted in ibid.

69. Du Shibin, quoted in ibid.

70. Quoted in Wong (December 31, 2011).

71. See official website: http://english.cntv.cn/special/6thmeeting_17thCPC/homepage/index.shtml.

72. Quoted in Edward Wong, "China's President Lashes Out at Western Culture," *New York Times* (January 3, 2012).

73. "CPC [CCP]Central Committee Kicks Off Sixth Plenum," Xinhua News Agency (October 15, 2011).

74. See Wong (January 3, 2012).

75. For an example of justified but unpersuasive spluttering, see Vicky Abt and Leonard Mustazza, *Coming After Oprah* (Bowling Green University Popular Press, 1997).

76. Tolson (2001), 15.

77. "Surviving Henan TV's Dating Reality Show," *Danwei* (May 4, 2010).

CHAPTER 4. FROM POP IDOL TO VOX POPULI

1. A Fremantle website: http://www.fremantlemedia.com/Production/Our_brands/Idols.aspx.

2. A seeming exception might be the *Eurovision Song Contest*, a program created by the fledgling European Broadcasting Union (EBU) in the mid-1950s. Conceived as a unifying event in which each nation submitted a song, the contest began early to incorporate telephone voting by the public. But there the resemblance to the pop idol genre ends, because all the contestants, the songwriters and performers, are professionals.

3. The memory of Bowes's haughty manner lived on for many former contestants, including the comedian Alan King, who while reminiscing about him on Johnny Carson's *Tonight Show*, stomped on the floor and shouted, "Can you hear me down there, Major Bowes?"

4. See mapping of television vs. digital penetration for sixty countries at the Center for International Media Assistance, National Endowment for Democracy: www.cima.ned.org/mapping/digital-media.

5. See MTV's Bill Roedy, quoted in D. Murali, "Television Anywhere, Anytime . . . ," *Hindu Business Line* (July 3, 2011).

6. See Evgeny Morozov, *The Net Delusion* (Public Affairs, 2011).

7. See *Serious Music and All That Jazz* (Fireside, 1971). For an extended discussion of the cultural ramifications of the Afro-American idiom, see my *Hole in Our Soul* (University of Chicago Press, 1996).

8. See Jacob S. Turner, "An Examination of Sexual Content in Music Videos," master's thesis, Communications Department, University of Delaware (Summer 2005).

9. Telephone interview, April 2005. See "Take Back the Music," *Essence* (January 2005). And for more on this debate, see my "Attacks on Rap Now Come from Within," *Wall Street Journal* (April 28, 2005); and my "Some of Rap's Fathers Start Taking Responsibility," *Wall Street Journal* (July 6, 2005).

10. In recent years the US Department of State has tried to capitalize on this tendency in hip-hop, sponsoring a program called "Rhythm Road," which sends "positive"

hip-hop artists to Latin America, Africa, North Africa, and the Middle East. The effectiveness of this program will be discussed in the conclusion.

11. Wael Ghonim, *Revolution 2.0* (Houghton Mifflin Harcourt, 2012), 86–87.

12. *Rock the Casbah* (Simon and Schuster, 2011), 121.

13. Interview, Jakarta, 4/5/07.

14. Interview, Jakarta, 4/3/07.

15. Interview, Jarkarta, 4/5/07.

16. See Johannes Nugroho, "Remembering the Dragon Spirit of a Wise and Noble Indonesian Leader," *Jakarta Globe* (January 01, 2010).

17. See Heru Andriyanto, Nivell Rayda and Anita Rachman, "Can Arifinto Be Charged Under the Porn Law?," *Jakarta Globe* (April 12, 2011). The title of the legislation is Law No. 44: "Bill Against Pornography and Porno-Action," passed October 30, 2008.

18. See, for example, Bryan Walsh, "Inul's Rules," *Time* (March 17, 2003); and Bret Stephens, "Hips Don't Lie," *Wall Street Journal* (April 3, 2007).

19. Interview, Jakarta, 4/4/07.

20. Quoted in Komal Sharma, "Playing It by Ear, Successfully," *LiveMint/Wall Street Journal* (September 11, 2011).

21. See David Page and William Crawley, *Satellites over South Asia: Broadcasting Culture and the Public Interest* (Sage, 2001), 149.

22. Interview, Mumbai, 3/27/07.

23. Anonymous filmgoer, quoted in "Bollywood Comes to Nigeria," *South Asian Magazine for Action and Reflection* (SAMAR, 2003).

24. By 2006 these included the Saudi-owned Rotana, Lebanon's ETV Music, Dubai's Music Plus and Nojoon ("stars") channels, and Egypt's Melody Hits and Mazzika TV. The largest was Rotana, whose parent firm, Rotana Audiovisual, was reported by *Forbes* to own "the most extensive Arab music catalog and film library." See "The Top 40 Arab Brands," *Forbes* (October 18, 2006).

25. By spring 2006, SMS messaging was taking up so much of the screen, some channels decided to forego all other programming, essentially creating a TV chat room. See Habib Battah, "SMS: The Next TV Revolution," *TBS* 16 (Spring 2006).

26. Marwan M. Kraidy, *Reality Television and Arab Politics* (Cambridge University Press, 2010), ch. 3; 90.

27. Media scholar Marlin Dick finds the same informal rule applied to fictional characters: "Saudi stations broadcast Western movies with women wearing skimpy clothes and it appears okay for Syrians and Egyptians to don such clothing as well, provided that Saudi characters do not engage in such objectionable practices." See "The Thin Red Lines: Censorship, Controversy, and the Case of the Syrian Soap Opera Behind Bars," *TBS* 16 (2006).

28. See Marwan Kraidy, "Reality Television and Politics in the Arab World," *Arab Media & Society* (formerly *TBS*), 1:2 (2005).

29. See Marc Lynch, "Reality Is Not Enough," *TBS* (Fall 2005).

30. "Ruby and the Chequered Heart," *Al-Ahram Weekly* (March 17–23, 2005).

31. Quoted in Salman Dossari, "A Talk with MTV Vice Chairman Bill Roedy," *Asharq Al Awsat* (July 23, 2007).

32. Quoted in Aleco, "Fredwreck Interview," mideastdynasty.com (April 13, 2011).

33. MTV Middle East website, program descriptions for 2012 season.

34. Interview, Sharjah, 3/20/07.

35. See Tara Parker-Pope, "The Kids Are More Than All Right," *New York Times Magazine* (February 5, 2012), 14.

36. See Navtej Dhillon and Tarik Yousef, eds., *Generation in Waiting* (Brookings Institution Press, 2009), 11, 21.

37. See Kraidy (2010), 160–62, 179–81.

38. Ahmad Ibrahim Bahzad, quoted in "The Reality of Reality TV in the Middle East," website of Al Bawaba Group: www.albawaba.com/ news/printArticle.php3?sid= 271966&lang=e (March 7, 2004).

39. See Kraidy (2010), ch. 4.

40. For example, *Star Academy* was condemned by the dean of the School of Islamic Law and *Shari'a* at Kuwait University; the Kuwaiti Parliament; Islamist youth websites; and Saudi Arabia's Permanent Committee for Scientific Research and the Issuing of Fatwas. See Kraidy (2005), 18–19.

41. Ibid., 20.

42. Mail Foreign Service, *Mail* [UK], "Brave Saudi Housewife Set to Win Arabic X Factor After Blistering Attack on Hardline Muslim Clerics on Live TV" (March 31, 2010).

43. Lynch (2005), 36–37.

44. Ibid., 43.

45. Interview, Hong Kong, 4/21/07.

46. See Jim Yardley, "An Unlikely Pop Icon Worries China," *International Herald Tribune* (September 5, 2005).

47. Raymond Zhou, "Secret Behind Idol-Making Super Girl Contest," *China Daily* (August 27, 2005).

48. Raymond Zhou, "Setting Record Straight," *China Daily* (October 15, 2005).

49. Xici Hutong, quoted on *EastSouthWestNorth* (August 26, 2005): http://www.zona europa.com/20050829_1.htm.

50. From *China Democracy*, quoted on *EastSouthWestNorth* (August 27, 2005): http://www.zonaeuropa.com/20050827_1.htm.

51. Thanh Nga Duong, "China's Super Girl Show: Democracy and Female Empowerment Among Chinese Youth" (master's thesis, Centre for East and South-East Asian Studies, Lund University, 2009), 7.

52. Ibid., 19.

53. Ibid., 23; and "Hu," seventeen years of age, quoted in ibid., 21.

54. "Ren," twenty years of age, quoted in ibid., 21.

55. Ibid., 32.

56. See Duong (2009), 39–40.

57. Gan Tian, "Not Everybody Happy with TV Singing Sensation," *China Daily* (September 8, 2009).

58. See Jane MacCartney, "TV Talent Contest 'Too Democratic' for China's Censors," *Times* (London) (August 29, 2005).

59. Zhu Dake, quoted in Zhou (August 2005).
60. Interview, Beijing, 4/17/07.
61. *Global Capital, Local Culture* (Peter Lang, 2008), 179.
62. Interview, Hong Kong, 4/21/07.
63. "The Daily Dish," *Atlantic* (June 13, 2009): http://www.theatlantic.com/daily-dish/archive/2009/06/the-revolution-will-be-twittered/200478/.
64. Evgeny Morozov may not have coined *cyber-utopianism*, but he put it on the map in his article "Texting Toward Utopia," *Boston Review* (March/April 2009).
65. Quoted in Philip Elmer-Dewitt, "First Nation in Cyberspace," *Time* (December 6, 1993).
66. The US military did not invent the Internet, but the Department of Defense did fund a crucial stage in its development: the Advanced Research Projects Agency Network (ARPANET), in 1969. See "A Brief History of the Internet," Internet Society: http://www.isoc.org/internet/history/brief.shtml.
67. For an early and influential use of this term, see Taylor C. Boas, "The Dictator's Dilemma? The Internet and US Policy Toward Cuba," *Washington Quarterly* 23:3 (Summer 2000), 57–67.
68. See Kathrin Hille, "China: The Big Screening," *Financial Times* (November 17, 2010).
69. See James Glanz and John Markoff, "Egypt Leaders Found 'Off' Switch for Internet," *New York Times* (February 15, 2011).
70. See Evgeny Morozov, *The Net Delusion* (Public Affairs, 2011), 130.
71. Quoted in Howard W. French, "As Chinese Students Go Online, Little Sister Is Watching," *New York Times* (May 9, 2006).
72. Morozov (2011), 95, 108.
73. Ibid., 97.
74. See Somini Sengupta, "Should Personal Data Be Personal?," *New York Times* (February 4, 2012); and J. P. O'Malley, "Little Brother Is Watching," *American Interest* (March–April 2012).
75. Mark Mazzetti and Scott Shane, "Threats Test Obama's Balancing Act on Surveillance"; and editors, "A Weak Agenda on Spying Reform;" in *New York Times* (August 10, 2013).
76. See, for example, Susan Murray and Laurie Ouellette, eds., *Reality TV* (NYU Press, 2009), ch. 9.
77. Interview, Delhi, 3/25/07.
78. See Hille (2010).
79. Quoted in Murali (2011).

PART TWO PROLOGUE. THE LESSON OF ODYSSEUS

1. Homer, *The Odyssey*, trans. Robert Fitzgerald (Vintage Classics, 1990), VIII: 440, 476.
2. Ibid., IX: 21–22.
3. "President Wilson's Fourteen Points," speech delivered before a joint session of the United States Congress, January 8, 1918; accessed at: http://wwi.lib.byu.edu/index.php/President_Wilson%27s_Fourteen_Points.

4. Theodore Streibert, quoted in Nicholas Cull, *The Cold War and the United States Information Agency* (Cambridge University Press, 2008), 102.
5. NSC action No. 936 (October 22, 1953) and NSC action No. 165/1 (October 24, 1953), quoted in ibid., 101–2.
6. My understanding of goals as defined by government agencies is derived from James Q. Wilson, *Bureaucracy* (Basic, 1989).
7. Cull's somewhat different list of the "core elements of public diplomacy" is found in Cull (2008), xviii.
8. Ibid., 498.
9. Telephone interview, 12/11/08.
10. Homer, *Odyssey* IX: 551–52.
11. For an early exposition of this view, see Charles Krauthammer, "The Unipolar Moment," *Foreign Affairs*, 70:1 (1990/91), 23–33.
12. These include: *America's Role in the World* (Business for Diplomatic Action, 2007); Hady Amr, *The Need to Communicate* (Brookings Institution, 2004); Richard L. Armitage and Joseph S. Nye, Jr., eds., *A Smarter, More Secure America* (CSIS Commission on Smart Power, Center for Strategic and International Studies, November 2007); *Cultural Diplomacy: The Linchpin of Public Diplomacy* (Advisory Committee for Public Diplomacy, US Department of State, 2005); Helle C. Dale, et al., *Strengthening US Public Diplomacy Requires Organization, Coordination, and Strategy*, Backgrounder #1875 (Heritage Foundation, 2005); Defense Science Board, *Report of the Defense Science Board Task Force on Strategic Communication* (Washington, DC, September 2004); Defense Science Board, Report of the Defense Science Board Task Force on Strategic Communication (Washington, DC, January 2008); Phyllis D'Hoop, ed., An *Initiative: Strengthening U.S.-Muslim Communications* (Center for the Study of the Presidency, 2003); Edward Djerejian, ed., *Changing Minds, Winning Peace* (US Department of State, 2003); *Finding America's Voice* (Independent Task Force on Public Diplomacy, Council on Foreign Relations, 2003); Kristin M. Lord, *Voices of America* (Brookings Institution, 2008); Christopher Paul, *Wither Strategic Communication?* (Rand Corporation, 2009); Peter G. Peterson, ed., *Public Diplomacy: A Strategy for Reform* (Independent Task Force, Council on Foreign Relations, 2002); and *Preserving Our Welcome to the World in an Age of Terrorism* (Report of the Secure Borders and Open Doors Advisory Committee, US Department of Homeland Security and US Department of State, 2008). See website of the Center for Global Engagement: http://www.thecgeinc.org/RelevantStudies .html.
13. Security expert Kori Schake faults the State Department's passive acceptance of public indifference to its efforts, comparing it unfavorably with the Defense Department's continual striving to build a domestic constituency. See *State of Disrepair* (Hoover Institution Press, 2012), 53.
14. USIA was established in 1953 under Reorganization Plan No. 8, authorized by the 1948 US Information and Educational Exchange Act (Public Law 402; 80th Congress), usually referred to as the Smith-Mundt Act after its sponsors Alexander Smith (R-NJ) and Karl Earl Mundt (R-SD). See Cull (2008), ch. 1.

15. National Defense Authorization Act for Fiscal Year 2013; H.R. 4310.

16. Eugene Kopp served under Presidents Nixon, Ford, and George H. W. Bush. Interview, Washington, 5/24/07.

17. I do not mean to belittle the security issue—it is real, as evidenced by the fact that in 2008, a little more than a year after my visit, a gun assault on the US consulate in Istanbul killed three Turkish police officers and three assailants. See Laura King, "Attack at the US Consulate in Turkey leaves 6 dead," *Boston Globe* (July 10, 2008).

18. See Patricia H. Kushlis and Patricia Lee Sharpe, "Public Diplomacy Today and Tomorrow," *WhirledView* (October 2011): http://whirledview.typepad.com/whirledview/public-diplomacy-today-and-tomorrow.html.

19. For a trenchant analysis of the civil rights movement as the embodiment of "prophetic witness" in the American grain, see Christopher Lasch, *The True and Only Heaven* (Norton, 1991), ch. 9; and David L. Chappell, *A Stone of Hope* (University of North Carolina Press, 2007).

20. Quoted in Fred Kaplan, "How 'Howl' Changed the World," *Slate* (September 24, 2010), http://www.slate.com/id/2268627/.

21. As mentioned in the introduction, "creedal passion" is political scientist Samuel Huntington's term for disputes over the meaning of American ideals. See *American Politics: The Promise of Disharmony* (Harvard University Press, 1981), 4.

22. See Donald Kettl, *Sharing Power* (Brookings Institution, 1993); and Allison Stanger, *One Nation Under Contract* (Yale University Press, 2009).

23. This free-for-all was once uniquely American, but no more. As Steve Green, director of cultural programs for the British Council, explained to me, "The days of government control over a country's image are gone. The British Council used to handle 100 percent of the cultural interaction between Britain and other countries, both ways. Today we have a micro-market share." The same is true of the British Council's counterparts in Europe, such as the Alliance Française and the Goethe Institute. Interview, London, 7/28/06.

24. Quoted on USC Center for Public Diplomacy website: http://uscpublicdiplomacy.org/index.php/about/what_is_pd.

25. Quoted in Frank Ninkovich, *The Diplomacy of Ideas* (Cambridge University Press, 1981), 13.

26. For an excellent overview of these instruments, see William A. Rugh, *American Encounters with Arabs: The "Soft Power" of U.S. Public Diplomacy in the Middle East* (Westport, CT: Praeger Security International, 2006), ch. 1.

CHAPTER 5. THE WASHINGTON-HOLLYWOOD PACT

Epigraph: Quoted in David Puttnam, *The Undeclared War* (Harper Collins, 1997), 132.

1. Remarks at "The Business of Show Business," MPAA-sponsored forum held at the Donald W. Reynolds Center for Art and Portraiture, Washington, DC, February 6, 2007.

2. The members of the MPAA are the "big six" studios: Walt Disney Company; Sony Pictures; Paramount Pictures; 20th Century Fox; Universal Studios; and Warner Brothers.

3. Remarks at "The Business" (2007).

4. Stephen E. Siwek, *The True Cost of Motion Picture Piracy to the U.S. Economy*, Policy Report 186 (Washington: Institute for Policy Innovation, September 2006), 21, 23.

5. Democratic Primary debate: Kodak Theater, Los Angeles, January 31, 2008.

6. *Projections of War* (Columbia University Press, 1999), 61.

7. *Irresistible Empire* (Harvard University Press, 2005), 289.

8. See William Uricchio, "The First World War and the Crisis in Europe," in *The Oxford History of World Cinema*, ed. Geoffrey Nowell-Smith (Oxford, 1996), 62–65.

9. See Philip M. Taylor, *Munitions of the Mind*, 3d ed. (Manchester University Press, 2003), 195–97.

10. Quoted in Matthew Fraser, *Weapons of Mass Distraction* (St. Martins Press, 2005), 40.

11. Formed in 1922 by the "Big Three" studios (Famous Players-Lasky, Metro-Goldwyn, and First National), the MPPDA immediately became the target of antitrust legal action. But none of the suits against it, which culminated in the 1948 Supreme Court decision *United States v. Paramount Pictures, Inc.*, involved the MPPDA's overseas operations. See United States v. Paramount Pictures, 334 U.S. 131, 166.

12. See de Grazia (2005), 305.

13. *The Undeclared War* (HarperCollins, 1997), 132.

14. Quoted in ibid.

15. See Ben Urwand, *The Collaboration* (Columbia University Press, 2013).

16. For a detailed account of the bureaucratic nitty-gritty, see Clayton R. Koppes and Gregory D. Black, *Hollywood Goes to War* (Free Press, 1987); for a more opinionated but lively version, see Thomas Doherty, *Projections of War* (Columbia University Press, 1999).

17. Original MPEA members included: Allied Artists, Columbia Pictures, Metro-Goldwyn-Mayer, Paramount Pictures, RKO Pictures, 20th Century Fox, United Artists, Universal International, and Warner Brothers.

18. Reinhold Wagnleitner, "American Cultural Diplomacy, the Cinema, and the Cold War in Central Europe," Working Paper 92-4 (Center for Austrian Studies, 1997), 5–6.

19. Ibid., 6.

20. Puttnam (1997), 211.

21. See ibid., 203; and Wagnleitner (1997), 7.

22. See Kyoko Hirano, *Mr. Smith Goes to Tokyo* (Smithsonian Institution Press, 1992), 38–39.

23. See Hiroshi Kitamura, "'Home of American Movies': The Marunouchi Subaruza and the Making of Hollywood's Audiences in Occupied Tokyo, 1946–9," in *Hollywood Abroad*, ed. Melvyn Stokes and Richard Maltby (British Film Institute, 2004), 99, 107.

24. See Puttnam (1997), 207–8.

25. According to Yale Richmond, who at age twenty-four served as a military governor in Bavaria, "'reorientation' was chosen over 'democratization' because the Russians, in their zone of Germany, had so abused the word democracy; and 're-education'

was rejected because it sounded too patronizing." See *Practicing Public Diplomacy* (Berghahn, 2008), 10.

26. Quoted in Heide Fehrenbach, *Cinema in Democratizing Germany* (University of North Carolina Press, 1995), 54.

27. Quoted in ibid., 54, 62.

28. For a thoughtful discussion of the Heimatfilm, see ibid., ch. 5.

29. *The International Film Industry* (Indiana University Press, 1969), 132.

30. Justice Joseph McKenna, quoted in Richard S. Randall, *Censorship of the Movies* (University of Wisconsin Press, 1970), 18. See also *Mutual Film Corporation v. Industrial Commission of Ohio*, 236 U.S.230 (1915).

31. See ibid.

32. One curious sidelight is that the co-chair of those anti-Nazi investigations, Rep. Samuel Dickstein (D-NY), was a paid informant for the Soviet spy agency, NKVD. See Allen Weinstein and Alexander Vassiliev, *The Haunted Wood* (Modern Library, 2000), 140–50.

33. Koppes and Black (1987), 10.

34. See Todd Bennett, "Culture, Power, and *Mission to Moscow*," *Journal of American History*, 88 (Sept. 2001).

35. For a dispassionate account of these events, see Ronald Radosh and Allis Radosh, *Red Star over Hollywood* (Encounter, 2005).

36. The other defendants in United States v. Paramount Pictures, Inc. (334 U.S. 131) were RKO Radio Pictures, Loew's, 20th Century-Fox Film Corporation, Columbia Pictures Corporation, Universal-International, Warner Bros., the American Theatres Association, and W. C. Allred. See Randall (1970), 23.

37. Indeed, *Il Miracolo* was favorably reviewed by the Vatican newspaper, *Osservatore Romano*. See Camille Cianfarra, "Vatican Views 'Miracle' Row," *New York Times* (February 11, 1951).

38. See *Joseph Burstyn, Inc. v. Wilson, Commissioner of Education of New York, et al.*, 343 U.S. 495.

39. Richard Pells, *Not Like Us* (Basic, 1997), 214.

40. United States Code, Title 22, Chapter 18, Subchapter I, § 144222, "Informational Media Guaranties," section 1933 (b). For a detailed account of the IMG, see Thomas H. Guback, *The International Film Industry* (Indiana University Press, 1969).

41. Puttnam (1997), 213; and Guback (1969), 23.

42. Puttnam (1997), 165–66.

43. Ibid., ch. 9.

44. Ibid., ch. 15.

45. See Pells (1997), 212–25.

46. "When Antonioni Blew Up the Movies," *Time* (August 5, 2007).

47. MPAA president Jack Valenti considered this change one of his greatest achievements, because the MPAA had long opposed a ratings system on the ground that classifying films would fragment the audience. Ironically, such fragmentation is now a cornerstone of the business.

48. Quoted in David A. Cook, *Lost Illusions*, vol. 9 of *History of the American Cinema*, ed. Charles Harpole (Charles Scribner's Sons, 2000), 12–13.
49. Puttnam (1997), 267.
50. Cook (2000), 12.
51. Puttnam (1997), 268–69.
52. Quoted in Colleen Roach, "The Movement for a New World Information and Communication Order: A Second Wave?," in *Media, Culture and Society*, 12:3 (1990), 286.
53. Interview, Washington, 9/26/08.
54. See Carol Balassa, *America's Image*, report for Curb Center for Art, Enterprise, and Public Policy (Vanderbilt University, 2008).
55. See Pierre Lescure, "Culture-Acte 2: Rapport de la Mission," Tomes I and II, at: http://www.culturecommunication.gouv.fr/Actualites/A-la-une/Culture-acte-2-80 -propositions-sur-les-contenus-culturels-numeriques.
56. Remarks to "America's Image Abroad," an Arts Industries Policy Forum of the Curb Center for Art, Enterprise, and Public Policy at Vanderbilt University, Washington, DC (April 24, 2008).

CHAPTER 6. "THE WORLD'S WORST PROPAGANDISTS"

1. See Bernard Bailyn, *To Begin the World Anew* (Knopf, 2003), ch. 3.
2. Ibid., 78.
3. USIA was established under Reorganization Plan No. 8, authorized by the 1948 U.S. Information and Educational Exchange Act (Public Law 402; 80th Congress), usually referred to as the Smith-Mundt Act after its sponsors Alexander Smith (R-NJ) and Karl Earl Mundt (R-SD). See Nicholas Cull, *The Cold War and the United States Information Agency* (Cambridge University Press, 2008), ch. 1.
4. For a full accounting of this history, see Cull (2008); Nicholas J. Cull, *The Decline and Fall of the United States Information Agency* (Palgrave Macmillan, 2012); and Richard T. Arndt, *The First Resort of Kings* (Potomac, 2005).
5. See Cull (2008), 52–53.
6. Quoted in Michael L. Krenn, *Fall-Out Shelters for the Human Spirit* (University of North Carolina Press, 2005), 90.
7. David Caute, *The Dancer Defects* (Oxford University Press, 2003), 612.
8. See Hans N. Tuch, *Communicating with the World* (St. Martin's, 1990), 65. Among the last remaining monuments to this era are the US libraries in India and Burma. As former public diplomat Donald Bishop recalls, the low postal rate for books in India made it possible to circulate books by mail: "People simply called or wrote the library, and the book would be mailed directly. There was a big staff in the basement that did only this." Bishop also notes that "most countries now have lending libraries, so American libraries in foreign capitals no longer need to demonstrate that particular democratic practice," especially "in an age when information is electronically distributed." Years of budget cuts in public diplomacy have led the State

Department to install "American Corners," recently renamed "American Spaces": small nooks in foreign universities and other such settings equipped with computers and informational materials that attract few users. In Bishop's view, these "shriveled" versions of the old US libraries are too often "a waste of money and effort."

9. Penny Von Eschen, *Satchmo Blows Up the World* (Harvard University Press, 2004), 4.

10. Quoted in ibid., 17.

11. Quoted in Yale Richmond, *Cultural Exchange and the Cold War* (Pennsylvania State University Press, 2003), 207.

12. Quoted in James Lester, "Willis of Oz," *Central European Review* 1:5 (26 July 1999).

13. *Talkin' Moscow Blues* (Ecco Press, 1990), 83.

14. For fuller accounts of this remarkable episode, see Caute (2003), 543–45; Michael Kammen, *Visual Shock* (Knopf, 2006), 102–4; and Krenn (2005), passim.

15. One of the auctioned works, Stuart Davis's *Still Life with Flowers*, was sold for $62.50 to a Winnetka, Illinois, public school. In 2006 that school made a tidy profit when Sotheby's sold the painting for $2.8 million. I am indebted to Richard Arndt for bringing this to my attention. Most of the other works were sold, at a steep discount, to the Universities of Georgia, Oklahoma, and Indiana, and to Auburn University in Alabama. See Dennis Harper et al., *Art Interrupted* (University of Georgia, 2012).

16. The "Agreement Between the United States of America and the Union of Soviet Socialist Republics on Exchanges in the Cultural, Technical, and Educational Fields," also known as the Lacy-Zarubin Agreement after its two chief negotiators, William S. B. Lacy (special assistant to Eisenhower) and Georgi Z. Zarubin (Soviet ambassador to the United States), was signed on January 27, 1958.

17. Cull (2008), 164–65.

18. Quoted in Krenn (2005), 165. Boris Pasternak's novel *Doctor Zhivago* had recently been banned in the USSR.

19. Krenn (2005), 165.

20. Quoted by Tuch, who served as translator. See Tuch (1990), 64.

21. *New York Times* (October 27, 2005).

22. See Hugh Wilford, *The Mighty Wurlitzer* (Harvard University Press, 2008), 7.

23. The publications founded by the CCF included *Preuves* in France; *Encounter* in England; *Der Monat* in Germany; *Cuadernos* in Spain; *Tempo Presente* in Italy; *Quadrant* in Australia; *Forum* in Austria; *Quest* in India; and *Science and Freedom*, as well as *Soviet Survey*, in the USSR.

24. See Peter Coleman, *The Liberal Conspiracy* (Free Press, 1989).

25. Quoted in Wilford (2008), 12.

26. Caute (2003), 617.

27. Wilford (2008), 10.

28. Quoted in Coleman (1989), 234.

29. Founded in 2006, EUNIC is a network of twenty-nine cultural relations institutes from twenty-four EU member states, with two thousand branches and activities in 150 countries. See http://www.eunic-online.eu/.

30. Steve Green, "New Directions," in *El discreto encanto de la cultura: Nuevas estrate-gias para la proyección exterior de la cultura,* ed. Elvira Marco and Jaime Otero (Madrid: Real Instituto Elcano y Ariel, 2012).

31. Interview, Washington, 10/15/05.

32. Ibid.

33. E-mail to author, 5/5/13.

34. Interview, Brighton, England, 7/27/06.

35. Quoted in Robert D. Kaplan, *The Arabists* (Free Press, 1993), 277.

36. Interview, Brighton, England, 7/27/06.

37. Timothy Ryback, *Rock Around the Bloc* (Oxford University Press, 1990), 32–33.

38. Michael Gray, telephone interview, 8/13/08.

39. See "Vaclav Havel," report of Czech Radio 7, Radio Prague (1996, 2008): http://www.radio.cz/en/article/36022.

40. Futurism arose in Italy in the early twentieth century and called for the destruction of the past in favor of a dynamic (and fascist) future; Dada arose in Zurich during World War I and emphasized spontaneous self-expression and the rejection of all meaning.

41. For more detail (and a few polemics) see my *Hole in Our Soul* (University of Chicago, 1996), ch. 16.

42. Quoted in Krenn (2005), 208.

43. Norman Geske, organizer of the US exhibit, quoted in Krenn (2005), 224.

44. Quoted in ibid., 228.

45. Krenn (2005), 209.

46. Quoted in ibid., 229.

47. Quoted in ibid., 230–31.

48. Krenn (2005), 230.

49. Telephone interview, 7/22/08.

50. E-mail to author, 12/6/12.

51. Cull (2008), 400, 407.

52. Ibid., 406, 478.

53. Wick did create one successful arts program. Called Artistic Ambassadors, it sent hundreds of musicians to every continent, not just to perform but to stay for several days and, in the words of director John Robilette, "interact with the musical com-munities." See Tim Page, "Numic Notes," *New York Times* (October 6, 1985).

54. Quoted in Cull (2008), 408.

55. Cull (2008), 437–38.

56. See Arndt (2005), 529.

57. Eugene Kopp, interview, Washington, 10/14/05.

58. See Edward P. Djerejian et al., *Changing Minds, Winning Peace,* report of the Advi-sory Group on Public Diplomacy for the Arab and Muslim World (2003).

59. The "X Portfolio" section of that posthumous Mapplethorpe show, *The Perfect Moment,* featured graphic photographs of gay sadomasochistic sex acts, including artfully composed shots of male genitalia and a self-portrait by the artist in which his naked buttocks are parted to reveal the handle of a bullwhip inserted in his anus.

60. Interview, Washington, 1/17/07.

61. Interview, Washington, 5/24/07.

62. For the definitive account of the last decade of USIA's existence, see Cull (2012).

63. For a polemical but engaging account of how free trade and free enterprise became the main message of US public diplomacy under President Clinton, see Nancy Snow, *Propaganda, Inc.*, 3d ed. (Seven Stories Press, 2010).

64. Cull (2008), 479.

65. Ibid., 481.

66. Lucyna Aleksandrowicz-Pedich, interview, Warsaw, 05/24/06.

67. Donald Bishop, e-mail to author, 12/5/12.

68. Interview, London, 7/18/06.

69. "Hollywood Disinformation," interview in *New Perspectives Quarterly* 15:5 (Fall 1998), 13.

70. E-mail to author, 5/28/13.

71. See John Lewis Gaddis, *The Cold War* (Penguin, 2005), 193.

72. "Millions Cheer as the Pope Comes Home," *On This Day* (June 2, 1979), BBC Online: http://news.bbc.co.uk/onthisday/hi/dates/stories/june/2/newsid_3972000/3972361.stm.

73. See Cull (2008), 122.

74. William A. Rugh, *American Encounters with Arabs* (Praeger Security, 2006), 37.

75. Ibid., 43.

76. One medical doctor who had studied in both countries joked that if the US embassy really wanted to turn Egyptians against communism, it should send them not to America but to the USSR, so they could see what "a terrible place" it was. See ibid., 53–54.

77. See ibid., 64–65; and Robert D. Kaplan, *The Arabists* (Free Press, 1995), 148.

78. *Jihad: The Trail of Political Islam* (Belknap Press, 2002), 27.

79. "The America I Have Seen," trans. Tarek Masoud and Ammar Fakeeh, in *America in an Arab Mirror*, ed. Kamal Abdel-Malek (St. Martin's, 2000), 11, 20.

80. John Calvert, "'The World Is an Undutiful Boy!': Sayyid Qutb's American Experience," in *Islam and Christian-Muslim Relations* 11:1 (2000).

81. "Sayyid Qutb's America," *All Things Considered* (NPR, May 6, 2003).

82. Ibid.

83. See Calvert (2000), 89, 98.

84. See Chapter 7 for a full discussion of this and other US government–sponsored broadcasting efforts.

85. Telephone interview, 5/20/08.

86. *Egypt After Nasser* (Paragon House, 1989), 18.

87. See Hind Rassam Culhane, *East/West, an Ambiguous State of Being* (Peter Lang, 1995), 29–30.

88. Lippman (1989), 247–49.

89. Culhane (1995), 29–30.

90. Lippman (1989), 249.

91. For a magisterial treatment of the religious roots of the secularization thesis, see

Charles Taylor, *A Secular Age* (Harvard University Press, 2007). For the lucid retraction of a former believer in that thesis, see Peter L. Berger, ed., *The Desecularization of the World* (William B. Eerdmans, 1999). And for a penetrating look at how different "secularisms" shape world politics, see Elizabeth Shakman Hurd, *The Politics of Secularism in International Relations* (Princeton University Press, 2008).

92. *Democracy in America*, trans. George Lawrence (Doubleday, 1969), Vol. I, Part II, ch. 9, 297.

93. Ibid.

94. See Chapter 9.

CHAPTER 7. US INTERNATIONAL BROADCASTING

1. Carnes Lord, *Losing Hearts and Minds* (Praeger Security International, 2006), 86.

2. "Statement by the President upon Signing Order Concerning Government Information Programs," August 31, 1945 (Text No. 120, Harry S. Truman Library and Museum), accessed at: http://trumanlibrary.org/publicpapers/viewpapers.php?pid=127.

3. *Impact Through Innovation and Integration: BBG Strategic Plan 2012–2016*, accessed at: http://www.bbg.gov/wp-content/media/2012/02/BBGStrategicPlan_2012-2016_OMB_Final.pdf.

4. See Philip M. Taylor, *British Propaganda in the Twentieth Century* (Edinburgh University Press, 1999).

5. Quoted in Alan L. Heil, Jr., *The Voice of America* (Columbia University Press, 2003), 57.

6. *Mein Kampf*, vol. I, ch. X; trans. James Murphy. Accessed at Project Gutenberg, Australia: http://gutenberg.net.au/ebooks02/0200601.txt.

7. Quoted in Heil (2003), 35.

8. Public Law 402, also known as the Smith-Mundt Act.

9. See Heil (2003), 45–57.

10. Public Law 94–350, signed into law on July 12, 1976, by President Gerald Ford. Quoted in ibid., 35.

11. Quoted in Alexander Kendrick, *Prime Time: The Life of Edward R. Murrow* (Little, Brown, 1969), 466.

12. Nicholas J. Cull, *The Cold War and the United States Information Agency* (Cambridge University Press, 2008), 194.

13. Quoted in ibid., 190.

14. See Philip M. Taylor, *Munitions of the Mind* (Manchester University Press, 2003), 269–70.

15. Quoted in "The Nixon Years: Down from the Highest Mountaintop," *Time* (August 19, 1974).

16. See "Covering Watergate: Success and Backlash," *Time* (July 8, 1974).

17. Quoted in Dan Kubiske, "Truth vs. Propaganda," *The Correspondent*, Online Publication of the Foreign Correspondents' Club of Hong Kong (December 2002–January 2003): http://www.fcchk.org/correspondent/corro-dec01/dec-voa.htm.

18. According to VOA veteran Alan Heil, the producers had originally been planning to include comments from the exiled king of Afghanistan, a respected US

scholar of Islam, and a spokesman from the anti-Taliban Northern Alliance. On its website the VOA notes the State Department's objections but reports that it did eventually air segments of the Mullah Omar interview as part of a larger piece framing President Bush's statement to a joint session of Congress. See Heil, *Voice of America* (Columbia University Press, 2003), 409–25; and VOA website, accessed at: http://www.insidevoa.com/content/a-13-34-2007-innovations-for-a-new-century-history-111602669/177527.html.

19. Quoted in Heil (2003), 412–13.
20. Quoted in ibid., 423–24.
21. See "Ted Landphair's America," at: http://blogs.voanews.com/tedlandphairsamerica/.
22. See Cull (2008), 379–80, 416–17.
23. See, for example, http://editorials.voa.gov/.
24. Telephone interview, 3/21/12.
25. Mardo Sogham, e-mail to author, 3/23/12.
26. E-mail to author, 3/21/12.
27. "US TV for Iran Might Be Free, Doesn't Have to Be Cheap," *Bloomberg* (February 20, 2012). Accessed at: http://www.bloomberg.com/news/2012-02-21/u-s-broadcast-for-iran-might-be-free-but-doesn-t-have-to-be-cheap-view.html.
28. *The Daily Show with Jon Stewart* is a satirical take on the news that is popular not only in the United States but also overseas, in an edited version carried on CNN International and prefaced with this disclaimer: "The show you are about to watch is a news parody. Its stories are not fact checked. Its reporters are not journalists. And its opinions are not fully thought through." *The Daily Show: The Complete Guide* (Google e-book, open source PDF), 12; accessed at: http://books.google.com/books?id=tapguflQI9AC&dq=%E2%80%9CThe+show+you+are+about+to+watch+is+a+news+parody.+Its+stories+are+not+fact+checked.+Its+reporters+are+not+journalists.%22+CNN+International&source=gbs_navlinks_s.
29. Tara Bahrampour, "Iranian Daily Show, Meet 'The Daily Show,'" *Washington Post* (January 21, 2011).
30. "USTV for Iran," *Bloomberg* (2012).
31. Telephone interview, 4/12/12.
32. "Inside Russia Today: Counterweight to the Mainstream Media, or Putin's Mouthpiece?," *New Statesman* (May 10, 2013).
33. Interview, Dubai, 3/18/07.
34. Susan McCue and Michael Meehan, quoted in "Governors Seek to Expand U.S. International Media Efforts in Russia," BBG press release (May 7, 2013).
35. See Arch Puddington, *Broadcasting Freedom* (University Press of Kentucky, 2000), 118–20.
36. Interview, Prague, 8/29/06.
37. Unfortunately, RFE/RL's research unit was phased out when the services moved to Prague. The archives were sold to billionaire democracy activist George Soros, who closed them down after two years. A few analysts were subsequently rehired, and, according to Liz Fuller, a Georgia analyst who worked for RFE/RL at the time, Soros donated some archived material to the Central European University in Budapest,

including bound volumes of newspapers. But Fuller also noted that a collection of *samizdat* publications, "a wealth of information about how people opposed the system" gathered in the 1980s, was lost because no one bothered to make copies of it during the move. Interview, Prague, 8/30/06.

38. Interview, Brighton, England, 7/27/06.

39. Interview, Prague, 8/27/06.

40. Back in Washington, where Facebook and Twitter are all the rage, this reliance on shortwave is frequently criticized. But Ron Synovitz, an American journalist who has worked in Afghanistan for RFE/RL, offered this reply to Azadi's critics: "Anyone who calls shortwave an outdated, horse-and-buggy technology has never been in southern Afghanistan—or in a refugee camp." Interview, Prague, 8/31/06.

41. Interview, Prague, 8/30/06.

42. Ibid.

43. E-mail to author, 3/21/12.

44. See Graham Bowley and Sharifullah Sahak, "Beheadings Raise Doubts That Taliban Have Changed," *New York Times* (February 23, 2012).

45. Tayyeb Afridi, "Why Fighting Mullah Radio Is Not Easy," blog post, *Express Tribune* (Lahore, March 12, 2012), accessed at: http://blogs.tribune.com.pk/story/10611/why -fighting-mullah-radio-is-not-easy/.

46. The music was also changed, from relentlessly upbeat dance music produced by the Iranian community in Los Angeles, to "underground" music made in Iran. As one émigré staffer with Radio Farda in Prague told me in 2007, "Underground does not mean any one genre, just whatever is not allowed." In 2009 the director of the Farda music program (also an émigré) emphasized the importance of respecting audience sensibilities: "I spend an hour every day vetting the songs, and if they are too street-wise or suggestive, I don't play them. Iran is still 50 to 60 percent religious, and people don't like soft porn in their songs." Interviews with Farda staff, 6/22/07 and 3/7/09.

47. According to Internet World Stats (http://www.internetworldstats.com), 46.9 percent of Iranians were online in 2010. The percentage has probably risen since then.

48. "Our Iranian Colleagues Believe in Radio Farda's Mission," *Middle East Quarterly* (Fall 2008), 53–56.

49. Mardo Soghom, e-mail to author, 12/14/12.

50. Gedmin (2008).

51. Office of the Inspector General, *Report of Inspection: U.S. Interests Section in Havana, Cuba* (ISP-1-07-27A, July 2007), 18.

52. *Cuba: Immediate Action Is Needed to Ensure the Survivability of Radio and TV Martí*, S. Report No. 111–46, 111th Cong., 2nd sess. (April 29, 2010), 9.

53. Consider: the OCB was able to spend millions of dollars trying to circumvent the Cuban government's jamming by means of blimps and, at one point, a specially built airplane. See Office of the Inspector General, *Review of the Effectiveness and Implementation of Office of Cuba Broadcasting's New Program Initiatives* (IOB-A-03-01, January 2003).

54. *Fiscal Year 2013 Congressional Budget Request*, http://www.bbg.gov. Accessed 3/3/12.

55. According to Freedom House's 2012 report, all six countries served by RFA are "not free." See *Nations in Transit* (June 16, 2012).

56. See Office of the Inspector General, *Inspection of Radio Free Asia* (ISP-IB-11-29, March 2011), 1, 3.

57. Ted Lipien, "Leader of Federal Agency with Lowest Leadership Ratings Justifies Cash Awards for Executives," tedlipien.com (December 29, 2011).

58. Lord (2006), 86.

59. One of the problems plaguing the BBG is the lack of members with experience in public diplomacy or noncommercial media. Another problem is the *lack of members*, period: in recent years the board has gone for long periods with less than eight members and/or no chairman.

60. Lord (2006), 86.

61. Telephone interview, 8/8/06.

62. Ironically, at the VOA's seventieth anniversary celebration in Washington (also in 2012), a video was shown of Aung San Suu Kyi, the Burmese democracy leader, recalling how the VOA's Burmese service was a sustaining presence during her eighteen years of house arrest.

63. *Fiscal Year 2013 Congressional Budget Request*, BBG.

64. "Public Diplomacy and the Transformation of International Broadcasting," *Cardozo Arts and Entertainment Law Journal* 21 (2003), 83.

65. The US-USSR Bilateral Information Talks. See Chapter 6.

66. E-mail to author, 5/15/13.

67. Robert Reilly, unpublished essay, e-mail to author, 8/30/05. A similar criticism is made in my essay "Good Will Hunting," *Wilson Quarterly* (Summer 2005).

68. Remarks of Jordanian journalist Salameh Nematt at "International Broadcasting: The Public Diplomacy Challenge," Fourth Annual Forum of the Public Diplomacy Council, School of Media and Public Affairs, George Washington University, Washington, DC, November 16, 2006.

69. Kleinman, e-mail to author, 5/15/13.

70. Reilly (2005).

71. Remarks at "International Broadcasting" (2006).

72. Excluding production and transmission costs. See *Fiscal Year 2013 Congressional Budget Request*, BBG, 6.

73. See Dafna Linzer, "Lost in Translation: Al-Hurra—America's Troubled Effort to Win Middle East Hearts and Minds," *ProPublica* (7/22/08): http://www.propublica .org/feature/Al-Hurra-middle-east-hearts-and-minds-72/.

74. Quoted in ibid.

75. *An Evaluation of Alhurra Television Programming*, conducted for the Broadcasting Board of Governors by the USC Center on Public Diplomacy at the Annenberg School, University of Southern California (July 31, 2008), 5–7.

76. See Dafna Linzer, "Does Obama Snub of Alhurra Signal a Shift?," *ProPublica* (January 27, 2009): http://www.propublica.org/article/does-obama-snub-of-alhurra-signal-a -shift.

77. E-mail to author, 5/15/13.

78. For a persuasive statement of this conclusion, see William A. Rugh, "Repairing American Public Diplomacy," *Arab Media & Society* 7 (Winter 2009).
79. E-mail to author, 5/27/13.
80. Interview, Prague, 8/29/06.
81. Tom Vanden Brook, "Pentagon Drops 'Strategic Communication,'" *USA Today* (December 3, 2012).
82. According to a 2009 report from the GAO, both the State Department and the BBG are required by Congress to provide detailed breakdowns of their proposed budgets. But "*the DOD* [Department of Defense] *does not have a separate budget covering its strategic communication activities*" (emphasis added). See United States Government Accounting Office, *U.S. Public Diplomacy*, GAO-09-679SP (May 2009), 7–9.
83. See Enders Wimbush, "Fixing Public Diplomacy and Strategic Communications," Report for the Hudson Institute (January 8, 2009), accessed at: http://dspace.cigi library.org/jspui/bitstream/123456789/26761/1/Fixing%20Public%20Diplomacy%20 and%20Strategic%20Communications.pdf?1.
84. See, for example, the remarks of Gen. Vincent Brooks at "Winning Hearts and Minds," public forum at American Enterprise Institute, Washington, DC (December 8, 2004): http://www.aei.org/eventtranscript953.
85. OSI report, quoted in "How Rocket Scientists Got into the Hearts-and-Minds Game," *US News* (April 17, 2005).
86. See James Dao and Eric Schmitt, "Pentagon Readies Efforts to Sway Sentiment Abroad," *New York Times* (February 19, 2002); and Donald Rumsfeld, press conference (February 26, 2002): http://www.defenselink.mil/transcripts/transcript.aspx? transcriptid=2798.
87. Worden et al., "Information War: Strategic Influence and the Global War on Terrorism" (2002), unpublished document quoted in Daniel Schulman, "Mind Games," *Columbia Journalism Review* (May–June 2006).
88. Interview, Washington, 5/24/07.
89. The request came from then Undersecretary of State for Public Affairs and Public Diplomacy Karen Hughes.
90. "The Fernandez Problem," *Abu Aardvark* (October 22, 2006).
91. Quoted in ibid.
92. That same year, Fernandez won the Edward R. Murrow Award for Excellence in Public Diplomacy, and in 2008 he received a Presidential Meritorious Service Award. He subsequently went on to become chargé d'affaires of the US embassy in Sudan; US ambassador to Equatorial Guinea; and the State Department's coordinator for strategic counterterrorism communications.
93. In September 2012, two US diplomats fell off the high wire: US Ambassador to Libya Christopher Stevens, who, after playing a key role in the US effort to unseat Muamar Gaddafi, was killed in an attack on the US consulate in Benghazi; and Larry Schwartz, chief PAO at the US embassy in Cairo, who, after issuing a statement condemning an anti-Muslim video that had gone viral in the Arab Middle East, was denounced by Republican presidential candidate Mitt Romney and (according to insiders at the State Department) "thrown under the bus" by his senior officers.

CHAPTER 8. BEARERS OF GLAD TIDINGS

1. Phrases translatable as *glad tidings* appear in the Hebrew Bible (Isaiah 52:7); the Christian New Testament (Romans 10:15); and the Quran (Sura 165).

2. *Federalist Papers*, No. 51.

3. Much of what is said in this chapter also applies to the path of the businessman or woman. Two other paths, that of the democracy promoter and that of the student or professor, are discussed in Chapter 9.

4. William Lederer and Eugene Burdick, *The Ugly American* (Norton, 1999; first published 1958), 277, 247, 263.

5. Like most of the characters in *The Ugly American*, Homer and his wife, Emma, are based on real people: Otto and Helen Hunerwadel, part of the first cohort of Fulbright recipients, who spent two years in Burma providing "technical assistance" of the kind long offered to US farmers through the Department of Agriculture Extension Service. See Robert L. Clifford, with Helen B. Hunerwadel, "Burma Beginnings," in *The Fulbright Difference, 1948–1992*, ed. Richard T. Arndt and David Lee Rubin (Transaction, 1993), 21–23.

6. Lederer and Burdick (1999), 208–9, 205, 210.

7. Ibid., 218, 277.

8. *All You Need Is Love* (Harvard University Press, 1998), 61.

9. Lederer and Burdick (1999), 216.

10. Hoffman (1998), 61, 179.

11. See Peace Corps website: http://www.peacecorps.gov/about/.

12. Hoffman (1998), 254.

13. "Core Expectations for Peace Corps Volunteers," peacecorps.gov.

14. Ibid.

15. Emilie Jacobs, quoted in Anna Schecter and Brian Ross, "Peace Corps Gang Rape" and two subsequent reports, 20/20, ABC News (January 12–26, 2011).

16. Schecter and Ross (January 12–26, 2011).

17. The Kate Puzey Peace Corps Volunteer Protection Act (S.1280) was passed on November 1, 2011, and signed into law by President Obama on November 21, 2011.

18. Quoted in Angela M. Hill and Randy Kreider, "Obama to Sign Kate Puzey Peace Corps Volunteer Protection Act," website of Representative Ted Poe (November 21, 2011): http://poe.house.gov/index.php?option=com_content&view=article&id=8465%3Aobama-to-sign-kate-puzey-peace-corps-volunteer-protection-act&catid=130%3Aarticles&Itemid=1.

19. The Kate Puzey Peace Corps Volunteer Protection Act (S.1280).

20. Quoted in Mark Landler, "A New Gender Agenda," *New York Times* (August 23, 2009).

21. "Her 'Crime' Was Loving Schools," *New York Times* (October 10, 2012).

22. See Landler (August 23, 2009).

23. See Gerry Mackie, "Female Genital Cutting: The Beginning of the End," in *Female "Circumcision" in Africa*, ed. Bettina Shell-Duncan and Ylva Hernlund (Lynne Reiner, 2001), 272–77.

24. For a biographical account of Melching's career, see Aimee Molloy, *However Long the Night* (HarperOne, 2013).

25. *Tostan* means "breakthrough" in Wolof, the most widely spoken language in Senegal.

26. Kerthio Diarra, resident of Malicounda Bambara, Senegal, speaking with Molly Melching at "FGC Zero Tolerance Day," sponsored by Population Reference Bureau, US Agency for International Development; Washington, DC (February 6, 2004).

27. Tostan website: http://www.tostan.org. Accessed 10/11/12.

28. See "V-Day Annual Report (2012)": http://www.vday.org/annual-report/documents/VDAY2012AR.pdf.

29. *The Vagina Monologues* (Villard, 1998).

30. V-Day website: www.v-day.org. Accessed 10/12/12.

31. See Christopher Walker, "Vagina Monologues Stirs Up Cairo," *Women's eNews* (February 26, 2004): http://www.womensenews.org/article.cfm/dyn/aid/1727/context/archive.

32. A fistula is a tear in the vagina caused by rape, assault, or difficult childbirth. Such injuries allow urine and feces to leak uncontrollably, making the sufferers social outcasts.

33. See Lydia Polgreen, "Massacre Unfurls in Congo, Despite Nearby Support," *New York Times* (December 11, 2008).

34. *Power, Terror, Peace, and War* (Knopf, 2004), 37.

35. *Making the Corps* (Scribner, 1997), 22–23.

36. "Confidence in Institutions," Gallup poll (July 2012): http://www.gallup.com/poll/1597/confidence-institutions.aspx.

37. Ricks (1997), 23.

38. "On Forgetting the Obvious," *American Interest* 2:6 (July–August, 2007).

39. The terms *hard power* and *soft power*, along with *smart power*, were of course made famous by Joseph S. Nye, Jr. See, most recently, Joseph S. Nye, Jr., *The Future of Power* (PublicAffairs, 2011). For historian Walter Russell Mead, these terms are not sufficient. So he would add three more: *sharp power*, meaning military force; *sticky power*, covering trade and economic relations; and *sweet power*, referring to "attraction to American ideals, culture, and values." See Mead (2004), ch.2.

40. For an impassioned and exhaustive account of the tragic blunders committed by the US military in Iraq, see Thomas Ricks, *Fiasco* (Penguin Press, 2006).

41. Telephone interview, 6/12/09.

42. See Allison Stanger, *One Nation Under Contract* (Yale University Press, 2009), ch. 5.

43. *Mugged by Reality* (Encounter, 2007), 160–61.

44. Ibid.

45. Ibid., 166–67.

46. For a critical look at the general failure of oversight and accountability in US government contracting, see Stanger (2009) and Donald F. Kettl, *Sharing Power* (Brookings Institution Press, 1993).

47. Stanger (2009), 92.

48. In 2012 there were two Abu Ghraib–like incidents involving US soldiers in Afghani-

stan: in January, a group of Marines posted a video of themselves urinating on dead Taliban fighters; in April, an anonymous soldier posted photos of paratroopers posing with the severed body parts of insurgent suicide bombers.

49. Quoted in Thom Shanker and Eric Schmitt, "The Struggle for Iraq," *New York Times* (May 8, 2004).

50. *Fobbit* (Grove/Atlantic, 2012), 3. The older derogatory term for noncombatant personnel is, of course, REMF, for "rear echelon mother-fuckers."

51. "The Military," in *Understanding America*, ed. Peter H. Schuck and James Q. Wilson (Public Affairs, 2008), 266–67.

52. *Twenty-Eight Articles: Fundamentals of Company-Level Counterinsurgency*, 1st ed. (March 2006), Article 10.

53. Interview, Boston, 4/23/12. For a similar account of a census being used, this time by a Marine unit officer, see Lieutenant Colonel Jim Crider, *Inside the Surge*, Center for a New American Security (June 2009).

54. Kilcullen (2006), Article 10.

55. Interview, Boston, 4/23/12.

56. E-mail to author, 8/20/12.

57. Kilcullen (2006), Article 27.

58. Interview, Boston, 4/23/12.

59. "What Is an ETT anyway," *Embedded in Afghanistan*, Blogspot (June 6, 2009): http://bc235.blogspot.com/.

60. See *Afghanistan: Green on Blue Attacks Are Only a Small Part of the Problem*, Center for Strategic International Studies, Washington, DC (September 4, 2012).

61. "Not Losing in Afghanistan," *Washington Post* (October 19, 2012).

62. Javid Ahmad, "Cultural Cluelessness Can Be Deadly," *Washington Post* (October 5, 2012).

63. Alaudin, quoted in Richard A. Oppel, Jr., and Graham Bowley, "Afghan Attacks on Allied Troops Prompt NATO to Shift Policy," *New York Times* (August 18, 2012).

64. Sayed Rahman, quoted in ibid.

65. Among the complaints lodged by Afghans against Americans were cursing, urinating in public, humiliating Afghan officers in front of their men, and disregarding the honor of families during night raids. Among the accusations leveled by the Americans against the Afghans were "illicit drug use," "massive theft," "cowardice," "disgusting personal hygiene," and "religious radicalism." See Jeffrey Bordin, *A Crisis of Trust and Cultural Incompatibility*, unclassified report for US Army N2KL Red Team (May 12, 2011), 32–47: http://www.gwu.edu/~nsarchiv/NSAEBB/NSAEBB370/docs/Document%2011.pdf.

66. Ibid., 37.

67. Interview, Boston, 2/22/13.

68. *Countering the New Orthodoxy: Reinterpreting Counterinsurgency in Iraq* (New America Foundation, June 2011), 3.

69. E-mail to author, 11/26/12.

70. Telephone interview, 6/9/09.

71. David Rohde, "The Obama Doctrine," *Foreign Policy* (March/April 2012).

72. See Max Boot, *Invisible Armies* (Liveright, 2013).

73. "Go Army, Beat Navy," *Foreign Policy* (September 28, 2012).

74. Army Sargent Dwight Williams, quoted in Staff Sargent Tony M. Lindback, "Three-Day Camp Teaches Iraqi Kids Basketball," in *Blackanthem Military News* (March 31, 2008): blackanthem.com.

75. Quoted in e-mail to author, 8/20/12. A foreign service officer of my acquaintance who served in Afghanistan recalls receiving a proposal from the field requesting funds to award Qurans to the participants in a certain program. The request was denied by a State Department official as a violation of the separation of church and state. In Chapter 9 I will address this and other bureaucratic obstacles pertaining to such gestures of religious respect.

76. For example, the nondenominational Arabian Mission, founded by the Dutch Reformed Church in America in 1889, built hospitals in Oman, Bahrain, and Kuwait. The roster of schools started by US Protestants includes the Lebanese American University, founded by Presbyterians in 1835; the American University of Beirut, founded by Congregationalists and Baptists in 1863; Robert College in Istanbul, founded by Unitarians in 1863; and the American University in Cairo, founded by Presbyterians in 1919.

77. For a fascinating look at this history, see Robert D. Kaplan, *The Arabists* (Free Press, 1993).

78. "The Pioneering Protestants," *Journal of Democracy* 15:2 (April 2004), 52.

79. See Mary Kissel, "The Pastor of China's Underground Railroad," *Wall Street Journal* (June 2–3, 2012); and http://www.chinaaid.org.

80. See David Aikman, *Jesus in Beijing* (Regnery, 2003), 275–82.

81. "Jesus Loves China, Too," *Foreign Policy* (May 14, 2012).

82. It is hardly surprising that twenty-first-century missionary work should overlap with humanitarian aid, since they have a common origin in the missionary outreach of the nineteenth century. See Michael Barnett, "Where Is the Religion?," in *Rethinking Religion and World Affairs*, ed. Timothy Samuel Shah, et al. (Oxford University Press, 2012), 165–81.

83. See Michael Montgomery and Stephen Smith, "The Few Who Stayed," produced for American Public Media by Radioworks (2002): http://americanradioworks.publi cradio.org/features/rwanda/index.html.

84. See Philip Jenkins, *The Next Christendom* (Oxford University Press, 2007; first published in 2002). See also Todd M. Johnson and Sun Young Chung, "Tracking Global Christianity's Statistical Centre of Gravity, AD33–AD2100," in *International Review of Mission* 93:369 (April 2004), 166–81.

85. Todd M. Johnson et al., *Atlas of Global Christianity* (Edinburgh University Press, 2010), 261.

86. *World Christian Database*, Center for the Study of Global Christianity, Gordon-Conwell Theological Seminary (Brill, 2011).

87. A. Scott Moreau, "A Current Snapshot of North American Protestant Missions," *International Bulletin of Missionary Research* (January 2011), 12–16.

88. The 10 percent figure comes from Robert Wuthnow, *Boundless Faith* (University of California Press, 2009), 42. The estimate of the total number of US missionaries comes from the *World Christian Database* (2011).

89. Wuthnow (2009), 42.

90. "Mission and Service Opportunities for Senior Adults and Recommended Young Adults," Latter Day Saints website: http://www.lds.org/csm.

91. See Dotsey Welliver and Minnette Northcutt, eds., *Mission Handbook 2004–2006: US and Canadian Protestant Ministries Overseas*, report for Evangelism and Missions Information Services at Billy Graham Center, Wheaton College (Wheaton, IL, 2004).

92. Wuthnow (2009), 171.

93. Ibid., 168.

94. See Brian M. Howell, "Mission to Nowhere: Putting Short-Term Missions into Context," *International Bulletin of Missionary Research* (October 2009), 206–11.

95. Fu (2012).

96. Quoted in "10 Things I Hate about American Mission Programs," *Mission Maker Magazine* (STEM Press, Minneapolis, MN, 2007), 32.

97. *To Give or Not To Give?* (Authentic, 2006), 141–44.

98. "Short-Term Missions and Dependency," World Mission Associates website (2009): http://www.wmausa.org/page.aspx?id=242674.

99. "10 Things I Hate about American Mission Programs," (2007), 28.

100. Interview with Carol Huang, Pasadena, 7/5/07.

101. The travel agency in question, Praying Pelican Missions, leads church groups to Belize, Costa Rica, Dominican Republic, Haiti, Jamaica, Mexico, Puerto Rico, and South Africa, as well as to "international churches" in Miami, Tucson, and Chicago. The price per person ranges from $295 (for a week in a US city) to $1,495 (for ten days in South Africa). All packages include promotional materials such as caps and T-shirts, and "35+ hours of ministry": ballgames, church services, construction projects. At some destinations, an additional $100 buys "a day/night on a tropical island, including boat transportation and hotel." See Praying Pelican Missions website: http://www.prayingpelicanmissions.org/priceinfo#jamaica.

102. For an incisive discussion of gospel tourism, see Richard Slimbach, "First, Do No Harm: Short-Term Missions at the Dawn of a New Millennium," *Evangelical Missions Quarterly* 36:4 (2000), 428–41.

103. See Jeffrey Gettleman, "Americans' Role Seen in Uganda Anti-Gay Push," *New York Times* (January 3, 2010); Jeffrey Gettleman, "Ugandan Who Spoke Up for Gays Is Beaten to Death," *New York Times* (January 27, 2011); and Kapya Kaoma, "The US Christian Right and the Attack on Gays in Africa, *Public Eye* (Winter 2009/Spring 2010).

104. Quoted in Michael Levenson, "Shift in Mission for Religious Firebrand," *Boston Globe* (January 5, 2011).

105. Lederer and Burdick (1999), 263.

106. C-SPAN, Interview with Brian Lamb, *Booknotes* (June 27, 1993).

CHAPTER 9. "FREEDOM'S JUST ANOTHER WORD"

1. NED contains a number of subsidiary organizations: the National Democratic Institute (NDI), the International Republican Institute (IRI), the US Chamber of Commerce Center for International Private Enterprise (CIPE), and the AFL-CIO's American Center for International Labor Solidarity (Solidarity Center). Similar democracy-promotion efforts have been mounted by the US Agency for International Development (USAID), the International Foundation for Election Systems (IFES), and Freedom House. In Europe, democracy promotion has been carried out by the UK-based Westminster Foundation for Democracy, the Netherlands Institute for Multiparty Democracy, the Heinrich Böll and Konrad Adenauer Foundations in Germany—and, at the level of the European Union, the European Network of Political Foundations and European Partnership for Democracy.

2. "Repairing Democracy Promotion," *Washington Post* (September 14, 2007).

3. For a well-developed version of this criticism from the American left, see Gerald Sussman, "The Myths of 'Democracy Assistance,'" *Monthly Review* (December 2006).

4. "Reenergizing Democracy Promotion," website of Carnegie Endowment for International Peace (November 29, 2012): http://carnegieendowment.org/globalten/?fa=50142.

5. Timothy Samuel Shah, "Introduction," in Timothy Samuel Shah et al., eds., *Rethinking Religion and World Affairs* (Oxford University Press, 2012), 2.

6. For a lucid overview of this contrast, see Ian Buruma, *Taming the Gods* (Princeton University Press, 2010).

7. "The Lesson from America," *Economist* (November 1, 2007).

8. Alexis de Tocqueville, *Democracy in America*, ed. J. P. Mayer, trans. George Lawrence (Perennial Classics, 1969), Vol. I, Part II, ch. 9, 297.

9. *A Religious History of the American People* (Image, 1975; Yale 1972), 462.

10. Tocqueville (1969), Vol. I, Part II, ch. 9, 295.

11. Remarks at Saddleback Church, Lake Forest, California, June 30, 2006; quoted in Andrew Preston, *Sword of the Spirit, Shield of Faith* (Knopf, 2012), 611.

12. For the definitive treatment of the central role of "prophetic religion" in the African-American civil rights movement, see David L. Chappell, *A Stone of Hope* (University of North Carolina Press, 2007).

13. Thomas F. Farr, "America's International Freedom Policy," in Shah (2012), 272.

14. "Islam's Way to Freedom," *First Things* (November 2008).

15. Frederick D. Barton et al., "Navigating in the Fog," in Shah (2012), 283.

16. Jennifer A. Marshall and Thomas F. Farr, "Public Diplomacy in an Age of Faith," in *Toward a New Public Diplomacy*, ed. Philip Seib (Palgrave MacMillan, 2009), 201.

17. Telephone interview, 11/24/08.

18. Public Law 105-292, International Religious Freedom Act (October 27, 1998); amended by Public Laws 106-55, 106-113, 107-228, 108-332, and 108-458.

19. Current US ambassadors-at-large deal with war crimes, counterterrorism, global women's issues, HIV and AIDS, and human trafficking. Freedom House is a government-supported NGO founded in 1941 to inform Americans of the dangers

of Nazism. After World War II it continued to oppose Soviet and Chinese Communism, and today it monitors the ebb and flow of political liberty around the world. Its annual reports and other research are highly regarded. See http://www.freedom house.org/.

20. In August 2013 Secretary of State John Kerry announced a new office of Faith-Based Community Initiatives, a similar effort with a more blue-state coloration.

21. Farr (2012), 267–68.

22. "Rethinking Islam and Democracy," in Shah (2012), 88.

23. Pippa Norris and Ronald Inglehart, *Sacred and Secular: Religion and Politics Worldwide* (Cambridge University Press, 2004), 146–47.

24. Hefner (2012), 86.

25. Norris and Inglehart (2004), 146–47.

26. Hefner (2012), 86.

27. Norris and Inglehart (2004), 146–47.

28. See "Religion, Democracy, and the 'Twin Tolerations,'" in Shah (2012).

29. Hefner (2012). The quoted phrase is from John L. Esposito and Dalia Mogahed, *Who Speaks for Islam* (Gallup, 2007).

30. Interview, Jakarta, 4/5/07.

31. "Fast Facts," *Open Doors* (Institute of International Education, 2012).

32. See William Lawton and Alex Katsomitros, "International Branch Campuses: Data and Developments" (Observatory on Borderless Higher Education, January 12, 2012): http://www.obhe.ac.uk/documents/view_details?id=894; and "International Branch Campuses: Even More Developments" (Observatory on Borderless Higher Education, March 2, 2012): http://www.obhe.ac.uk/newsletters/borderless_report_march_2012/international_branch_campuses_even_more_developments.

33. See James S. Coleman, "The University and Society's New Demands upon It," in *Content and Context: Essays on College Education, Report for the Carnegie Commission on Higher Education* ed. Carl Kaysen (McGraw-Hill, 1973), 374, 360ff.

34. Morrill Act of 1862 (7 U.S.C. § 301 et seq.).

35. R. W. "Brock" Powers, interviewed by Carole Hicke, *American Perspectives of Aramco, the Saudi-Arabian Oil-Producing Company, 1930s to 1980s* (Regional Oral History Office, University of California at Berkeley, 1995).

36. *Cultural Exchange and the Cold War* (Pennsylvania State University Press, 2003), 25, 79.

37. "Fast Facts" (2012). See also Ellen Knickmeyer, "Saudi Students Flood in as U.S. Reopens Door," *Wall Street Journal* (July 28, 2012).

38. F. I. Al-Harithi, "Saudi Undergraduates in the United States," *Dissertation Abstracts International* 49 (1987).

39. "Fast Facts" (2012).

40. For an evenhanded discussion of growing inequality in US higher education, see Andrew Delbanco, *College* (Princeton University Press, 2012), ch. 4.

41. "Hate Your Policies, Love Your Institutions," *Foreign Affairs* (January/February 2003).

42. Interview, Jarkarta, 4/5/07.

43. For a lucid overview of the system's many advantages, see William E. Odum and Robert Dujarric, *America's Inadvertent Empire* (Yale University Press, 2004), ch. 6.

44. Interview, Mumbai, 3/27/07.

45. See *Experience and Education* (Macmillan, 1938) and *Democracy and Education* (Free Press, 1966).

46. E-mail to author, 5/20/12.

47. This account is taken from Laurence Veysey, "Stability and Experiment in the American Undergraduate Curriculum," in *Content and Context: Essays on College Education, Report for the Carnegie Commission on Higher Education*, ed. Carl Kaysen (McGraw-Hill, 1973), 1–63.

48. See, for example, the statement of the University of Wisconsin Regents, published in the Madison *Democrat* (September 19, 1894) and quoted in full in Theodore Herfurth, *Sifting and Winnowing* (Wisconsin Electronic Books): http://www.library. wisc.edu/etext/wireader/WER1035-Chpt1.html; the *Declaration of Principles* of the American Association of University Professors (AAUP) (1915): http://www.aaup.org/ file/1915-Declaration-of-Principles-o-nAcademic-Freedom-and-Academic-Tenure.pdf; and the AAUP's *Statement of Principles on Academic Freedom and Tenure* (1940): http://www.aaup.org/report/1940-statement-principles-academic-freedom-and-tenure.

49. "America the Popular" (editorial), *Wall Street Journal* (11/21/08).

50. Dixon v. Alabama, 294 F. 2d 150 (5th Cir. 1961).

51. Peter Lake of Stetson University, quoted in Eric Hoover, "'Animal House' at 30," *Chronicle of Higher Education* (September 5, 2008).

52. See Marlon P. Mundt and Larissa I. Zakletskaia, "Prevention for College Students Who Suffer Alcohol-Induced Blackouts Could Deter High-Cost Emergency Department Visits," *Health Affairs* 10.1377 (March 14, 2012).

53. Lisa Wade and Caroline Heldman, "Hooking Up and Opting Out," in *Sex For Life*, ed. Laura M. Carpenter and John L. Demater (New York University Press, 2012), 144. See also Elizabeth Marquardt, *Hooking Up, Hanging Out, and Hoping for Mr. Right* (Institute for American Values, 2001).

54. When asked to estimate the number of sexual partners their fellow students had had the previous year, 14 percent estimated one, and 3 percent estimated none. But when asked to report the number of their own sexual partners, 46 percent reported one, and 30 percent reported none. See National College Health Assessment, Spring 2008 Findings: http://www.acha-ncha.org/. I thank Tim Muldoon of Boston College for bringing this study to my attention.

55. Michael Driessen, e-mail to author, 5/20/12.

56. William Lederer and Eugene Burdick, *The Ugly American* (W. W. Norton, 1999; first published 1958).

57. *Open Doors Report on International Educational Exchange*, Institute of International Education (2012): http://www.iie.org/opendoors.

58. "Fast Facts," *Open Doors* (2012): http://www.iie.org/Research-and-Publications/ Open-Doors. In June 2009 Congress voted to spend $120 million on the goal of sending one million US students overseas by 2020. See H.R. 2410, Title VII: Senator Paul Simon Study Abroad Foundation Act. The bill was referred to the Committee

on Foreign Relations on March 2, 2009. But while Senator Simon's name continues to be associated with efforts to increase American study abroad, the bill itself has proceeded no further.

59. Ibid.

60. William P. Kiehl, "Global Intentions Local Results," (PhD. Diss., University of Pennsylvania, 2008).

61. Roula Khalaf and Heba Saleh, "Mohamed Morsi Has Squandered Egypt's Good-will," *Financial Times* (30 November 2012).

62. Jerrold Keilson, interview, Washington, 5/24/07.

63. *Open Doors* (2012). David North, "Who Pays?," Center for Immigration Studies (June 2009), 9.

64. I base this on interviews in Egypt and the UAE, especially in Dubai, and at the American University of Sharjah, 3/17–20/08.

65. Philip Altbach, interview, Boston, 5/30/08.

66. Assma, a student in the Georgetown University School of Foreign Studies in Qatar; quoted in "Education City," *NOW on PBS* (May 15, 2008).

67. E-mail to author, 5/14/13.

68. Ibid.

69. See Coleman (1973), 374.

70. Just to cite one example, MIT has played a significant role in developing the Skokolvo Institute of Science and Technology in Russia; the Masdar Institute of Science and Technology in Abu Dhabi; and two facilities in Singapore: the Singapore Alliance for Research and Technology, and the Singapore Institute of Technology and Design.

71. See Karin Fischer, "MIT Adopts a Quiet Global Strategy," *Chronicle of Higher Education* (October 26, 2012).

72. See James L. McGregor, *No Ancient Wisdom, No Followers: The Challenges of Chinese Authoritarian Capitalism* (Prospecta Press, 2012).

73. *River Town* (Harper Perennial, 2001), 45.

74. The battle began with Allan Bloom's *The Closing of the American Mind* (Free Press, 1988); then continued with Roger Kimball's *Tenured Radicals* (Harper and Row, 1990) and Dinesh D'Souza's *Tenured Radicals* (Free Press, 1998).

75. "Nothing Wrong with Teaching What's Right About U.S.," *Los Angeles Times* (December 30, 2001).

76. See Spencer Witte, "Transnational Higher Education: Who Benefits?," *International Higher Education* 58 (Winter 2010).

77. Saadiyat Island is also home to the lavish Zayed National Museum and branches of the Guggenheim and Louvre.

78. Suzanne Daley, "N.Y.U. in the U.A.E.," *New York Times* (April 15, 2011).

79. See Ursula Lindsey, "NYU–Abu Dhabi Behaves Like Careful Guest in Foreign Land," *Chronicle of Higher Education* (June 3, 2012).

80. See Shafeeq Ghabra and Margreet Arnold, "Studying the American Way," Policy Focus #71, Washington Institute for Near East Policy (June 2007), 11.

81. Interview, Sharjah, 3/20/07.

82. According to Jihad Fakhreddine, Middle East and North Africa regional research
    director for the Gallup World Poll, the UAE produces the highest percentage of
    educated women in the world. Ninety-five percent of Emirati women apply to
    university, and large majorities of the students at most UAE universities are female.
    Interview, Dubai, 3/16/07.
83. Quoted in Daley (2011).
84. Ibid.
85. Bryan Garsten, e-mail to author, 5/16/13.
86. Ibid.
87. Bryan Garsten et al., *Yale-NUS College: A New Community of Learning* (Yale
    University, April 2013: Yale-NUS http://www.yale-nus.edu.sg/images/doc/Yale-NUS-
    College-Curriculum-Report.pdf.
88. *World Report 2012: Singapore* (Human Rights Watch, 2012): http://www.hrw.org/
    world-report-2012/world-report-2012-singapore.
89. Garsten et al. (2013), 29.
90. Hoffman (2001).
91. See, for example, Richard Arum and Josipa Roksa, *Academically Adrift* (University
    of Chicago Press, 2011); and Professor X, *In the Basement of the Ivory Tower* (Viking,
    2011).

CONCLUSION

1. Military doctrine distinguishes between two different kinds of "information operations": "psychological operations" ("psyops") and "deception." Most psyops do not
   rely on untruth or deception.
2. See my treatment of classic popular culture in *Hole in Our Soul* (University of Chicago Press, 1996); and "Popular Culture," in *Understanding America*, Peter Schuck
   and James Q. Wilson eds., (Public Affairs, 2008).
3. B. F. Keith and Edward F. Albee, quoted in Charles W. Stein, ed., *American Vaudeville as Seen by Its Contemporaries* (Knopf, 1984), 17, 24.
4. "At the Edge of Respectability, a Celebration," *New York Times* (November 19,
   2005).
5. One egregious example was the awarding of a $15 million contract, soon bumped up
   to $82 million, to Science Applications International Corporation (SAIC) to estab-
   lish a "free and independent indigenous media network" in post-Saddam Iraq. With
   no demonstrated expertise in news reporting, SAIC was an odd choice, given that
   RFE/RL was already running a service, Radio Free Iraq, that would have benefited
   greatly from a larger budget. For a detailed account of what followed, see Monroe
   Price, "Foreword: Iraq and the Making of State Media Policy," in *Cardozo Arts &
   Entertainment* 25:5 (2007), 9–11.
6. Remarks by Donald Rumsfeld at the Council on Foreign Relations (February 17,
   2006) and by Robert Gates, Manhattan, Kansas (November 26, 2007); cited in William A. Rugh, "Repairing American Public Diplomacy," *Arab Media & Society* 7
   (Winter 2009): http://www.arabmediasociety.com/?article=709.

7. *The Decline and Fall of the United States Information Agency* (Palgrave Macmillan, 2012), 186–87.

8. See CGE website: http://www.thecgeinc.org/uploads/CGE_Plan_FINAL_copy.pdf.

9. It was Hughes who encouraged the forceful engagement with Arab media by Alberto Fernandez described in Chapter 7. See Rugh (2009).

10. Telephone interview, 12/17/10.

11. Telephone interview, 12/17/10.

12. Interview, Wheaton, Illinois, 4/26/07.

13. See comments at Patricia H. Kushlis, "Detroit on the Potomac," *WhirledView* (May 12, 2009): http://whirledview.typepad.com.

14. Craig Hayden, "Public Diplomacy and the Phantom Menace of Theory," *Whirled-View* (May 19, 2009): http://whirledview.typepad.com.

15. *Practicing Public Diplomacy* (Bergman, 2008), 9.

16. See Kapya Kaoma, *Globalizing the Culture Wars* (Political Research Associates, 2009).

17. Secretary of State Hillary Clinton stopped short of doing this in her main speech on the subject, "Free and Equal in Dignity and Rights," delivered at the Palais des Nations, Geneva, on Human Rights Day, December 6, 2011.

18. See "New BBG Governor Sworn In," BBG press release (August 7, 2013).

19. See M. E. Jacobs, posted comment on David S. Jackson, "The Case for an International Broadcasting CEO," Public Diplomacy Council website (July 20, 2012): http://publicdiplomacycouncil.org/topics/broadcasting-board-governors-bbg.

20. In a "town meeting" program, studio audiences in two different countries are linked by live satellite to participate in a shared discussion. The first such broadcast, between the United States and the Soviet Union, occurred in 1982 under the auspices of the USIA. See discussion of WORLDNET in Cull (2008), 434. For an overview of America Abroad Media, see http://www.americaabroad.org/.

21. See my "Public Diplomacy, TV-Style," *Wall Street Journal* (February 16, 2007); "On the Road—Again," *World Affairs* (March 22, 2010). For an overview of Layalina Productions, see http://www.layalina.tv/.

22. See A. Ross Johnson and R. Eugene Parta, *A 21st Century Vision for U.S. Global Media* (Wilson Center, November 2012).

23. Quoted in Stefan Kanfer, "The Voodoo That He Did So Well," *City Journal* (Winter 2003).

24. The most famous challenge to this view is sociologist Paul DiMaggio's study of cultural institutions in nineteenth-century Boston, which argues that their main purpose was to assert the superiority of the Brahmin elite by intimidating the largely immigrant working class. I have no doubt that many working-class Bostonians have been intimidated by the grandeur of the Public Library and Museum of Fine Arts. But the fact remains that these institutions, unlike their aristocratic European counterparts, were designed to open their doors, free of charge, to ordinary citizens. See Paul J. DiMaggio, "Cultural Entrepreneurship in Nineteenth-Century Boston," Parts I and II, *Media, Culture and Society* 4:1 and 4:4 (Winter and Autumn, 1982).

25. These terms come from John A. Kouwenhoven, *The Arts in Modern American Civilization* (Norton, 1948).

26. For example, NEA supports American Masterpieces, a program bringing exhibitions and performances to "under-served" communities; NEH funds Ancient Greeks/ Modern Lives, a project that invites military veterans to discuss war-related passages from Homer, Aeschylus, and other classics; PBS produces two excellent documentary series, *American Masters* (focusing on artists) and *American Experience* (focusing on US history); and NPR and APM host two fine music programs, *Piano Jazz* and *Performance Today*.

27. Robert Conrood, telephone interview, 8/7/12.

28. The importance of fees was clarified for me by Bambang Rachmadi, the former CEO of McDonald's in Indonesia. To show his goodwill to the owners of the *khaki lima* (five legs) food stalls lining Jakarta's streets, he offered a two-day course in hygienic food handling. When offered for free, the course was poorly attended. When Rachmadi charged a small fee, attendance shot up. Interview, Jakarta, 4/3/07.

29. *Arts, Inc.* (University of California Press, 2008), 37–38, 291.

30. E-mail to author, 5/13/13.

31. Interview, Cairo, 3/13/07.

32. E-mail to author, 9/15/08.

33. E-mail to author, 5/29/13.

34. *Between You and Me: Egyptian Treasures from the Archives of the Voice of America* (US Embassy, Cairo, 2007). For material in the public realm, public diplomats might do well to encourage distribution via the Internet and inexpensive VCDs (with the US embassy name attached, of course). For copyrighted material, such piggybacking on existing distribution channels will have to wait until the world finds a solution to the problem of intellectual property rights in the Internet age.

35. See *Mightier Than the Sword* (Brookings Institution, 2008).

36. President George W. Bush, address to a joint session of Congress, September 20, 2001. To be fair, the president was not talking about most foreigners or even Muslims, but about the violent extremists who had attacked America just nine days before.

37. Justice Joseph McKenna, commenting on *Mutual Film Corp. v. Industrial Commission of Ohio*, 236 US 230 (1915); quoted in Richard S. Randall, *Censorship of the Movies* (University of Wisconsin Press, 1970), 18.

38. David Puttnam, *The Undeclared War* (HarperCollins, 1997), 345; quoted in Carol Balassa, *America's Image Abroad: The UNESCO Cultural Diversity Convention and US Motion Picture Exports* (Curb Center for Art, Enterprise, and Public Policy, Vanderbilt University, 2008), 27.

39. Balassa (2008), 35.

40. See Thomas Doherty, *Projections of War* (Columbia University Press, 1993), 46–49.

41. This change is reflected in the contrast between two speeches by Secretary of State Hillary Clinton: "Remarks on Internet Freedom," at the Newseum, Washington, DC (January 21, 2010); and "Internet Rights and Wrongs," at George Washington University, Washington, DC (February 15, 2011).

42. See Evgeny Morozov, *The Net Delusion* (Public Affairs, 2011); and Rebecca MacKinnon, *Consent of the Networked* (Basic, 2012).

43. See Bruce Elting et al., "Political Change in the Digital Age," *SAIS Review* 30:2 (December, 2010).

44. Interviews, Mumbai, 3/29/07.

45. See *Understanding the Mission of U.S. International Broadcasting* (McCormick Tribune Foundation, 2007), 26.

46. Interview, Washington, 5/24/07. Firestein invited me to attend a similar presentation before fifty-five foreign secondary schoolteachers visiting the United States from Muslim-majority countries and India. He captured and held the group's attention through the simple device of playing hit songs and talking about their themes, which included small-town life ("Boondocks," by Little Big Town); pride in humble origins ("Redneck Woman," by Gretchen Wilson); the cowboy work ethic ("Hardworking Man," by Brooks and Dunn); family ("Watching You," by Rodney Atkins); and religion ("Jesus Take the Wheel," by Carrie Underwood). About the last, Firestein told his rapt listeners, "You don't have to be Christian to appreciate this song. I'm not Christian, I'm Jewish, but I get goose bumps whenever I listen to it." The event, which capped off an academic year in which the participants studied at US universities and team-taught in US high schools as part of the International Educators Program (IEP), was held at the Kellogg Conference Hotel, Gallaudet University, Washington, DC (June 19, 2007).

47. Interview, Washington, 5/6/07.

48. As noted in Chapter 5, *hip-hop* is a broader term than *rap*, referring not just to the music but also to related styles of dance, graffiti, and fashion. *Rap* refers to the all-important spoken element.

49. Hishaam Aidi, "The Grand (Hip-Hop) Chessboard," *Middle East Report* 260 (Fall 2011).

50. See Penny von Eschen, *Satchmo Blows Up the World* (North Carolina Press, 1980).

51. Interview, Boston, 8/21/07.

52. For a cogent discussion of this problem, see Aidi (2011).

53. Remarks before "Hip Hop Diplomacy," conference of the Institute for Public Diplomacy and Global Communication; co-sponsored by the Elliott School of International Affairs and the School of Media and Public Affairs, George Washington University, Washington, DC (March 27, 2012).

54. Ibid.

55. *Federalist Papers*, No. 55.

56. Lederer and Burdick (1999), 266–67 and 284–85.

INDEX